GALILEO'S READING

Galileo (1564–1642) incorporated throughout his work the language of battle, the rhetoric of the epic, and the structure of romance as a means to elicit emotional responses from his readers against his opponents. By turning to the literary as a field for creating knowledge, Galileo delineated a textual space for establishing and validating the identity of the new, idealized philosopher. *Galileo's Reading* places Galileo in the complete intellectual and academic world in which he operated, bringing together, for example, debates over the nature of floating bodies and Ludovico Ariosto's *Orlando furioso*, disputes on comets and the literary criticism of *Don Quixote*, mathematical demonstrations of material strength and Dante's voyage through the afterlife, and the parallels of his feisty note-taking practices with popular comedy of the period.

CRYSTAL HALL is currently Assistant Professor of French and Italian at the University of Kansas.

GALILEO'S READING

CRYSTAL HALL

CAMBRIDGE
UNIVERSITY PRESS

CAMBRIDGE
UNIVERSITY PRESS

University Printing House, Cambridge CB2 8BS, United Kingdom

Published in the United States of America by Cambridge University Press, New York

Cambridge University Press is part of the University of Cambridge.

It furthers the University's mission by disseminating knowledge in the pursuit of education, learning and research at the highest international levels of excellence.

www.cambridge.org
Information on this title: www.cambridge.org/9781107047556

First published 2013

Printed in the United Kingdom by CPI Group Ltd, Croydon CRO 4YY

A catalogue record for this publication is available from the British Library

Library of Congress Cataloguing in Publication data
Hall, Crystal, 1981–
Galileo's reading / Crystal Hall.
pages cm
Includes bibliographical references and index.
ISBN 978-1-107-04755-6 (hardback)
1. Galilei, Galileo, 1564–1642. 2. Galilei, Galileo, 1564–1642–Language. 3. Galilei, Galileo,
1564–1642–Literary style. 4. Ariosto, Lodovico, 1474–1533. Orlando furioso. 5. Ariosto,
Lodovico, 1474–1533–Influence. I. Title.
QB36.G2H35 2013
195–dc23
2013020833

ISBN 978-1-107-04755-6 hardback

Contents

Acknowledgments

I owe thanks to a great number of individuals and institutions for their assistance in bringing this book to press. The editors and the anonymous readers at Cambridge University Press offered priceless advice for refining and strengthening the presentation of my arguments. This research was made possible by the support and collaboration of several institutions: the University of Pennsylvania, the University of Kansas, the Galileo Museum in Florence, the Biblioteca Nazionale Centrale di Firenze, the Archivio di Stato di Firenze, the Huntington Library, the Houghton Library, the Linda Hall Library, and the Spencer Research Library.

I am particularly in debt to Victoria Kirkham, in whose course I first discovered Galileo as an author of literature. At the University of Pennsylvania, when this book only existed as a kernel inside my dissertation, I am fortunate to have had the support of Kevin Brownlee, Fabio Finotti, Michael Gamer, and E. Ann Matter. I found guidance and inspiration in many places outside my home institutions, but I would like specifically to thank Arielle Saiber, Eileen Reeves, Patrizia Ruffo, Michele Camerota, Tom Settle, Renée Raphael, Marilyn Migiel, Bill Wallace, and Albert Ascoli for their contributions to my research.

The support of the Department of French and Italian at the University of Kansas has been consistent and abundant, with particular thanks owed to Caroline Jewers, Jan Kozma, Van Kelly, Karen Cook, Sally Cornelison, Cara Polsley, the KU Libraries, and Interlibrary Loan Services.

Finally, a list of personal thanks to colleagues who became close friends and the friends who became colleagues after many hours spent listening to me talk about this project: Lillyrose, Sarah, Federica, Stefano, Kim, Charlie, Bruce, Michelle, Louis, Alethea, Leigh, Nicole, Rebecca, and Kraig. I do hope that Ingrid Horton and Misty Schieberle will want to read this book one more time after patiently reviewing so many early drafts. In the end I hope to have produced a book that my mother will enjoy reading, with the precision that my father expects, written in the good spirit that my sister exemplifies.

Introduction

Galileo's Reading developed around Galileo Galilei's (1564–1642) frequent claims in his philosophical texts that he was playing the part of one of the Christian knights in Ludovico Ariosto's (1474–1533) Renaissance masterpiece *Orlando furioso* (1516, 1521, 1532). The studies in this book show that Galileo methodically and consistently incorporated the literary elements from his favorite poem and similar works into the philosophical arguments he championed. This authorial choice intersects with issues of wider concern in the seventeenth century: the definitions of truth and fiction, the interdependence of philosophy and poetry, reader reception in both specialized and courtly audiences, and the generation of knowledge. *Galileo's Reading* brings Ariosto's and Torquato Tasso's (1544–1595) Christian knights, pagan warriors, and ferocious monsters face to face with the Paduan Aristotelians, Jesuits of the Collegio Romano, and the fictitious interlocutors in Galileo's final works. By chronologically considering specifically the appearance of epic poetry within Galileo's entire corpus, this book compares the fictional works Galileo read with the subsequent literariness of his writing, uses the material history of Galileo's library to examine the interplay of natural philosophy and epic poetry in creating knowledge, and suggests a more widely based literary and cultural genealogy for Galileo's new epistemology than that previously considered by scholars.

The conflicts in which Galileo was involved erupted during a fruitful period of innovation and interdisciplinarity, making the identification of key terms a necessity for any discussion of the fields in which he operated. Learned men like Galileo wore many complementary hats: mathematician, poet, astronomer, dramatist, philosopher, artist, and scientist. Accordingly, finding a tidy label for Galileo and his associates is problematic. When Galileo moved to the Medici court in Florence in 1610, he asked to be called a mathematician and philosopher, that is, an intellectual who used geometric and numerical demonstrations to inform hypotheses about the causes of natural phenomena generally described in terms of dialectical, logical reasoning. For that reason, I will refer to Galileo as a mathematician, philosopher, or natural philosopher. His opponents also distinguish the territory of these fields from astronomy, making the terms critical to an identification of the presumed conventions of practitioners in these disciplines.

Operating hand in hand with philosophical best practices are also Galileo's concerns with the role of the literary in this new paradigm. In many ways the literary was precisely what Galileo was working against with geometric, numerical, and logical analysis. Literary language continues to be constructed in such a way as to invite, if not necessitate, multiple interpretations of the author's text. The literary points to not just one physical objective reality of the kind that Galileo was trying to describe, but many. These include the traditions of the genre, the need to ingratiate a princely or imperial court, establishing symbolic or allegorical claims about society and the human condition, and presenting models of behavior for readers. Thus, while Virgil's verses can accurately describe the received tradition of the movement of constellations, the language in which the poet expresses that idea is suspect (to Galileo) owing to its role in the much larger, subjective project that is the *Aeneid*. According to Galileo's perspective, descriptive terms were not necessarily chosen for their direct correspondence to an object or phenomenon, but to satisfy requirements of meter, form, and style in the service of the literary elements listed above. His preference for things, *res*, has been well documented by modern criticism, but the mechanism for his success was still dependent on a tradition of words, *verba*.[1]

Because the implications of the Copernican reconsideration of the place of the Earth in the heavens were so dramatic, so too was the opposition. Since the means of expression of these ideas were critical to the success or failure of Galileo in intellectual debates of the period, literary models and sources became catalysts in the acceptance of a philosophical idea. Authors in these debates speak widely of the philosophy and poetry that inform their theories. This is an era in which Tycho Brahe (1546–1601), famous for his compromise solution to the Copernican–Ptolemaic debates, could claim that the Book of Proverbs was written by "Poetae."[2] Pliny's prose *Natural History* was as authoritative on matters of natural philosophy as the verses of Virgil's *Aeneid* and Lucan's *Pharsalia*. For that reason, "poetry" in *Galileo's Reading* will refer to verses indicated as poetry by the authors of these works. Epic poetry and the epic project are specifically poems depicting large-scale conflict often written with the intent of providing a foundational narrative to glorify the poet's patron. For the period, the interconnection of poetry and philosophy is not novel, but Galileo's particular meditated and evolving incorporation of epic poetry into his philosophical prose is.

In other contexts, recent interdisciplinary studies have offered partial solutions to this consideration of the mutual influences of philosophy and literature including poetry. New, bizarre, or otherwise intriguing discoveries about the natural world had been popular fodder for poetic and prose-fiction writers in many cultural contexts. In *Galileo's Glassworks*, Eileen Reeves provides a history of lenses and mirrors in literature that included a sizeable group from the early epic and romance traditions: the ancient cycle of stories *Romance of the Seven Sages*, Gower's *Confessio Amantis*, the tournament chronicles *Chroniques de Tournoy*, the anonymous French chivalric poem *Roman de Renart Contrefait*, the medieval French romance *Cleomadés*, the Carolingian cycle on the sack of Rome *Destruction de Rome*, the medieval Grail story *Parzival*, and the later French *Romance of the Rose*.[3] Reeves has observed that optics in these literary contexts are frequently tied to the rise and fall of empire; often to the victors belonged the technology.[4] In Patrick Grant's study of method in the English Renaissance, he argues that the development of method in philosophy modeled by Francis Bacon (1561–1626) challenged poets to renew their investigation of the relationship between fictive images and the truth.[5] Isabelle Pantin has shown how French poets of the sixteenth century used Plato, Apollonius of Rhodes, the Bible, Giovanni Pontano (*c.* 1429–1503), Marsilio Ficino (1433–1499), Philipp Melanchthon (1497–1560), and Tycho Brahe as sources and inspiration for a poetry that reflected prejudices, illusions, experiments, and debates otherwise reported in treatises of the period.[6] In the case of Jean Edouard du Monin's *Uranologie* (1583), the poet broke with Aristotle as an authority on comets and subsequently adopted Seneca's *De cometis* as his primary text of engagement.[7] This rupture suggests that some poets were attuned to ideological shifts in the philosophy of the period and accordingly exercised discretion about their sources for inspiration. But what of the philosophers who turned to verse for everything from allegorical structure, to rhetorical flourish, to examples of word usage and descriptions of natural phenomena? More pressing still, what of authors such as Galileo who manipulated the literary qualities of these poetic sources in order to craft a philosophical argument?

At the most accessible level, philosophical texts turn to poetry for didactic reasons. Quite simply, verse was (and remains) a tool for memorization. Work by Francis Yates and Lina Bolzoni has demonstrated Renaissance readers' use of mnemotechnics, the practice of committing to memory large amounts of information.[8] Verse played a role in this skill. Mnemonic verses were used to teach syntax and grammatical rules, or became part of larger memorization schemes. French philosopher and follower of Galileo, Pierre Gassendi (1592–1655), includes several mnemonic verses in his works on various mathematical and astronomical topics. One such example is the following Latin couplet: "Livor, mente latens insultat honoribus, horret / Grandi gesta, harens insigni laude notates."[9] The translation of these verses is less important than what the words represent in the mnemonic scheme. Each of the twelve words corresponds to one of the twelve months of the year in chronological order: *livor* is March, *mente* is April, etc. Using this information, the words are used to determine how many days of each month are spent in a given zodiac sign. The first letter of *livor* is the tenth in the alphabet, and there are thirty-one days in the month of March. Thirty-one less ten makes twenty-one, leaving twenty-one days under the sign of Aries in March.[10] This kind of quick aid for factual recall is not subjective, figurative, argumentative, or literary. The words are mathematical indicators, the meter a vehicle for memorization.

Verse was also a means for transmitting material with educational and informative value on a much larger scale. Classical didactic authors such as Aratus, Manilius, and Lucretius wrote their encyclopedic works of natural history in epic hexameter, and early modern philosophers frequently excerpted from those texts in their own books. Authors of classical epic poems such as Homer, Virgil, and Lucan were also cited for their statements on natural phenomena as though they were witnesses to these events rather than transmitters of classical literary expression. This is a use of the literal meaning of these poems. Galileo raises his first objection to his detractors' texts because of this poetic testimony and he will turn that practice against its practitioners by exploiting the literariness of those same sources.

Aside from being factual sources and memory aids, poets were also models for rhetorical moves that could assist an author in clarity, persuasion, or both. Studies have shown that other early modern philosophers incorporated verses into their texts in a structurally significant way. The premise of Brian Vickers' work on Francis Bacon is that the fascination created by Bacon in his own time was not just the result of his science, but also his prose. Through close linguistic analysis, Vickers connects the rhetorical structure of Bacon's prose to his method, demonstrating the powerful interpretative combination of the two. For example, Bacon's frequent use of analogy often results in magnifying the object originally under discussion.[11] Elizabeth Spiller points out that Robert Boyle (1627–1691) read *Amadis de Gaule* and *Orlando furioso*, and was himself aware of the influence of the poems' wandering narratives on his thought and writing.[12] These are stylistic elements with roots in poetry.

Galileo's Reading proposes to identify the literary discourses, not just the rhetorical flourishes, active in the conflicts between Galileo and his opponents. Recent scholarship on the early modern period has established both the philosophical and literary as sites of knowledge production by arguing that the practices of both disciplines emerge from the premise that knowledge can be made rather than found.[13] Galileo would have readers believe that he provides found information about the natural world, but he must also make a new philosopher willing and able to find it. By revealing these strategies of making the new philosopher, my analyses shed light on the larger question of the interaction of these two means of expression without subjugating the one, poetry, to the needs of the other, philosophy. Galileo's effective use of analogy has been well studied, as has his highly praised syntax, and digressive dialogue structure, but when seen in light of his explicit use of verses that I analyze, the breadth of this literary attack on his opponents becomes apparent.[14] The combination of his passion for reading and annotating authors such as Ariosto and Tasso (along with dozens of other authors of epic poetry) with the frequently vivacious defense of his philosophical ideas suggests a natural pairing that nonetheless has gone unanalyzed. *Galileo's Reading* examines the specifically literary nature of these elements to reveal a complex project of textual one-upmanship played by the Tuscan philosopher and his opponents.

For Galilean studies, the context and import of this relationship between literary and philosophical discourses in the conflicts of the late sixteenth and early seventeenth centuries have been concerned primarily with the overlap between the very structures of reasoning and communicating: dialectic and rhetoric. Both disciplines were at the fore of publications in Galileo's lifetime, both with roots in Aristotelian philosophy.[15] Traditional logical investigation for determining the causes of natural phenomena typically involved syllogistic examination of known true principles related to them. When those true statements were elusive, dialectical reasoning furnished the means for arriving at an apparent truth by using principles commonly held to be true. This use of common opinion fundamentally unites dialectic and rhetoric.[16] The probable and the persuasive form a powerful alliance for determining what seems to be true.[17] I argue that Galileo moves poetry out of the realm of fact-bearing vehicle of tradition and into the world of the probable via his strategy of revealing the literariness of its language. Notably, this strategy calls attention to the tenuous link between objects in the physical world and the words used to describe them. At the same time, the literary space allows Galileo to craft the person of the philosopher using the persuasive force of rhetoric and the creative capacity of the literary to bring him (because these are overwhelmingly men) most fully to life in his final works.

The aim of these allied forces of philosophy and literature was to promote a hypothesis about what Fernand Hallyn has called the *mythos* or *poesis* of the natural world. This kind of *poesis*, or making, stands in sharp contrast to that of the plastic or visual arts, a distinction that Galileo will repeatedly draw in his works when he compares his opponents' work to marquetry, paintings, and collages.[18] According to Hallyn, the very actions of proposing probable truths about the natural world involve accessing or recreating a divine poetics of the natural world.[19] Galileo, through mathematics, embraces that optimism of revealing the structure of the natural world. Through a literary epistemology he establishes a *poesis* of the new philosopher. For further epistemological connections, we might look to Cristoforo Landino (1424–1504), whom Galileo would have known through his commentary on Dante's *Comedy*. In that commentary he explores the demarcation of making and creating:

> The Greeks said "poet" from this word *piin*: which is in the middle between "creating," which is appropriate to God when out of nothing he brings something forth into being, and "making," which is appropriate to men when in any art-form they compose out of matter and form. Therefore, although the figment of the poet is not completely out of nothing, yet it departs from "making" and comes very close to "creating."[20]

Philosophers who construct a world become poets. For Copernicus and Kepler, this involves the instruments of rhetoric and dialectic: an inventory of topics, intertextual insertions that expose a network of relationships, and tropological analysis. Instead, Galileo, while he still adopts those Aristotelian elements of investigation to explain this *poesis*, also develops a means of incorporating literary poetics to aid his arguments.

Moments of textual criticism against an author's presentation of theory are the instances in which Galileo is most likely to cite from epic poetry, make reference to fantastical monsters, resort to a language of chivalric combat, or declare that his own work is a poetic fiction. This should not be a surprising connection, since the practices of both philosophical and poetic *poesis* were hermeneutically intertwined and the humanist project at the base of each was, after all, one founded on textual analysis.[21] Rebecca Bushnell describes reading for the early modern humanist in an apt way for imagining the approach to classical poets by these philosophers that will be outlined in Chapter 1: "harvesting or mining of the book for its functional parts – useful to borrow for the reader's own writing or to serve as practical conduct rules or stylistic models."[22] Texts written by authoritative authors then, to use Bushnell's terminology, were veritable mines for facts, phrasing, and form, as suited the purpose of the discerning reader. The contemporary method of commonplaces – that is, copying out and categorizing passages based on their rhetorical, dialectical, or informative value – was also an integral part of the natural philosophical writing of the period, what has been called: "a seemingly unending cycle of textual selection and assessment."[23] Galileo's opponents could thus use Tasso as a witness of an eclipse as easily as they could for a spirited alliterative verse. To establish the paradigm for the new philosopher to follow, Galileo instead will turn to poets to evoke literary tradition, courtly practice, and exemplary behavior, not as piecemeal models for style or pleasing ornaments.

Determining and validating an authoritative source for these aims involved similar techniques in the disciplines of philosophy and literature. For example, in Anthony Grafton's outline of Leon Battista Alberti's (1404–1472) reading process, he identifies certain humanist techniques that I would argue are the same ones that informed Copernicus' *De revolutionibus* (1543): "collation of witnesses, the setting of testimonies into their proper chronological order, and the denunciation (and explaining away) of scribal error."[24] As is well documented, Copernicus contrasted close readings of traditional works of geocentric philosophy with star charts generated on the assumption that the Earth rotated around the Sun.[25] Using this approach he pointed out the inconsistencies of the Ptolemaic theory of the structure of the universe for predicting planetary and stellar motion. By presuming that the Earth moved around the sun, the resulting charts were far more accurate in their accounting for the movement of celestial bodies. The selection of a poetic source involved the same textual challenges. Practices in both epistemologies include seeking out patterns of copy error, establishing the individuality of each manuscript, considering every version to compare possible errors, searching for ancient confirmation, making provisional readings, and separating criticism from hermeneutics.[26] Galileo applied similar critical reading strategies to both Aristotelians and the most popular poets of the period.

The *poesis* of these philosophers created a proliferation of printed materials that both aided and hindered fact-finding. The disparity of learned opinions on a topic destabilized monolithic truth claims and invited renewed investigation. As Grafton succinctly states about the relationship between books and the development of new ideas: "The laboratory could not exist without the library."[27] Such disagreement came into sharp focus as printed volumes made the direct comparison of theories and measurements available to a wider reading public. This world in print comes under much scrutiny in Galileo's dialogues as his interlocutors compare it to the physical world around them. Already recognized by Erasmus (1466–1536) and others in the period, the problem of books in the late Renaissance was twofold: the overwhelming quantity of material to read, and the recognized power of words to persuade and deceive, if not edify.[28] The particular choice of poetic authority amid this crowd of authors was, then, considered and meaningful. Galileo's interlocutors navigate through this sea of books, and the hermeneutical choices they make reflect their characteristics as philosophers and as literary figures.

Because the Copernican controversy was based on reading, either of books or of natural phenomena, and because reading was such a personal endeavor, the identities of the reader and the author come to the foreground in these debates in a way that Galileo will exploit by turning to the literary elements of poetry where his opponents turned to it for fact. The personal, individual nature of criticism in the early modern period views an individual text as the direct result of historical conditions, which allows for the general criticism of the authority of the text itself.[29] Moreover, through an author's repetition or imitation of the art of the past, his or her art becomes an obvious product of human craftsmanship and therefore open to a critique of its authority for truth claims.[30] Already in Alberti's work, Grafton sees this implicit program of overturning classical predecessors in the Renaissance revival of Latin texts.[31] As more competing voices enter into a conversation, the authority of a single one diminishes. For example, such confusion permits the Jesuit Paolo Donati to de-authorize Plato and others as viable resources in a 1575 work on celestial motion that Galileo owned: "if Plato were of this opinion, that it is certain that the stars move themselves on their own, then even in this he deceived himself. Who doubts the lies of Herodotus, being esteemed by everyone a fantastical [*favoloso*] historian? And Pomponio Mela does not tell this as a true thing, but as very marvelous and impossible to believe."[32] While discussions of Galileo's Platonism persist in modern scholarship, Aristotle remained the figure with whom most of his contemporaries and he himself contended in written work and public debates.[33] If such an authority as Aristotle could be contested, then the philosophers of the day were equally open to attack. Galileo was not willing faithfully to accept the authority of someone else's written account, whether philosophical or poetic. He balked at reading citations of poetry as presentations of facts about nature in the works of other astronomers and philosophers, which allows a discursive opening for the creation of a new authority, a new philosopher, crafted, as it were, in literary terms.

In the dialectical reasoning as well as the persuasive rhetoric that underlie the two epistemologies at work in establishing this new paradigm, the importance of the word cannot be understated. Words themselves needed to be defended from attack. According to Grafton, Leon Battista Alberti "picked his Latin words and phrases with a watch-maker's delicate precision from a wide range of sources, some of them newly discovered."[34] Galileo accordingly collected as many contemporary volumes on a subject as he could and also collected their source texts to conduct comparative readings.[35] For this reason, *Galileo's Reading* draws its comparative texts from books that were in Galileo's library and that he likely read. Since he heavily annotated volumes of poetry, mathematics, astronomy, and philosophy, and since he was frequently sought out for his opinions on matters of both poetic and philosophic interest, his comments on the acts of reading, interpretation, analysis, and drawing conclusions provide the most fruitful moments of intersection for *Galileo's Reading*. His collection of books establishes the tradition and, in some cases, also the negative model for literary and philosophical writing. His bookshelves represent Bushnell's humanist mine for form and phrasing. Returning to such territory is important because the Copernican controversy reflects problems of interpreting words as much as it does problems of interpreting the physical world – that is, the *res* and *verba* dichotomy of such importance to Galileo. As Lisa Jardine states in the contemporary context of Francis Bacon, dialectical reasoning requires "analysing natural relations as embodied in discourses, and manipulating language to gain insight into the natural world."[36] In a complementary way, by looking at the debate on the characteristics of the Moon's surface, William Shea summarizes the importance of analogy and metaphor in the early seventeenth century: "To see more, scientists had to see otherwise."[37] Galileo's library itself is a testament to these practices. In *Galileo's Reading* nearly every example of how authors approached matters of fact and designed their literary language is taken from a book Galileo owned.

In many ways the collection reflects the ideals outlined by Gabriel Naudé in his prescriptive *Advice on Establishing a Library* (1627). Naudé insists that book owners seek out many authors on one topic, both the principal authors and commentators, modern and ancient alike.[38] Galileo's collection shows the wide range of voices that compete for authority in debates on the mountains of the Moon; the satellites around Jupiter; sun-spots; floating bodies; and, of course, heliocentrism. In this way his library is similar to many of his contemporaries, though the uses to which he put it can be categorized along a spectrum. At one end can be found Galileo's friend, the abbot Orazio Morandi, whose collection in the service of Santa Prassede was subject to investigation by Inquisitorial authorities.[39] At the other end, one might look to the princely collection of Federico Cesi (1585–1630), founder of the Accademia dei Lincei into which Galileo was inducted in 1611, whose personal library of several thousand books and manuscripts became the foundation for that organization's research.[40]

Modern research on other philosophers has primarily focused on their figurative speech, with fruitful conclusions about the role of language in intellectual investigation. Again in reference to Bacon, Jardine's and Vickers' research has shown the range of rhetorical devices that Bacon employed with his new sense-based methodology: parable, *exempla*, apothegms, and proverbs, to name a few.[41] Bacon's *exempla* fall into distinct image groups: building, journeying, growing, and illuminating.[42] For example, as Bacon explains his intellectual journey to readers, the paths to knowledge need to be cut, or are blocked, or he simply gets lost along them. The sea voyage imagery is equally fraught with peril as his ideas face metaphorical shipwrecks and storms.[43] Hunting metaphors are another common motif in early modern natural philosophy.[44] William Eamon, primarily in the context of Bacon and Hooke, ties the hunting metaphor to the princely court and the new cultural ideals of the period.[45] For Galileo, such rhetorical choices are not merely flourishes or occasional gestures to the court, but work together to create a rich literary text of philosophy.

The particular focus of these literary elements on images of epic conflict is emblematic of fundamental courtly ideals and also carries with it distinct ties to Galileo's habits as a reader, his dislike of poetry in philosophical works, and even modern critics' descriptive language for the conflicts in which he was involved. This genre is tied to the princely court from its foundations in a way that was recognized by practitioners of natural philosophy prior to Galileo. In the dedicatory letter of Peter Apian's *Cosmography* (1584), the editor Johannes Bellerus writes to a group of noble adolescents: "indeed literature everywhere sets forth as testimony in famous records the exploits of the highest princes and heroes: just as Mathematics is useful and necessary to the understanding of the *Cosmographia*."[46] The study of letters and mathematics will create the ideal blend of studies for these young nobles. At first Galileo adopts similar parallel roles for epic poetry and his philosophical content in a courtly context. Later he chastises a Jesuit mathematician for the same faults he saw in the work of Tasso; uses oblique references to Ariosto, slyly to deride the valor of a critical astronomer; and begins to establish the new model of the philosopher via a literary epistemology. Finally, he characterizes the interlocutors of his dialogues not just according to their support (or lack thereof) for the Copernican theory, but also according to the literary elements of epic poetry, knight-errantry, and popular romance. As the complexity and number of debates expands, epic poetry and his reading of it provide an opportunity for attacking the codes of conduct of his opponents, using the familiar structure of poetry in philosophical treatises in an unfamiliar way.

Galileo's Reading responds to Pierpaolo Antonello's call for a reading of Galileo's prose that combines "literary-artistic outcomes with intellectual intent, socio-historical background with the scientific undertaking."[47] Galileo's library, annotations, citations, and metatextual comments demand an interpretation of the interplay between philosophy and literature that moves beyond the fact that a man of letters was also a revolutionary mathematician and natural philosopher. Likewise, for early modern readers overwhelmed by the complexities of kinetics and physics, these literary elements would have made the works accessible; likely generated sympathies for the author in his battle against the knights of Aristotelianism; and also outlined the paradigm for the new philosopher with all of his intellectual, moral, and courtly valor. *Galileo's Reading*, then, re-establishes the value of these literary, poetic elements in Galileo's new philosophy.

Chapter 1 explores Galileo's mathematical and poetical preparation as a young man. By looking not only at the collection of epic poetry that Galileo owned, but also at the ways in which his father incorporated literary elements into his musical works on harmony, I establish the context for Galileo's use of epic poetry in later works. Similar in content though his library may have been to those of other learned men of the time, in Galileo's hands these volumes became a new tool in the war of words over the structure of the universe: fertile literary ground for negatively characterizing the very philosophers who would otherwise use them for fact. An examination of other philosophical writing at the time shows the ways in which his contemporaries turned to poetry as authoritative testimony of natural phenomena, and establishes the model against which Galileo works in his own writings.

Chapter 2 demonstrates how these epistemologies begin to overlap in the period surrounding the development of the telescope while Galileo was in Padua. During the debates on the supernova of 1604, thought by observers to be a new star, Galileo entered the conversation under one, and possibly two, pseudonyms, with texts written in Paduan dialect. One of the responses to these masked works, Lodovico Delle Colombe's *Risposte piacevoli e curiose* (*Curious and Pleasant Responses*; 1607), sets a remarkable precedent for the place of contemporary epic in philosophical treatises. Shortly thereafter, Galileo expressed a desire to incorporate poetry into his preparations for the second edition of the *Starry Messenger* (1610), the treatise that revealed the contours of the Moon's surface and the previously unseen satellites around Jupiter identified with his telescope. For him philosophy could not be informed by poetry, but could be assisted by it: following the norms of publications for a courtly audience, he invited fellow poets to contribute prefatory material to the volume, but not to offer factual accounts of their observations as support. As the debate over the validity of the heliocentric Copernican theory versus the geocentric Ptolemaic theory erupted, Galileo wrote his frustrations in the marginalia of his detractors' works in a language similar to his commentary on Tasso and Ariosto. These annotations outline a method of reading, and in turn writing, natural philosophical treatises that he expresses in the language of contemporary literary criticism. This prescription for intellectual engagement frames my analysis of Galileo's literary language and shows his early attacks on the intellectual vices and lack of courtly decorum in these opponents.

Chapters 3 and 4 analyze the more mature incorporation of the literariness of epic poetry and its satire in the *Assayer* (1623), a book written as part of the so-called "Controversy on the Comets of 1618." In what I demonstrate to be an elaborately crafted literary contribution to this battle of words, Galileo cited poets directly and indirectly to insult the methods of his opponent. In this work he offered the most vivid examples of rhetorical *ethos*, or emotive effect, and epic poetry working to challenge authority. The use of this language of epic has the rhetorical ability to connect with an early-sixteenth-century audience enamored of paladin heroes. Chapter 3 shows that what modern critics have referred to as an epic battle was reflected as epic at the level of the language used to debate the theories of the nature of comets. Via references to epic poetry Galileo shows a keen ability to characterize an intellectual opponent as a treacherous, bloodthirsty foe without courtly or academic virtues.

Chapter 4, "Galileo's Lesson on *Don Chisciotte* (1622–1625)," specifically uses Cervantes' parody of epic in *Don Quixote* to frame Galileo's ridicule of that same opponent. Cervantes' critiques of reading and interpreting reality in Quixote's adventures parallel Galileo's own attacks on the misconceptions of philosophical tradition. I suggest that through his own engagement with epic poetry, Galileo, via his stylization of the fictional Sarsi and his creation of the interlocutor Simplicio in his subsequent work, proposes a modification to the otherwise tragic outcome of Cervantes' work through the creation of a new figure that will be dramatized in his dialogues. When considered in light of his use of Ariosto in the *Assayer*, this reading shows the dual purpose of epic that underlines Galileo's attack on philosophers.

Chapter 5 shows how different types of epic journeys and conflicts are manifest in Galileo's final two works, the *Dialogue on the Two Chief World Systems* (1632) and the *Discourses on Two New Sciences* (1638). When compared to the styles of other dialogues on similar topics, the characterization of Galileo's speakers stands out for its incorporation not just of the epic values and characteristics that Sarsi so lacked, but also for the overtones of romance and picaresque traditions that illuminate the intellectual preparation of the participants in the debate. The chapter demonstrates that as the three men discuss theories of the structure of the universe, the tides, and mechanics, their method borrows narrative elements from these literary traditions to define and model the successful and unsuccessful means of exploring natural phenomena.

The conclusion shows how one Aristotelian responded to these literary elements. Scipione Chiaramonti's *Difesa al suo Antiticone, o libro delle tre nuove stelle* (*Defense of His Anti-Tycho; or, A Book on the Three New Stars*; 1633) not only confronts Galileo's philosophical ideas, but fights epic poetry with epic poetry. He recognizes Galileo's rhetorical strategy, if not the literary one, and departs from his usual tone and style in order to reply directly to the multiple levels of attack that Galileo had launched. Particularly with his use of Tasso, Chiaramonti's response indicates that the charges Galileo had made in his use of poetic authorities had not gone unnoticed. Rather, the virtues and vices brought to life by Galileo's literary use of epic poetical sources set the tone for the new science and the praise of Galileo's prose by later writers.

CHAPTER ONE

The poetry of early modern philosophy

In August of 1610, Galileo (1564–1642) wrote to the German mathematician and astronomer Johannes Kepler (1571–1630) about his discoveries with the telescope related to Jupiter. In this letter he also described the criticism he subsequently received related to the discovery of the apparently new stars he found orbiting the planet and the mountains on the Moon. In order that he and Kepler might ridicule the critics together, Galileo said of these early detractors: "This race of men think that philosophy is a certain book, as it were, the *Aeneid* and the *Odyssey*: not true in the world or in nature, but to be sought in the confrontation of texts (to use their words). Why can I not laugh with you for a long time?"[1] As part of the standard practice of early modern philosophy, Galileo's predecessors and contemporaries incorporated not only the classical Latin didactic poems, but epic poems such as the *Aeneid* into their mathematical, astronomical, and cosmological texts, and they applied similar reading strategies to all of these texts in a way contrary to Galileo's own precepts about philosophy. Here, then, is the root of a series of topoi that will frame Galileo's ideology for his later works: that early philosophy, written by human authors, was opaque, not transparent as he believed nature to be.[2] Thirteen years later, in 1623, Galileo claims publicly, in print, that philosophy is not "a book of fiction created by some man, like the *Iliad* or *Orlando furioso* – books in which the least important thing is whether what is written in them is true."[3] Ariosto's *Orlando furioso* replaces Virgil's *Aeneid*, and Homer's *Iliad* takes the place of the *Odyssey* in this 1623 iteration of the idea, but the two genres of philosophy and poetry remain opposed in what one critic has called the "stretched" version of this metaphor.[4] Galileo goes on to explain just what he means in one of the most frequently cited passages from his work:

> Philosophy is written in this grand book – I mean the universe – which stands continually open to our gaze, but it cannot be understood unless

one first learns to comprehend the language and interpret the characters in which it is written. It is written in the language of mathematics, and its characters are triangles, circles, and other geometrical figures without which it is humanly impossible to understand a single word of it; without these, one is wandering about in a dark labyrinth.[5]

For Galileo, epic poems and the books of philosophy created a fruitful juxtaposition that highlighted what he proposed as different textual structures, content, and reading strategies for the two genres. Paradoxically, in order to insist upon this division between poetry and philosophy, in his later works Galileo would use that poetry and its devices to create literary philosophical works that demonstrate the power and danger of literary texts as witnesses to natural phenomena. To begin, this chapter seeks out Homer, Virgil, and even Ariosto in the texts of Galileo's contemporaries to expose the affinities between the works of the poets and those of early modern philosophers that Galileo tried to dissolve with this new methodology based on the geometric book of philosophy.

Poetic precedents in mathematics, astronomy, and philosophy

Traditionally, some of this affinity was a matter of practice. Several of the authors in Galileo's library, those that he cited in his own work, as well as Galileo himself, had firsthand experience of poetry and the other arts. For instance, Galileo owned seven volumes of the natural philosophical works by Giovanni Battista [Giambattista] Della Porta (1535–1615), the Neapolitan polymath likely most famous for his work *Magiae naturalis* (*Natural Magic*; 1558), a lengthy compendium of studies ranging from alchemy to animal husbandry. Della Porta's work can lay claim to one of the earliest mentions of a telescopic device in print, and the Neapolitan magus was also a celebrated dramatist whose theater and science had much in common.[6] Moreover, Della Porta translated the complete works of the early Roman playwright Plautus (now lost) and was author of fourteen extant comedies, some of which have been traced as sources for English theater.[7] In addition to the late medieval Tuscan poets Dante, Petrarch, and Boccaccio, Della Porta's sources also include episodes from the Renaissance novellas of Matteo Bandello (1480–1562) and Ariosto's works. Another example highlights these multiple talents of natural philosophers. The Sienese moral philosopher Alessandro Piccolomini (1508–1579) was also inclined to write in other genres. His comedy *Alessandro* (1544), of which Galileo owned a copy, was written for carnival and performed at the royal court of Henry II in France. His comedies are marked by typical elements of the genre in

this period such as transvestism and misidentification, often employed to
ridicule age or social status.[8] The Danish philosopher Tycho Brahe (1546–
1601) wrote his own poetry, including an epigram in praise of Maurice,
Landgrave of Hesse (1572–1632), the generous patron of his philosophical
projects.[9] Kepler, who worked with Brahe during the last year of his life,
translated the first book of the first-century Tacitus' Roman *Histories*.[10]
Galileo gave lectures on Dante, wrote poetry, and also drafted comedies.[11]

Beyond this experience as authors, most philosophers used poetry as
prefatory or otherwise paratextual material in their works. Tycho Brahe,
born shortly after Copernicus published *On the Revolutions of the Heavenly
Spheres*, was not satisfied with the Copernican explanation of celestial
motion. Using vast resources that included the island of Uraniborg, which
itself became an instrument for the detailed measurement of changes in
apparent stellar and planetary locations, Brahe posited the theory that the
Earth was stationary and the Sun orbited around it while the other planets
and celestial spheres orbited the Sun in turn. His *Astronomiae instauratae
mechanica* (*Instruments for the Restoration of Astronomy*; 1590) provides a
strong example of the paratextual use of poetry in a natural philosophy
context. The *Instruments for the Restoration of Astronomy* explained the
construction and operation of the tools that Brahe used in his observations and the subsequent calculations to predict the motion of stars and
planets. In the preface Brahe included his own epigrams and cited verses
from the didactic poet Manilius. His diagrams show that he inscribed allegorical phrases on his measuring instruments. He concluded sections of
the work with his own distichs or Latin hexametrical verses written by
others, and then closed the book with a series of poems written in his
honor by others.[12] Brahe's presentation of his instruments followed not
only the convention of using a classical authority such as Manilius, but a
courtly practice of publication as well. Paratextual poetry could be found
in dramatic, historical, technical, poetic, and commentary texts aimed at a
noble class of patrons. Allegorical inscriptions adorned sculptures, paintings, doorways, and more. Recent research has shown that Brahe even
reappropriated classical images such as Titan, specifically in order to connect with a larger, noble audience.[13] Still, none of these instances of poetry
in a philosophical text influences the message of the content of the work.
The verses are not integral to the comprehension or plausibility of Brahe's
or any other author's arguments, nor do they produce knowledge.

Alessandro Piccolomini eloquently explained the widely held, early, more
fundamental relationship between poetry and philosophy in his edition of
the *Sfera del mondo* (*Sphere of the World*; 1540), a treatise that elaborates

upon the books of the same title by English mathematician and astronomer Johannes Sacrobosco (d. *c.* 1256) and the Austrian Georg von Peurbach (1423–1461). Piccolomini anticipated Giambattista Vico (1668–1744) with his declaration that all early philosophers were poets: "Learned men are certain that most anciently, from the beginning, men, almost new to the world, began to philosophize. All of the parts of Philosophy were handled with the help of the poetic faculty, in such a way that the poets were those who, with the arts and sciences, taught the world."[14] In this way poets were frequently relied upon as sources of matters related to the rules of natural philosophy.[15] Piccolomini espouses a style of reading in the *Sfera* that Galileo supports for a reading of scripture, but rejects in the understanding of philosophy.[16] Piccolomini had written of the need for poetry to veil philosophy and give it a pleasing form that would be acceptable to audiences. He said that the early philosopher-poets were aware that their audience might resist the ideas they presented. As a result, these authors were:

> as those who well knew that those unrefined masses of the first ages would have supported hearing or learning things with difficulty if they had been placed in front of them covered only with the usefulness and honesty that come with them without any other enjoyable covering. This is why Poetry, by means of imitation and verse, which are two things in their nature pleasing to man, can cover up the useful things in a way, with the charm of sweetness, that our souls will drink them up in the guise of some sweet liquor that doctors often use to surround a bitter medicine that they want to give to children, so that, lured in by the sweetness, they drink the victuals that are to be useful to them. From this it was born that the Poets (as I said a little earlier) were those who in the first ages dealt with all of the sciences.[17]

Without using the term, Piccolomini discusses the rhetorical practice of *accomodatio*, accommodating difficult ideas to the intellectual level of an audience by simplification or the use of figurative language. He borrows the topos from classical traditions, perhaps most notably from Lucretius. In an emotional presentation of his infatuation with the Muses, in *De rerum natura* (*The Nature of Things*) Lucretius explains the reason why he has wedded poetry with his philosophy:

> Because I teach great truths, and set out to unknot
> The mind from the tight strictures of religion, and I write
> Of so darkling a subject in a poetry so bright,
> Nor is my method to no purpose – doctors do as much;
> Consider a physician with a child who will not sip
> A disgusting dose of wormwood: first, he coats the goblet's lip

All round with honey's sweet blond stickiness, that way to lure
Gullible youth to taste it, and to drain the bitter cure,
The child's duped but not cheated – rather, put back in the pink –
That's what I do. Since those who've never tasted of it think
This philosophy's a bitter pill to swallow, and the throng
Recoils, I wished to coat this physic in mellifluous song,
To kiss it, as it were, with the sweet honey of the Muse.[18]

Galileo reacted against using this type of poetic source in matters related to observation, particularly because the sweet and charming verses are not in fact the useful, honest material – only their covering. Having to analyze the language of this poetic veil suggests the possibility for a multiplicity of interpretations of the words themselves and therefore uncertainty about the truth contained in their message.

This aligns with contemporary thought outside Italy, specifically French mathematician Charles de Bovelles (c. 1475–1566). In Bovelles' work one modern critic sees the expression of a solution to finding truth in slippery language: "the idea that mathematics could provide certainty of order that language had lost."[19] Accommodation in Galileo's case then relies not on poetic veils, but a return to the useful and honest understanding of principles that Piccolomini had identified at the heart of philosophy, though now expressed in mathematical and geometrical terms instead of those of poets.[20] As later chapters will show, Galileo will reserve the literary elements of poetry for a different kind of knowledge production.

The broad-based humanist preparation of Galileo's readers nonetheless reflects that the disciplinary boundaries Galileo desired to see between Homer or Virgil and Euclid did not in fact exist. Either as a call to action or a call to patient philological study, authoritative texts from all genres were treated as models of eloquence and information on a variety of topics. On the ways in which students in the Renaissance were taught to approach books, Robert Black provides an apt example: "a basic schoolbook such as Boethius' *Consolation*, far from being used as a text of moral philosophy, appears to have been read in the thirteenth, fourteenth and fifteenth centuries as a convenient anthology of Latin prose and poetry, filled with valuable grammatical, mythological, geographical, lexical and metrical material."[21] Black's comment about the *Consolation of Philosophy*, a sixth-century philosophical text that explores the nature of evil, fortune, and happiness in a world ruled by a beneficent God, lays bare the possibility for a widespread application of this convention. Classical Latin texts were veritable mines of information for fields likely far beyond what the author had intended. For example, Kepler's mentor Michael Maestlin unsuccessfully asked him to collaborate on a commentary on Homer that involved calculating the dates of the conjunctions of the planets that correspond to the encounters of the gods in the *Iliad* and *Odyssey* as a means to solving hidden allegories of those poems.[22] Fortunio Liceti (1577–1657) interpreted the jealous lovers' quarrel that ended with Jupiter's punishment of Juno as described in *Iliad*, XV.17–21 as an allegory of the relationship between earth, water, air, and aether.[23] If, then, accounts of the battle of Troy could contain hidden star charts and allegorical insight into the human condition, what other value did those verses possess for natural philosophers?

The ancients and the moderns could both hold a place in the intellectual preparation of an early modern student for a variety of pedagogical ends.[24] Beyond the classical epics of Homer and Virgil, Paul Grendler's work on Venetian schools in the Renaissance has also shown that chivalric romances were often part of classroom reading.[25] These texts were not the *Odyssey* and *Aeneid*, but the heroic vernacular poems that were so popular in the sixteenth century. Recently Marina Beer tallied close to 500,000 extant copies of titles from the epic genre alone published between 1470 and 1600.[26] As Grendler reports, a survey of Venetian teachers in 1587 shows that some were teaching "libri de batagia [*sic*]" in an effort to appease the desires of parents and pupils.[27] Other teachers were using Laura Terracina's moral rewritings of epic poetry.[28] Teofilo Folengo (1491–1544) included an episode in his poem *Baldus* (1517) in which the protagonist reads chivalric romances and drops out of school to become a knight after beating up his teachers.[29] Grendler links this episode to the teaching of epic and chivalric poetry in schools.[30] In the case of *Buovo d'Antona*, the fourth book of Andrea da Barberino's early-fourteenth-century prose *I reali di Francia* (*The Royal House of France*), Grendler suggests that the work could have had value in classrooms for its parallels with contemporary life, its presentations of morality and punishments, as well as the historical chronicles it presents, though he does caution: "whether teachers and students read it as popular romance, sophisticated poetry, or both, is difficult to determine."[31] Other modern criticism has shown that both instances could be possible. For instance, in the case of the Ferrarese chivalric poems of Boiardo and Ariosto, JoAnn Cavallo has demonstrated the programs of education, or rather the ethics of action, that both the *Orlando innamorato* (*Orlando in Love*; 1495) and *Orlando furioso* promote.[32] On the other hand, as Dennis Looney has said: "Ariosto's allusions to the classics, for example, encourage a reader to return to the authorities to whom he alludes with a raised brow, to read them anew."[33] Here then is a key difference between the ways in which readers encountered these poetic texts: *Orlando furioso* was a literary document that prompted rereading in order to analyze, explore, or otherwise revise the meaning of the text, but the poetic texts of Virgil, Homer, and Lucan that were seen as authorities on natural philosophy were repositories offering a reliably predictive order to the universe.[34]

Galileo's contact with poetry

Galileo's preparation to confront the problem of poetry within philosophy was both formal and familial. In his *Racconto istorico della vita di Galileo Galilei* (*Historical Account of the Life of Galileo Galilei*; 1655), Vincenzo Viviani (1622–1703), Galileo's final direct disciple, amanuensis, and caretaker at the end of his life, gave a sample of Galileo's reading habits that included primarily poets. Even though Viviani likely indulged in hagiography with his biography, when compared with books Galileo owned this account of his intellectual preparation is indicative of certain trends. Where Viviani distinguished between the languages in which the following authors wrote, their appearance in Galileo's library and written work suggests an amicable relationship between Galileo and poets:

> He was blessed by nature with an exquisite memory; and enjoying poetry immensely, he had memorized, among the Latin authors, a large part of Virgil, Ovid, Horace, and Seneca; among the Tuscan authors, almost all of Petrarch, all of the rhymes of Berni, and slightly less than all of the poem of Ludovico Ariosto, who was always his favorite author and whom he celebrated above all the other poets, having made particular observations about him and made parallels with Tasso in many places.[35]

Viviani established a lineage of reading, and perhaps of writing, when he described Galileo's passion for poetry. Peter Armour evaluates the impact of this literary preparation on the philosophy that Galileo proposed: "Without the literary awareness which he possessed and the sense of form which this gave him, Galileo would not have been such a danger to his opponents or such an influential campaigner for the heliocentric world-system."[36] A poetic preparation, then, was not inconsequential to Galileo's approach to philosophical questions. Critics have also seen the indications of Galileo's philosophical aims in these early literary inclinations: what Lanfranco Caretti characterizes as "genuine and concrete authors, that is ... writers of *things* and not *words*."[37]

Viviani mentions the classical authors Horace, Seneca, and Ovid, who are minimally represented in Galileo's library compared to the importance given them in his biographies. In Antonio Favaro's catalog of Galileo's book collection, Seneca appears only once, as the author of the *Tragedies*. Horace similarly appears just once, as the author of the *Poemata*, Galileo's annotated copy of which is currently held by the Biblioteca Nazionale in Florence.[38] Ovid appears more frequently in the inventories used to compile the catalog, with the Latin and Italian editions of the *Metamorphoses* and *Letters* (likely the *Heroides*) listed. Still, Galileo did not cite any of these authors explicitly in his published writing. Virgil has three entries in the original catalog: "Virgilius," a tiny Latin volume in 32mo, and two vernacular translations of the *Aeneid*. Since there were more than 275 editions of Virgil's *Opere* during the period 1469–1600, determining the specific editions that Galileo owned is unlikely with current resources.[39] Surprisingly, Virgil is the only classical author in Viviani's list cited by Galileo in his writing.[40]

Viviani's genealogy of Galileo's Tuscan influences is chronological, and bypasses Dante to name Petrarch (1304–1374); the humorist Francesco Berni (*c.*1497–1536); and Galileo's favorite poet, Ariosto, as those worthy of memorization. Petrarch appears with three titles and likely five editions between them in Galileo's library.[41] Other materials further support Viviani's claims about Galileo's interest in Petrarch. In Lorenzo Ceccarelli's letter about the death of Galileo's daughter Maria Celeste in 1635, he cites Petrarch (*Canzoniere* 365, line 4) and thanks Galileo for teaching him the verse.[42] Marginalia in an edition of Petrarch's *Canzoniere* that included the *Trionfi* suggest that Galileo worked with several editions (including that by the popular contemporary poet Alessandro Tassoni (1565–1635)) to compile his own critical summary of the poems.[43] In addition he owned at least two copies of Ariosto's *Orlando furioso*. He also owned three editions of Dante and delivered his two lectures to the prestigious literary *Accademia fiorentina* on the size of the *Inferno*, but the poet escapes direct mention as a poetic or literary influence in the earliest biographies of Galileo.[44]

This interest in poetry reflects not only what could be seen as canonical taste in the Italian literary tradition, but a passion for poets known for their raucous, if not obscene, subject matter. Canon Niccolò Gherardini (d. 1678) said in Galileo's biography, *La vita del Signor Galileo Galilei* (*The Life of Mr. Galileo Galilei*; *c.* 1654): "He was very familiar with a book titled the *Ruzzante*, written in Paduan dialect, taking great pleasure from those coarse stories and ridiculous accidents."[45] Angelo Beolco (1502–1542), also known as Ruzzante, mentioned several times by Galileo in his letters, had a successful publishing history in the sixteenth century, but only appears in the catalog with the 1565 edition of his *Comedies*.

According to Gherardini, Galileo also "quite often cited the chapters of Francesco Berni, whose verses and quotations in many propositions he adapted to his position, no less than if they had been his own, and with great pleasure."[46] Berni, another burlesque poet, although cited repeatedly in Galileo's letters, was not present in documents related to his library. In spite of Berni's absence in these sources, he is present in flavorful spirit in Galileo's writing.[47]

In the first decades of Galileo's life, his father was working on musical studies of harmonics, dissonance, acoustics, and monody informed by observation with the senses. Written within a courtly setting, these works make reference to the poetry and fables that will become part of Galileo's repertoire in his own philosophical writing. For a sense of the tone of Vincenzo Galilei (*c.*1520–1591) in his *Dialogue on Ancient and Modern Music* (1581), the work in which he courteously corrects the theory of his instructor Gioseffo Zarlino, one example notably anticipates the kind of insult that will be found in Galileo's own work, particularly the *Assayer*.[48] Typically Galilei uses the poems of Homer, Virgil, Ovid, and Lucan for examples of musical instruments or sounds, and even the horn of the despot Caligorante from Ariosto's *Furioso* appears in the text.[49] Yet, in response to critics who display what Galilei labels the vice of ignorance, he summarizes the tale from Aesop of a mouse whose tail becomes white with flour and, fancying himself a master of ground wheat, proclaims himself miller and kicks out the legitimate, knowledgeable mouse who had held the position.[50] Galilei goes on to critique the style of certain singers who similarly know nothing of the mathematics or musical theory involved in their art: "Without a knowledge of these things, God knows how they manage. Instead they have on their lips as evidence of their knowledge more proverbs of Burchiello and Berni than any other pedagogue of our mother tongue. What, please, have the burlesques of these two ridiculous poets to do with demonstrating the distances and ratios of the musical intervals?"[51] Burchiello and Berni, the two satirical poets, play a similar role in this expression of frustration as do Virgil, Homer, and Ariosto in Galileo's later remarks that poetry has no place in the geometrical, philosophical explanations of the natural world. Of such stubbornness, Galilei had already written: "But to persuade such people that they are ignorant of the true music would take not the rhetoric and eloquence of Cicero or Demosthenes, but the sword of the paladin Orlando or the authority of some very great prince who is a friend of the truth."[52] If eloquent rhetoric cannot vanquish the ignorant, the only solution would seem to be the epitome of courtly force: Orlando or the prince himself. These references to Aesop, Berni, Burchiello, and Orlando are not made to draw on the authority of fables and poetry to demonstrate matters related to musical theory. Aesop's moral tale calls into question the morality of the singers; the satirists are mentioned to satirize the next group of singers; Orlando is brought in when reason fails to convince the stubbornly ignorant.

Each of these instances belittles the behavior and practice of opposing theorists or practitioners of musical arts, and here we see the early traces of a literary development within a philosophical work. The *ethos* of these figures is put in doubt by references to poetry that require analysis to understand. Galilei will make this connection explicit in his later work, again in response to Zarlino's theories. In a particularly feisty moment in the subsequent *Discorso intorno alle opere di Gioseffo Zarlino* (*Discourse on the Works of Gioseffo Zarlino*; 1589), Galilei complains that Zarlino has unnecessarily relied on a reading of Ptolemy's description of syntonic diatonic tuning as a basis for vocal intonation. As part of the list of faults he finds, he claims that Zarlino added the modifiers "natural" and "artificial" to Ptolemy's definition. Galilei takes Zarlino to task, saying: "I respond that he is hung up on the ideas of natural syntonic and artificial syntonic, and I say again that Ptolemy created just one syntonic diatonic, to which he gave neither a name nor a last name like natural or artificial."[53] Galilei goes on to make a direct comparison between Zarlino's slippery, ill-conceived linguistic program and the paladin Orlando when he has lost all of his courtly, knightly qualities: "Saying then that as such it is pleasing to him, seems to me the same faculty of reason that Orlando used at the height of his fury."[54] He explicitly pairs reasoning skills with honor: "if in his escape he has no other defense than this, it would have been more honorable to bow to the truth immediately, knowing himself to be in error, rather than try to defend himself with means such as these and make the offense much greater."[55] Orlando is once again called upon to place the character of Zarlino in question. Ariosto may not be an authority on tonality, but his poem is a mine for matters of courtly decorum.

While Galileo's father was working on these polemical discourses, Galileo was gaining introductions to courtly and academy life in Tuscany. Galileo's recent biographer Heilbron reminds us that his first contact with patrons was via a literary academy, the *Accademia degli Alterati*.[56] For the literary elite the academies became "a forum to rehearse erudition, to imitate greatness, and to temper their characters."[57] Galileo met the artist Ludovico Cardi, "Il Cigoli" (1559–1613), in the 1580s through connections with the Florentine *Accademia del Disegno*.[58] He delivered lectures on the size of Dante's *Inferno* to the *Accademia fiorentina* in 1588. This contact with the Medici-inspired academies invited, if not necessitated, attention to questions of courtliness, honor, and decorum. Mario Biagioli has clearly demonstrated Galileo's concern for these questions while marketing his instruments, and I will argue that his literary, instead of factual, use of poetry achieves the same end.[59]

The *Accademia degli Alterati* was also involved in the Ariosto–Tasso debate in which Galileo took a very active interest. During the last decades of the sixteenth century and the first years of the seventeenth, men of letters in Italy rigorously argued about definitions of genre, the necessity for the unity of narrative, and the status of heroic protagonists in the *Gerusalemme liberata* and the *Orlando furioso*, in attempts to define and legitimate heroic poetry.[60] Because of their relevance to the linguistic and stylistic controversy surrounding their masterpieces, Galileo's comments on Tasso and Ariosto have garnered so much modern critical attention that they have taken on identities of their own: the *Considerazioni al Tasso* (*Considerations of Tasso*) and the *Postille all'Ariosto* (*Glosses on Ariosto*).[61] These titles suggest an independence of the criticism in the margins from the texts they analyze, when in fact the *Considerazioni* and *Postille* would make no sense if extracted from the poems. Tibor Wlassics dates Galileo's *Considerazioni* to as early as 1586 and as late as 1627, a period after both the *Gerusalemme liberata* (1581) and the *Gerusalemme conquistata* (*Jerusalem Conquered*, 1593), noting that their first mention in letters appears in May 1609, and the last in May 1640.[62] Paolo Beni (1553–1625) hurriedly published his commentary on Tasso in 1607 thinking that he needed to beat Galileo to the press, though Galileo's letters suggest that he was still grappling with how best to present his comparison of the poets as late as 1640.[63] The *Postille all'Ariosto* indicate an equally lifelong fascination with the *Furioso*, but one aimed at the poem's perfection rather than its critique.[64]

Of the many volumes that Galileo annotated, the only *postille* to receive intense modern critical treatment have been these comments on the *Liberata* and the *Furioso*, but even then, the interest in Galileo's copies of these epic poems has been frequently limited to the question of the philosopher's aesthetic principles. While the traditional critical approach to these marginalia can provide insight on what Galileo valued in his poetry, they, perhaps more than others, also can be pushed further to help us understand the steps of Galileo's intellectual encounters with books and the links he creates among texts in his library. Galileo's notes in the margins of the other works are less studied, and to my knowledge, have not been compared to the Tasso and Ariosto commentaries.

Even though much has already been written about Galileo's annotations of the *Orlando furioso* and the *Gerusalemme liberata*, a consensus has not been reached. Tibor Wlassics suggests that philological, psychological, geographic, chronological, and aesthetic explanations of Galileo's dislike of Tasso are incomplete. He concludes that the most satisfactory reason for the polarizing tone of Galileo's *Considerazioni* is the sociological phenomenon of academic literary debate in the period.[65] I will argue in Chapter 3 that the tone of these annotations matches that of other debates on sunspots, floating bodies, and comets. Heilbron suggests a slightly different context for them: "Galileo's cuts and thrusts should be regarded as material for sprightly debates among brash young literary men, private notes for knockdown confrontations with members of the *Alterati*, who tended to favor Tasso, not formal literary criticism for later depth analysis."[66] On the other hand, Peter Armour argues that the *Considerazioni al Tasso* and *Postille all'Ariosto*, given their format and structure, were not part of the literary debate of the early Seicento.[67] Yet, Fernand Hallyn comments on what he sees as Galileo's anti-mannerist criticism of Tasso in line with literary aesthetic concerns of the period, which follows the similar analyses by Giulio Marzot, Raffaele Colapietra, and Raffaelo Spongano.[68] Both Wlassics and Armour suggest that Galileo's extreme reaction against Tasso is a refusal, or at the least a miscomprehension, of the protoromanticism of the *Gerusalemme liberata*.[69] Then again, on one aspect of Galileo's marginalia in the *Furioso*, Peter DeSa Wiggins writes: "In the realm of character, at least, he might be considered among the earliest of readers of the novel, even though the Italian novel itself, as we know it, did not exist in his time."[70] When seen together, these analyses of the *Considerazioni* and *Postille* suggest that Galileo's lifelong fascination with the poems of Ariosto and Tasso – one that likely began while he was starting his studies at the University of Pisa – was either an active and formal part of the debates of the period or not, a reaction to changing literary taste or not, and a reaction against the novel or not. For this reason I propose to read these annotations in tandem with his marginalia in philosophical documents to show the consistency that exists between them.

Most frequently modern literary critics associate Galileo's attacks on Tasso with a negative response to mannerism that would seem to ally Galileo's prose with poetic and aesthetic ideals of previous centuries, but only recently have they explored the ways in which his criticisms of poetry overlap with his philosophical concerns. In fact, much of Galileo's commentary on Tasso is related to the question of rhetoric and the rhetorical more than the aesthetic, concerns that are found in his commentaries on

philosophical writing. Jonathan Unglaub recently and succinctly summarized what Galileo saw as the primary fault in Tasso's poetic language: "a
mere accumulation of words that function not as bearers of meaning, as
seeds of a palpable image, but as gratuitous poetic interference."[71] Unlike
Ariosto's or even Galileo's own language of description that appealed to
the senses, Tasso's reliance on previous poetic models asked readers to rely
on their intellects to connect the dots between phrasing and tradition in
order to construct images in the narration. This kind of language left far
too much to the imagination to be part of the language Galileo championed for the book of nature.

While Galileo will utilize material from his poetic and philosophical
sources in different ways, the structure and content of the annotations in
the *Furioso* and *Liberata* show the consistency with which he was reading all of his books. The modern editor Alberto Chiari groups the various *Postille all'Ariosto* according to type in a way that we could apply to
Galileo's *postille* across the books in his library: "excerpts, comparisons,
hyperboles, difficult and confusing passages, generic references, corrections to the 1572 printing, Galileo's amendments, comparisons and annotations, cancellations, underlines, duels, astronomical descriptions, harsh
constructions, citations and generic signs."[72] Apart from the duels and the
astronomical descriptions, which are unique to the *Furioso*, examples from
each category can be found in at least one other volume annotated by
Galileo, if not several, and many of them are works of natural philosophy.
The attention to astronomical descriptions is limited to four instances
of short, hand-drawn lines where Ariosto marks time according to the
location of celestial bodies.[73] The only physical phenomenon to receive
extended attention in a poem is what Galileo sees as Tasso's exaggeration
of visual acuity at long distances under dusty and chaotic conditions.[74] By
bowing to the poetic conventions of identifying the host of men attacking
a city, Galileo feels Tasso stretches the reader's credulity beyond the limits
of verisimilitude when he has Erminia identify the Christian warriors at
great distance through clouds of dust. Because the work of annotating
these two poems was a lifelong endeavor, the criticism of poetry developed alongside the criticism of philosophical ideas during Galileo's career
in Pisa, Padua, and eventually Florence. For this reason, they will be considered together in each conflict.

Aside from these debates about Ariosto and Tasso, who do figure most
prominently in Galileo's work, critics also tend to overlook the overwhelming number of epic, chivalric, heroic, and mock-heroic works that Galileo
owned. Building on research on Galileo's library begun by Antonio Favaro

in the 1880s, my archival work on Favaro's sources significantly expands the titles in this category. Favaro had already identified that Galileo owned many of the classic epic poems. Homer and Virgil appear in his catalog in vernacular translations by the Venetian Lodovico Dolce and Anibal Caro.[75] Galileo mentions an episode from the *Aeneid* in his *Assayer* (1623) and part of his deposition by the Inquisition in 1633 involves a presumed discussion between Galileo and Giambattista Della Porta on Virgil and Naples.[76] He also owned at least two of Boccaccio's romances, the *Commedia delle ninfe fiorentine* (or *Ameto*), and *Filocolo*, as well as the pastoral *Arcadia* by Jacopo Sannazaro. In addition Favaro listed the editions of the *Orlando furioso* and *Gerusalemme liberata*; the earlier *Orlando innamorato*, produced at the Este court of Ferrara by Matteo Maria Boiardo; and the chivalric epic written by Torquato Tasso's father, Bernardo, the *Amadigi* (1560), inspired by the Spanish romance cycle of Amadis of Gaul.

Beyond these mainstream epic poems, Galileo owned many minor works that were primarily related to the Carolingian cycles presented by Boiardo and Ariosto. These titles include Luca Pulci's *Il Ciriffo Calvaneo* (*c.* 1470), two copies of Giambattista Dragoncino da Fano's *Innamoramento di Guidon Selvaggio che fu figliuolo di Rinaldo da Montalbano* (*The Enamored Guidon Selvaggio, Son of Rinaldo of Montalban*; 1516), Marco Guazzo's *Astolfo borioso* (*Vainglorious Astolfo*; 1523), Bartolomeo Oriolo's *I quatro canti di Ruggiero* (*The Four Canti of Ruggiero*; 1545), and Pietro Lauro's translation of the *Historia delle gloriose imprese di Polendo figliuolo di Palmerino d'Oliva* (*History of the Glorious Feats of Polendo, Son of Palmerin de Oliva*; 1566).[77] Galileo's collection also includes several anonymous works in this same category: *Libro chiamato Aspramonte* (*The Book Called Aspramonte*; 1516), *Libro del Gigante Morante & de re Carlo & de tutti li paladini, & del conquisto che Orlando fece de la Citta de Sania* (*The Book of the Giant Morante and of Charlemagne, the Paladins and Orlando's Conquest of Sania*; 1531), the *Aggiunta al secondo volume di don Rogello di Grecia, che è in ordine quarto libro di don Florisello* (*The Addition to the Second Volume of Don Rogello of Greece, Fourth Book of Don Florisello*; 1564), and *Libro chiamato Antifor di Barosia* (*The Book Called Antifor of Barosia*; 1584).[78] Another subset of this category was a series of madrigals written in Paduan dialect by Bertevello delle Brentelle about Ariosto's characters Bradamante, Isabella, Zerbino, and Orlando.[79] His library also contained a translation of the mid-sixteenth-century picaresque tale *Lazarillo de Tormes* (1554) that will be discussed in the fourth chapter.[80]

This interest in epic poetry and its variations persisted well into the seventeenth century. Galileo's library reflects a series of international epic and heroic poems composed after the turn of the century. For example, he owned a copy of Scottish poet John Barclay's *Argenis* (1621). The French astronomer Nicolas-Claude Fabri de Peiresc (1580–1637), a correspondent of Galileo, was a friend of Barclay, and this popular Latin epic had a fortunate life of reprints in translation in Italy after 1629.[81] Carlo Bocchineri's *Il Palladio poemetto* (1611) takes inspiration from the death of Henry IV of France, an event about which Galileo owned several other volumes.[82] Andrea Salvadori's *Medoro* (1623), of which Galileo also owned a copy, brings to life the story of Angelica and Medoro as told by Ariosto in the *Furioso*, then imagines what would have happened had Sacripante persisted in his pursuit of the princess and if she had repented her desire to leave him. In this group also is Giovanni Battista Calamai's *Il Parto della Vergine. Poema eroico in 20 cantici* (*Birth of the Virgin: Heroic Poem in Twenty Canticles*; 1623), a religiously themed heroic poem.[83] Galileo owned a copy of Raffaele Gualterotti's *L'universo, ovvero il Polemidoro, poema eroico* (*The Universe; or, Polemidoro: Heroic Poem*; 1600).[84] Gualterotti was a frequent correspondent of Galileo's, asked him for lenses for telescopes, and also claimed to have invented a weaker telescope prior to Galileo's refinement of the instrument in 1609.[85] Gualterotti wrote to Grand Duke Cosimo II de' Medici in 1610 saying that after having read Galileo's *Starry Messenger* he was inspired to compose a third poem in the series that began with *Polemidoro*, and this next poem would be based on the new stars and the four new "planets" around Jupiter.[86] Galileo also owned at least one seventeenth-century follow-up to Tasso's *Gerusalemme liberata*, Francesco Rasi's *Lamento d'Emireno poemetto primo* (*Lament of Emireno: First Poem*; 1619),[87] and his library included an Italian translation of Cervantes' mock-heroic, picaresque *Don Quixote* (1605, 1615) that will be discussed at length in Chapter 4.[88]

A final subset of these works of epic and heroic poetry includes those that Galileo owned in which he or his telescope also appeared. These include Gabriele Chiabrera's *Firenze* (*Florence*; 1615), Giovanni Domenico Peri's *Fiesole distrutta* (*Fiesole Destroyed*; 1621), Giulio Strozzi's *La Venetia edificata* (*Venice Edified*; 1623), and Giambattista Marino's *Adone* (*Adonis*; 1623).[89]

Galileo's involvement with poetic production extends beyond reading poems and engaging in literary debate. We know that we have lost much of the material related to his literary efforts from letters that suggest his peers considered him to be an influential critic of literature. Through letters of the mathematician Luca Valerio, we learn of Galileo's involvement in the corrections made to Margherita Sarrocchi's epic poem *Scanderbeide* (Rome, 1623).[90] An investigation of this exchange opens a new dimension for understanding Galileo's relationship to epic poetry. In 1609 Valerio writes of Galileo's role in shaping Sarrocchi's historical epic poem: "Lady Sarrocchi thanks you for the favor done to her by sending your opinions of the style of her poem, and the diligence you express that you want to show to every part of it."[91] In response to a request several months later from Sarrocchi herself asking Galileo to consider the changes made to her epic poem based on his first edits, he writes that he is too ill to complete the work a second time.[92] How many other similar requests did Galileo receive?[93] This practice may explain the presence of a copy of Piero Bardi's (Beridio d'Arpe) mock-heroic *Avino Avolio Ottone Berlinghieri* in the lists of books in Galileo's library, even though it was not published until after Galileo's death, in 1643.[94] As a final note, it must be mentioned that very little evidence exists about what manuscripts Galileo may have owned. The above list of titles is undoubtedly incomplete.

Notably absent from this collection of epic poems are the didactic texts that are fundamental in the presentation of philosophy written by so many of Galileo's contemporaries, opponents, and supporters alike. Instruction and epic poetry were related as early as the first didactic poets who adopted epic hexameter for their verses. Epic carried a weight of seriousness and import; poetry had a didactic quality. Both were closely associated with divine inspiration and therefore held a unique truth value.[95] Beyond natural philosophy, didactic poetry became a source on matters linguistic, poetic, metaphorical, allegorical, philosophical, and moral. The popular and well-received *Phaenomena* by Aratus (315 BCE–240 BCE) owes much of its style to Homeric phrasing and has many Homeric glosses in its verses. This can be observed to such an extent that D. Mark Possanza has argued that Germanicus Caesar's translation of Aratus used the poetry of Homer and Hesiod not only to understand the *Phaenomena* but also to rewrite passages using them as models.[96] Cicero and Ovid both benefited from translations they made of this work early in their careers.[97] Possanza identifies the central proposition of the poem as: "the geocentric universe is a well ordered system presided over by a rational, beneficent deity whose presence is revealed by signs."[98] This explains perhaps why Ptolemy's *Almagest* contains diagrams, tables, and explanations, and why the only verses cited are from the *Phaenomena*.

Other didactic epic poems used this template, but with lasting implications for post-Reformation philosophy. Following the model of Aratus, the first-century BCE Latin didactic poet Lucretius is best remembered for his six-book *De rerum natura*.[99] The Epicureanism of this work was likely part of the foundation for the heresy charges against Galileo in 1632.[100] The revolution of Lucretius' text resided in the notion that all matter is made of eternal, invisible particles that are infinite in number and common to all living and inanimate beings.[101] Moreover, neither they nor humans have a creator or an eternal soul, which suggests that religion is a false belief. Though scandalous in its implications, copies of Poggio Bracciolini's rediscovered manuscript circulated quickly and in great quantity, and the work was not placed on the early Index of Prohibited Books. Thus it was that contemporary readers had direct access to *The Nature of Things* as well as the classical authors who had also relied on the Lucretian text. Some scholars have seen the Lucretian influence on Galileo as early as his preparatory pages of the *De motu antiquiora* (1589–1592), but he could have also known atomist teachings by Democritus that had been transmitted through Aristotle and Galen and were part of the scholarly environment at Pisa when Galileo was a young man.[102] Atomism had implications for investigating the density of solids and the resulting differences in their motion, which were Galileo's concern in his works on floating bodies, comets, and motion more generally. Lucretius is the only printed didactic poem in the documents related to his library.[103] Galileo's closest colleagues were also engaging with Lucretian thought in their own work: Virginio Cesarini, dedicatee of the *Assayer* and author of Lucretian inspired poetry, wanted to write a poetic commentary for *The Nature of Things*; and Giovanni Ciampoli, influential for procuring permissions to print Galileo's *Chief World Systems*, was composing an atomist dialogue in the 1620s.[104]

Virgil's *Georgics*, written slightly later, were a common linguistic and moral authority that was even used as a source for interpreting weather signs into the eighteenth century.[105] The work was a popular touchstone for the language of natural philosophy because it was received as truth presented directly to the reader without any pleasing veil. Della Porta turns to the *Georgics* for use of the word *distillatio*, the Lincean Fabio Colonna for the definitions of shades of purple, and Galileo's French follower Pierre Gassendi for the use of the word *vertice*.[106] A recent scholar of the *Georgics* concisely explains the methodology of the work: "The Virgilian farmer thus predicts weather because Jove himself has *revealed* to him the true correspondence between signs and signified events, and not because the farmer has established a link or an independently humanly manufactured basis – by, say, a statistical manipulation of observations or by means of an 'empirical' method of discovery."[107] Much in the same way that Aratus interprets the signs of a deity through the natural world, so too does Virgil.

This deity-down approach, laden with poetry, revealing a divine *poesis*, is antithetical to the natural-world-up approach that Galileo begins and his followers in later centuries wholeheartedly adopt.

The first-century CE work by Manilius, the didactic poem *Astronomica*, was patterned after the *Georgics*. Dividing the poem into five books, Manilius recognizes the daunting task before him and specifically brings his didactic work into dialogue with the classical epic poems of the centuries prior. At the beginning of Book III Manilius declares that he will not copy Hesiod's *Theogony* on the war of the gods; nor the *Iliad*; nor the *Argonautica* of Apollonius Rhodius; nor the epic poem *Messeniaca* by Rhianus, the *Persica* by Chocrilus of Samos, the story of the Seven against Thebes, the tragedies of Oedipus or Thyestes, or the *Annales* of Ennius. Instead, he writes, "I must wrestle with numerals and names of things unheard of with the seasons, the changing fortunes and movements of the sky, with the signs' variations, and even with the portions of their portions. Ah, how great a task it is to put into words what passes understanding! Ah, how great to tell in fitting poetry, and this to yoke to a fixed metre!"[108] As an example of this challenge, Manilius spends nearly sixty verses of epic hexameter explaining how to determine the degree of movement for each zodiac sign.[109]

The problematic uses of poetry

Typically the poetry used by early modern astronomers and philosophers is not just the didactic hexameter of Manilius or Lucretius, but also the narrative poetic texts of Virgil, Homer, Lucan, and other epic poets who had been used for centuries as sources for various disciplines. The persistence of this use of these classical authors, particularly from works of epic, suggests a continued mediation of the contents and means of expression of these poems for philosophers. As Anthony Grafton states, most sixteenth- and seventeenth-century scientists were: "commentators by vocation, they saw their duty not as discovering facts never before seen and drawing inferences from them but as assembling facts from reliable sources in a new and revealing order."[110] In many cases, Galileo's contemporaries followed a textual tradition of citation with medieval, and earlier, roots. Aristotle's *On the Universe*, Chapter 6 particularly, uses verses from Homer to echo concepts of geography, cosmography, and natural philosophy.[111] One of the most popular uses of the classics by these astronomers and philosophers was for establishing etymologies and rules of word usage that allowed them to incorporate the widest variety of sources. Fortunio

Liceti uses Pliny and Ovid for the definition of "circumference," and Virgil's *Georgics* and *Aeneid* for the term "fire."[112] In *De terra unico centro motus ... coeli ... disputationes* (*Disputations on the Earth, Only Center of the Motion of the Heavens*; 1641) Liceti goes beyond etymological concerns and uses three places from the *Aeneid* and the *Georgics* that for him support the equal division of the months.[113] Later, the *Georgics* are used as evidence of the division of the tropics into zones.[114] In another of his works, *De luminis* (*On Light*; 1641), he mentions the beginning of *Aeneid*, VIII as a source for the behavior of reflecting light.[115]

In a more specific example, Dido's death is indicative of several natural phenomena. In *De luminis* Liceti explores the tangential topic of astral light helping those of weak disposition live to their seventieth year provided that other obstacles do not hinder their aging:

> on account of many errors in lifestyle, and other reasons, it is easily possible to weaken a disposition of this sort for oneself, and to diminish the extent of one's own life; whence the poet spoke well and in the sweetest meter that the young lady Dido, transfixing herself with her sword because of Aeneas' departure, ought not to have perished by fate or by death:
>
>> Then omnipotent Juno, pitying her prolonged pain
>> And her difficult death, sent down Iris from Olympus,
>> So that she could release the struggling soul and knotted joints.
>> Since in fact she perished neither by fate nor deserved death,
>> But wretched before her day ...[116]

I provide the passage at length to show how Liceti introduces the quotation from Virgil. Because Dido's actions (and her suicide) accelerated the arrival of her death, Virgil's verses are proof that his theory about the ways in which individuals weaken the positive effects of astral light is true. Similarly Dido's death appears in Giambattista Della Porta's work on refraction, in a discussion of seeing one image doubled. He cites Virgil from the moment when the Queen of Carthage interprets the omens of her death: "She was like Pentheus, stripped of his mind, seeing armies of Furies / Seeing the sole Sun double, and Thebes in duplicate presence."[117] The context of the *Aeneid* surrounding these verses adds nothing to a reader's understanding of Liceti's or Della Porta's arguments.

This tradition of poetic quotation persists, for instance, in a text that is central to the Ptolemaic–Copernican debates, Johannes de Sacrobosco's *Tractatus de sphaera* (*Treatise on the Sphere*; c. 1230). Sacrobosco becomes a pivotal figure because *On the Sphere* was the authoritative explanation of the Ptolemaic system and therefore foundational for not only medieval astronomy, but studies for subsequent centuries. Sacrobosco himself makes use of this poetic tradition in his analysis of Ptolemy, and his commentators amplify that style in turn. One of the most influential commentaries on the *Sphere* (considered by some the greatest) was written by Christoph Clavius, S.J. (1538–1612), an important educator for generations of Jesuit astronomers and a cordial colleague to Galileo.[118] Clavius' commentary on Sacrobosco was printed multiple times between the first edition in 1570 and the author's death. In addition to being part of the Gregorian calendar reform, he wrote several textbooks on mathematics and was part of the Jesuit project to evaluate and accept Galileo's discoveries with the telescope.[119] While Clavius did disagree with the implications of those discoveries, he shared Galileo's comfort in the clarity of mathematical solutions and skepticism of divergent philosophical opinions. Galileo, along with many other mathematicians and philosophers, revered Clavius' work on algebra and the astrolabe, and they maintained a respectful relationship in which the Jesuit sent Galileo copies of his books as they were published.

At times, Clavius can supply nearly ten pages of commentary on ten lines of Sacrobosco's text. These glosses include indications of word usage, measurements, calculations, and predictions. He quotes heavily from biblical passages and Aristotelian texts, but these are not his only sources. More substantially, and with greater implications for the generation of meaning in the text, Clavius inserts lines of poetry into his commentary to augment Sacrobosco's own use of other authorities. For example, Sacrobosco cites two incongruous lines from the *Georgics* when he describes the Arctic and Antarctic zones – "Five zones form the heavens, of which one is always ruddy … Through both when the twelve signs' slanted ranks might revolve" – and on the next page he cites two incongruous lines from Ovid's *Metamorphoses* to distinguish the other zones of the sky: "The god divided the sky into two zones, two on the right and two on the left … Two he placed in between and made temperate regions, where heat and cold are mixed."[120] The divine ordering of chaos that Sacrobosco cites is the first metamorphosis of Ovid's poem that will eventually lead to the creation of mankind, whose transformations are its overarching subject. Yet, Sacrobosco approaches the verses as a literal description of creation without its thematic or figurative implications. He says he uses Ovid "in confirmation" of his theories, and Clavius subsequently calls Virgil a "witness" to these phenomena.[121] For a final authoritative touch, Clavius adds his own poetic source to Sacrobosco's inclusion of Virgil and Ovid by citing from Lucan's *Pharsalia*, III.248: "You Arabs arrived in a world you found unfamiliar, / marveling at trees whose shadows fail to fall to the left."[122] Clavius' addition extends the discussion of the zones of the sky to an examination of how light from these zones falls differently on the Earth's spherical surface so that shadows appear to move in opposite directions in the northern and southern hemispheres.

Clavius represents the multiple approaches to the question of how to utilize textual authority. For example, he wrote arithmetic and geometry textbooks in an elementary Latin (or translated into simple Italian), heavily supplemented with diagrams, tables, and charts of predicted stellar and planetary locations. He also composed manuals for the construction and use of instruments, and supplied commentary on foundational texts of astronomy using no quotations from other sources. At one point Clavius includes his own mnemonic verses on the formula for calculating the dimensions of a circle, but only after he provides a description of the method in prose.[123] In his glosses he mentions only a few commentaries on Archimedes, in particular that of Federico Commandino.[124] The same is true for Clavius' work *De cochlea* (*On the Screw*; 1615). The *Gnomonices* (1581), named for the gnomon, or indicator, on a sundial, direct the reader to specific passages of texts by classical authors such as Pliny, Euclid, and Ptolemy, as well as contemporary mathematicians Guidobaldo del Monte (1545–1607) and Giovanni Battista Benedetti (1530–1590).[125] Clavius' manual for the construction of an astrolabe mentions many of these same mathematical texts to demonstrate a tradition of calculating methods using the instrument.[126] Taken together, this accumulation of classical authorities establishes the veracity of contemporary hypotheses derived from them. These are not moments of metaphor or hyperbole. By comparison, when Galileo refers to the episode from the *Aeneid* of Alcestes lighting his path by the lingering glow of a flaming arrow shot into the night, he discounts its factual nature by saying: "This effect is not to be seen except in poetry."[127]

These sources are not without their problems even for those who adopt them wholeheartedly, and Galileo's contemporaries often engage questions of discrepancies between classical *auctores*. The absolute authority given to Homer or Virgil often ignores discord among poetic sources. An example from Alessandro Piccolomini's *Sphere*, discussed earlier for its presentation of these poetic authorities as philosophers, demonstrates the conflicting stories presented by them. Piccolomini points out that their aim was not necessarily to provide literal, objective descriptions:

> For which reason, among several things, they needed many and diverse descriptions of their own to adorn their poems, since by being able to vary their verses better they would bring greater delight through describing the

same things in different ways. They used this same thing in Astrology in the birth and the disappearance of stars, among other things. So that by assigning different ways of appearance and disappearance they would be able variously to describe and nearly sketch out the different seasons of the year, the diverse times of hours and days, and other similar things, according to what we see used by Homer, Virgil, Horace, Ovid, and other great Poets."[128]

At the end of Chapter 6 he goes on to say that the new knowledge of the seasons and stellar motions will help to reread the poets and understand them better, not vice versa: "with this doctrine many places in their texts can be understood. In order to weave a more beautiful tapestry and make their poem more varied and rich, they proceed in various ways describing the seasons of the year, the days, and the hours according to the rules of good poets, as I take great pleasure doing myself, which anyone can see for themselves very well."[129] Homer and Virgil are not necessarily the best first steps for understanding a natural phenomenon since they are bound by rules of poetry. Later Piccolomini will attribute these discrepancies between poetic and philosophical explanations to *accomodatio* once more. He claims that many of the errors of astrology come from the "fragility" of man, who is limited in understanding by his senses:

> just as Aristotle affirms in his books on the soul and even elsewhere, and as Dante equally makes clear, when he says: 'Such signs are suited to your mind, since from / the senses only can it apprehend / what then becomes fit for the intellect' and what follows. Being as such, it would be no wonder if the Astrologers, in many things, and especially in showing quantities and sizes of the aforesaid luminous bodies of the Heavens, and their distances from Earth, did not arrive at their target at all.[130]

Again, this style of writing, with multiple ways of interpreting the words of the poets and understanding the truth of their verses, is the very style against which Galileo must work as he presents his observations that challenge the Ptolemaic theory of the structure of the universe.

Beyond questions of misinterpreting poetic form or working backward to knowledge from *accomodatio*, the poets also disagree, and then their instructional value is called into question. Pierre Gassendi, a French follower of Galileo in many of his philosophical investigations and an intellectual who took an anti-Aristotelian stance in his works, explores the intricacies of dealing with these sources in a passage in his treatise on meteorology. He uses the example of the Pleiades, a bright cluster of stars whose motion was the basis for determining the seasons for millennia. The motion of the Pleiades appears repeatedly in the discussions of the

Copernican and Ptolemaic systems once Galileo publishes observations
of previously unknown stars in this cluster in the *Starry Messenger* (1610).
Both sides use data on the motion of these stars to argue for the validity
of their theories. Gassendi discusses their cosmical (happening at sunrise)
and acronychal (happening at sunset) rising or setting in relation to the
accounts by Virgil, Ovid, and Lucan:

> In this place you see in passing that the same autumn is described, by Virgil
> indeed through the setting, but by Ovid through the rising of the very same
> Pleiades. But clearly the former understands the setting as cosmical; for the
> Pleiades go down at that time in the morning: the latter understands the
> rising as acronychal; for at that time in the evening they begin a decline.
>
> There are fewer instances of acronychal settings. For example, since they
> in fact maintain that Sagittarius is recognized to fade with this setting, when
> Lucan is about to describe twilight close to the summer solstice, he says,
>
>> For the Sun occupied the stars of Leda,
>> when its light is highest in the neighboring Cancer,
>> then a brief night urged on the Thessalian arrows.
>
> It is indisputable that Sagittarius is not able to set at that time, unless cos-
> mically, for example, with the Sun rising with Gemini; and strictly speak-
> ing it can only be an acronychal setting, as long as the Sun is in the very
> constellation, and sets together with it.[131]

Lucan is not used here to describe epic conflict, but because he creates
a hermeneutical problem with his presentation of the constellation of
Sagittarius (the Thessalian archer with his arrows), which sets as the Sun
rises. This is not Virgil using the *Georgics* for epic similes in the *Aeneid*, or
Aratus using the *Iliad* for the same in the *Phaenomena*.[132] Gassendi does
not borrow phrasing, syntax, or imagery from Lucan; he is borrowing the
observation and trying to reconcile it with more recent data and theories
without disputing Lucan's authority.[133]

    In addition to these concerns for multiplicity of meaning, at the most
fundamental textual level the incorporation of verses into an early modern philosophical book creates a host of interpretative problems for both
contemporary and modern readers of the texts in which they are found.
Frequent variations of the Latin verses are to be found among editions,
authors have a tendency to paraphrase lines, or they cite inaccurately
from memory.[134] Typographical errors abound in the printing process.
Working from different manuscripts or *exempla*, early modern editors
could often release works of poetry laden with errors. Some of the errors
in transcription are insignificant, but others alter the meaning of the
verse. Paraphrases too are problematic, since they assume a reader who

has equal familiarity with the source text as the author. In theory, the transposition of the classical or poetical source (or its equivalent paraphrase) into an author's text should allow the reader to forgo a rereading of that source text, yet their practices explain why the strategy was frequently unreliable.

For example, in Liceti's *Litheosphorus* (1640), the work on phosphorescence that disputed Galileo's theories about the luminescence of the Moon, one passage of textual sampling is particularly noteworthy for the confusion it generates. In a section where Liceti apparently cites four consecutive lines from Virgil, the quotations are actually from two different authors.[135] They are combined as though they were from a single passage in *Occult Philosophy or Magic* (1531), but the author, Cornelius Agrippa, was pairing his own verses with Virgil's. Liceti's erroneous pairing even continued in subsequent texts that used him as an unnamed source.[136] Agrippa had created his supporting verses from a patchwork of Virgilian texts, and Liceti subsequently created a collage of Agrippa's own verses and Agrippa's selection of Virgil's verses that later readers treated as four lines of Virgilian text. How are readers meant to navigate such confusion among source texts? Liceti's presentation suggests that the fact that the words came from an authority are sufficient, not their context or importance to the source texts overall.

Methods of citing from authorities are haphazard. Della Porta, one of the most prominent authors in Galileo's library, exemplifies the variety of ways to include or omit poetic authorities from philosophical works. In *Problemata astronomicorum libri septem* (*Seven Books of Astronomy Problems*; 1609) Della Porta discusses stellar incline and decline; celestial distances; the zodiac; the distance from the Earth to the Sun; and other topics that usually warrant frequent citations of Virgil, Seneca, and the usual host of poets, but without mentioning them. Likewise, his revised *Elementorum curvilineorum libri tres* (*Three Books on Curved Lines*; 1610) is a work that includes definitions, problems, propositions, diagrams, axioms, without any citations from poetry, but uses what Arielle Saiber has called "semiotic acrobatics" and a host of curious words that seem to be of his coinage to explain curved lines and how to square the circle.[137] Yet, when Della Porta does turn to other sources, for example in *Natural Magic* in a chapter on the usefulness of rain, the reader might quickly be disoriented. In this chapter Della Porta cites at length from both the didactic poet Aratus and Virgil. The excerpt from Virgil contains thiry-one lines of verse, printed as though they were continuous in a single Virgilian source text. In fact, the verses correspond to *Georgics*, 1.373–392, 427–429,

440–443, and 450–453.[138] He cites all of the verses without indicating that he is skipping lines from the original passage. Both author and editor assume that the reader will be familiar enough with the *Georgics* and Latin to know that sampling has occurred. The mathematician Benedetti similarly extracts Ovid in his *Diversarum speculationum mathematicarum, & physicarum liber* (*Book on Diverse Mathematical and Physical Speculation*; 1585) when arguing with another author about diurnal motion. In a section called "That which Ovid passes over from diurnal motion in addition to annual motion," based on the section of the *Metamorphoses* in which Phaethon asks Apollo to use his chariot for a day and Apollo begrudgingly offers his advice to his son, he distills 120 lines into just 34 verses broken into 8 quotations cited out of order.[139] Galileo will have an interlocutor in his later dialogue chastise this approach:

> you are not bothered by things being scattered here and there, and you think that by collecting and combining various parts you can squeeze their juice. But then, what you and other learned philosophers do with Aristotle's texts, I will do with the verses of Virgil or Ovid, by making patchworks of passages and explaining with them all the affairs of men and secrets of nature.[140]

This kind of commentary and style does not transfer to every author or every writer of glosses or every text within their corpus. Galileo's contemporaries adopted various styles of citation and quotation in their texts, often turning to the same core group of sources, sometimes using lesser-known authors to lend intellectual weight to their arguments.

Poetry and mathematics

One explanation for the differences in presentation rests in the methodology of mathematics and the position of what had previously been seen as a lesser art within the princely court system. While the growth of mathematics in the Renaissance shares roots with the humanist recovery of manuscripts, the rediscovery of perspective and proportion in the visual arts, and the revision of texts for clarity, mathematical demonstrations could not be rearranged piecemeal like a commentary or poetry.[141] The logic of a geometrical proof was not enhanced by a quotation from Virgil. Yet mathematicians were trying by other means to validate their skill within a system that valued that very cultural capital as part of its self-fashioning. For example, the lifelong search by Mutio Oddi (1569–1639) for patronage at different courts demonstrates the ways in which early modern mathematicians were sensitive to the concepts of *disegno*, *grazia*, virtuosity, and *sprezzatura*.[142]

Critics have argued that the mathematical method at the core of Galileo's revolutionary philosophy was contingent upon the social legitimation of practitioners of the mathematical disciplines.[143] The other mathematicians upon whom Galileo relied, his supporters and subsequent followers alike, overwhelmingly adopted a style of minimal citations and maximum use of objective language supplemented with diagrams. These authors were often working in many capacities at once at the court, demonstrating a certain level of social mobility, and gained a significant presence in the higher levels of society as engineers became occupied with practical concerns related to ballistics, fortifications, and urban development. In Galileo's library these include Rafael Bombelli's algebra texts, Niccolò Tartaglia's *Nuova scientia* (*New Science*; 1537), Girolamo Cardano's work that opposed it, and the two volumes by geometer Luca Valerio that Galileo owned. Even with patronage concerns, these are all mathematical works that rely on charts, tables, definitions, postulates, propositions, proofs, corollaries, and lemmas, leaving no room for figurative language.[144] Giovanni Antonio Magini's mathematical texts are quite similar in their style and structure. In his work on mirrors, his authorities are the notable figures of mathematics, astronomy, and optics Witelo, Alhazen, Euclid, Ptolemy, and Copernicus.[145] In some works he does not include a single quotation from another author, but relies on diagrams and charts to demonstrate the validity of his theories expressed in the prose.[146] The mathematician Giovanni Battista Benedetti's preface to his book remains the only place for quotation. It is here that he mentions classical and medieval mathematicians and philosophers Euclid, Pythagoras, Plato, Nichomachus, and Boethius.[147] Niccolò Aggiunti, a disciple of Galileo who became chair of mathematics at Pisa and was also literature tutor in the Medici court, makes no mention of poets nor employs quotations of other authors in his work on mathematics.[148] These are mathematical texts, not astronomical ones, which demonstrates a first way in which the two fields divided over Copernicanism differed.

The emotions of these authors, when they are allowed a place in a book, are frequently the only expressions couched in poetic, if literary, terms. Niccolò Tartaglia, whose mathematical works were inspirational to Galileo, does precisely this in *Ragionamenti sopra la sua travagliata inventione* (*Reasoning about His Tormented Invention*; 1551). The scope of the work was not just to explain algebraic or geometrical principles, but to earn a higher station through service to the princely court. Samuel Edgerton has touched on what he calls the "bootstrap humanistic ambitions" of Tartaglia and others, who use their publications on practical mathematics

to approach the court for patronage.[149] Tartaglia has the English interlocutor in this series of dialogues quote from Ariosto in response to the character Nicolò's explanation of why he gave his work such a sad title. Nicolò
speaks of his suffering in Brescia and laments about broken promises: "it
seems that to them a promise isn't a promise if it is not made publicly and
at the hand of a notary."[150] Richard responds:

> With what you said, you have brought to mind a saying of Ariosto on such
> matters, which goes like this:
>
>> Faith should never be tarnished
>> whether to just one or to a thousand at once,
>> and just as in a wood or a cave
>> far from cities and homes
>> so too in front of courts, with a pack
>> of witnesses, writings, and seals
>> without taking any oath or other more expressive sign
>> it suffices that a promise were made just once.[151]

This is a lengthy citation that closes this section of the *Ragionamenti*.
Richard alludes to the moment in the *Orlando furioso* when the paladin
Zerbino is compelled to protect the hag who had held his lady hostage
in a cave while pirates found a buyer for her virginity. Richard's quotation is a criticism of the Brescian court for not living up to the ideals he
sees espoused by this scene in the *Furioso*. If Zerbino could keep his oath,
pledged in the woods to a warrior who has since ridden away, to safeguard
a woman who takes joy in tormenting him about his lost lady, surely the
Brescian court should be able to uphold its pledge of support to Tartaglia.
Once again though, this is a case where the author's emotions, not facts
about their material, are couched in quotations from poetry.

Kepler was more emotional and more figurative still with his use of
poetic sources. Like Brahe before him, Kepler too includes his own verses
in his work, but they do not form part of the argument.[152] Anthony
Grafton has shown that "Kepler clearly rejected the notion that one could
find precise astronomical data in the ancient epics."[153] Yet Kepler's relationship to poetic sources is different from the examples we have seen
so far. A closer analysis of his works will reveal the ways in which poetry
established Kepler's investigative tone. The vivacity of this voice can be
seen in his *Mysterium cosmographicum* or *Secret of the Universe* (1596), published just as Galileo was refining the theories on the tides that led him
to support the Copernican Theory. Kepler makes frequent addresses to
the reader, speaks often of himself, and poses numerous rhetorical questions in the *Secret*. Throughout that work, to support his arguments, he

cites from Euclid, Plato, Copernicus, and Pythagoras. In the preface of the work though, to make emotional claims about his search, he turns to Seneca, Ovid, Virgil, Horace, Terence, and Cicero. Early in the book, he uses Ovid's *Fasti* to highlight the ability of the subjects of his book to elevate the reader, citing: "Happy the souls whose first concern it was / To gain this knowledge and soar to heavenly homes."[154] When Kepler laments about his joy being scattered to the winds, the Latin text he provides is a likely allusion to the *Aeneid*. When he claims to have ignored the advice of the satirist who counsels writers to delay the distribution of their books for nine years, Kepler borrows the maxim from Horace's *Ars poetica*.[155] To defend his haste in publishing his discoveries, he turns to Cicero's *De amicitia*. The last line of the preface, which claims that by the end of the book the reader "will have an answer for the peasant who asks what hooks the sky is hung on to prevent it from falling," is an allusion to the second-century Roman dramatist Terence's *The Self-Tormentor*.[156] Sometimes Kepler uses figurative allusions in his emotional outbursts in the body of the text, such as his apostrophe to the "daughters of Pieris" in which he asks these mythological sisters who competed with the Muses to explain how a round object such as the Sun could produce rays in a straight line.[157]

Very infrequently, Kepler's prose itself borrows phrasing or similes from the poets; usually he is direct about the philosophical sources he uses. For example, when he speaks about the kinship of the planets in the *Secret of the Universe*, he writes: "In the case of Venus and Mars their turbulence and changeability are due to their large number of faces. Woman is always fickle and capricious; and the shape of Venus is the most capricious and variable of all."[158] The phrase "Woman is always fickle and capricious" is an allusion to Mercury's admonishment of Aeneas for his delay in Carthage with Dido in Virgil's *Aeneid*.[159] Kepler does not indicate that he quotes from another text, either by introducing Virgil before quoting him or with hyphens, indentation, or italicized font, the traditional editorial indicators of a borrowed verse. For comparison, in his *Almagest*, Pietro Pitati uses similar figurative language when he talks of Venus acting like a wife in her relative motion to other planets, but he does not cite from poetry to punctuate the statement.[160] These are all examples of figurative language that do not contribute to the generation of meaning in the work.

The only other use of a non-philosophical or non-mathematical source in the *Secret* appears in Chapter 18, but in this second instance, the borrowed line is indicated by Kepler and the printer as a quotation, unlike the subtle incorporation of a Virgilian verse just mentioned. By using a common trope of discovery as a journey, Kepler claims that Copernicus repaired much in the way of astronomical calculations, but that modern methods are no more perfect than the ancient ones:

> The way to the truth of the matter is long and has many windings. The ancients have shown it to us; our predecessors have started on it; we go on ahead of them, and stand on a closer level, but we have not yet reached the goal. I do not say this to show contempt for Astronomy – "You can get somewhere, if you can't get further."[161]

The quotation is from Horace's *Epistles* (1.2.32) and is indicated as a quotation by hyphens in the first edition. Kepler's choice of idiom is once again made for emotive effect. This is not Virgil's description of Dido's death or Lucan's verses on Sagittarius, which support a conclusion about natural philosophy. Kepler displays his erudition in the realm of his own *ethos*, not philosophical logic.

Thus, as Galileo entered into the debate over the validity of Copernicanism from his position at the University of Padua, he faced a text-based, emotional, and poetic journey. The fact that heliocentrism was a bitter pill is confirmed by Kepler's letter to Herwart von Hohenber in 1586, which I cite at length because his phrasing speaks to the exasperation of natural philosophers encountering opponents to Copernicanism even at this relatively early stage in the debate, and returns us to the Lucretian passage that opened this chapter. In response to objections against the heliocentric theory based on the relative smallness and unimportance given to the Earth in a decentralized location in infinite space, Kepler says that size and import are not related:

> If the planets were the most unimportant part of the world because the entire planetary system practically disappears when compared with the fixed star system, according to this same argument man would belong to the absolute trifles of the world, since he can in no way be compared with the earth, and this, the earth, in turn cannot be compared with the world of Saturn. Yes, the crocodile or the elephant would be closer to God's heart than man, because these animals surpass the human being in size. With these and other sugar-coatings on the pill, maybe, this huge morsel could be digested.[162]

Before the advent of Copernicanism, Piccolomini and Lucretius before him had spoken of the bitter medicine of philosophy that needed the sweet coating of poets to make the ideas more palatable to the intellect. Kepler claims that Copernicus resorted to this kind of sugar coating as well. In the *Secret of the Universe* Kepler had spoken of the heavenly circles surrounding the Earth like a kernel around a seed. In his notes, he attributes the simile to Copernicus and offers two possibilities for his use of the figurative language: "whether he wished to accommodate our capacity for understanding, or whether he himself was truly caught in perplexity over the point."[163] This annotation encapsulates Kepler's overall view on the use of figurative language: for thought experiments, emotional expression, or to accommodate abstract ideas into the realm of the tangible.[164] The geometric language that Galileo proposed to Kepler fourteen years later is somehow still insufficient for the explanation of the ideas that he supports. The traditional remedy had been verse, and as Galileo begins to write and criticize, he also begins to experiment with the literary, not factual, potential of the epic poets who might help him to make his case.

This snapshot of poetry at the various levels of text in works of natural philosophy serves as a reminder that poetry is at once everywhere in the lives of these authors and their presumed readers, and nowhere does it stand out as anything other than the usual kind of resource. Galileo enters a printed, textual philosophical world that is starkly different from the natural, geometrical physical world he will champion in his own writing. As we will see in the next chapter, his own philosophical and poetic enterprises, while both involved in polemic, are nonetheless almost entirely separate at the beginning of this journey.

CHAPTER TWO

Starry knights

As the controversies in which Galileo was involved became as personal as they were philosophical, the character of the philosopher, understood both as an invented figure and as a collection of personality traits, became as important to argumentation as the theories themselves. Character was not determined so much by philosophy as it was by literature; not by university formation, but by the court and academies. Where William Eamon has shown that science depicted as a hunt (the topos of *venatio*) is an attempt to mirror the court's self-image, I suggest that references to and images from epic poetry achieve the same goal.[1] As Mary Baine Campbell argues that Galileo maps courtly space onto extraterrestrial space in his philosophical works, my reading suggests that via the mechanisms of epic poetry the literary elements of his prose reflect courtly ideals that should be mirrored in philosophers.[2] In a parallel vein of research Steven Shapin has done considerable work on the way in which English philosopher Robert Boyle (1627–1691) crafted his experimental identity to reflect the integrity and freedom of action that defined the gentlemen of the day in order that it would positively affect his philosophical project; *ethos* was of considerable importance in truth claims.[3] Galileo attempts this very thing, and his use of the popular poetic fiction of the period demonstrates that he is a cultured player on every level. By engaging with thematic, figurative, and epistemological elements of poetry, Galileo can establish a new paradigm for his philosophy, one that generates a truth claim for his work but also dismisses the truth claims of literal readings of poetry. The way this tension plays out on both sides of the debates indicates the fierce competition for this territory in the courtly intellectual setting.

This chapter brackets Galileo's publication of his lunar observations with an examination of the vocabulary of the epic in his writing before and immediately after the publication of the *Starry Messenger* (1610) in order to explore his early experimentation with the literary as a space for knowledge production. Given the impassioned nature of the conflicts surrounding the *nova*, the compass, the Moon, the apparently new stars seen by the telescope, floating bodies, and sunspots, the texts are rich with rhetorical experimentation in search of the most efficacious way to attack a philosopher or his ideas. Galileo's annotations to these works and his published books establish a profile of him as a reader actively engaged with the language and the content of a work, quick to cite epic poets and fables to make his critical point. Expanding the analysis of this use of epic poetry to the other authors in these debates shows the ways in which each side was aware of the other's strategies and attempted to navigate a path less taken in the use of poetic authorities.

In October of 1604, observers such as Kepler and Galileo could see what Kepler later called a new star (*stella nova*), now known to have been a supernova.[4] Because of the absence of parallax in the different observations of this *nova* in the Milky Way, its appearance became evidence that celestial bodies beyond the lunar sphere were in fact susceptible to change, not changeless as Aristotelian and Ptolemaic dogma declared.[5] At this point, Galileo had been in Padua for over twelve years as chair of mathematics at the university, supplementing his income with tutoring in various mathematical disciplines and distributing his geometric and military compass. After Galileo had delivered public lectures on this new star, the Paduan professor Antonio Lorenzini (perhaps a pseudonym for the Paduan Aristotelian Cesare Cremonini [1550–1631]) and the Padua student Baldassare Capra (1573–1624) both printed works that tried to reconcile the phenomenon with Aristotelian precepts. The response was a work written in Paduan dialect, likely by Girolamo Spinelli with some tenuous evidence of collaboration with Galileo, given the latter's familiarity with and fondness for the burlesque poetry in the language, and his participation in the local circle of followers of the humorist Angel Beolco (1502–1542) – known as Ruzzante – a writer of jocose poetry in Paduan dialect.[6] Written under the pseudonym Cecco de' Ronchitti, a name likely derived from the irreverent Tuscan jocose poet Cecco Angiolieri (1260–*c*. 1312) and a diminutive form of the stony, jagged stone or *ronchione*, the *Dialogue Concerning the New Star* (1605) openly ridiculed the staunchly Aristotelian professoriate. The structure of the professor–pupil team wearing masks of pseudonyms like that of Cremonini, Lorenzini, and the disguised Cecco prefigures the remarkably similar form of the conflict over comets that develops in 1618 and will be discussed in the next two chapters.[7]

This chapter will examine one response to Galileo's position that came from Lodovico Delle Colombe (1565–1616), a Florentine scholar whose own work on the *nova* at the end of 1605 prompted yet another

response in dialect published in 1606, this time written by the pseudonymous Alimberto Mauri, often also considered to be Galileo himself.[8]
At the same time, Galileo was also involved in the defense of his intellectual property from none other than plagiarist Baldassare Capra, who had
copied Galileo's manual and instrument to sell them as his own. The disputes with Delle Colombe were also renewed after Galileo had moved to
Florence and was working on questions related to the buoyancy of floating objects. Shortly thereafter, in 1612 and 1613, Galileo was involved in
yet another debate, this time on the nature of sunspots, and once again
with an opponent writing under a pseudonym. With all of these debates
and false identities, the fact that Galileo had refined the telescope and first
looked at the Moon and the planets in 1609 seems relatively uninterest-
ing stylistically. Yet, as my analysis will show, the resulting treatise touches
upon themes related to epic poetry as well.

Tradition and novelty in the words of epic poets

The *nova* debates were in part a battle for intellectual territory between
mathematicians and philosophers. As chair of mathematics, when Galileo
delivered his lectures on this celestial phenomenon using numerical data
and made claims about its nature suggesting the possibility that the
Ptolemaic theory was erroneous, he trespassed the disciplinary bound-
ary with philosophy.[9] Lorenzini's clumsy response to these lectures, the
Discorso intorno alla stella nuova (*Discourse about the New Star*; 1605),
was in turn attacked from three different directions. The first came from
his compatriot Baldassare Capra, who weakened Lorenzini's physical
claims and supported Tycho Brahe in his *Consideratione astronomica
circa la stella nova dell'anno 1604* (*Astronomical Consideration of the New
Star of 1604*; 1605). The second response to Lorenzini was Kepler's Latin
treatise on the new star.[10] The third was Cecco de' Ronchitti's dialogue
in Paduan. In its own way, each work tried to destabilize the authority
of Lorenzini and the devout Aristotelian philosophers at the University
of Padua.

In his work on the supernova seen in 1604, *De stella nova in pede
Serpentarii* (*The New Star in the Foot of Ophiuchus*; 1606), Kepler makes
evident the conflicts that arise between mathematical and what he calls
poetic accounts of stars, as part of his larger project of identifying and
critiquing the human inventions such as astrology that had been used
to describe celestial phenomena.[11] Part of Kepler's analysis examines the
history of the constellation Ophiuchus, the snake-bearer, formerly called

Serpentarius, of which he says: "after the image was assumed in the sky, the Poets began to think about their tales."[12] He goes on to summarize the tale of Avienus, a translator of the didactic poet Aratus, who says that the snake-bearer is the god of medicine Asclepius. Then Kepler more generally refers to other accounts that claim the figure is alternatively Hercules, Triopas, or Glaucus, or even Orpheus' lover Eurydice. He copies verses from the humanist Giovanni Pontano that suggest this last possibility, and expresses his wonder at such variety: "So great is the Poets' creative license that they change this specter daily rising from the sea into a woman: what wonder is it if it is even imagined womanly by some?"[13] Kepler subsequently moves into an exhaustive, if not exasperating, list of the possible interpretations of the constellation's image. The combination of rhetorical questions and rhetorical *accumulatio* make all too clear Kepler's insinuation that the poets cannot offer uniform, authoritative testimony on this phenomenon:

> Therefore it is all right for Pontanus to call it either Apollo of Pytho, or Cadmus, slayers of the Boeotian dragon, or Jason who put to sleep the dragon of Colchis, or Aesacus, avenging on the serpent the murder of the muse Egeria, or Eurydice, as he says: But what if you claim that it is the dragon of Lesbos, turned to stone by Phoebus – that dragon who gnawed at the famous head of Orpheus? Do you see how, with its neck turned back towards the Crown and Orpheus' Lyre, which follows this at a short distance, it seems even now to seek in the Crown the head of Orpheus, who was lord of the lyre? On the other hand, if this is less satisfying, Identify Aristaeus in Serpentarius, Proteus in the Serpent, so that there is an obvious reason for a woman grieved.
>
> But nothing is more fitting than Virgil's Laocoön, whom, as he wards them off from the death of his sons, the serpents
>
> > Seize and bind with their mighty coils, and already Entwined twice about his middle, twice about his neck with their scaly backs, they overcome him with head and lofty necks; At the same time, he strains to tear apart the knots with his hands.
> >
> > [*Aeneid*, II.217–220]
>
> Indeed, all in vain. No tale is suitable [*Nulla fabula quadrat*]. Manilius quashes it with one verse:
>
> > The pair will always be at war, because they are even in strength.
> >
> > [*Astronomica*, I.336]
>
> But all those related to this point either have conquered or have been conquered. Now, let us come from playthings to calculations, from Poets to Mathematicians.[14]

The reference to the poets' "playthings," translated from the Latin term *ludicris*, specifically characterizes these activities of identification as anything but serious or authoritative. As Kepler's analysis transitions from these poetic tales to mathematics, he makes a statement that summarizes succinctly the tensions between geometry and poetry: "Nulla fabula quadrat." Literally: "No fable squares." No poetic story creates a uniform frame for the evidence. The figurative language of poetic veils and the precise descriptions of geometry cannot be reconciled. As Galileo will write to him a few years later, the natural world is not the *Iliad* or the *Aeneid*, but a book of geometrical figures.

Kepler persists in this attitude toward the poetic. He opens Chapter 24 of the *De stella nova* saying that opponents to his theories like the German astronomer Matthias Bernegger (1582–1640) will argue that this new star is a miracle of God:

> I hope that I will be received by patient ears, especially by Bernegger and by the others who thought that this star could not be ascribed to nature unless we also devise a new physics for celestial bodies. Let me be the first, then, to express my opinion, so that the rest have very much more abundant material for speaking. And some Pythagorean may at this point interrupt me, singing something or other of Virgil's.
>
> > In the beginning sky and lands and limpid seas,
> > And the conspicuous sphere of the moon, and Titanic stars –
> > Life within nourished these; and infused through their limbs,
> > Mind stirs the whole mass, and mixes itself with the great body.
>
> > [*Aeneid*, VI.721–727]
>
> By these words Scaliger judged that we are drawn into the hidden secrets of nature.[15]

Immediately following these verses, Kepler writes "Aristoteles vero sic" ("And so Aristotle …") and provides a paraphrase of his belief in the spirituality of the natural world.

Kepler removes a literal reading of Virgil's *Aeneid* from the same authoritative level as Aristotle's *Metaphysics*. His tone is dismissive of both the idea of miracle and the possibility that he will need to respond to "some" Pythagorean's anticipated "singing" of "something or other from Virgil." Kepler is likely making a sarcastic reference to the tradition of viewing Pythagorean, and by extension mystical, undertones in Virgil's works such as the *Eclogues* and *Aeneid*.[16] These perfunctory poetic inclusions are obstacles to the task of his chapter, which is to demonstrate the efficient cause of the supernova. While Kepler will continue periodically to cite Virgil in

De stella nova, his attitude toward these sources subordinates them to the more important and convincing mathematical and philosophical discussions at the core of his demonstrations.

Already in the *nova* debate, then, the traditional forms of authority are called into question. Notably, even though Galileo's simultaneous response to Lorenzini and Capra has been called "a farcical exercise in a popular comic form," the players in the *Dialogue* of Cecco de' Ronchitti resort to practical knowledge and the experiences of perspective, parallax, and measurement as they climb trees and wander the countryside – not the authority of books.[17] Although the authorship of Cecco's dialogue is still debated, as Stillman Drake said: "Admittedly some other explanation might be found for the use of a pseudonym by a different writer, but when it is added that the author spoke as an astronomer, was unsympathetic to philosophers, and cited with approval the dialect work of Cecco di Ronchitti, the field of candidates is pretty limited."[18] For all of the rhetorical elements that make this dialogue so entertaining, the speakers Matteo and Natale, by their very roles as inversions of the esteemed professor of philosophy, do not display the classical erudition so often associated with the late Renaissance humanist education described in the previous chapter. Their physical activities and language of the body lend earthliness, corporeality, and tangibility to what would otherwise be the abstract, inaccessible material of the stars. Cecco's model is not Aratus, Lucretius, or Virgil, but Ruzzante, one of Galileo's favorite authors.[19]

Ruzzante's style appeared again the following year. In early 1606 the Florentine Lodovico Delle Colombe joined the debate on the *nova* with his own *Discorso*, which attempted to argue that this celestial body was not new (and therefore not a negation of Aristotle's declaration of the immutability of the heavens), but newly seen. This approach prompted a response from yet another pseudonymous figure, Alimberto Mauri. The attribution of Mauri's *Considerations of Some Places in the Discourse of Lodovico Delle Colombe* (1606) to Galileo is plausible, but contested.[20] Importantly, Delle Colombe believed Galileo was Mauri. Delle Colombe's response to these attacks sets the tone for the use of Ariosto and Tasso in his later debates with an unmasked Galileo on the behavior of floating bodies. Not only does Galileo in turn adopt that same style for disputes with a masked author in the later controversy on the comets, but he is then also able to draw on that material for the literary creation of his speakers in his dialogues.

As pleasant as the title *Risposte piacevoli … alle considerazioni di certa Maschera saccente nominata Alimberto Mauri (Pleasant Responses … to*

the Considerations of a Certain Arrogant Mask Named Alimberto Mauri;
1608) claims his text will be, Delle Colombe immediately places himself on
the defensive with bellicose language. In the opening pages of the *Risposte
piacevoli* he writes: "I, who try to enjoy the sky, philosophizing about its
beautiful lights, and flee conflicts if, when attacked, I strike the enemy –
why should I not deserve pardon? Instead, I could well say with Venier
the same that he said in his tragedy *Idalba*: 'My defenses, forced, have
punished their faults.'"[21] According to Delle Colombe's figurative description of his philosophical approach, he flees, yet in his philosophizing there
are fights, blows, enemies, defenses, and conquests. A battle has com-
menced. Delle Colombe's reference to Maffio Venier's posthumous tragic
story of *Idalba* (1596) would bring to the mind of contemporary readers
the Aristotelian drama of a princess trying to regain her throne from a
cousin who usurped it upon the death of the King. Venier (1550–1586) was
perhaps most famous for the provocative and obscene poems in Venetian
dialect that he wrote against the courtesan Veronica Franco (1546–1591).[22]
While *Idalba* is not written in dialect, the reference to Venier moves the
debate toward Cecco's and Mauri's linguistic realm of Paduan. The allusion to a usurped throne speaks to the disciplinary concerns of philosophers who felt that mathematicians should play no part in discussions of
astronomy.

Delle Colombe calls attention to the theatricality of the debate and
explains the structure of his treatise, which comes to resemble a duel
between books:

> Now, because we, Lady Mask, or rather Alimberto Mauri, desire that those
> to whom the reading of these responses and defenses will be pleasing are
> not bothered by the double task of having to hold many books in their
> hands … but that they can in just this one for ease and greater clarity com-
> fortably see everything related to this subject, with purity [*ischiettezza*] and
> sincerity of writing copied over, we will begin at the start of your consider-
> ations and immediately after each one will follow the response.[23]

In order to carry out this close textual analysis with *ischiettezza*, Delle
Colombe lists Mauri's considerations and provides a response under-
neath each one, a much more ambitious undertaking than Mauri's own,
in which he had only copied the first few words of passages from Delle
Colombe's original *Discourse on the New Star of 1604*. This popular style,
which Galileo adopts in the Controversy on the Comets a decade later,
turns the treatise into a discourse by virtue of inserting a second author's
voice into the original text. It also eliminates the need for readers to buy a
competitor's work. The blows and parries that Delle Colombe mentioned

at the start of the book become verbal lunges in the continued debate over the *nova* in his *Risposte piacevoli*.

Delle Colombe's use of epic blends figurative language from different sources to describe the debate. He even engages directly with the content of epic poems at a literary level that prefigures what Galileo will do more skillfully, consistently, and comprehensively years later in the *Assayer*. Mauri had frequently used journey imagery to describe the actions of philosophy, and at one point called Delle Colombe's opinions sirens: "treacherous young ladies [apt] to check the voyage of any who may aspire to come to know that most ancient, most noble, and most useful Dame Astronomy."[24] This is a likely allusion to the sirens that threaten Ulysses' voyage home in Homer's *Odyssey*, since Mauri will later refer to them and other obstacles in this epic journey, Scylla and Charybdis.[25] Delle Colombe replies to this general allusion to the figure of sirens with a specific reference to Tasso, and he converts Mauri's story of a journey into one of war: "I am certain that if Torquato Tasso could have usurped such a beautiful description, he would have thrown it into his poem, to paint in a more lifelike way the tempting swimmers that aspired with their lures to halt the passage of those two warriors so that they would not recall to camp the valorous Rinaldo, who was with Armida in her garden of delights and wantonness."[26] Delle Colombe alludes to *Gerusalemme liberata*, XV.58, in which the two Christian warriors Carlo and Ubaldo, sent by Godfrey to rescue the hero Rinaldo, stumble upon two sirens at the Fount of Laughter, a pool formed by a mountain stream. As modern criticism has shown, the scene exposes a tension between courtly virtues since it highlights the conflict between participation in emasculating, seductive games of song and displays of military strength.[27] Could Delle Colombe be suggesting that Mauri is better at these games of song than at confronting philosophical battles? By casting the exchange in terms of Tasso's Rinaldo, rather than the obvious classical referent, Homer's Ulysses, Delle Colombe also aligns himself with the Aristotelian supporters of the *Liberata* in the ongoing debates about the superiority of Tasso or Ariosto as authors of epic poems.

This support of Tasso continues as Delle Colombe persists in his line-by-line analysis of Mauri's introduction. When Mauri says that it should be no surprise that a man so well known in one field, like Delle Colombe is known in philosophy, might be corrected or reproached in another, mathematics; Delle Colombe responds by citing the *Liberata*: "Do you not see that this sugar-coated sting twists again back at you, since, not being satisfied with the art of seeing the future, you want to pass yourself off as a philosopher, as a theologian, in such a way that one could gracefully recite this verse of Tasso about you: 'He confuses the two laws poorly known to him'?"[28] The moment from the *Liberata* is a description of Ismen, the magician who assists the Muslim ruler of Jerusalem while they defend the city from the Christian forces. He was once a Christian, then converted to Islam, and as a result confounds the practices of both religions. The implication is that Mauri, who Delle Colombe thinks is Galileo, is not only a traitor to his faith (which Delle Colombe implies is astrology, not astronomy) by trying to speak of philosophy or theology, but has polluted his practice of both by using instruments of one, mathematics, for the study of the other. By drawing on readers' awareness of context, themes, and the poetic tradition Delle Colombe has implied that Mauri has usurped his position, dabbled in effeminate practices, is a traitor to his own faith – and all this before beginning to discuss the question of the *nova*. This is already a large epistemological step away from the factual use of poets seen in the first chapter, and Delle Colombe's choice of comparison texts places the debate with Mauri into a context of chivalry, honor, and courtly ideals.[29]

Continuing the imagery of concepts as either virtuous damsels or wicked temptresses, Mauri had said that he would reclothe the ideas so that they were not shameful. In response, Delle Colombe references Petrarch, Boccaccio, and Tasso to call into question Mauri's motives and his relationship with these womanly ideas, which he believes are anything but virtuous:

> Beware that love does not trick you, and make them seem like they did to Petrarch, "Ladies and damsels that are firs and beeches." Because they may appear like Tasso says, "Daughters of wild tree bark." Come on, do you want me to tell you? To me they appear pure, exactly like the daughter of the Sultan of Babylon was. She was contaminated nine times, but still sold herself as a maiden. But you have not known how to cover them well, so that they do not appear as violated women, and since you want to bear witness to their purity, one should not lend credence to your words, because you call yourself their father, but you may be their corruptor.[30]

Delle Colombe begins this retort with Petrarch's amorous, courtly hallucination of *Canzoniere*, CLXXVI.8 set in the forest of Ardennes. Petrarch believes he sees Laura surrounded by ladies who are in fact only fir trees and beeches. That unadulterated love becomes something more deceitful and corrupting when Delle Colombe goes on to cite from *Liberata*, XVIII.27.6. Here the false creations of Armida try once again to seduce Rinaldo and lead him away from his holy purpose. Rinaldo must disenchant Armida's sylvan ladies, and reclaim the forest in order to furnish the Christian army with weapons and supplies that will ultimately allow them to liberate Jerusalem from the Muslim captors. From there, Delle Colombe's reference becomes more insidious. He speaks of Alatiel, the daughter of the Sultan of Babylon, whose story is told by Boccaccio on the Second Day of the *Decameron*. Through a series of misadventures that begin with a shipwreck on her way to marry her intended husband, Alatiel becomes a silent subject to the desires of nine different men before she is finally returned home and then presented to her intended husband as a virgin. Delle Colombe implies that Mauri plays an active role in the corruption and violation of these ideas, these damsels, and then repackages them in a way that deceives the reader about their true nature. The context of these citations and even their literal interpretations are not essential to understanding the argument at hand about the *nova*, but they are quite effective at undermining the *ethos* of the philosophers involved.

Delle Colombe also includes further insults from Dante, Petrarch, Boccaccio, Giambattista Gelli, and others to this effect, though without the range or insistence with which he uses Tasso.[31] One representative example shows that he chose passages from these authors with similar implications about Mauri's – and by extension, Galileo's – presumed character. At one juncture in the text Delle Colombe relies on two heavily charged poetic references to highlight Mauri's faults:

> Go slowly, Mr. Alimberto, since things are going very well; because you have conceded to me that reasonably the new star could be in the Primum Mobile, so there remains one difficulty for you, and it is this, that, because the crystalline sky is not penetrable to our vision, it cannot be true that this star was seen in the Primum Mobile. In a minimal difficulty, in a hair, consists all of your force. Come on, let's remove this hair from this Nisus, because it is in truth a hair that sustains you, that keeps you, so that you do not surrender. And I can well say these words of Petrarch against you: "See, noble Lord, from what trivial causes comes such cruel war."[32]

Nisus is a minor character from Virgil's *Aeneid*, always paired with his close friend, the younger Euryalus. The two men appear twice in the Virgilian story, first in Book V as competitors in a foot race, in which Nisus slips while in the lead and trips the contestant behind him in order that Euryalus can win. As strong as their love for one another is, Nisus is willing to cheat and risk his honor. They next appear during a night attack on sleeping soldiers in the Rutulian camp in Book IX, a demonstration of their strength that ends in tragedy when they collect so much loot that they draw attention to themselves and are killed. The characters

are at once comic and tragic, but carry serious implications about virtuous and right actions. To compound the severity of Delle Colombe's
attack, the quotation from Petrarch is taken from the sixth *canzone* of the
Canzoniere, poem 128, "Italia mia": an overtly political poem addressed
to the warring leaders of a 1340s Italy overrun by foreign invaders. The
poem calls for peace, but highlights the brutality and destruction that
the poet sees throughout Italy. Delle Colombe recasts Mauri's language
of insult into a specific language of battle, one based on poets, epic,
and others, in order to win a war he thinks he is fighting with fellow
Florentine Galileo.

Delle Colombe continues to shape the conflict with Mauri specifically within a courtly framework identified by characteristics presented
in Tasso's various works, at times even touching on the shared foundations of literary and philosophical conceits. While discussing the absolute
immobility of the Earth, Mauri claimed that Delle Colombe and others
state that the Empyrean sky is entirely without motion. Following upon
citations to this effect from Aristotelian texts, Delle Colombe closes his
counterattack by arguing that there can be immobility among mobility,
and he uses an example from Tasso's dialogue on the visual *impresa*, a her-
aldic device:

> following this sentiment Cardinal Don Luigi d'Este made his own *impresa*,
> which was a Sphere, or Celestial Orb, and the motto *Immobility in motion*.
> And truly this *impresa* he imprinted well into his soul, since, as Torquato
> Tasso says in his *Dialogue* on the *impresa*, amongst the motions of fortune
> and of wars he always remained immobile and constant, exactly like my
> doctrine is in combatting yours.[33]

Tasso's dialogue on the *impresa*, called *Il Conte, ovvero dialogo delle imprese*
(*The Count; or Rather, Dialogue on "Imprese"*; 1594), is set in Rome, where
the interlocutors discuss the hieroglyphics on the obelisk that stand in
front of the Church of San Giovanni Laterano and, from there, analyze
the relationship between words and images in the *imprese* of illustrious
men. Delle Colombe suggests that at the heart of three types of creation,
the plastic, poetic, and philosophical, one can find an immobile mobility.
His authority rests on this unity of characteristics between epistemologies.
As later chapters will show, Galileo works against this approach by undermining the authority of each component.

Delle Colombe has repeatedly characterized his opponent as an unvir-
tuous enemy worthy of being defeated for his trespasses against philosophy. Yet, overwhelmingly, these insults remain only insults. They do not
engage with the literariness of their sources beyond analogies, and they are

not interconnected in a way that would make his text literary in the fashion we shall see in Chapter 3. Although Delle Colombe later says that he was eventually convinced that Galileo played no part in the Mauri debate, his work, his use of Tasso, and his conflicts with Galileo will return in a matter of years when a new duel erupts over floating bodies.

Although slightly anachronistic, because the work in question was published near the end of Galileo's life, one response to questions raised by Galileo's observations of the Moon deserves particular attention for its return to earlier literal styles of incorporating poetry into philosophical works. Fortunio Liceti (1577–1657) was a prolific author on natural philosophy and medicine, working primarily as a professor at the University of Padua, where he overlapped briefly with Galileo. Liceti and Galileo were frequently in contact with one another, though they did disagree courteously on the nature of the light of the waning Moon. Liceti argued that the Moon could retain light like a recently discovered phosphorescent stone from Bologna, while Galileo maintained that the Moon's illumination was due to the reflection of the Sun's rays from the Earth's surface. Liceti has a notable presence in Galileo's library with sixteen titles to his name, more than any other author in the collection.

Liceti makes no use of extended metaphors or fables in his work on the light of the Moon, but his supportive quotations are other authors' authoritative quotations. He copies passages from Strabo in which Strabo quotes from Lucan and Martial, from Plutarch when Plutarch cites Homer, and from Seneca's quotations of Ovid.[34] Daniel Javitch has elaborated on the potential implications of a similar citation strategy in Galileo's favorite epic poem, Ariosto's *Orlando furioso* which when applied to Liceti highlights the literal versus literary uses of these sources.[35] Ariosto's imitation of poetic passages from texts that also imitate their predecessors shows not only his erudition, but his acknowledgment of the poetic sampling present in great works. Here Liceti seems only to double the authority of his authorities with these telescoping references, but the potential for making similar assumptions about the richer overall message of a text still exists with other natural philosophical works that use epic war poetry, mythology, and love poetry to punctuate key moments or passages.

In the *Litheosphorus* (1640) Liceti provides one indication of the potential for this strategy, a move that will provide a suitable introduction to the nexus of poetic problems that Galileo tackles throughout his career writing in the vernacular. Liceti's work typically relies on a notable use of Virgil and Lucan, but at one point he cites from none other than one of Galileo's favorite burlesque poets, Francesco Berni (1498–1535). After going to great lengths to outline the history of the word *silex*, stone, Liceti begins a long digression on the different types of stones and how they should be called by different names. He gives an example of popular usage of the term from Berni's sonnet that is now called "Contro la moglie" ("Against the Wife"). Notably, when he quotes Berni, he actually quotes from a secondary work written by Giovan Maria Cecchi (1518–1587) writing under the pseudonym of "Bartolino from the neighborhood of Canto de' Bischeri in Florence": *Lezione o vero cicalamento di maestro Bartolino dal canto de' Bischeri sopra 'l sonetto Passere e beccafichi magri arrosto* (*A Lesson, or Really Jabbering of Bartolino from Canto de' Bischeri on the Sonnet "A Roast of Skinny Sparrows and Quails"*; 1582). Cecchi's pseudonym plays on the Florentine association of the name Bischeri with people who are not very clever. Liceti stays true to form with his citation of Cecchi's citation of Berni, which differs slightly from the original by its first word: "Cancheri" ("Curses!") in Berni's collection of poetry appears as "Passeri" ("Sparrows") in the *Cicalamento*. This burlesque commentary on Berni's burlesque sonnet ridicules the entire structure of authoritative commentaries and glosses. He would seem an odd choice for Liceti's authoritative use of the word "stone," particularly since Liceti's text is in Latin and his source text, Cecchi, is Italian. After citing Isidore of Seville, Virgil, Pliny, and others on the various terms used for stone, Liceti begins this peculiar digression. His introduction to the sonnet is worth citing at length to draw out the oddities of this inclusion:

> I do indeed concede that a rough pebble, by name a sharp stone, is tread on with greater annoyance than a pebble with a smooth surface; but I am unable to concede that the hardest stone is not troubling to those who tread on it merely because it is smooth, and if by chance it should fall inside a shoe, that it does not grow and injure the one walking; with its meagerness contributing in vain to a lack of annoyance. For by hardness alone it wounds vehemently, whence our fine poet has very fittingly placed it in a position which is not last among the most annoying annoyances when Bartolino, with his name derived from Canto de' Bischeri, carried a pebble in his shoe in this short poem:
>
>> A roast of scraggy quails [and sparrows], a bit
>> Of salted pork to cram down a dry throat;
>> To be dead tired and find nowhere to sit;
>> To have the fire nearby, the wine remote;
>> To pay cash down but to be paid at leisure;
>> To be compelled to grant a profitless boon;

Not to see aught when you've gone out in pleasure;
To stew in January as you did in June:
To have a pebble lurking in your boot;
To feel a flea a-running round about
Your stirrup-leg, inside your sock; to know
One hand is clean and one as black as soot,
One foot is with a shoe and one without;
To be kept waiting when you're wild to go;
Add to all this what tries you most in life,
Vexation, care, grief, every sort of strife,
You'll find that far away the worst's a wife.

But yet this man perhaps had wed some Xanthippe, or Megera. Galen, delivering On the Faculties of Simple Medicines, makes the stone a common sort the same as pumice, cadmia, jasper, lodestone, lignite, limestone, and many other kinds ...[36]

This poem appears after nearly a page of analysis of the names for small stones. Liceti continues for four pages of text to tease out the nuances of terms for tiny rocks to conclude finally that the generic term *lapide* is best for the Bolognese phosphorescent rock that he is comparing to the Moon.[37] Within this inventory of stones stands Berni's "Against the Wife" in its entirety, a catalog of dislikes, an example of the Provençal *enueg* or Italian *noia* genre of poetry devoted to nuisances. Is this an oblique comment on the hassle of providing the lexical history for such a trifle? The word Liceti cares about, *sassolino*, a small stone, is buried at the midpoint of the sonnet, and it is Italian, not Latin! If he needed a source for *scrupum*, the Latin term he discusses just before this digression, he could have just as easily used Lucan's *Pharsalia*, v.675, which talks about a shore free of sharp-edged stones.

Why Berni's *sassolino*? The choice of Berni requires a meandering introduction to the poem that includes musings on the relative discomforts of these stones in one's shoe, only to have Liceti's final word on the matter relate to the kind of wife described by the poet, not the stone presumably in question. Without pause, he then launches into Galen's categories of stones. This kind of poetic use seems to be unique in Liceti's work. As a vernacular, burlesque poetic composition, found in Cecchi's commentary which also is not meant to be taken seriously, Berni's "Against the Wife" destabilizes the entire philological exercise of Liceti's chapter. This example, however unique, is a warning that for all of the norms associated with this borrowing of textual authority in early modern philosophy, exceptions and outliers are quite possibly the choices that reflect an extra message for the knowing reader.

The beginnings of a chivalric code among philosophers

Liceti's hidden messages, while not courtly, suggest the potential for similarly analyzing other poetic content. In the summer of 1609, word reached Galileo of the first telescopes, and by the end of the year he was observing the sky with his own refined instrument that would prove essential in his move from university life to the court of the Medici in Florence.[38] He published these observations in a short Latin treatise, the *Sidereus nuncius* (*Starry Messenger*; 1610), which he dedicated to Grand Duke of Tuscany Cosimo II de' Medici (1590–1621), the man for whom he named the satellites he was able to see orbiting Jupiter by virtue of the telescope. Although Galileo did not write an epic poem to describe the mythical origins of the Medici family, as Ariosto did when he made Bradamante and Ruggiero ancestors of the Este family, and as Virgil before him did with Aeneas for Augustus, his project in the *Starry Messenger* was no less grandiose. Richard Westfall has already pointed out that Galileo originally referred to the *Sidereus nuncius* as the *Cosmica sydera*, Cosimo's stars, in honor of the Grand Duke.[39] In the introduction to the *Starry Messenger* Galileo suggests ways of honoring heroes and famous men, including statues, columns, pyramids, and entire cities, and he adds: "Others, however, looking to more permanent and long-lasting things, have entrusted the eternal celebration of the greatest men not to marbles and metals but to the care of the Muses and to incorruptible monuments of letters."[40] Two things are notable in this list. First, Galileo cites the elegiac poet Propertius to describe the expense of these earthly monuments. Second, according to Galileo, literary monuments are inferior only to giving names of famous men to the "familiar and eternal orbs of the most brilliant stars."[41] Beyond this implied superiority of naming the stars to writing a literary monument for the Medici, Eileen Reeves has shown the epic nature of this introduction to the *Starry Messenger*, and Ladina Lambert has specifically connected Galileo putting the Medici name on the stars to the rhetorical effect of Ariosto placing the Temple of Earthly Fame on the Moon.[42] Jean Dietz Moss even finds poetic elements in the prose of the *Sidereus nuncius*, in phrases such as "flooded with light" and "ablaze with glowing splendor," which give a certain vivacity to these static observations.[43] To complement those analyses, I will show that Galileo's self-aware allusions to his project as equally important or greater than that of a poet, particularly the epic, are present even in the materials leading up to its publication and his departure from Padua to Florence.

A draft of the letter from Galileo to Grand Duke Cosimo II's secretary Belisario Vinta on March 19, 1610 directly voices the relationship that Galileo created between his own work and an epic poetic project. The letter announces the dedication of the newly discovered moons of Jupiter to the Medici family and accompanies the present of the telescope with which Galileo made the first observations of what became known as the *stelle medicee*, the Medicean stars. It is a letter of great importance to Galileo's career, since it represents a major step in his move from Venice to Florence. In the draft of this letter, we read: "It remains now that we make sure that this act, which by its nature is the most heroic and sublime way to explain and propagate for eternity the glories of great princes, be received by the world with the greatest splendor and grandeur."[44] Galileo planned to send copies of the *Starry Messenger* and a copy of the telescope to church officials and European royal families as part of a larger project to claim ownership for his improvements and negotiate a larger courtly environment.[45] He made preparations for a second edition that would have been translated into Italian and prefaced by the poems written by the "beautiful intellects" who wrote about his discoveries.[46] Material that Galileo assembled for this edition (which was never published) shows that the poetry for the second edition of the *Sidereus nuncius* included forty hexameters, ten Sapphic odes, two epigrams, and four distichs, all in Latin, all written by Jesuits.[47] These were not epic octaves, but still a traditional use of prefatory poetry in a courtly philosophical setting.

The final version of the letter that Galileo sends to Vinta, his future employer's secretary, includes the suggestions for a second edition and the desire to send the telescope to the same list of personages as stated in the draft, but the substance of the comment on the heroic nature of writing the *Sidereus nuncius* underwent considerable revision between versions. In the final letter Galileo says: "I am most certain that God, knowing my most ardent affection and devotion for my most merciful Lord, although he did not make me a Virgil or a Homer, wanted me to be the giver of a no less precious and excellent means of exalting his name, registering it in those eternal annals."[48] The heroic task in the draft, a term that combines the religious with the epic, is here broken into its constituent parts in the final version. Galileo positions his authorial voice in relation to the epic poets Virgil and Homer. He distances himself from writing epic poetry, but suggests that his writing glorifies God, just via a different path. Rather than the "cantare," the singing, of the poets he will "decantar," exalt, the glories of the Medici family.

Contemporary responses to the *Starry Messenger* generally took one of two rhetorical forms: the technical, literal engagement with the function of the telescope and the discoveries it made possible, or a more figurative, poetic discussion of the same.[49] When Girolamo Sirtori wrote his description of the telescope in 1612 (published only in 1618), complete with diagrams of lenses, tables of proportions for lenses, and tools for forming lenses and constructing the tube, he returned to the mathematical, technical presentation of the instrument free from poetics at any level.[50] Even Simon Mayr, who Galileo believed was responsible for Capra's plagiarism of the military compass, maintained this technical style in the *Mundus Jovialis* (*World of Jupiter*, 1614), which claimed primacy of the discovery of Jupiter's moons and provoked Galileo's ire in the opening pages of the *Assayer* a few years later.[51] Aside from one mention of Ovid, everything else in the book was composed of measurements and direct engagement with Galileo's observations.[52] On the other hand, one of Kepler's responses, the *Somnium* (1634), placed a fantastical and allegorical dream frame around what a modern critic has summarized as: "a detailed and accurate astrophysical account that tallies point for point with the then current state of knowledge in Copernican astronomy."[53] The *Starry Messenger* had not then established a model for writing about philosophical discoveries.

The year following the publication of the *Starry Messenger* was a busy one for Galileo. He had moved to Florence in September of 1610 and by March of 1611 was making a trip to Rome to meet the philosophers and mathematicians of the Collegio Romano to discuss his observations. The flurry of interest and arguments surrounding the claims of mountains on the Moon, new celestial bodies around Jupiter, observations of Saturn, and even the spots on the Sun had tremendous implication for the debates on heliocentrism. The 1611 trip to Rome was an important opportunity to make connections among Jesuits and at the papal court.[54] Heilbron calls this period "knight-errantry," highlighting both the courtly aspect of the journey and its dangers.[55] The trip also marked the beginning of two disputes that occupied much of Galileo's time in the following years: the nature of sunspots and the behavior of bodies in water. The sunspot debates involved foreigners and lasted until 1613. The quarrel over explanations of floating bodies was significantly shorter, but entirely set in the ambiance of the Medici court in Florence. Galileo was living the life of a nobleman at the ducal court, called upon to display his virtuosity as desired, often with little time to prepare, and certainly under the constraints of entertaining by a display of wit and ingenuity.[56] This also helped to distinguish Galileo as a philosopher rather than a mathematician. Even though the books published in relation to this material are labeled as discourses or letters, they are essentially dialogic. As one critic writes: "it is nothing other than a more or less polemical reply to criticisms and oppositions brought against him by adversaries all the more combative and tenacious, since they were ill-equipped in the realm of epistemology."[57] These opponents were equally ill-equipped in both the philosophical and literary epistemologies, and in these conflicts Galileo begins to explore their weaknesses with the latter as he undermines their claims in the former.

The telescope allowed for more detailed investigation of phenomena that were only barely discernible to the naked eye, and sunspots were one of them. In late 1610, Thomas Harriot in England made the first report of these dark areas that appear on or in front of the Sun's surface. A few months later the father–son team of David and Johannes Fabricius in Germany did the same, nearly at the same time as the Austrian Christoph Scheiner, S.J. While Galileo was in Rome the following spring meeting with the Jesuits, he showed them sunspots as well. Later that year Scheiner sent three letters to his ally Marc Welser, arguing that these spots behaved like stars and were to be found near the sun, but not on it. The letters went to print early in 1612 as *Three Letters on Solar Spots*, but he used the pseudonym of "Apelles hiding behind his painting." His choice of secret identity refers to the classical Greek painter who displayed his works in front of his shop and eavesdropped on passers-by who commented on the quality of the paintings.[58] Galileo responded quickly to the errors he perceived in Scheiner's work by writing two letters in May and August of 1612 to Welser, who had asked for Galileo's opinion of them. Modern critic Jean Dietz Moss uses the subheading "The First Sally in the Sunspot Duel" for her analysis of the works in this period, calling attention to the perceived elements of epic poetry and its parody in the exchanges between these intellectuals.[59]

Scheiner next published a follow-up treatise in September, the *Accuratior sisquisitio* (*A More Accurate Discussion*; 1612), and Galileo wrote a final letter of reply, which argued that the spots are solar material, a position that would have later implications for showing that the Sun rotates on an inclined axis. Even though his response was aggressive, he chose a subtle and holistic means of attack. On the sunspot quarrel, Dietz Moss writes of Galileo: "He knew how to shatter an adversary's image through disparaging analogies, how to destroy an argument by characterizing its assumptions as hopelessly antiquarian. The ingenious comparisons, the lively progression of each clause and sentence, the apt phrase, all contrive to build a marvel of rhetorical refutation."[60] Recognizing the tone of Galileo's letters of criticism, Scheiner signed his second treatise *"Apelles hiding behind his painting* or, if you prefer *Ulysses, under the shield of Ajax."*[61] In March of 1613 Galileo's letters appeared in print, some published with Scheiner's work, others without, marking Galileo's official public declaration in support of Copernicanism. This was done with a minimum of references to poets or poetry. Galileo's reply to the masked Apelles was not laden with quotations from the *Furioso* in the way that Delle Colombe's responses to Alimberto Mauri were punctuated with verses from Tasso's various works. The debate was still contentious, but without the poetic substructure of many previous texts in the field.

There is one notable exception, when Galileo seeks clear definitions of terms from his opponent. Relying on the typical authority for etymologies, a poet, Galileo also accesses a common ground between the literary and philosophical. Given Schiener's insistence that the spots were stars, Galileo returns to the question of how to define the term star, which had also been discussed in the debates on the *nova*. In a passage similar to Liceti's lengthy study of the names of stones Galileo says:

> neither the Jovian nor [the fixed] stars are spots and shadows, and the solar shadows and spots are not stars. In truth, I am not insisting on nomenclature, for I know that everyone is free to adopt it as he sees fit. As long as people did not believe that this name conferred on them certain intrinsic and essential conditions, I would care little about calling them "stars," for it was thus that those of 1572 and 1604 mentioned earlier were also named. Meteorologists use the name "star" for those with hair, those that fall, and those that race through the air; and finally, lovers and poets are permitted to call their ladies' eyes "stars": "When Astolfo's successor sees [*sic*] / Those smiling stars appear above him." For like reasons one might also call solar spots "stars," but they have, in essence, characteristics that differ considerably from those of actual stars.[62]

With this quotation from *Furioso*, VII.2.1–2, Galileo suddenly takes attentive readers to the island of the sorceress Alcina, known for seducing men and then turning them into trees once she has grown tired of their lovers' games. Astolfo's successor in this cycle is Ruggiero, who very nearly succumbs entirely to Alcina's wiles. Eileen Reeves has recently pointed out that this citation presents more than a mere demonstration of the flexibility of the word "star": "A double illusion is at stake here: unlike the lovers Astolfo and Ruggiero, the poet knows that the lady's eyes, elsewhere described as 'dark, or rather as two brilliant suns,' are not really stars; Ruggiero discovers after his dalliance that she's no lady either, but rather an ancient, shrunken, and toothless hag."[63] Following Reeves' analysis, Galileo is Ariosto, whose far-reaching gaze, prior to the reveal, has seen through the disguises of trickster characters. Heilbron pushes this analysis one step further, suggesting that Galileo presents himself as Ruggiero, who defeats the siren Alcina with Angelica's Ring of Reason and escapes to the court of Alcina's twin sister, a place described as the abode of reason and philosophy.[64] Importantly, on the surface, Galileo has simply included the verses as an example of the different meanings that lovers and poets have for the word "star," similarly to the technique that Liceti parodied with his study of stones. For its full effect, for the implication that Galileo's reason will see through Apelles' disguise or even Aristotelian dogma's untruths, readers needed to know the *Furioso* and be well versed in Ariosto's literary strategies. Galileo's Italian readers, at least those who had not spent years in academies disparaging Ariosto's poetics, would be aware of these connotations, but for the authors, like Scheiner himself, who had to wait for Galileo's letters to be translated into Latin before they could read these replies, the veiled insult would have likely remained hidden.

In part, this could explain why Ariosto has a more notable presence in Galileo's works intended for a courtly Italian audience. In late 1611 he became involved in debates in Florence on the reason bodies in water float or sink: their shape or their specific gravity.[65] Florentine Lodovico Delle Colombe, fresh from the *nova* debates, is one of the chief protagonists in this dispute because he claimed that shape determines floating or sinking, which Galileo refuted if the shapes were already wet (to remove the factor of what we now call surface tension). A dispute with demonstrations was arranged, but each philosopher claimed that the other failed to appear at the designated time and place.[66] Delle Colombe (according to Galileo) took the debate to the public square, rather than meet him in the way that Galileo felt was best to reach the appropriate audience and to satisfy the Grand Duke's expressed desire of maintaining decorum – in a courtly setting or in print.[67] In September 1611, at the request of the Grand Duke, Galileo wrote out what would have been an oral argument, immediately placing the debate in an erudite courtly setting via a short letter that makes ample use of Ariosto, particularly considering its brevity. After the topic again appeared at a court lunch in October, Galileo formalized his ideas in the *Discourse on Bodies in Water* (1612), in which he again employs the language of warfare, but eliminates the poetic references found in the draft.

In the fifteen-page document that predates the *Discourse*, Galileo raises his preliminary objections to Delle Colombe's theories on the behavior of solids in water. Composed as a letter to the Grand Duke, Galileo concludes by saying:

> Most Serene Lord, I have taken the trouble (as your Highness has seen) to keep alive my true proposition, and along with it many others that follow therefrom, preserving it from the voracity of the falsehood overthrown and slain by me. I know not whether the adversaries will give me credit for the work thus accomplished, or whether they, finding themselves under a strict oath obliged to sustain religiously every decree of Aristotle (perhaps fearing that, if disdained, he might invoke to their destruction a great company of his most invincible heroes), have resolved to choke me off and exterminate me as a profaner of his sacred laws."[68]

Galileo goes on to compare his situation as a savior of truth to that of Orlando as he rescues the inhabitants of the cursed Island of Tears from the monstrous *orca*. As told in the *Furioso*, every day the residents of Ebuda offer a virgin to Proteus, King of the seas, in hopes to appease the god after their King killed his own daughter and her child fathered by the sea god. Proteus never accepts the offering, and the maidens are devoured by his sea monster, the *orca*. The island location is a pivotal space for the stories of both Orlando and Ruggiero, whom Galileo will mention in relation to events on this island in the *Assayer*, discussed in the next chapter.

Like the paladin Orlando, Galileo has killed a monster that threatened a sequence of "shes," women and propositions, but the consequences may not be those he anticipated. In this letter on floating bodies Galileo speaks of his efforts to "keep alive my proposition and, together with it [*lei*], many others that will follow, saving them [*le*] from the voracity of the lie brought down by me and killed."[69] The proposition in question relates to the effect of shape on an object floating and its motion in water. Since Orlando was chased by an angry mob driven by fear of their angered god, Galileo subsequently questions how his own act will be received by the academic community: "I do not know if any of my adversaries will hold me in good esteem for such a deed as I have done."[70] Galileo wonders if the Peripatetics will feel liberated from their erroneous thinking, or: "rather, if finding themselves under such severe judgment obliged to uphold almost religiously every decree of Aristotle, fearing maybe that he, insulted, would send forth to destroy them an enormous host of his most undefeated heroes, they will resolve to throw me in the water and exterminate me as a profaner of his most holy laws."[71] The words "religious," "host," "profane," and "holy" are all included in the verses of the *Furioso* to which Galileo alludes.[72] Edits to the passage show that Galileo even changed the language in this draft better to reflect its connection with the octaves from the *Orlando furioso*. In the original, the "undefeated heroes" were simple "followers."

This is one moment where readers need not know Ariosto, because Galileo provides the necessary context, including the key vocabulary used by the poet. The literary concerns of courtly virtues, morality, and tradition are assumed completely into the philosophical and courtly context. The Peripatetic opponents would be, according to Galileo: "as such imitating the inhabitants of the Island of Tears, who, irate with Orlando, as recompense for his having liberated thousands of innocent young virgins from the horrible holocaust and voracity of the ugly monster, move against him, pricked by strange religion [*rimorsi da strana religione*] and scared in vain by the fear of Proteus' wrath, to submerge him in the vast ocean."[73] The phrase "by strange religion and scared" is added in Galileo's hand in the margin of the fragment, as is the modifier "vain." The additions echo Ariosto's description of the islanders' reaction: "A deed so holy seems profanity / to those who would hold to heathen creeds in vain" ("i quai da vana religion rimorsi").[74] Perhaps for dramatic effect, Galileo continues to make reference to the episode: "and they well would have done it, if he, impenetrable, even though naked, against their arrows had not done with them that which a bear tends to do with small pups, such that with vain and uproarious barking they importunately stun him."[75] The islanders, and by extension all followers of vain religions, risk being torn to shreds by their opponent, a particularly disastrous fate for the paper texts the Peripatetics continue to defend and study.

These concerns have no place in mathematical discussions, but are essential to the philosopher himself either as a guide for conduct or as a model of expression. As Galileo incorporates more of this literary self into his philosophical writing, that epistemology, particularly in later works, will create the space for this new figure. Galileo breaks from the metaphor to conclude: "But I, who am not Orlando, I have nothing impenetrable except the shield of truth; unarmed and naked otherwise, I turn to the protection of Your Highness, at whose simple gaze will fall to the ground the weapons of whosoever, outside reason, against reason, will imperiously want to move assaults."[76] According to his own description, Galileo's battle, though philosophical, is no less epic and his valor no less heroic. While this is not a use of literary elements to generate knowledge of a philosophical topic, the comparison that Galileo makes does serve to ingratiate him with the Grand Duke in a parallel way to the veracity of his arguments on the behavior of floating bodies.

This experimentation with the implications of literary references continues sporadically in each of Galileo's works through the 1616 edict that banned direct published support of the Copernican hypothesis. When not relying on Ariosto to supply the erudite, courtly, or dramatic subtext for his self-presentation, Galileo turned to the same material in order to undermine those characteristics in his opponents. In his marginal annotations to Lodovico Delle Colombe's response to this work on floating bodies, *Discorso apologetico* (*Apologetic Discourse*; 1613) he returns to a motif that Delle Colombe had raised in the *nova* disputes nine years prior: philosophical choices depicted as religious ones. Galileo's follower and student, Benedetto Castelli, drafted a response to this detractor, the *Risposta alle opposizioni del S. Lodovico delle Colombe e del S. Vincenzio di Grazia sopra il trattato del Sig. Galileo Galilei sulle cose che stanno sull'acqua, ò che in quella si muovono* (*Response to the Oppositions by Lodovico Delle Colombe and Vincenzo di Grazia about Galileo's Treatise on Bodies in Water*), which was eventually published in 1615 in Florence. This book is the first example where the manuscript is as much, if not more, in Galileo's hand than in his pupil's.[77] One passage has a particularly Galilean flair to it, since the "foolishness" of the Peripatetics' understanding of floating bodies, the inappropriate brevity of Lodovico Delle Colombe, and his epic dislike of one of Galileo's solutions are all subject to ridicule and word play based on a citation from Ariosto. Castelli's text says:

> To another experiment of some Peripatetics, who had written that an egg floats in salty water and sinks in sweet water because the salty is more dense and corpulent, Galileo responds that this is great foolishness because with other reasoning and the same methods it will be proven that sweet water is more dense than salty. To this Mr. Colombo [*sic*] responds: "this experience with the egg has the same flavor as the others"; and he goes no further with his response. But that he does not like the flavor could possibly not be the fault of its tastelessness, but in that which Ariosto writes of Rodomonte:

> > But the Saracen, who was born with bad taste,
> > Not even did he taste it, he disliked it.

> But if you do not show with a better reason the foolishness of this phenomenon, I believe the response of Mr. Galileo will remain such that it is, most efficacious.[78]

For this moment of insight Galileo refers to a passage from the *Orlando furioso* in which the Saracen Rodomonte tries to dissuade a young virgin from joining a convent. Her traveling companion, a monk, comes to her defense and lays out a feast of spiritual food to save Rodomonte's soul, but the pagan cannot stomach such talk and kills the monk. The comparison of a philosophical opponent to a Saracen establishes an early dichotomy that will persist through Galileo's later published work in which he characterizes himself as a paladin hero.

The 1613 letter to Tolomeo Nozzolini, which had a limited circulation, contains similar references to the *Orlando furioso* and demonstrates an instance where Galileo is able to achieve both ends. The letter is yet another defense of the *Discourse on Bodies in Water*. Unlike Delle Colombe's earlier insinuations that his opponent was an unfaithful usurper and corruptor of women, Galileo's choice of literary foundation allows him to explore the philosophical implications of this opponent's actions. Of his adversaries, Galileo says: "like the poorest, or rather totally naked of any defense, they make up their minds, inhibited by extreme destitution, to confess as errors and falsehoods their own propositions, not being able to find them among mine, even though there remains some hope that they may be able to make their propositions appear to be mine."[79] Galileo's defenseless adversaries cannot admit their error, but would rather try to make their readers believe that error to be a product of Galileo's own philosophy, not their own. Our philosopher claims that this brings to mind "the strange departure of the rival of Grifone at the banquet of Norandino," a reference to *Orlando furioso*, XVII.[80] Grifone, the nephew of Orlando, took part in a tournament organized by the King, Norandino, only to have his first competitor flee out of cowardice before the event concluded, subsequently undermining the strength of Grifone as a knight.

For a reader unfamiliar with the nuances of the *Furioso*, the implications of the reference might go unnoticed, since Galileo compares a reshuffling of philosophical concepts to the sudden departure of a tournament competitor, an unlikely but permissible similitude. After the coward Martano is shoved into combat and reins his horse away from contact with the competitor's lance, Ariosto says:

> with his sword his conduct was far worse –
> Demosthenes himself could not defend him.
> As though of paper (it was steel, of course)
> His armor was, he feared each blow would rend him.
> Then breaking through the ranks, he fled, and laughter
> From all the crowd arose and followed after.[81]

Martano, here the representative of Galileo's detractors, fights steel with paper, and even the rhetoric of the orator Demosthenes could not hide his, or their, lack of skill. Fighting with paper will be a common image in the remainder of the philosophical debates in which Galileo is involved. He claims that his opponents use a world on paper, the world of printed, received tradition, instead of their own senses and that natural, physical world – steel, as it were – to defend their beliefs.[82]

Accordingly, as such a weak combatant, Martano shames Grifone, just as the Peripatetics have done to Galileo with their attempts to defend themselves. Ariosto describes the audience response to Martano's cowardice at length:

> The clapping and the mockery became
> So boisterous that, as Martano fled,
> Grifone, who remained, was filled with shame,
> As though *he* had been guilty of the deed,
> And brought dishonor down upon his name;
> At his companion's flight he hung his head
> And rather would he seek the fire's embrace
> Than stay, defiled and tainted, in that place.[83]

Such derision forces Grifone into vicious combat, and he defeats numerous other knights in the tournament. Ariosto describes the moment of Grifone's decision to triumph:

> As inwardly, so outwardly, he burns,
> As if his were the shame and only his.
> The crowd of onlookers at once discerns,
> And longs to see him test, his expertise.
> Much on Grifone's skill and courage turns.
> Perfection more than ever needful is,
> An inch, a fraction of an error will
> Appear an even grosser blunder still.[84]

Suddenly the reason for Galileo's casual reference that almost seems out of place is evident. Within the literary context of the poem, this scene is rich with implications for virtuous behavior, chivalry, and triumphing over not only a cowardly opponent, but a deceitful one as well. The vague mention of the departure of Martano incorporates the shameful performance of Galileo's Peripatetic adversaries and the perfection that Galileo hopes to maintain to defeat all of his future opponents. One has to wonder if Galileo's intense reading of Ariosto allowed him to recognize Delle Colombe's (and others') slippery strategies, or if Ariosto simply provided the way of making that accessible to his readers. In either case, the realm of the poem opens the avenue for discussing method, expression, and intent while natural philosophical elements are treated with mathematical rigor.

The final example from this period dramatizes yet another rhetorical strategy in terms recognizable from Ariosto's poem. Perhaps Galileo anticipated the vicious attacks he would suffer after the publication of the

Letters on Sunspots. Midway through the *Letter to Benedetto Castelli* on the discrepancies between scripture and interpretations of natural phenomena – another letter with a limited circulation from 1613 – he writes that there needs to be a forum for discussion, not a field for battle, in philosophical investigation. Furthermore, the debate must be a debate, not a moment of shining the shield of religious truth to scare the speakers into silence. He laments the lack of strategy and respect his opponents seem to demonstrate amongst themselves and outside their circle:

> but if they, contending amongst themselves over natural terms, not producing other weapons than philosophical ones, know that they are superior to their adversary, why, when coming to the match, do they reach for an inevitable and tremendous weapon, that with one look terrifies each most dexterous and expert champion? But if I have to tell the truth, I believe them to be the first to be terrified, and that, feeling themselves unable to stand strong against the assaults of their adversaries, they attempt to find a way to not let themselves be hit.[85]

Here Galileo's incorporation of the poem is subtle, calling to mind, but not mentioning specifically, the way Ruggiero uses his magic shield and Astolfo his magic horn in the *Furioso*. These enchanted weapons have a troubled place in the poem, functioning well against monstrous, magic creatures, but with disastrous repercussions when applied to other knights.[86]

Galileo did not simply invent an epic battle simile to explain the argument of his opponents, but chose an existing set of images that allowed him to reach certain conclusions about his own opponents. The literary and philosophical epistemologies are here working inseparably and equally to make a delicate interpretative point about the role of scripture in debates about celestial bodies. Ariosto provides the paradigm that allows Galileo to demonstrate how his adversaries depart from those ideals.

As these examples from materials that mostly had limited circulation demonstrate, Galileo's approach to poetry moved from jest and biting comments about logic to jesting the logician and finally becoming a model for thinking through philosophical problems. As Shapin has shown in the early years of the Royal Society, disputes were as much about things as they were about people: "Veracity was understood to be underwritten by *virtue*."[87] The use of epic poetry to exemplify that virtue achieved a dual purpose: by its very nature as valorous, it was an authority on virtue, and it was part of the princely court culture that supported Galileo's investigations. Similar to Delle Colombe's implications about Mauri's character via Tasso, Galileo's tendencies to use Ariosto have already implied that the

Paduan Aristotelians and his Florentine detractors were a horde of scared and misinformed peasants, dishonorable and cheating combatants, a lustful and treacherous sorceress, and a blood-thirsty and vicious Saracen. This is in line with what Jean Dietz Moss has written more generally about Galileo's prose style: "Had he simply exposed his opponent's lack of logic he would have had no need of rhetoric; dialectics would have been enough, but he preferred to destroy his opponent's *ethos*."[88] Moreover, the literary space of the poem provides opportunities to explore the problems facing the new philosopher.

This literary program nonetheless exists in tandem with the fact that Galileo has already discounted poetry and will continue to write against it in philosophical works to the extent that Wlassics says the separation of poetry and science "is in part, in great part, an initiative of Galileo himself."[89] Battistini has even provided a careful survey of the ways in which Galileo deploys caricatures of the very poetic elements against which he is arguing in order to win over his readers.[90] This use of poetry, here in its infancy, requires the reader to be more involved with the source text and Galileo's own writing, but does not yet reflect a comprehensive and organized incorporation of the literary for philosophical ends. The Controversy on the Comets of 1618 will provide the necessary environment for bringing that to fruition.

CHAPTER THREE

Sarsi and the Saracens

While Lodovico Delle Colombe had made his reliance on Tasso clear in published work, Galileo's use of Ariosto in a philosophical context had a limited circulation until the *Assayer* (Rome, 1623). In subsequent works Galileo's points of criticism mirrored those he made of Tasso's poem, but he refrained from the explicit use of poetic quotations to prove his philosophical points. The *Starry Messenger* indicated the courtly value of epic poetry but, again, without the poetic preface its author had envisioned. The remaining references to the *Furioso* seen in the previous chapter appeared in drafts that were likely not read by anyone other than Galileo and in letters that were presumably read only by the intellectual circle of the addressee. The notable exception was Galileo's self-presentation as the masterful Ariosto and brave Ruggiero fighting with the Ring of Reason in the dispute on sunspots. The more mature incorporation of the language of epic poetry in the *Assayer*, part of the controversy on comets over a decade later, exploits a literary strategy that has the ability to connect with an early-sixteenth-century audience enamored of paladin heroes, and to persuade them of the valor of their author when faced with trickster opponents. Moreover, as an epistemological discourse, these literary elements as much outline the characteristics of the new philosophical epistemology as help to generate them.

Criticism has often acknowledged the bite of Galileo's rhetoric in the *Assayer*, and critics have adopted a vocabulary of epic conflict to discuss the historical events of this period. Pietro Redondi evokes military strategy and foundational epics such as the *Aeneid* when he calls this period "Operation Sarsi" or the "Sarseide," and organizes his description of events leading up to the publication of the *Assayer* in the form of a play-by-play analysis of a battle.[1] John Heilbron remarks on the epic nature of Galileo's personality in his recent biography, in which he calls the *Assayer* "a heroic poem in prose, a 'Sarsiad', a protracted tale of right against wrong, good against evil, innocence against deceit."[2] Mario Biagioli mentions the letter that Federico Cesi wrote to Galileo, in which he specifically uses the language of jousting related to Sarsi.[3] Many scholars indicate Giambattista Marino's praise for Galileo in his epic mythological poem *Adone*, published at the same time as the *Assayer*, but without an indication of potential literary connections between the two works.[4] Even letters to Galileo in this period show that his friends were enthusiastic about a vivacious response, but without anticipating the kind of prose Galileo would generate. Cesi wrote to Galileo in 1620 that he should quickly write a response, but not aimed directly at Sarsi, advising: "do not come out in a direct duel."[5] Cesi specifically called the debate a duel ("duello"), noting the biting and bitter response that Galileo needed to compose, but even these battle metaphors did not foresee what Galileo would accomplish in the *Assayer*.

In this work, Galileo offers the most vivid examples of rhetorical attacks on the *ethos*, or character, of his opponent. The citations from epic poetry challenge authority and suggest a new philosophical paradigm. Determining the function of this rhetorical strategy has the advantage of expanding previous work on Galileo's style and also suggesting a literary component to that language that seems to have been overlooked in the face of the formal, technical rhetorical elements that are undoubtedly present in his works. For this analysis I rely on the precedent set by the research of Jean Dietz Moss who argues that rhetoric displaced dialectic in the Copernican Controversy, thereby giving space to emotion in philosophical argumentation.[6] In terms of rhetorical training, Galileo has been linked to the Jesuit Ludovico Carbone and his contemporary in Padua, Antonio Riccobono, both notable scholars of rhetoric.[7] As their works on rhetoric show, for both Carbone and Riccobono, the end goal of rhetoric is persuasion based on what Riccobono calls the "persuasible" – that is, argumentation that depends not only on logic, but also on character, emotions, belief, and above all persuasion.[8] When combined with the question of character, either of the opponent or the reader, the "persuasible" can hinge on a reader's response to Galileo's claims about the person of the philosopher, not the claims he makes, leading one critic to call this "murderous wordplay" in the *Assayer*.[9]

Certain stylistic elements contribute to this reader involvement. As William Kennedy argues, the tone of false naivety that Galileo often adopts creates a distance from the text that allows readers to be directly involved in acts of judgment.[10] *Ethos* and *pathos*, appeals based on the character of the speaker and appeals that elicit an emotive response from the audience, are the elements of rhetoric that enlist the participation of the reader or listener in creating the argument or drawing conclusions. The slip from negative evaluation of character to rejection of a theory would seem to go hand in hand. My analysis will show that in order to achieve this effect fully, Galileo must exploit the literary richness of the sources he chooses to connect poetic themes and images to his philosophical project. This type of examination does more than compare and contrast. It documents a shift in Galileo's understanding of the poetic from a place of mere ornaments and traditionally accepted factual observations that he dismissed outright to a discursive space that allowed for the creation of an essential part of his new philosophy, the philosopher himself. In this sense, I follow a similar style of analysis to Eileen Reeves. Her study of Galileo's use of the commentary tradition surrounding Daniel 5 in the *Assayer* shows how he casts Orazio Grassi and Tycho Brahe as Chaldeans. With this allusion he claims that they are able to see, but not to interpret, the writing on the wall that indicates their imminent demise.[11] But as I show, the Bible is not the only source for Galileo's intertextuality, since he makes similar use of the poems of Ariosto and Tasso. This analysis develops a framework to then show how embedded this style of critique and creation became in the *Chief World Systems* and the *Two New Sciences*.

The work began as a series of Galileo's marginal annotations that reflect an ideological position similar in tone and style to his *postille* in Tasso's *Gerusalemme liberata*. His marginalia about imprecise vocabulary, relative language, decorum, loquacity, and feigned or demonstrated ignorance demonstrate the energetic and spirited way in which he pored over the pages of a book. They are the closest recreation of being with the philosopher during his interpretative process and demonstrate the similarities between the Pisan philosopher's poetic aesthetics and his standards for astronomical, physical, and mathematical expression. Galileo does not pull his punches in these private annotations. Texts fall victim to Galileo's fondness for epideictic rhetoric, particularly *vituperatio* (name-calling), something that does not appear with such intensity in the published documents in which he addresses his adversaries. For example, aside from identifying bizarre, pedantic, idiotic, and cursed passages, Galileo compares some philosophers' activities to following the scrotum of another, indicative of the linguistic register of much of his marginal criticism of intellectuals for whom he had no respect. The annotations establish the personal and visceral tone of Galileo's reading, and their presence indicates the elements of writing that triggered such vituperation. Peter Armour has also noticed the linguistic similarities between the notes that make up the *Considerazioni al Tasso* and the marginal annotations in Galileo's copy of the *Libra astronomica ac philosophica* (*Astronomical and Philosophical*

Balance; 1619) that would eventually become the text of the *Saggiatore*, suggesting that like the comments in Sarsi's work that were a draft for a longer, formal text, so too the notes in Tasso may have been the beginning of a more substantive treatise.[12] Armour primarily focuses on linguistic elements such as the similar adjectives that describe Tasso and Sarsi, and he acknowledges that Ariosto is cited or mentioned more in the *Assayer* than in any other work by Galileo.[13] By contrast I examine what Galileo criticized, the literary elements with which he did it, and the result for the changing identity of the new philosopher.

When framed by two other sets of feisty annotations – those in Baldassare Capra's plagiarized manual on the operations of Galileo's military compass, *Usus et fabrica circini cuiusdam proportionis* (*Use and Construction of Proportional Compasses*; 1607), and Antonio Rocco's *Esercitationi filosofiche* (*Philosophical Exercises*; 1633) – the development of this style of intellectual attack becomes apparent. Galileo criticizes his philosophical opponents for the same faults he finds in Tasso's epic poem and, in his annotations, with the same disparaging vocabulary. Using these moments of criticism, we can reconstruct his standards for well-written philosophical prose. Identified *ex negativo*, this prose would then be the good model to inspire new philosophers in their careful observations and search for effective demonstrations.

Baldassare Capra and Antonio Rocco are useful foils to Sarsi given their relationships with Galileo. Aside from the annotations in their work being, alongside those in Sarsi's *Balance*, some of the most vicious examples of Galileo's *postille*, Galileo's reasons for marking the margins are similar. Capra had directly refuted Galileo's lectures in Padua on the supernova of 1604 and then clumsily plagiarized the booklet that Galileo distributed with copies of his geometric and military compass. Galileo's annotations are the preparatory material for a planned rebuttal. Capra's blunders while he copied Galileo's text are similar to Sarsi's. Instead of maintaining the integrity of a passage, Sarsi excerpts phrases or sentences to which he gives a new context. The problem is twofold: Sarsi is a poor reader, and he misdirects other readers. Galileo suggests that in order to understand the literal message of Sarsi's text in the *Astronomical and Philosophical Balance*, readers need Galileo's text to reveal the layers of passionate rhetoric that hide the truth. He criticizes Sarsi for not faithfully reproducing the passages he cites, then for taking them out of context: "you do not produce (even in abbreviated form) other than those places from which it seems to you possible to show contradictions or other fallacies. One could recognize all too clearly the falsity of your tactic if one had available my work."[14] To amend this fault Galileo will copy Sarsi word for word to maintain the integrity of the text, all the while impugning Sarsi's integrity as a philosopher.

Antonio Rocco was a rebellious defender of Aristotle and a scandalous commentator who exposed contradictions in exegesis.[15] The work discussed here was published as a response to the *Chief World Systems* while Galileo was preparing his treatise on motion that would become the *Two New Sciences*. Galileo organized his annotations of Rocco's *Esercitationi filosofiche* – seventy-five marginal notes with some longer commentary – and they were partially incorporated into the First Day of the *Two New Sciences*.[16] There is some evidence that these annotations can be tied back to the earlier disputes on the *nova*.[17] Like Sarsi, Rocco represents a case of marginal annotation becoming a published document. All three, and some of the authors I have discussed in previous chapters too, are subject to Galileo's same sharp rhetorical blade, but Rocco was alive and publishing under his own name, which arguably limited Galileo's expressive potential out of concern for decorum.

When Galileo switches from critical *postille* in the margin of an opponent's work to writing the body of a text, he casts aside the language of derision reserved for Tasso and Tasso-like philosophers, and instead uses citations from Ariosto's epic to ridicule the ideas and the authors he challenges. Personal attacks are softened, translated into a formally appropriate vocabulary, and contextualized when Galileo's commentaries are published in the form of a new discourse, in this case the *Assayer*. As an intellectual debate, the structure of these arguments on comets is once again part of a back-and-forth publishing game, one that parallels Galileo's earlier works on floating bodies and sunspots, but the polemic builds on the concerns and strategies outlined in those disputes with a new layer of depth in the use of Ariosto and Tasso in his prose. Galileo cites poets directly and indirectly to insult the methods of his opponent in what becomes a program of explicit incorporation of epic poetry into his writing on astronomy and physics. Instead of the marginal jibes against his opponent that resemble his comments on Tasso, the published *Assayer* uses language borrowed from his favorite Renaissance poet, Ludovico Ariosto, to describe Galileo's experience as a philosopher and mathematician. For readers who can recognize the literary clues, Galileo keenly characterizes a philosophical opponent as a treacherous, bloodthirsty foe without courtly or academic virtues. An analysis of his citations from the *Furioso* in the *Saggiatore* shows that these excerpts are not only enunciations of simple metaphors, but also moments of double meaning that can be read as direct insults understood by readers with an extensive knowledge of the author's favorite epic poem. Taken together they outline a new model of behavior for Galileo's ideal philosopher. These moments of poetry suggest a prose style indicative of equal investment in the literary culture of the period and the philosophical argument of the day.

In what is now called the Controversy on the Comets of 1618, both Galileo's supporters and the Jesuits produced a series of texts, rebuttals, and counterattacks over the course of six years.[18] The publishing flurry began with Orazio Grassi's treatise that used Tycho Brahe's theories to suggest that comets had orbits similar to planets: *On the Three Comets of the Year 1618*, published anonymously in 1619. Galileo's student Mario Guiducci responded with a *Discourse on the Comets* (1619) that describes a rectilinear motion for comets (and implies the movement of the observer and therefore terrestrial motion).[19] Galileo himself wrote many sections and supervised the rest.[20] Grassi responded later that year with the *Astronomical and Philosophical Balance*, no longer anonymous, but published under the pseudonym Lothario Sarsi. Galileo was also perhaps involved in a dispute on the place of comets in the Tychonic system in another format with literary foundations – the *Assemblea Celeste radunata nuovamente in Parnasso sopra la nova cometa* (*The Celestial Assembly Newly Convened in Parnassus about the New Comet*; 1619) – and the unpublished response, "Esopo in Parnaso" ("Aesop in Parnassus").[21] Rhetorical posturing occurred on both sides of the debate: Grassi created a screen for himself by publishing the *Balance* under the pseudonym of Lothario Sarsi, and giving Sarsi the identity of Grassi's own fictitious student. Galileo's marginalia to this volume are in many cases the direct inspiration for his 1623 reply, the *Assayer*.[22] Whereas Grassi's and Guiducci's texts had the traditional structure of a treatise, Galileo's reply took the form of a letter addressed to a promising young colleague, Virginio Cesarini, Pope Urban VIII's Maestro di Camera when the book was published. In spite of its purported epistolary structure, Galileo adopts a popular printed debate structure by copying Sarsi's *Balance* word for word in his text, interspersed with paragraphs of analysis and biting commentary on what Galileo sees as faulty methodology and sneaky rhetoric in the Jesuit's work on comets. The *Assayer* is so dependent on the idea of critical interpretation that Armour calls the *Saggiatore* "a parody of the peripatetic commentary."[23] Both Guiducci and Grassi publish follow-up pieces, and Kepler too had a part in this dialogue between books, including his response to, and critique of, the *Assayer* as an appendix to his *Hyperaspistes* (1625), itself a defense of Tycho Brahe's theories about comets against Scipione Chiaramonti's *Antitycho* (1621).

The "Controversy on the Comets of 1618" was not unlike other battles of books. Notably, Leonardo Salviati, of the Accademia della Crusca, had adopted this same structure for his *Degli Accademici della Crusca Difesa dell' "Orlando furioso" dell'Ariosto* (*Defense of Ariosto's "Orlando furioso" by the Academics of the Crusca*; 1584) against the attacks of Camillo Pellegrino. The style also appeared in the natural philosophical realm, for example in the disputes between the Italian humanist Julius Scaliger (1484–1558) and the Italian mathematician Girolamo Cardano (1501–1576). Scaliger's 1557 refutation of Cardano's *De subtilitate rerum* (*On the Nature of Things*; 1551) has been aptly described by a modern critic as "a mixture of philological learning, references to common sense, *reductiones ad absurdum*, scorn, and flippancy."[24] Scaliger's rebuttal took the form of *Exercitationes* (1557), or 365 exercises that copied excerpts from the work of Cardano in order to prove directly his errors. Cardano next responded in 1560 with a refutation presented in the form of a dream sequence, though his opponent was already dead. As this example shows, some of the rhetorical and formal elements of the Galileo–Grassi tussle have roots in works of natural philosophy from at least sixty years prior.

The communicative value of the knightly imagery from the *Orlando furioso* in the *Assayer*, more so than that from the *Gerusalemme liberata* in Delle Colombe's earlier example, can then be seen as more than a nod to popular literature or mere courtly allusion. In light of my elaboration of Dietz Moss' approach, references to Orlando, Ruggiero, Angelica, and the Saracens are then not just pleasant reminders of Galileo's fondness for Ariosto, but well-chosen pieces of a literary project themselves. These poetic interludes in the *Assayer* aim to persuade the reader of the superior character of the author and engage his emotion in a debate on comets in order further to persuade that same reader of the logic of those ideas and spur him to active decision making. In so doing, Galileo creates a literary-philosophical text that invites rereading and critical analysis, not simply study of philosophical ideas.

Sarsi and Tasso: marginal similarities

Galileo's detractors, such as Capra, Delle Colombe, and Sarsi, are all prone to writing works that Galileo dismisses immediately in his annotations with a particular set of modifiers. Notably, this kind of attack is not found in the annotations of Rocco's *Esercitationi*. Galileo identifies one of Tasso's parenthetical phrases as labored (*stentato*), searching (*mendicato*), pedantic, swollen (*gonfio*), and haughty (*burbanzoso*).[25] A later verse is "junk [*robaccia*] for filling empty corners, insipid, disgraceful, and as usual, pedantic."[26] Sarsi produces "arch-pedantries" and "tall tales" (*fanfaluche da niente*).[27] Galileo says of Tasso's work: "you will dirty many pages and you will make a bed for dogs."[28] Ludovico Delle Colombe is guilty of "revealing himself above all of the other ignorant the most ignorant" alongside the *ignorantone*, Lothario Sarsi.[29] In his pejorative language of condemnation, Galileo is argumentative and exploits Italian flexibility in suffixes, not just to indicate the superlative seen here, but also to insinuate the diminutive. In the margins of the *Esercitationi filosofiche* Rocco is criticized for an *esclamazioncella* ("exclamationlet") and Galileo provides him with a final *considerazioncella* ("considerationlet").[30] Tasso is accused of writing *scherzetti* ("jokelets"), needlessly including a *concettino* ("conceptionlet"), and writing *fanciullaggini* (childishness).[31] These suffixes set the mocking tone for most of the marginalia.

The scatological insults appear frequently with simple animal-inspired name-calling, a linguistic element not found in published work. Galileo marks many passages for their appropriateness (or lack thereof) in content and presentation. In these marginal comments, likely not intended for wide circulation, but inspiration for works that would be published, Galileo adopts an unadulterated language that does not heed his own standards for writing. For example, he makes a sarcastic comment in the margins of Lodovico Delle Colombe's *Contro il moto della terra* (*Against the Motion of the Earth*; 1611), in which he refers to the luck of not always urinating on oneself if the Earth carries stationary objects such as people and artillery pieces forward in space as quickly as their projectiles, if not faster.[32] In the dedication of the *Consideratione Astronomica circa la nova, et portentosa Stella* (*Astronomical Consideration of the New and Portentous Star* [Padua, 1605]) by Baldassare Capra, the author of the dedication, Giovanni Antonio Dalla Croce, proclaims himself "the only lover and defender of the mathematical sciences, against the ignorant slanderers."[33] Next to the phrase "lover and defender" Galileo writes that Dalla Croce is the "only testicle" (*solo coglione*) in the mathematical sciences and goes on to label the entire talk a "chatter" (*ciarlare*).[34] He chides Tasso for the "nice asinine courtesy" (*bella creanza assinina*) of Clorinda, and Tasso and his characters are subject to a host of name-calling: Goffredo becomes a "big baby" (*bamboccio*) and Tancredi a "coward" (*vigliacco*); Tasso himself a "little dwarf" (*omettino*), "poor little painter" (*pittorino poverino*), and a "shabby and miserable painter" (*pittor gretto e meschino*).[35] In Galileo's marginalia, Capra was a "dumb ox" (*bue*) and an "ignorant thief" (*ladro ignorante*).[36] The title of "dumb ox" is bestowed upon several authors in

Galileo's collection of annotated volumes: Baldassare Capra, Ludovico Delle Colombe, Lothario Sarsi, and Antonio Rocco. While hardly poetic, I include these to show that neither poets nor philosophers were immune to this register of criticism. Sarsi joins the plagiarist Capra, the Tassist Delle Colombe, and Tasso himself in this cohort of authors who produce unphilosophical and unpleasant works.

Galileo repeatedly categorizes the writing of these men as pedantry, and those comments are frequently found in publication. In the 1612 edition of the *Vocabolario degli Accademici della Crusca*, the entry for *pedante* redirects to the definition of *pedagogo*: "He who leads children, and teaches them, to which we say *pedant*."[37] However, historically in this period the pedant is not simply a teacher: the figure abounds in comedies, most obviously Francesco Belo's *Il pedante* (1529). In the Prologue, the figure of Silence explains to the audience: "The comedy is named *The Pedant*, which is a person that, with letters in hand, will defend his reasoning."[38] She equates figures of this type to "abject pedants that speak worse than a German when he forces himself to speak Italian."[39] This theatrical phenomenon highlights the literary nature of the term "pedant," particularly in comedy, and particularly as the object of ridicule. For a reader as steeped in the literary culture of his day as Galileo, a term as charged as "pedant" would conjure images of dozens of characters from the comedies and jocose poetry that he so enjoyed by Berni, Burchiello, or Ruzzante.

My sense is that typically this literary element is removed from the interpretation of Galileo's comments about the pedantic habits of his contemporaries. Yes, epistemological pedantry can certainly apply to the poets and philosophers that Galileo so heavily criticized, but this divorces the term from its rich, literary connotations. The figure quickly represents the precariousness of the line between wisdom and folly: erudition and *sprezzatura*, or graceless antiquarianism and anachronism.[40] Torquato Tasso is called many variants of "pedant" along with Lothario Sarsi and Antonio Rocco.[41] Tasso is accused of writing material for *giovani* (the young), *principianti* (beginners), and *fanciulli* (little kids) in Galileo's comments to Canto II alone.[42] When considered alongside the comments of *grezzo*, *povero*, and *meschino*, criticisms that Tasso doesn't have a poetic ear to distinguish sonorous verses from those that are not, and finally that he is like the little pedant (*pedantino*) who shivers with excitement at pleasing his mother, the complete picture of Tasso as pedant looks more and more like the comic figure.[43] Whether or not the annotations of Tasso circulated, they provided the background for the creation and interpretation of the pedantic Sarsi that Galileo wished his readers to acknowledge.

The image of Tasso as a pedant bears striking resemblance to Sarsi, enough so that the implied literary connotations should not be overlooked. In his comments on Sarsi's *Libra astronomica* that will become the *Assayer* Galileo writes: "We learned from Ptolemy and not from lowly pedants; so do not be surprised that we did not know these things [about the cosmos] and you did: and if you had learned from the same teacher, you would not make such blunders [*gofferie*]."[44] In the *Assayer*, Galileo has the luxury of treating Sarsi like the student that he claims to be, and slyly insinuating to readers that Grassi is the *pedante*: "At my age, these altercations simply make me ill, though I myself used to plunge into them with delight during my childhood, when I too was under a schoolmaster [*pedante*]."[45] Elsewhere, he compares Sarsi to a man who scrutinizes fine cloth for imperfections even though the clothes made from it will be filthy by the time the night ends, a traveler so focused on saving time on his trip to India that he spends hours walking the city to inquire about which gate is the most expedient for the shortest trip, incompetent secretaries of unknown crimes, and the arrogant bluffer who flees when his insufficiency is exposed.[46] In particular, the reference to the pedantic departure for India could have resonated with the Jesuit audience, given their missions in the Portuguese colony of Goa in India.[47] Taken together, these presentations of Sarsi are more of the comic, literary type. Pedantry here carries the implication of being juvenile, ill-prepared, pompous, and even poorly dressed. Sarsi is a mask, and Galileo treats him as such – a character from a comedy. Such a lengthy pause for a single term would itself seem pedantic, but for the resulting sense that, even in comments such as these, Galileo's attitude toward Sarsi is decidedly literary. While calling Sarsi a dumb ox would have violated rules of decorum, pedant was a safe term of criticism to use.

This literary, comical understanding of the term was more widespread at the time, for there exists a later example from the aftermath of the controversy on the comets. Giovanni Camillo Glorioso was part of Galileo's intellectual circle in the Veneto, but wary of declaring himself a Copernican and doubtful of the role of parallax in determining the location of comets. He succeded Galileo as chair of mathematics at Padua when the Tuscan returned to Florence. His *Responsio ad controversias de Cometis Peripateticas* (*Response to the Peripatetic Controversies on Comets*; 1626) is part of a polemic that included Fortunio Liceti. This response is primarily a philological exercise to undermine Liceti's earlier *Controversiae de cometarum* (*Controversies on the Comets*; 1625). In the preface Glorioso reacts to Liceti's comparison of the two philosophers to the epic poets Homer and Virgil:

And finally he reminds me to be assured that learned men never will consider that I am such a man as Homer, from whom his own Virgil was willing to nibble at little blossoms of eloquence; certainly if I am not Homer, neither is he himself Virgil: yet I am certain that fellow has nibbled much more from me than little blossoms of eloquence; and who are those learned men never to think this? Perhaps those two, or at most three, novice scholars, and beardless men, with whom he parades through the Gymnasium, and through the town? Indeed, I do not believe there are others.[48]

Glorioso's characterization of Liceti's followers as "beardless men" signals Liceti as the pedant, the teacher of uncertain educational background pompously leading pupils into erroneous lessons. I do not wish to suggest that every use of pedant carries only this comedic, literary connotation, but rather to propose that this definition exists simultaneously and in a complementary way with the pedantic slave to erudite minutiae that Galileo will also deride.

The pedantic Sarsi, Tasso, and others share with the literary figure another linguistic element that Galileo seeks repeatedly to correct in his philosophical writing: the laughable language of confused terminology. The consistency of these complaints in annotations across the poetic and philosophical books that Galileo owned shows the great importance of carefully chosen words. Galileo's library is populated by authors who neglect to define their terms, and in so doing leave their texts open to multiple interpretations – a possibility that works against the very transparency of meaning he saw in the geometric book of nature mentioned in the previous chapter. Galileo even brings Ariosto to task for incorrect use of the verb to name, *chiamare*, saying about one verse: "people, not names, are named."[49] When Rocco suggests repeating an experiment keeping the distance the same, but altering another variable, Galileo asks in an annotation: "The distance from whom, Mr. Rocco?"[50] Delle Colombe comes under attack for using "contrary" without offering examples both of the object or principle and of its opposite.[51] Tasso is chastised for first speaking of a short manuscript, *breve foglio*, and then later calling it a book, *libro*.[52] Galileo further derides Tasso for the use of relative terms:

I believe that without other presumptions, everyone will be able to know for themselves how much this "Yet in the guise of a great and uncaring man" is pedantic and pompous; I warn only that he is beginning to put his hand in the box of *greats*, to season, as will be seen as the poem progresses, many upon many soups with *great* heads … *great* bulls … *great* bodies … *great* horses, and many other *great* things. Such a condiment, according to the taste of this poet, if I am not deceived, is very appropriate for making his style *great*.[53]

Galileo goes on to list six more instances of Tasso's inappropriate use of *gran* and its variants. Later, when he describes the two sons of a warrior killed by Clorinda as *gran* he exclaims in frustration: "Up already and take care with that cursed *grande*! They must have been two huge boors, because that's what it means in Tuscan to say *gran figli*."[54]

In this language of annotations, Galileo blends linguistic criticism with the animalesque insults and the flexibility of suffixes in Italian to create a rich series of complaints about lax word choice. His comments on Tasso's use of *gran* resonate with his jabs against a series of authors such as Sarsi, Delle Colombe, and Rocco for their ambiguous phrasing. Galileo generally bristles at the possibility that one word can refer to a number of physical realities, not a single signified object, yet he claims immunity for himself from this flaw in argumentation. In his *Philosophical Exercises* Rocco attacks Galileo for presumably contradicting himself by using a vague term when talking about the known fixed stars. In a marginal note to the work Galileo claims that he simply uses the vocabulary employed by others at the time when he refers to two phenomena as stars: "[from] the name therefore … with you, is derived, as a consequence, the identity of the substance? O, dear sir, don't you all still call a star that little white mark for which a horse is called starred on the forehead? Is not the spinning wheel of a spur called a star? Not one of these is distinct from the real star in the sky."[55] Galileo had done something similar in the *Dialogue of Cecco de' Ronchitti* when Matteo says of Lorenzini: "Who the devil told him that this new star is a starry star? Maybe it's just a bright spot with no star. I didn't call it a star till now, because it isn't one; it just looks like those others."[56] Problems of the inadequacy of language to describe physical reality later lead Galileo to create new words and adopt lexicons from other disciplines, even colloquial kitchen terms, to describe celestial phenomena accurately.[57] Not only does a philosopher need to describe the physical world instead of constantly rewriting the words of another, but he must do so with precision.

In Sarsi's response to the *Assayer*, the *Ratio ponderum librae et simbellae* (*A Reckoning of Weights for the Balance and the Small Scale*; 1626), he has certainly noticed how often questions of precise language vex Galileo. Sarsi deliberately misinterprets Galileo's term for the title – *saggiatore*, the assayer of fine metals – as *assaggiatore*, the taster of wines.[58] When Galileo comments on this passage, he again keeps to the themes of poor choice of vocabulary by offering an alternative definition for *simbellatore*, weigher, the term Sarsi used to identify Galileo in his title: "I, imitating you, could say that the name *Simbellatore* [a hunter who uses decoys] comes from the decoy birds, which are little sachets full of bran, tied at the head with a little cord, with which our farmers at carnival tend to lure in and to strike masqueraders."[59] These little sachets tied with their little cords are reminiscent of the other pejorative diminutives seen earlier.

Until this point, nearly all of the above examples derive from handwritten marginalia, that is, from private commentary that did not have a wide circulation. The shift from reactionary marginalia to polished and published criticism reflects a complete linguistic change and a new point of poetic reference. Relative language, for example discussing size or length without measure, is probably the stylistic element that Galileo criticizes most frequently in his published work, yet his expression is most boisterous in the private annotations. One particular example from the *Assayer* that has its roots in the notes to the *Libra* shows how he modifies his tone, but retains his criticism from postil to publication. Sarsi frequently uses relative adjectives without providing points of reference, to which Galileo responds in the *Assayer*:

> From indeterminacy of this sort, it comes about that the same things may be called very near and very far; the closer may be called distant and the farther close; the larger may be called small and the smaller large. Thus one might say, "This is a very small hill," and "This is a very large diamond." A courier calls the trip from Rome to Naples very short, while a great lady grieves that the distance from her house to the church is too great.[60]

In the annotation that inspired the above passage, Galileo had written something more biting:

> Mr. Lothario, you would like to change cards on us while they are in our hands; and like the nursemaid that takes the jewel from the baby, and showing him the sky says: "look, look, the little angels," and exchanges in the place of the gem a chestnut, so you would like with tiny diversions to throw dust in our eyes, and to treat us like imbeciles. This is not Jesuit doctrine.[61]

In the publication the sneaky nursemaid from the marginal note is reduced to the morally neutral figures of an enthusiastic courier and a lazy noblewoman. All references to misdirection on the part of Sarsi have been removed. Galileo's point remains the same: such vague terminology confuses the situation.

Just like Tasso's indeterminate and multipurpose "great," Sarsi's "large" and "far" are not precise enough for Galileo. Elsewhere in the *Assayer*, Galileo criticizes, in a tone of jest, this kind of relative language by identifying what Sarsi has called the "nobility of shapes":

> As for me, never having read the pedigrees and patents of nobility of shapes, I do not know which of them are more and which less noble, or which more and which less perfect. I believe that all of them are, in a way, ancient

and noble; or, to put it better, that there are none which are noble and perfect or any that are ignoble and imperfect, except in so far as for building
walls the square shape is more perfect than the circular, while for rolling or
for moving wagons I deem the circular more perfect that the triangular.[62]

Galileo, an avid collector of Greek, Roman, Danish, French, Italian,
and other chronicles, invents a subgenre related to the science of comets in order to poke fun at Sarsi's problematic categorization of shapes.[63]
These are obviously qualities that are difficult to quantify and therefore
do not fit easily into a geometrical analysis of natural phenomena. Yet,
with Ariosto, Galileo suggests that a repetition of a word with different
meanings in relationship would improve the *Furioso*, VII.66.2: "The verse
would read better 'Reasoning such the sorceress arrived,' and the word
venne [arrived] would be placed three times, always with a different meaning."[64] The above comments form one category of criticism that would
imply the need to avoid meticulously all vague vocabulary choices, except
to demonstrate erudition in a literary context. What Galileo practices on
these texts is what we would refer to now as literary criticism, and he does
so while at the same time he also challenges the philosophical conclusions
made by his opponents.

In a similar critique, this time on appropriate content rather than style,
Galileo reacts against authors who fill their pages with items of no importance to distract the reader from the inadequacy of the text. On the proliferation of worthless words that generally results from poor interpretation
or poor texts to interpret, Galileo writes in response to Delle Colombe and
his colleagues in criticism: "It is not worth setting oneself out to confront
one who is so ignorant that, to confront all of his little stupidities (those
being more in number than the lines of his writing), it would be necessary to write enormous volumes, with no utility for those who do understand, and without any advantage in the face of the common crowd."[65]
He excuses his own prolixity in all three of the *Letters on Sunspots*, and in
the third criticizes Scheiner for the unnecessary length of his geometrical
explanations.[66] Galileo makes the same interpretation of what he sees as
Tasso's superfluous content – "We shall say that he who does not know
what to say, and yet wants to fill a page, must write of these niceties" –
and in the *Assayer* he suggests about one of Sarsi's arguments that he
"capriciously introduced it in order to swell the size of his book."[67] Worse
still, according to Galileo, is magnifying the minuscule and minimizing
the moment of greatest importance to a few lines, again distracting the
reader from the central theme or argument of the text. Even Ariosto, with
whom Galileo often identifies, is not exempt from the criticism of this

sort: "By the grace, Sir Lodovico, content yourself that these two stanzas be removed, because this exaggeration is a little bit long, and in the end begins to languish and diminish the agitation."[68] He criticizes the same misappropriation of energy in a number of places in Tasso's *Gerusalemme liberata*, but particularly when the sentinel announces the arrival of the Christians at the gates of Jerusalem: "An entire stanza is consumed to recount the cry of the watchtower guard; and now the provisions that Saladin must make to defend Jerusalem, as the enemy approaches, are dismissed with two words."[69] Repeatedly Galileo chides Sarsi and Tasso alike for their lack of brevity where it is required and garrulity where it is not. He warns readers of the *Assayer* that their examination of the *Libra* will include "a sea of diagrams introduced into a long discourse designed to corroborate an experiment which in the end fails to achieve the slightest assistance for the main point under consideration there."[70] Even geometric loquacity is not an endearing quality for Galileo as a reader, particularly when an author pairs it with an apparent misunderstanding of, or deliberate deviation from, the task at hand.

The question of originality began early in Galileo's career with the proprietary debates over his military compass, and continued through the controversy on the comets. When he quickly points out omissions, transcription errors, and impossible calculations that Capra created by trying to alter numbers provided in examples from Galileo's original manual, he turns to poetic phrasing to attack his foe. Galileo criticizes Capra for an inexact citation (poor plagiarism in fact), but he does it by inexactly citing a poet: "Here is his cruel destiny [*fiero destino*], which makes evident, from the falseness of what he says here, that what he said above is not flour from his own sack."[71] Capra's method is doomed as soon as he begins to copy blindly. "Fiero destino," for a reader like Galileo, who had memorized Petrarch and Ariosto, evokes both the "Triumph of Fame" in the *Trionfi* and several moments in the *Orlando furioso*.[72] Galileo wrote the word "destino" in the margin near Petrarch's passage on Plotinus not being able to escape a lifelong malady in the *Trionfi*, which indicates its importance to him.[73] In the *Furioso* "fiero destino" refers alternatively to the fate that leads the paladin Ruggiero toward what his guardian has foreseen as certain disaster in France, King Agramante's failure to follow advice that would have spared the city of Biserta, and Rinaldo's unrequited love for Angelica.[74] Given his identity as a reader, Galileo has quietly borrowed a semantically recognizable phrase and used it to criticize another author for doing something similar, though on a much larger scale and with far less skill. Like the ill-fated love of Rinaldo and the doomed figures of Ruggiero and Agramante, Capra's stolen mathematics are destined for ruin. The Venetian courts recognized Capra's plagiarism of Galileo's text, and he was banned from the university.[75] Similar to what we will see with more elaborate examples, Galileo's poetic borrowing creates an unproblematic intertextuality that highlights the writer's literary erudition and here stands in the face of Capra's (incorrectly) borrowed terms that ultimately discredit his authority.

During the comet exchanges, Orazio Grassi, using the identity of his invented student Lothario Sarsi, accused Galileo's real student, Mario Guiducci, of being nothing but a copier. Sarsi called Galileo's student a "copiatore," since he recognized Galileo's role in Guiducci's *Discourse on the Comets*, but Galileo insisted that he had written unique theories where Sarsi has only repeated, poorly and inaccurately, things said by others. Galileo's retort emphasizes the value he places on originality in an author: "If Sarsi charges in one way as a copier Mr. Mario, he who nonetheless writes many things not written by others, how is Sarsi not the same as Father Grassi, who only writes things said by many others? This would be pardoning oneself for those defects condemned and reproached in others."[76] Sarsi did not master the primary texts, let alone improve upon them. Plagiarists and scribes are stymied by their limited intellectual vision. By borrowing without being critical, they no longer hide behind shields, but expose themselves to the most damaging kind of attack on their fraudulent authority.

These annotations continue to circle around a comic figure, one who is laughable with a silly language and a questionable intellectual preparation. Sarsi is not the classical, skilled, ideal philosopher. As much as Galileo demonstrates this through philosophical arguments and geometrical demonstrations, these moments of what amounts to literary criticism move this intellectual exercise into the realm of satire. Galileo's characterization of Sarsi as comic in private notes would at least partially serve to imply a code of action and explanation that this purported Jesuit pupil did not follow. Distinguishing the worthy philosopher from the unworthy is in line with what modern intellectual historian Steven Shapin has seen in England a few decades later. When discussing the discrepancies among observations of much later comets, those of 1664 and 1665, Shapin elucidates the moral management that took place in their support: "Reports from the vulgar might be costlessly negated in order to build up or hold stable some valued representation of nature whereas representations of nature might be adjusted in order to hold stable the moral order of skillful and sincere colleagues."[77] By extension then, if Galileo can discredit Sarsi's courtliness and intellectual preparation, essentially making him a member of what Shapin calls the vulgar crowd, Sarsi's conclusions or observations can be negated and Galileo can preserve the reputation of what he sees as proper philosophy.

The literary connotations associated with this criticism are precisely what prevent Galileo from maintaining the style of comment found in the marginalia once he uses those notes to compose the *Assayer*. Taken together, Galileo's criticisms in the margins of Sarsi's work echo a tale translated by Anton Francesco Doni (1513–1574) in the *Moral Philosophy* (1552). Galileo owned a copy of this work along with others by Doni, so we might even assume his knowledge of this anecdote as he was writing.[78] Doni's translation of the fourth-century Sanskrit instructional text *Panchantantra* includes an introduction taken from Abdullah Ibn al-Muqaffa's eighth-century Arabic translation and elaboration of that same text, titled *Kalīla wa Dimna*.[79] Doni's presentation of this story reflects an idea that had been circulating in the wider cultural consciousness for centuries:

> Let us not be like that indiscreet, ignorant man who desired to be held as a learned and an eloquent speaker. He asked a good friend (both poet and skilled rhetorician) to provide him with some erudite and eloquent writings, so that once learned, he could recite them in the company of other intelligent men and not appear lesser than they. The friend satisfied his request, upon which, in a small, gold-trimmed book that was well bound, he wrote many knowledgeable sayings and maxims. The man began to learn by heart this authority, and for a time toiled night and day to commit them to memory. He resolved to show himself to be learned. Finding himself in conversation (not knowing what the words he had learned meant because they were in a language he did not know), he began to link his maxims out of place, and as a result he was reprimanded and made the object of ridicule. The man, nearly angry, responded like a stubborn fool: "How can I be in error since everything I learned was from a book written by such a valiant man? And it is all covered in gold!" At this everyone laughed at his ignorance.[80]

Doni's tale highlights the comedy of false erudition. Everyone laughs as the narrative lays bare the speaker's empty intelligence as a mask. For Galileo, these authors have exposed themselves as ridiculous – their works earn them the title of ignorant, dumb oxen. Beyond their foolishness, their blunders and inattention show the signs of pedantry in their slippery vocabulary choices and superfluous, incongruous content. Publicly though, this kind of attack does not follow rules of decorum, and Galileo still had not severed all ties of support from the Jesuit community. In the margins we have seen that Galileo arms himself for his attack on these masked intellectuals with the same language he uses to criticize Tasso, but the use of Ariosto becomes a soft way of achieving that goal and simultaneously mocking one of the structures of classical philosophy – that of citing authoritative poets for support. Sarsi's mask gives Galileo the opportunity to maintain a vivacious level of attack in the *Assayer*, but engaging with the *Orlando furioso* will permit him to fight public character battles, display his own virtuosity, and achieve his philosophical goals at the same time.

Sarsi and Ariosto: courtliness and comets

The remainder of this chapter will look specifically at Galileo's use of Ariosto as an apparent source in the *Assayer*. Galileo's citations from the *Furioso* structurally appear to serve the purpose of supporting his conclusions by turning to an intellectual authority for similar observations, but their function is quite different from those of his predecessors and opponents. In this same work Galileo generally attacks this method of argumentation any time he sees it. Every time Sarsi includes a quotation from one of these poetic sources (hyperbolic and fictitious though they may be) as proof of a natural phenomenon, Galileo laments that his mind must be satisfied by "a little poetic flower" (*fioretto poetico*) instead of a demonstration.[81] The reference to the poetic flowers would have immediately evoked for an early modern reader the popular genre of florilegia, collections that compiled excerpts from various authors on different topics or themes. The reference is as critical of the use of poetry as a source as it is of the piecemeal recycling of early texts. Repeatedly in the text of the *Assayer*, he discounts all such references that Sarsi makes. Galileo himself, aside from an allusion to Dante, and one citation from Boiardo, uses only Ariosto as an apparent poetic source in the *Assayer*. Yet at one point he even suggests that the reliability of Sarsi's poets is comparable to that of Ariosto using Turpin. So why then turn to Ariosto for verses and images in his own text?

Through the excerpts from Ariosto Galileo effectively calls Sarsi (and therefore Grassi) a deceitful woman trickster, a shrieking bird, and a brutal Saracen warrior, but only if a reader probes the references to the *Orlando furioso* that Galileo makes. These are not the single-dimension, literal uses of poets seen in the first chapter, nor are they the obvious insults seen in the second. At the surface, the citations from the *Furioso* seem to be casual references and metaphors, not insults. In the first example we will see that

Galileo practices linguistic "slippage" to achieve a hidden and insulting effect. This slippage, described by Andrea Battistini in a philosophical context, allows Galileo to use the vocabulary and images from two different semantic fields (here a debate on comets and an eighth-century epic war) to create meaning and add understanding to one aspect of one field.[82] As Battistini shows for thought experiments in the later *Chief World Systems*, Galileo navigates through systems of meaning slyly in a way that resembles the literary strategy I am about to outline: to talk about something known, for example the motion of a cannon ball, and suddenly expand the discussion to something unknown or intangible, such as stars. Similar to analogy used so frequently in philosophical thought experiments, my analysis here will show that Galileo uses metaphor to achieve his desired literary result. As the first two chapters have shown, Sarsi is not the first to fall victim to this kind of attack, but he is the first to earn these insults in print. The use of poetry would seem to be in line with the ornamented verses seen in the texts of Galileo's detractors and even Kepler, but for the meaning they carry in their literary context, which also has implications for philosophy.

The program of Ariosto citations in the *Assayer* begins when Galileo asks if Sarsi believes that entire hosts of good philosophers can be imprisoned behind the gates of walls. Galileo extends the metaphor by insisting that the best philosophers are free, rare, and quiet like eagles, not like starlings who "fly in flocks, fill the sky with shrieks and cries wherever they settle," an implicit citation from *Furioso*, XIV.109.7, which has been identified by modern editors as such, but without explanation.[83] While Heilbron mentions the starlings, he does not credit the source to Ariosto.[84] Lanfranco Caretti, editor of the *Orlando furioso*, when talking about Galileo's prose, quotes this passage including the original Italian phrase "empiendo il ciel di strida e rumori," but makes no mention of the connection to the poem, since he focuses only on Galileo's tone in the paragraph.[85] At the simplest level, Galileo implies that he is not a noisemaker like Sarsi and the others, who have published frequently but without much merit. Every metaphor functions in two semantic fields, but, similarly to Ariosto, Galileo creates his metaphors by citing metaphors to achieve this type of insult.[86] The way Galileo uses the verse suggests that the screeches and noise belong to birds alone, and only serves to finish the metaphor he began about good philosophers being eagles. Attentive readers of the *Furioso* would recognize that the quotation comes from the moment Ariosto breaks a metaphor to describe the beginning of a battle. The octave that Galileo cites is an extended metaphor that compares the din of swarms of flies over a summer meal and starlings among grapevines to the cries of the Saracens in a surprise attack on the Christians. The "grida"/"cries" and "rumori"/"noises" of the *Furioso* belong to the Moors, and in that system of signification, if we see Sarsi and his noisemakers as the screaming besiegers of truth, the passage then hides a warning. After these lines in the *Furioso*, we read: "The Christian army, waiting on the wall / With axes, lances, fire and stones and swords, / Defends the city, fearing not at all."[87] Reading intertextually shows that Galileo is unthreatened by the rabble of Sarsi and his followers. Like Ariosto's Christian army, he remains confident that the enemy will be forced to retreat.

As the program of citations from the *Furioso* progresses throughout the *Assayer*, this confidence becomes superiority as Galileo uses references to Ariosto to criticize, illustrate, and insult. Shortly after implying that noisemakers will neither silence his work nor penetrate his philosophical stronghold, Galileo goes on to criticize Sarsi for two linguistic points: for wanting to call a long or short telescope a telescope all the same, and for arguing that it is applied differently to terrestrial and extraterrestrial objects. Galileo disagrees that the instrument is the same regardless of size though it is applied in the same manner; the distance between the lenses on a long or short telescope would change the instrument dramatically. Against Sarsi's claims that a long telescope is the same as a short one and that each must be used differently for looking at near or distant objects Galileo writes: "The same instrument is said to be differently applied when it is put to different uses without suffering any alterations; thus the anchor was the same when applied by the pilot to secure the ship and by Orlando to catch whales [*balene*], but it was differently applied."[88] With this allusion, Galileo would seem to be making reference to an episode from the poem already discussed in Chapter 2, when Orlando kills the monstrous *orca* to which the islanders of Ebuda had been sacrificing virgins in hopes to appease the sea god Proteus, a reading that modern editors have followed without recognizing the word play at hand.[89] Editors traditionally interpret this line by saying the anchor is still an anchor in both examples, but the applications are different by the pilot and by Orlando.

For careful readers of the *Orlando furioso*, the reference to Orlando's use of the anchor to "catch whales" is an excessively vague reference to the paladin's use of an anchor to prop open the mouth of a sea monster in order to kill it.[90] The paraphrase is ambiguous to the point of being erroneous, particularly when compared to Galileo's other verbatim citations of the *Furioso*. Such a careless description of a unique event in his favorite poem could not happen without reason. Ariosto never uses the word *balena* to describe the *orca* of Canto XI which Ruggiero and Orlando fight. *Balena* is a noun reserved for the whales that the sorceress Alcina controls, particularly the one so large that it eventually ferries Astolfo to her enchanted realm after he and his companions mistake it for an island. Galileo has already mentioned the aftermath of this episode in the *Letters on Sunspots*, when Astolfo's successor Ruggiero uses the Ring of Reason to see through Alcina's incantations. Galileo also reduces to the single word "catch" the entire narrative episode in which Orlando braces the jaws of the beast with the anchor so that it cannot bite him while he attacks, another deliberately erroneous statement. Orlando does not catch whales in the *Furioso*; Alcina catches whales to do her bidding. Galileo's suggestion that Orlando uses an anchor to catch whales is simply not true without generously taking advantage of the flexibility of the definitions of the terms. Neither Tasso nor Sarsi would be permitted such a factual or linguistic slip, but Galileo can use such an opportunity to access the likely literary preparation of his readers in order to demonstrate the fallacies of applying inappropriate terms to the objects of philosophy, and the dangers of relying on poets as witnesses or authorities on natural phenomena. The chaste, chivalric Orlando is not the lusty seductress Alcina, neither are enchanted whales murderous sea monsters, just as the long telescope is not the same as the short.

When viewed together with this implied, albeit erroneous, reference to Orlando killing the *orca*, the next mention of Ariosto's poem in the *Assayer* demonstrates a larger poetic strategy afoot in this philosophical debate. The third reference to the *Furioso* appears as Galileo accuses Sarsi of attacking weak arguments instead of the ones that are well founded and most likely to be true. He does so by making what would seem to be a passing reference to *Furioso*, XI. After suggesting that Sarsi invented outrageous numbers for the distance of comets to use in a syllogism that would disprove Galileo's theory of comet locations, Galileo offers a hypothetical Aristotelian counterargument to Sarsi's criticism and then says:

> Here there is nothing for the opponent to do except shrug his shoulders and remain silent. If one is to win over his adversaries, he must confront them with their own most favorable assertions, and not with those most prejudicial to them; otherwise he always allows himself to retire with immunity, leaving his enemy feeling stunned and senseless, as Ruggiero felt at the disappearance of Angelica.[91]

Without tracking down the reference in the *Furioso*, the remark simply seems to suggest that Galileo is as shocked when the argumentation is interrupted as Ruggiero was when Angelica fled from him.

There are many moments of vanishing and disappearing in the *Furioso*, so we need to ask, why did Galileo choose this one, particularly when it would imply that he plays the part of a lustful, unknightly Ruggiero? Ruggiero's rescue of Angelica that leads to her disappearance from his sight is the antecedent to the scene just described in which Orlando rescues yet another damsel about to be sacrificed to the same *orca* by placing the anchor in its mouth in order to kill the beast. Both scenes find classical precedents in Perseus saving Andromeda. In the hypothetical argument of the *Assayer*, the Cathay princess Angelica acts out what Galileo claims Sarsi does when trying to debate ideas that do not conform to tradition. In the poem, the exotic object of desire, Angelica, recently liberated from an impending death by sea monster, quickly realizes that her liberator Ruggiero will soon be her violator after his sexual appetite overcomes his chivalry.

Here Galileo risks implicating himself in unchivalrous actions by positing this allusion, though his contemporary readers may not have read the scene in this way. Daniel Javitch has effectively argued that Ariosto's rewriting of Ovid's tale of Andromeda's rescue by Perseus denies allegorical interpretations and calls attention to its sameness to classical tradition via the praised Renaissance rhetorical technique of *variatio*.[92] When read in the light of a strategy of *variatio*, Galileo's use of Angelica's disappearance places the philosopher at the level of his favorite poet. Rather than continue explicitly to berate Sarsi for deceptive argumentative practices and faulty physical investigation, Galileo has found a creative, lively way to demonstrate these characteristics of the *Libra astronomica ac philosophica*. The poetic allusions for Galileo, as for Ariosto, skillfully demonstrate the potential variety for describing the same topic. While Ariosto's Ruggiero–Angelica scene precedes the Orlando–Olympia episode in the *Furioso*, in the *Assayer*, Galileo's references reverse their order, but they are placed concurrently in the commentary. Given their placement they maintain their function as variations on the same theme. For Ariosto this theme was classical imitation; for Galileo it is the opportunity to devalue the claims of his opponent and to imitate his favorite poet.

Furthermore, by casting the scene in terms of the physical senses and immediately characterizing Angelica as the deceiver, Galileo rewrites the episode in such a way that Ruggiero becomes the victim. In the *Furioso*, naked and defenseless, Angelica sees the Ring of Reason on her hand and: "So filled with stupor and with joy is she / That all appears a dream, or else in vain / Imaginings her sight and touch must be / Deceiving her."[93] Angelica proceeds to remove the ring from her finger and secretly place it in her mouth so that she can take advantage of another of its magical qualities and disappear from Ruggiero's sight. The occurrence of the word *vano* (vain) here resonates with the same derivatives of the word that punctuate a reading of the *Assayer* as part of Galileo's criticism of Sarsi. When reread in light of the philosophical context that Galileo provides in the *Assayer* Ariosto's octave highlights deceit, concealment, and a blurred reality based on the act of seeing. We can think of the importance of seeing to Galileo in this moment, as he tries to convince people via geometry that although they see a comet that looks larger than stars, it is actually smaller (or really the result of refracting light), or, in the context of the larger philosophical conflict, that people see the Sun move when the Earth is actually in motion.

Through his allusion to the *Furioso*, Galileo accuses Sarsi of the same doubt and ultimate subversion of the physical senses as Angelica. There is particular emphasis on the misuse of the senses, primarily sight, to confirm reality in these verses. She disbelieves reality, she doubts, she thinks she is dreaming without purpose. Angelica has difficulty believing her vision (*gli occhi*) and her sense of touch (*la man sua*), which Galileo argues is the case with Sarsi, who he believes relies only on received tradition, not sensory observation, to draw conclusions about comets. Once Angelica does believe (*dà fede*), she resorts to magic, a subversion of the senses, to escape, just as Sarsi dodges a difficulty in his argument by rhetorically disappearing. Ruggiero is left to search for her "like a blind man," a man who cannot use his senses to achieve his goal. Galileo himself puts emphasis on this very characteristic, reminding us that the opponent subject to Sarsi's style of argumentation will be left not just "stunned," but also "senseless," literally without his senses to guide him. The literary and the philosophical are here working together, neither subservient to the other, to create a full picture of Sarsi that invites a rereading of not just Sarsi's text, but Ariosto's.

Later we see that Galileo offers what appears to be a truce to Sarsi: that they contend courteously. From what we have seen however, we know that such terms are difficult to meet in this dispute. Once again Galileo uses a moment from the poem in which he finds the same philosophical elements at work as in the treatise on comets. He writes: "Still, I prefer to 'Let gentlemanly strife prevail between us' [*Tra noi per gentilezza si contenda*], as the great poet says, and I shall consider the strength of your proofs."[94] The citation comes from the scene in Canto XXIII of the *Orlando furioso* in which Mandricardo approaches Orlando to avenge the death of his Saracen master Agrican. They battle for Durindana, Orlando's rightful sword, which he has only recently reclaimed, and which Mandricardo mistakes for the stolen property of the Saracen he has come to avenge, the same man who was in fact the original thief of the sword. The scene is one based on the incompatibility of appearance and reality in a way that rings true with the challenge facing Galileo on a philosophical level. Each party interprets visual cues and derives from them a coherent narrative of events. Based on his sources, the Jesuit Sarsi has deduced one theory that he believes correct, and, based on his observations, Galileo has done the same. When Galileo addresses Sarsi, he only cites the second verse of the octave, and omits the first line: "Although the sword belongs to me by right." Galileo is at once Orlando locked in an epic battle with his Saracen foe, and also the epic poet Ariosto using his all-inclusive gaze masterfully to invoke an entire series of signifiers to imply his authority on comets.

Using a variation on this theme of sword ownership, but taking a step backward in the genealogy of epic poetry, Galileo next writes in the *Assayer* that the great expenditure of words that Sarsi and his colleagues have generated to debate a relatively small issue of physics reminds him of a short monologue in the *Orlando innamorato* (1495) by Matteo Maria Boiardo (*c.*1440–1494), spoken by the paladin Rugiero (the character continued by Ruggiero in the *Furioso*). Just prior to this passage Galileo had been particularly critical of the use of poets to support claims that rapid motion caused arrows to catch fire (which would then suggest that comets are ablaze because of their quick motion). He compares the debate to a duel between warriors: "And here the passage brings to mind a saying from the shrewdest Poet: To win Orlando's sword, which they / Don't have, and maybe never will, / They blindly beat themselves so much."[95] The quotation from the *Innamorato* paints the picture of the energy wasted in battling over an item, in a philosophical case the truth about the fiery nature of comets, but the lines that Galileo does not cite from the poem cut to the quick of the matter. Rugiero explains to the heroine Brandimarte his previous attempts to separate the pagans Mandricardo and Gradasso, who fight for rights to Orlando's sword, which neither possesses. The octave in full reads:

> Rugiero said, "I've tried, but I
> am powerless to part those two.
> To win Orlando's sword, which they
> don't have, and maybe never will,
> they blindly beat themselves so much
> that I can hardly bear to watch [*Che pietà per me ne vien pur a vedere*].
> They surely are, from their appearance,
> two leading lights of strength and skill!"[96]

Rugiero's frustration easily parallels that of Galileo, trying "in vain" to direct his detractors toward a new way of thinking instead of following a predetermined path. In the octave to which Galileo alludes, for all of their bravery and strength in attempting to beat one another, Mandricardo and Gradasso uselessly expend their energy. Rugiero says that the two warriors have the skill and strength, but neither is victorious, and neither is in the right. The same could be said, if it has not already been implied by Galileo in his choice of citations, of the Jesuits and Peripatetics making claims about the nature of comets. Rugiero literally exclaims that *pietà* moves him as he watches. We have to wonder if that sense of *pietà* is also shared between Galileo and Rugiero.

The final example from the *Assayer* confirms the underlying duplicitous role of these poetic citations in this otherwise philosophical prose. In the *Assayer* Galileo has continually derided Sarsi and the philosophers on whom he relies for believing in chimeras and other *vanità*. He equates their believing that heat is created by motion (based on the accounts in the tenth-century *Suidas lexicon*) with believing the hyperbolic statements of Ariosto. Galileo responds critically to the story of the Babylonians cooking eggs by whirling slings around rapidly: "I do say that the cause of such marvels is very different from that which philosophers have attempted to maintain when they have reduced it to attritions of air, or of exhalations, and such chimeras which are all foolishness. Do you want to know the real cause?"[97] With his rhetorical question, Galileo seems to signal to his reader that he has the authoritative answer. Instead, he subverts his own authority by casting the response in Ariosto's voice:

> Listen to the peerless poet commenting upon the encounter of Ruggiero and Mandricardo, and the breaking of their lances:
>
>> The shafts, ascending, to the heavens came;
>> And Turpin, writing here with truth entire,
>> Says two or three fell back again in flame,
>> These having mounted to the sphere of fire.
>
> Do you think the great Ariosto raised no question about the truth of this when he bolstered it with Turpin's testimony? Everyone knows how veracious Turpin is, and how far one is obliged to believe him. But let us leave the poets in their proper place.[98]

Galileo's sarcasm is evident. Sarsi citing other philosophers and poets parallels Ariosto the poet citing the hyperbolic language of Turpin, the imaginary historian.[99] This allusion lays bare Galileo's attack on a strategy he will later call hiding behind the shield of another. Perhaps not accidentally, this quotation on the minimal trustworthiness of poets is the final such use of Ariosto in the *Assayer*. The reference slyly indicates to readers who understand the *Orlando furioso* that they should reconsider Galileo's own use of poetic sources, if they haven't already understood the program of veiled insults from the beginning. Not only does Galileo prove that he can use poetry more effectively than his counterparts, but his efforts also highlight the impotence of literal poetic testimony in the debate of philosophical truths. What they are able to do instead is give dimension to the voice behind a text and ridicule this faulty rhetoric and comedic waste of energy.

This poetic program does not end with the close of the book. Galileo makes a similar move in his first comment on Sarsi's *Ratio ponderum*, the response to the *Assayer*. The annotation appears immediately following a Latin verse that Sarsi cites to conclude the dedicatory letter to Cardinal Buoncompagni: "Settle these discordant minds, oppress these flames."[100] Sarsi's choice of verse strikingly echoes Galileo's final poetic image of Ruggiero's and Mandricardo's lances ablaze. In his copy of the *Ratio* Galileo has written a poetic response borrowed from Ariosto: "'Peace' the face pretends, but 'vengeance'/ the heart demands and awaits nothing else."[101] This is the only annotation (rather than published critique) I have found where Galileo quotes Ariosto. His response to Sarsi's polite, poetic request that the patron end the bitter dispute on comets recalls the moment before Drusilla revenges the death of her husband in the Marganorre episode of the *Furioso*, evoking a dramatic tone for Sarsi's project. In the poem Drusilla uses trickery to carry out her bloody project, but only after having been the victim of machinations herself.[102] It would seem that even in the battle of *fioretti poetici*, Galileo again has the last word.

Ariosto and Tasso in later works

Galileo's use of Ariosto does not end with the Controversy on the Comets of 1618. While my analysis of the literariness of Galileo's subsequent works, the *Chief World Systems* and the *Two New Sciences*, will be more thorough in Chapter 5, it is opportune to consider all of the examples of this use of Ariosto together. When they are viewed as a group, the richness of these poetic allusions indicates a deliberate and evolving use of Ariosto, and even Tasso, in Galileo's philosophical project.

Here, I will choose just one example of the Aristotelian character Simplicio's roots in epic poetry. In a moment of consternation in the *Chief World Systems* he says of fellow interlocutor Salviati's defense of

Copernicanism: "This manner of philosophizing tends to subvert all natural philosophy and to throw into disorder [*mettere in conquasso*] and upset the heavens, the earth and the whole universe. But I believe the foundations of the Peripatetics are such that one need not fear that upon their ruins one can erect new sciences."[103] The word *conquasso*, a violent shaking up, is a hapax in the *Chief World Systems*, just as *conquassato* is in the *Orlando furioso* and *Gerusalemme liberata*.[104] Though different forms of the same word, each stands out for being unique in the respective works, and given Galileo's familiarity with both poems, I suggest that there is a rich connection. Simplicio describes the somersault of the heavens and the Earth, one now still, the other in motion. This is analogous to the situation in which the passengers on the boat with Marfisa find themselves in the middle of the *Furioso*: "On the sea and often up close to the sky / the afflicted and shaken boat jibes."[105] We can imagine a wave-tossed vessel rising and falling, and creating a sense of disorientation among the passengers. Simplicio's second sentence builds on the imagery from the verse where *conquassato* appears in the *Gerusalemme liberata* that describes the walls of Jerusalem being shaken. Galileo has artfully placed a word plucked from poetry into the dialogue of Simplicio, implicitly tying him to the image of epic hero as well as supporting the claim that the contemporary Peripatetics argue with poetry instead of philosophy.

Yet Salviati is the only interlocutor to cite Ariosto explicitly and verbatim. Given his frequent identification with Galileo and Copernican philosophy, Salviati's use of the *Furioso* further characterizes him as the speaker most aligned with Galileo's style in other works. The first time he adopts this practice, on the Fourth Day of the *Chief World Systems*, he describes his own intellectual difficulties in an attempt to console his fellow confused interlocutors. Salviati gives Sagredo and Simplicio reason not to despair that they are not easily understanding a certain concept as he remembers: "how many hours, how many days, and how many more nights I spent on these reflections; and how often, despairing of ever understanding it, I tried to console myself by being convinced, like the unhappy Orlando, that that could not be true which had been nevertheless brought before my very eyes by the testimony of so many trustworthy men."[106] Salviati alludes to Orlando's discovery of his beloved Angelica's new love for Medoro by reading messages carved into trees.[107] Medoro's declarations of love are also inscribed in both Italian and Arabic on the entrance to the cave the lovers shared. Salviati's statement indicates Orlando's subsequent search for confirmation or denial of the veracity of these words.[108] The parallel reading is not without internal tensions, as Maurice Finocchiaro has shown in a careful analysis of the parallel between Salviati forcing himself not to believe the claims of the Peripatetics that the Earth does not move in spite of the evidence he clearly sees.[109] Beyond this, even though Sagredo is cheered by the news, he adds what Salviati has not: "Well, thank God for not letting your despair lead you to the end that befell the miserable Orlando, or to that which is perhaps no less fictitiously related to Aristotle; for then everyone, myself included, would be deprived of the revelation of something as thoroughly hidden as it is sought after."[110] Salviati, and therefore Galileo, have cited the series of readings that Orlando completes immediately before the moment from which the *Furioso* takes its name.

This pivotal moment in the poem brings together Italian and Arabic, the written words of the lovers, and the spoken words of the shepherd who hosted them. The identity of Orlando as an ideal knight or an uncivil madman hinges on the act of reading these signs. Ariosto presents the destruction of one imagined reality (Orlando imagining that Angelica loved him) and the admission of a reality so unimaginable that Orlando subsequently loses his mind and every vestige of what made him the perfect courtly knight. In the context of the *Chief World Systems*, the two languages are the written tradition of Aristotle and the language of heliocentrism that suggests a reality so *conquassato*, to use Simplicio's term, that it could drive men mad. But Salviati cleverly overcomes the situation of this epic hero – he is not Orlando gone mad, nor is he Simplicio who refuses to look at the other language that would drive him mad. As Salviati works through the complicated philosophical ideas, he subtly erodes the trustworthiness of the men who would argue against the motion of the Earth, thereby destabilizing their claims that would otherwise lead to his insanity.

The only other time Salviati uses explicit Ariostan language is in the *Two New Sciences*. In this instance, Salviati's analogy exemplifies *slittaggio*, the slippage between linguistic systems discussed earlier. Salviati suggests the impossibility of proportionately increasing the size of natural and man-made structures to extreme dimensions through an examination of disproportionate sizes of cylinders that support their own weight without breaking. A wooden oar enlarged 100 times to row a boat enlarged by the same amount would break without thickening the handle disproportionately to the length of the original oar. Speaking about bones, Salviati gives the example that only by changing the anatomy of an animal could such distortions be possible, and such creatures would then be unrecognizable as a man, horse, or other animal, because they would be "monstrously wide" (*mostruosamente grosso*), as he says.[111] Salviati goes on to cite Ariosto: "This is perhaps what our most wise Poet indicated while describing a huge giant, when he said: 'Impossible it is to reckon his height / it is all so disproportionately wide.'"[112] Ariosto had borrowed the story of the Orco, or land giant, from Boiardo, who had said "He's not tall, but as fat as six."[113] Boiardo's and Ariosto's words indicate the giant's impossibly large size. Erwin Panofsky has offered a compelling analysis of this passage:

> even if Galileo's interpretations were correct, he would not have adduced Ariosto as an authority for a statement about physics (as did those who attempted to prove a scientific theory by examples taken from classical literature) but, on the contrary, would have paid a graceful compliment to his *accortissimo poeta* by crediting him with a quasi-prophetic insight into what he, Galileo, had discovered more than a hundred years later.[114]

Based on my analysis thus far, this interpretation is entirely in line with Galileo's complaints about "poetic flowers" and his praise of Ariosto over Tasso.[115] Panofsky's conclusion and my analysis would seem to establish a pattern if it were not for the final example of Galileo's use of an epic poet.

To conclude, I would like to address the one exception to this overall trend. If Tasso is the poet of private marginal derision, and Ariosto the poet of sly public allusion, then why does Galileo put a direct quotation from Tasso in the mouth of Salviati during the Fourth Day of the *Dialogues on the Chief World Systems*? Salviati, while speaking of the tides, says that we are wrong to expect that the way water and air behave on a planet in motion be "sensible [*sensibile*] and evident"; as he explains: "in fact, quite the opposite happens."[116] He goes on to demonstrate what he means:

> How strongly water is disposed to preserve a disturbance once received, even after the cause impressing it has ceased to act, is demonstrated to us by the experience of water highly agitated by strong winds. Though the winds may have ceased and become tranquil, such waves remain in motion for a long time, as the sacred Poet so charmingly sings: *Qual l'alto Egeo [As the waves on the deep Aegean Sea]*, etc. The continuance of the commotion in this way depends upon the weight of the water.[117]

The "sacred Poet" of this passage is not Dante, though Favaro indicates him as the source in the index of the national edition of Galileo's works.[118] Rather, through Salviati, Galileo cites a simile from Tasso, *Gerusalemme liberata*, XII.63 – the octave that precedes the description of Clorinda's mortal wound and subsequent baptism at the hands of her unknowing lover, Tancredi: "As the waves on the deep Aegean Sea / when the air grows calm after the ocean's shaken / and pounded by the winds: they rock and sway/ and rumble from the buffeting they've taken."[119] This is the only explicit

citation of Tasso in Galileo's published works. Beyond making reference
to a poet that Galileo attempted so vivaciously to deauthorize in his private annotations, Salviati calls upon Tasso's verses to prove the veracity of
a natural phenomenon, a strategy of using poetry in philosophical works
that Galileo has criticized vehemently in earlier texts. We need only think
of Sarsi's use of *fioretti poetici* from Ovid, Lucan, and Virgil.

The choice of Tasso over Pliny or other *auctores* of natural science would
seem to undermine Galileo's project of rejecting the fictions and fables
that are, to borrow Galileo's terms, "in a sense essential to poetry," and
that are antithetical to his methodology of observation and demonstration.[120] The image of turbulent waves remaining choppy after the wind
can no longer be felt fits well into Salviati's argument on the tides, but
the verses are chosen from a simile that describes the warriors Tancredi
and Clorinda, still battling even though the force to do so has long since
left them. This use of Tasso is problematic more than just for the fact
that it presents a poet as an authority on natural phenomena, and beyond
the fact that Galileo constantly derided Tasso. Galileo, through Salviati,
cites the simile, the figurative language, not the literal narrative fact being
described in this canto of the *Liberata*. Is Salviati signaling the exhaustion
of both sides in these arguments? Is he alluding to the mutual damage
caused to both sides during these conflicts? After all, Tancredi is about to
kill the woman he loves. Is this is a subliminal call to conversion for the
Peripatetic detractors of Galileo's new science? Or is this simply a citation
of a poetic genius to prove a point about the motion of water? The episode escapes annotation in Galileo's *Considerazioni al Tasso* leaving us with
no indication of his private response to the passage that might inform his
use of the verse in a philosophical context. Editor Ferdinando Flora's note
on the passage merely suggests that Galileo had softened toward the poet
near the end of his career.[121]

I would like to suggest that this is yet another charged citation, placed
at a moment when Salviati had already explicitly said that instead of the
expected conclusion making itself "manifest and available to the senses,"
rather what happens is "the exact opposite." There are several sea episodes
in the *Furioso* that would have given Salviati similar imagery. Readers
expect Ariosto, Favaro expected Dante, and Galileo provides Tasso. My
second suggestion is that this use of Tasso is a type of *accomodatio* for
the Aristotelian in these dialogues, Simplicio, to whom Salviati explains
this theory of the tides. Recourse to a poetic authority, typically expressed
in heroic verse, is, after all, the traditional way of supporting an argument. Alternatively, the Italian verse has distinct echoes of a line from the

Furioso: "As the hoary Aegeus" ("Quale il canuto Egeo").[122] The line is one that Ariosto changed in the revisions to the poem from 1516 to 1532, and comes from a scene in which King Aegeus of Athens realizes that Medea has tricked him into nearly killing his own son Theseus.[123] Could this be Galileo craftily indicating his own sneaky switch to knowledgeable readers? Then again, under Salviati's own rubric of expectations being defied by reality, perhaps this inclusion is nothing more than form following function. Regardless, it is clear that a program of citing the *Furioso* does exist in Galileo's works outside his marginalia with rich significance for those who are willing to go beyond their literal message to their literary connotations.

Compared to other works of natural philosophy of the period, the *Assayer*'s use of poetry is unique. Unlike Liceti, who turned to myriad sources for verse testimony on phenomena; or Delle Colombe, who found several poetic texts to impugn Mauri; or even Kepler and Tartaglia, who relied on poets to express their emotions, Galileo specifically chose only recent epic poems to demonstrate the perils of unquestioningly incorporating received tradition into philosophical arguments. Doing so not only allowed him to create a text that invites rereading, but also suggests new ways of reading Ariosto. Moreover, this literary space in the text gives rise to questions about knowing the truth, trusting the senses, applications of terms and uses, and the successful characteristics of a philosopher. These questions – not by chance, I would argue – are the very ones that face Cervantes' protagonist Don Quixote, the subject of the next chapter. Working alongside the program of Ariostan poetics in the *Assayer* is also a strategy of literary criticism similar to Cervantes' that undermines tradition further but also seeks to erect a new epistemology that can address the concerns outlined above.

CHAPTER FOUR

Galileo's lesson on Don Chisciotte *(1622–1625)*

Galileo's sustained criticism of the myriad books that utilized poetic authority in matters philosophical and Miguel de Cervantes' satirical presentation of the outdated ideals of chivalry have more in common than many readers may anticipate. Galileo owned a copy of Lorenzo Franciosini's Italian translation of *Don Quixote, Dell'ingegnoso cittadino don Chisciotte della Mancia* (*The Ingenious Citizen Don Quixote of la Mançia* [Venezia: Andrea Baba, 1622-1625]), but his relationship with the volume transcends material history. In many ways Cervantes illustrates the tragic outcome that Galileo too had tried to warn against with his invectives against *fioretti poetici* as eyewitnesses to the natural world. The conflict of *Don Quixote* is rooted in part in the relationship between *res* and *verba*: that is, the most exact correspondence between objects and language, a language that can only be read literally to describe the natural world. The success of Galileo's new philosophy relies instead on forging a better correspondence between the one and the other. The comedy of *Don Quixote* functions on the breakdown of this relationship when a literal reading no longer corresponds (if it ever did) to a lived reality. Cervantes imbibes Don Quixote with a passion for the literal Ariosto equivalent to Galileo's opponents' passion for Homer, Virgil, and Lucan.[1] The similarities between Cervantes' comic protagonist and Galileo's parody of Aristotelianism – what he refers to as believing the "world on paper" – make clear that Galileo was as steeped in the literary culture of the day as Cervantes, the proponent of aesthetic and social critiques via the figure of Quixote.[2] This chapter will examine how Galileo's criticism of astronomers and philosophers from this period mirrors the same literary and stylistic critiques that Cervantes offers in the *Quixote*: literary aesthetics, verisimilitude, and modeling behavior for readers. By mapping the striking similarities between the concerns of the two texts, the chapter will show how Galileo adopts a literary cultural methodology to create a space for his philosophical ideals and their representatives.

An analysis of the Cervantean elements of the *Assayer* offers an interpretative lens through which to identify the literariness of Galileo's strategy for deauthorizing Sarsi's philosophy. The analysis will also show that
Galileo's criticism of Torquato Tasso's heroic poem, *Jerusalem Delivered*,
resembles the critique of the Canon of Toledo near the end of the first part
of *Don Quixote* on the genre in general. The Canon's criticism of books of
chivalry has often been cited as Cervantes' declaration of a theory of the
novel. Perhaps not surprisingly then, the short story known as the "Fable
of the Sounds" in the *Assayer* (1623), which is often taken as Galileo's statement of scientific method, bears a striking resemblance, albeit abridged in
length, to the form and content of these criticisms in *Quixote*. This aspect
of Galileo's prose suggests a double-pronged approach that uses Ariosto
to attack from one side and incorporates literary structures from the parody of Ariosto's very genre to undermine from the other. He thereby
destabilizes a tradition of authority on which he might lean to make new
claims in philosophy, but he also fashions a reader who can corroborate
these new interpretations of phenomena. Building once again on work by
Spiller and others, the conclusion of this analysis of the literary realm of
Galileo's writing in the *Assayer* demonstrates the potential for generating a
kind of knowledge essential to philosophy: that is, the knowledge of how
to be a philosopher.

We may all be familiar with the heroic Quixote who is so taken with
romance that he begins to imitate the life of a knight errant, jousting
at windmill giants and courting his lady Dulcinea, who is the farm girl
Aldonza. Yet, it is the *fool* Quixote that Cervantes uses to critique the role
of literature in society and it is the *fool* that contemporary readers would
have recognized. This Quixote is important for understanding Galileo's
literary method of philosophical dispute, in which Sarsi and the interlocutor Simplicio from his later dialogues are similarly fools that are instruments of criticism.[3] Recent editors of Juan Maldonado's pre-picaresque
works posit the successful recipe for the picaresque form to develop: a
first-person perspective of superiority combined with veiled expressions of
dissent acting within a compromised socio-political system.[4] In a philosophical context, these were the very conditions in which Galileo was
writing. Cervantes uses episodes such as the purging of Quixote's library
and the discussion of the ideal romance at the end of the first part of the
book to highlight the incongruity of a certain traditional narrative style in
a changed society. When we investigate the ways in which Galileo criticizes and attempts to supplant previous modes of philosophical thinking,
we can see that he employs techniques much like those of Cervantes, both

as an author of a literary document and as a reader of what he considers
to be literary texts on philosophical subjects. The moral of Galileo's story
applies to Quixote as well as it does to Galileo's opponents: the literal use
of literary works is rife with danger.[5]

Don Chisciotte in Galileo's library

As much as Galileo's library was a repository for literary models, a high
proportion of its contents also represented the printed tradition of erroneous accepted truths about the natural world, much in the same way that
the personal library that Cervantes invents for Don Quejana, the man who
will become Quixote, reflects an outdated tradition of behavior. Galileo's
constant antagonistic dialogue with the written tradition of Ptolemy, supporters of the heliocentric theory, and Aristotelian Peripatetics is akin to
Cervantes' juxtaposition of the "old" world of chivalry and his contemporary, late-sixteenth-century Spain. Nearly no Italian parodies of the epic
and chivalric traditions exist in Galileo's library aside from the *Quixote*.
Galileo did begin a translation of Homer's mock-epic *Batrachomyomachia*,
the *Battle of the Frogs and Mice* that plays on the themes of the *Iliad*, but
this appears in some of his earliest notebooks when he was a student at the
University of Pisa. The only Italian satirical epic in Galileo's library may
have been Piero Bardi's *Avino Avolio Ottone Berlinghieri*. Bardi's hyperbolic poem is one of the problematic entries in the inheritance inventory
of Galileo's books because it may have only seen its first edition the year
after Galileo died.[6] Even if Galileo did not read this genre extensively, he
and his circle of followers were nonetheless well versed in its language of
parody. We need only remember the mocking title *Sarseide*, which they
used to refer to the *Assayer*, playing on the names of epic foundational
poems to poke fun at the vain efforts of Sarsi to defend himself and his
philosophical Aristotelian citadel.[7]

In spite of this lacuna in the library, the element of parody, particularly
as it relates to clashes between the ancients and the moderns, nonetheless has parallels with the philosophical developments of the period more
generally. The Seicento in Italy saw the proliferation of the mock-epic,
satirical epic, and various parodies of the ever-popular poems of which
Galileo was so fond. Among the most notable is Alessandro Tassoni's *La
secchia rapita* (1622) – *The Rape of the Bucket* – a mock-heroic account
of a battle in 1393 between Bologna and Modena. Tassoni invented the
motivation for an actual conflict: quite literally the theft of the bucket
used to pull water from the city's central well. Although a printed copy

of the *Secchia rapita* does not appear to have found a place in Galileo's library, Tassoni's *Dieci libri di pensieri diversi* (*Ten Books of Diverse Thoughts* [Modena, 1608]) did.[8] The collection of Tassoni's thoughts is relevant to the *Quixote* arguments because it is best known for the chapters that compare (and at times berate) the books of ancient authors in favor of modern ones. Tassoni does try to keep an even hand in his evaluations, but he admits that the task is skewed even with the "sovereign beacons of the language," Ariosto and Tasso, because "the Ancients, having been without competitors for so many centuries, went along enjoying an excess of fame such that going beyond them seems to require a superhuman intellect."[9] Tassoni recognizes the power of sheer quantity in any debate. Ariosto and Tasso are only two voices with a few short decades of commentary on their works standing in the face of centuries-long proliferation of an aesthetic ideal. In that sense, Aristotle too enjoyed centuries of dominance in the philosophical field, while Copernicus had only been in print for a few decades.

Only slightly better represented in Galileo's library are picaresque novels, which are emblematic of further complexity in his presentation of philosophy.[10] I point this out with the usual word of caution that just because these titles appear in the manuscripts related to the books Galileo owned, we cannot know for certain whether or not he read them. In this case two key texts from the picaresque tradition appear: one of the most popular *picaros* in the Spanish tradition, and a popular encyclopedic presentation of Italian wayfarers. Barezzo Barezzi's translation of *Lazarillo de Tormes* (*Il Picariglio castigliano, cioè la vita del cattivello Lazariglio de Tormes* [Venice, 1605]) is listed among the books Galileo likely owned. *Il vagabondo ouero Sferza de' vianti, e vagabondi* (*The Vagabond; or rather, The Lash of the Wayfarers and Vagabonds* [Venice and Macerata: Grisei and Piccini, 1627]) is likely indicated in one inventory by the entry "Sferza de vagabondi."[11] Andrea Battistini is one of few critics who have mentioned the importance of the fact that Galileo owned copies of Cervantes and the anonymous *Lazarillo de Tormes*, along with collections of short stories by Geraldi Cinzio and Sebastiano Erizzo.[12] This is perhaps because Battistini sees Galileo as the "master of the carnevalesque."[13]

The Italian translation of *Don Quixote* joins *Lazarillo* and the *Vagabonds* in this collection. Even without evidence of citations or annotations, a parallel reading of Cervantes and Galileo shows the highly literary nature of Galileo's three works written after 1622: the *Assayer*, the *Dialogues on the Two Chief World Systems* (Florence, 1632), and the *Discourses on the Two New Sciences* (Leiden, 1638). A few questions remain about which edition

of Franciosini's translation Galileo owned, since the first part of the translation of the *Quixote* was published alone in 1622. The first edition of
the second part, again translated by Franciosini, was published together
with the second edition of the first part in 1625. One manuscript related
to Galileo's library lists separately "Don Chisciotte" and "Don Chisciotte
Parte 2:a," which suggests two distinct volumes. Galileo likely owned the
first edition of the first part and could have seen this translation of the
Quixote while he was writing the *Assayer*.[14]

A word is in order about the context of the *Quixote* as it moved from
its native Spain to Italy. As other scholars have pointed out, the *Quixote*
was published in Spain during a period of scientific and philosophical discovery in Europe – Johannes Kepler published the *New Astronomy*, and
the philosopher Francis Bacon the *Advancement of Learning* in the same
year as Cervantes completed the first part of *Don Quixote*: 1605. Among
natural philosophers, the discoveries of the *nova* in 1604 had not yet been
analyzed to a point where intellectuals were quarreling over the immediate theological and philosophical implications of such new information.
The Italian *Chisciotte* instead appears after Galileo's discoveries with his
powerful telescope in 1611, after the 1616 papal edict against support of
the Copernican Theory, and after intense debate had erupted between the
Jesuits in Rome and the Galilean school in Florence.[15] Discovery had led
to division. At the same time that Italian readers encountered the self-
proclaimed knight-errant of the old tradition who battled objects in
his contemporary society, the scientific and philosophical communities
played out their battle between the dusty tomes of Ptolemy and Aristotle
and the technical observations and lived experiences of an upstart Tuscan
mathematician.[16]

Galileo's career as an intellectual can be (and has been) bracketed by
proper noun pairs such as Renaissance and Enlightenment, Michelangelo
Buonarroti and Isaac Newton, or Copernicus and Shakespeare.[17] The previous chapters have focused on the relationship between Galileo's work
and the *Furioso* or the later *Liberata*. Rarely do critics situate his philosophical writing in the expanded literary sphere with which the Pisan
astronomer was intimately familiar: the evolution of the epic from the
High Renaissance debates about the poetic styles of Ariosto and Tasso
through the later romances and parodies of the genre during its decline
in popularity. Galileo's library and the style and content of his writing
reflect this trajectory. Galileo published the *Assayer* in 1623, the year after
Lorenzo Franciosini finished his Italian translation of the first part of *Don
Quixote* and the year after Alessandro Tassoni published his mock-heroic

Rape of the Bucket. In the *Assayer* Galilean prose leans toward the Ariostan epic, and Galilean methodology begins to show itself in the non-linear style of a *romanzo*. Not only are Galileo's later texts also recognizable for their constant digressions and zigzag logic, but the language he uses to describe these structural elements mimics those of the narrative elements in the parodies of romance. Most conspicuously, Galileo uses the so-called "Fable of the Sounds" and its wandering adventurer to give a sharp reprimand to Sarsi. The mocking tone of the contemporary fictional literature is precisely the one that the Tuscan mathematician adopts to criticize the supporters of the "old" tradition of Ptolemy and the geocentric theory of the structure of the universe.

Though rarely expressed in such terms, Galileo's greatest challenge was to defeat the convenient narratives about planetary and stellar motion that had been accepted as truth and passed from generation to generation as authoritative and factual. Galileo did not invent another story, but championed one narrative, that of the motion of the Earth. His inspiration, means of self-defense, and the source of the attacks against him can be found in two ancient literary-philosophical traditions: the geostatic theory of the structure of the universe and the heliocentric one. In the heliocentric model, Aristarchus in the third century BCE had attempted to account for planetary and stellar motion using one narrative: the Earth rotated around the sun, just as the stars did.[18] In the second century CE Ptolemy created a narrative that displaced the heliocentric theory to become the dominant narrative underpinning theology and philosophy for centuries to come: the Sun and the stars moved around the Earth. As centuries of observations accumulated, additional episodes appeared in the narrative because the stars do not follow a circular orbit around the Earth. These additions to the theory, called ellipticals, account for discrepancies between actual observations of stellar motion and the idealized single-circle orbit. An elliptical is a small circular detour to the orbit of any given star as it moves around the Earth. In Galileo's library, this received tradition is reflected in over 200 printed volumes.

Galileo, like the observers of Quixote's madness, finds himself at a point of collision between the book culture that described the traditional narrative, and the world of our physical senses. When investigation was aided by new instruments, the sensible world often appeared quite different from the one described in books. The old world in print looks foolish, as does Quixote, when compared to what Galileo sees as the reality of the book of nature, or Cervantes' presentation of actual Spanish culture. Turning to a military term, Galileo will eventually speak of a *schiera*, or troop, of philosophers that constantly attack his writings.[19] Notably, the term itself, according to the 1612 *Vocabolario degli Accademici della Crusca* refers primarily to soldiers, evoking a military connotation. Moreover, Victoria Kirkham has provided a history of the Italian literary tradition of referring to a *schiera*, from Dante to Petrarch and Boccaccio, with a continued use by the sixteenth-century *Petrarchisti*. The term used both with awe and with disdain to indicate a group of friends, a group of poets, or a group of women, but traditionally not a band of philosophers.[20] Galileo uses this literary term to indicate a troop of descendants of the geostatic theory who are readers, authors, and defenders of commentary on primary works that are centuries old.

In a similar way to the protagonist of *Don Quixote*, the Peripatetics find themselves living a narrative that belongs to the previous period. The authority these intellectuals followed was less that of Ptolemy, and almost entirely that of Aristotle. In spite of centuries of experimentation and observation contradicting the medieval and Renaissance heavy-hitters that commented on the texts, this *schiera* remain faithful to what they have read, to the point of discrediting what they see with their own eyes.[21] With Aristotle stands the doctrine of Saint Thomas Aquinas, and many of the Church Fathers that Galileo had tried to read in a way that suited his purposes in the *Letter to the Grand Duchess Christina of Lorraine Concerning the Use of Biblical Quotations in Matters of Science* (1615).[22] Likewise, in his attempts to uphold the values and ideals of the literature that he loves, to which he is faithful, Quixote calls an inn a palace, an innkeeper a lord, and a windmill a giant. As *Quixote* scholar Walter Reed demonstrates: "Don Quixote is a reader of *Amadis of Gaul* and *Palmerin of England*, but the world he inhabits is the world of *Lazarillo de Tormes* and *Guzmán de Alfarache*."[23] The *schiera* of detractors of the heliocentric theory of the universe do the same, particularly when we read Galileo's interpretation of their strategies for victory in the *Assayer*. In their faithful imitation of the doctrines of Aristotle, they call the Earth the center of the universe where Galileo and the new generation of philosophers see the Sun.[24] They see an orbit with ellipticals where Galileo sees a circular orbit around a different center. Galileo's theory of these orbits will eventually be proven wrong by Newton, placing his work in the position of the "old" literature and the "old" principles in the cycle of knowledge.[25] *Don Quixote* thereby provides a strikingly similar literary approach to the same problems Galileo was encountering in philosophical disputes.

The mechanisms for Galileo's philosophical criticism and Cervantes' literary one are the same: textual criticism. The fictional Curate and Barber carry out the same critical function as Galileo, in that they all see the insanity of trying to impose onto lived reality the literary world that does not exist but has been perpetuated in print. The Canon of Toledo in particular gives voice to the analyses that Galileo carries out in the *Assayer*: evaluations of verisimilitude and concerns for audience. Like Galileo, well-versed in the works of this false reality, so too all of these fictional representatives are well aware of what they consider to be incorrect realities. This intellectual preparation allows them to be selective and confidently answer any objections in the debates that arise. One of the frequent statements of Galileo's interlocutor Simplicio is that he hasn't read many of the books under discussion in the *Chief World Systems* or *Two New Sciences*, and for this he lives up to his name. In order to enter into the debate over the old and new cultures of literature or philosophy, one must have a familiarity with the books that represent them.

The epistemologies of this criticism are also remarkably similar. Galileo's adoption of this literary methodology carries the advantage of developing a discursive space for critique. He could not escape print culture and worked actively to find a means for it to become a useful tool in his arguments rather than a constant obstacle in his attempts to prove the heliocentric theory. Just as the Curate and Barber trick Don Quixote into returning home at the end of Part I by donning costumes and acting the part of figures from his imagined reality, Chapter 3 has shown that Galileo too turns the literary power of the poetry against the perpetrators of what he believes is its misuse as simply, and only, literal. At this juncture, the epics in Quixote's library function similarly to the poets in the Aristotelian source texts of Galileo's opponents as evidence of outdated beliefs that do not correspond to observed reality. Critic Andrea Battistini even refers to the Peripatetics as "paladins of tradition."[26] As part of their efforts to cure Quixote of his madness, the Curate and the Barber purge the library of what they believe to be the source of his misinterpretation of reality.

Early in the first part of the *Quixote* the Curate begins an inspection of the books to see if any should be spared from the flames awaiting the titles that arrive unceremoniously in the courtyard. Based on his annotations in them, the philosopher likely would have been happy to send many of these volumes to a pyre in his courtyard in this fashion too. The Curate and Barber take turns discussing the contents and styles of many future victims of the fire, but they also suggest pleasurable readings to one another, and do take a fair armful of books home for reading at a later date. Their rejection of the genre is not complete, just as Galileo's rejection of Aristotle is not outright. In their role as inquisitors compiling the list of banned books, the Curate and Barber suggest emendations, corrections, and the outright censoring of passages in order for certain titles to be spared. Where they grant clemency to the founders of the tradition, Galileo will cut straight to the source to launch his attacks against those who pervert that tradition with misinterpretations, false claims, and the rhetorical tricks for which he criticized Sarsi in philosophical as well as literary terms, as described in the previous chapter.

The spilled ink posed two critical problems: the proliferation of what Galileo saw as erroneous, outdated theories, and the dissemination of these ideas in what he saw as a sloppy, distasteful style. Using geometric demonstrations to challenge these authors will only convince readers who understand them. By proposing Sarsi's text as a literary document, as something that can be analyzed, interpreted, and glossed, Galileo can expose weaknesses that simultaneously discredit Peripatetic texts and also valorize those mathematical proofs in the eyes of readers. His language of criticism of both the form and content of these philosophical works takes shape in the same terms that are brought to light by the Canon of Toledo and Don Quixote as they debate the validity and aesthetic value of romance. Yet again we see the ways that Galileo manipulates this language of literary criticism to undercut his philosophical opponents by establishing himself as a reader superior to other authors who read the book of nature, with varying degrees of aptitude or ineptitude. Galileo corrects the misreadings both of the stars and of the printed word via the language and critical apparatus of a literary dispute. He tries to prove that the old world, or the old universe, never existed as it was written. Cervantes uses Don Quixote to show the futility of trying to prove that presentation of the old world real by having him act it out, just as the staunch Aristotelians consistently reaffirm their worldview with textual sources, not lived experience – that is, via a world on paper, not the world outside their windows.

When Galileo makes his famous claim about the book of nature not being an epic poem, he brings together this sense of being trapped by a text, being liberated by a mathematical language of geometrical symbols, and the madness of any other paradigm.[27] The line of demarcation in these languages is clear for him in his description of the book of nature: "its characters are triangles, circles, and other geometrical figures, without which it is humanly impossible to understand a single word of it; without these, one is wandering about in a dark labyrinth."[28] In Andrea Battistini's analysis of Galileo's labyrinthine imagery, the Aristotelians are Minotaurs, and the modern scientist is Ariadne, but this overlooks the hero of the tale, Theseus.[29] I think a more fruitful analogy with philosophy develops if

we consider the Galilean philosopher as the hero, Theseus; sensate observations that guide him out of the labyrinth as Ariadne; Aristotle as the
architect of the maze, Dedalus; and the Aristotelians as the Minotaur (or
his victims), imprisoned there without hope of escape. As this chapter and
the next will show, Galileo's corrective to the Quixote tale suggests that
wandering in an open space is the preferred way of philosophizing, not in
a labyrinth created by another.

I suggest this parallel structure to highlight the ways in which Galileo
sees the Aristotelians as prisoners of their own doctrine, limited, restricted,
and wandering in a fortified space, literally fixed in print. The very name
Peripatetic is associated with figurative, intellectual wandering since these
Aristotelians were so nicknamed for their literal, physical wandering while
lost in discussion. Tied to this language of philosophy is also the double meaning of *errare*, both "to wander" and "to err" in Latin and many
Romance vernaculars, including Italian. By distinguishing between open
and closed systems, Galileo also helps to delineate the space for each definition of the term. He will later demonstrate this correct way of wandering in the *Chief World Systems* and *Two New Sciences*. In the *Assayer*,
immediately preceding this image of books of philosophy as a labyrinth,
Galileo characterizes Sarsi in an unmistakably quixotic way:

> It seems to me that I discern in Sarsi a firm belief that in philosophizing it
> is essential to support oneself upon the opinion of some celebrated author,
> as if when our minds are wedded to the reasoning of some other person
> they ought to remain completely barren and sterile. Possibly he thinks that
> philosophy is a book of fiction by some writer, like the *Iliad* or *Orlando
> furioso*, books in which the least important thing is whether what is written
> in them is true.[30]

By structuring the passage in this way, Galileo implies that like Quixote,
Sarsi's reasoning is wedded to the reasoning of the epic poems of Homer
or Ariosto. The narrator had said of Don Quixote that after reading nothing but tales of knights and chivalry "his brain dried up and he went
completely out of his mind."[31] When seen with Galileo's evocation of a
sterile, barren mind and the reading of epic poems, the inspiration for his
description of Sarsi cannot be mistaken.

Galileo cannot follow Aristotle to the letter, even though the Peripatetics
had done so for centuries, and his characterization of Aristotle suggests the
possibility for revision and creation, not an unquestionable monolithic
presentation of the truth. Aristotle was, after all, only a human author
and reader, working under the constraints of history, subject to the same
limited intellect that Galileo saw elsewhere, which accordingly leaves his

work open to challenge. Aristotle may have imagined a telescope, but neither he, nor the astronomers with whom he was familiar, had an instrument as powerful as Galileo's.[32] In the dispute on sunspots Galileo had
already indicated that his colleagues were "those wise philosophers who
judged differently from Aristotle about the celestial substance and from
whom even Aristotle would not have distanced himself had he had knowledge of the present sensate observations."[33] Where the Peripatetics claimed
Aristotle as a guide, Galileo saw him as an inadequate dictator of one path
among the many possible in the maze of the intellect, the labyrinth of
nature, and the stacks of a library.

Literary criticism of philosophical texts: pleasure, instruction, and verisimilitude

Beyond these larger cultural, historical, and structural parallels, Galileo's
laments about the overpowering role of print culture in the approxima-
tion and determination of the truth are expressed in literary terms that
specifically resemble the discussions of the function of reading and the
art of representation in the *Quixote*. There the discussion of the value of
the printed word occurs between the various readers of books of chivalry.
They demonstrate the criticism that Galileo launches not only against
Aristotelians, but also against Tasso. Using *Quixote* as a frame brings
to light the literary nature of many of Galileo's judgments against the
Peripatetic philosophers. Just as Galileo's quotations of Arioso were part
of his demonstration of erudition and virtuosity that went hand in hand
with establishing the negative *ethos* of Sarsi, so too are the very literary
concerns that he shares with the critical characters of the *Quixote*. The
following analyses that use *Don Quixote* as a frame will show the ways
in which Galileo characterized Sarsi's work (and by extension that of the
other Peripatetics) as literary works open to multiple interpretations,
analyses, and criticisms instead of declarations of philosophical truths.
Working in tandem with the mathematical and geometrical demonstrations of the *Assayer*, this layer of reasoning operates on Sarsi's prose to
expose his faults as a writer and by extension as a philosopher.

One of the particular cultural aspects of the self-referential discussions
in these texts returns to the courtly ideals of poetic and prose production: the sense of pleasure derived from the text by a reader. Importantly,
pleasure must be regulated in order to be positively construed. Unchecked
pleasure prompts Don Quixote's unstoppable consumption of chivalric
romances, but useful pleasure is what spurs Galileo and his interlocutors

ahead in their investigations. The Horatian sense of *dulce et utile*, expressed in *Ars poetica* (verses 333-365) and championed by Castiglione and others in the Renaissance, was also an aesthetic sense adopted by Galileo. Although he clearly states in the *Assayer* that "nature takes no delight in poetry," the explanation and understanding of nature relies heavily on pleasure.[34] The entire premise of the *Chief World Systems* is based on the enjoyment and instruction that comes from gentlemanly conversation. Galileo's speakers in the *Chief World Systems* and the *Two New Sciences* repeatedly express the delight that they take from their conversation and the subject matter that they are learning. As we saw Lucretius, Kepler, and Piccolomini state in Chapter 1, the bitter pill of philosophical truth is much easier to swallow if it is wrapped in the form of pleasurable reading. On the second day of the *Chief World Systems*, Salviati also extends this sense of delight to the act of philosophizing itself, creating a hierarchy of the various joys of being a philosopher: "I have always derived very great delight from my discoveries; making them is the greatest, but next to that I take great pleasure in discussing them with a friend who understands them and shows he enjoys them."[35] Not by chance the character most closely associated with Galileo himself professes this nearly hyperbolic iteration of the *dulce et utile* dictum. Simplicio even abbreviates a reference to the Horatian passage on Day Two of the *Chief World Systems* as he is forced to admit that his source text is perhaps more *dulce* than *utile*. He quickly says of a passage in the book he is using to support his views: "This refuge appears insufficient to me because the variation is too great; in this case I can only say *quandoque bonus, etc.* ["whenever great," etc.]."[36] Simplicio cites the middle of the verse "indignor quandoque bonus dormitat Homerus" ("I resent whenever great Homer sleeps").[37] The verse is Horace's feigned expression of annoyance when Homer, very infrequently, is found to be sleeping on the job – that is, when he makes an error.

Without that sense of *utile* – without intellectual gain, that is – the value of the *dolce* is diminished. For Galileo this indicates a linguistic shift. Instead of the *diletto* Salviati expresses at hearing mathematically perfect harmonies or upon the instruction of his fellow gentlemen interlocutors, Galileo refers to what he sees as the whimsical, uninformed, or misinformed delights of his opponents with the word *piacere*. The same criticism holds true in the literary context of the *Quixote*. Near the close of the first part of the book the knight errant is carted back to La Mancha under the impression that he has been enchanted. As the prisoner's party approaches an inn, they are overtaken by the Canon of Toledo and his subordinates. The Canon and the Curate begin their discussion of the value of chivalric literature. The Canon declares "As I see it, this species of writing and composition is in the same class with what are called Milesian fables, which are nonsensical tales designed solely to amuse and not to instruct, in which respect they are unlike those apologues which afford entertainment and instruction at one and the same time."[38] Galileo will create an apologue of the new philosophy in the Fable of the Sounds discussed at the end of this chapter. The concern for being both enjoyable and educational remains the same across these two types of texts. Like Cervantes' staging of this conversation, Galileo's incorporation of the terminology into his philosophical works is not a case of mere ornament that makes the speakers more entertaining. The *dolce et utile* dictum operates in a literary realm, for literary readers, that immediately signals positive and negative attributes of a philosophical text and its author.

In the *Assayer* this integration of literary criticism persists in other ways that can be brought into relief by Cervantes' own concerns. Both Galileo and Cervantes are concerned with truth: discovering it, describing it, and identifying its perversions. Verisimilitude, with its beguiling similarity to truth, is as much Quixote's stumbling block as Sarsi's. In the discussion at the end of the first part of the *Quixote* verisimilitude is a primary concern for the Canon when he reads chivalric literature and, again, one shared by Galileo, who criticizes Tasso for faulty poetic aspects and also casts Sarsi and later Simplicio in a negative light with regard to their truth claims. The Canon continues his description of the ideal chivalric text by saying:

> … in works of fiction there should be a mating between the plot and the reader's intelligence. They should be so written that the impossible is made to appear possible, things hard to believe being smoothed over and the mind held in suspense in such a manner as to create surprise and astonishment while at the same time they divert and entertain so that admiration and pleasure go hand in hand. But these are things which he cannot accomplish who flees verisimilitude and the imitation of nature, qualities that go to constitute perfection in the art of writing."[39]

The Canon's statement brings together the problematic concern for *accomodatio* (which makes Galileo distrust poetry as an authoritative source), the important sense of pleasure, and the accuracy of the imitation of nature. Again, the parallels with the *Quixote* are similar to Galileo's criticism of Tasso's heroic poem, his adoption of Ariosto's style, and the literary concerns that surround the debate about epic poetry as a weapon in his philosophical debates.

Galileo's annotations show that he is attentive to the nuances of verisimilitude across texts. One of the first criticisms that Galileo launches

against the *Gerusalemme liberata* is against the likelihood of God expressing doubt. When annotating the twelfth stanza of the first canto Galileo
writes: "I am not sure how appropriate it is to make God speak in inter-
rogatives, asking why the war has stopped or has not been renewed; it
would be more divine to rule absolutely, without any ceremony."[40] The
complaints that Galileo repeats against the view Erminia has from the
battlements of Jerusalem are closely related to his concern for optics. He
argues for the impossibility of Erminia's identification of the Christian
soldiers from the top of a tower at least a mile distant "in the midst of the
dust of the skirmish, which are things that can't be done even in our time
at the distance of an eighth mile."[41] In a similar way, the Canon of Toledo
berates the bloody content of battle, the impression authors give that the
heroic knight can defeat an entire army single-handedly, and the improprieties of damsels who cast themselves into the arms of any paladin just
as Galileo will call out what he sees as Clorinda's improprieties and the
excessive sentimentality of male heroes of Tasso's poem.

This very literary concern with verisimilitude also finds a place in philosophical settings because the true narratives about the Earth's motion need
to be differentiated from the possible ones that are only similar to truth.
The concern for "true" versus "likely" remains vivid even later in the century as intellectuals such as Huygens and Fontenelle explore the boundaries of the credible in logical conjectures and in literature.[42] The ancient
and the modern, or the printed culture and the philosophy of experiences
and the senses, are also further differentiated by textual structure and literary content under the rubric of verisimilitude. Returning to the bellicose
language so often associated with these moments of literary criticism of
poor philosophy, in the *Assayer* Galileo says of Sarsi's efforts to obtain supportive linguistic testimony from any source:

> he had better pay attention to his cause, and consider that to a person who
> wants to convince others of something which, if not false, is at least very
> questionable, it is a great advantage to be able to use probable arguments,
> conjectures, examples, analogies [*verisimili*], and other sophisms, and to
> fortify himself further with unimpeachable texts, entrenching himself
> behind the authority of other philosophers, scientists, rhetoricians, and his-
> torians. To reduce oneself to the rigor of geometrical demonstrations is too
> dangerous an experiment for anyone who does not thoroughly know how
> to manage these.[43]

Galileo lays bare the structures of successful verisimilitude. He exposes
this logic of uncertainty based on the probable and the rhetoric of received
tradition (outside geometry) that acts as a shield, not as a foundation for

arguments. The method of the new philosophy embraces conjecture but does not treat the outcome as fiction.

When Galileo dramatizes these efforts in the figure of Simplicio, the presentation is more literary. On the second day of the *Chief World Systems* this criticism reappears when Simplicio demonstrates the fallacy of a logic that embraces verisimilitude instead of truth in his reaction to discussions of terrestrial rotation and critical reasoning. He says: "If the discussions so far had not produced in me such a high opinion of Salviati's well-founded understanding and of Sagredo's sharp intelligence, I (with their permission) would be ready to leave without listening to anything else. For it seems to me impossible that one can contradict such palpable observations; moreover, I would like to keep my old opinion without having to hear anything else, because it seems to me that even if it were false, the fact that it is supported by such likely [*verosimili*] reasons would render it excusable. If these are fallacies, what true [*vere*] demonstrations were ever so beautiful?"[44] Simplicio's declaration of deliberate adherence to the *verosimile* in the face of tangible evidence that disproves the verisimilar dramatizes the faults that Galileo had seen in Sarsi's critical reasoning in the *Assayer*. As the Canon describes, literature functions on successful and seductive conventions of verisimilitude. Galileo's comments on Tasso show that he agrees, but his labeling of Sarsi's work as verisimilar moves that old tradition into a realm of criticism where it risks appearing like Quixote's books of chivalry.

Part of Simplicio's rationale for preferring the verisimilar is its beauty. His rhetorical question in the *Chief World Systems* about the appeal of such demonstrations earns him a response from Sagredo tied to both the literary and philosophical aesthetic ideals of the day. Sagredo patiently suggests: "it would be good to hear Salviati's answers. If these should be true, they must be even more beautiful and infinitely more beautiful, and those others must be ugly, indeed very ugly; this would follow if there is truth in the metaphysical proposition that truth and beauty are the same thing, as falsehood and ugliness also are."[45] This reiteration of the Platonic conception of the harmony of beauty, proportion, and truth is in line with the fact that Galileo's work tends to support the metaphysical claim that truth is beautiful. As mentioned before, that concern was also literary.

Galileo often expressed the ugliness of falsehood or inferior attempts at verisimilitude in terms of the *intarsiatura* of poets and the chimeras of philosophers, neither of which have a place in geometrical demonstrations, but both of which help to authorize his own strategies. The image has particular resonance in the Copernican–Ptolemaic debate because

Copernicus himself used the figure of a monster to describe Ptolemy's geocentric system. In the dedicatory letter to Pope Paul II that opens *On the Revolutions* he writes that those in favor of epicycles do not understand the symmetry of the structure of the universe. Rather, he says, "their experience was just like someone taking from various places hands, feet, a head, and other pieces, very well depicted, it may be, but not for the representation of a single person; since these fragments would not belong to one another at all, a monster rather than a man would be put together from them."[46] The multiple identities of a chimera are easy enough to imagine, and the reference to *tarsie* is a tangible, easily recognizable fault. Many of Galileo's comments resemble the way he criticizes Tasso for the *intarsiatura*, or inlaid-wood, structure of the *Gerusalemme liberata* in his first annotation to the poem:

> One among other defects is very common to Tasso, born from tightness of veins and lack of conceits. It is this: often lacking in material, he is constrained to go around piecing together fragments of conceits that are not dependent on or connected to one another, so his narration comes out more like a picture made of inlaid wood than painted with oils. Since inlaid works are a jumble of little pieces of differently colored wood, which could never be paired or united in such a soft way that their edges do not remain sharp or crudely distinguished by the different colors, by necessity they make dry, rough shapes without roundness or relief.[47]

The conceit expressed in this annotation stems back to a passage in Cicero's *De oratore* inspired by Lucilius on the arrangement of words being similar to small stones in a pavement; the quality of the resulting mosaic is proportional to the closeness of the stones and the smoothness of the transition from one to the next.[48] Echoing the lessons on pedants and plagiarists in Chapters 2 and 3, Galileo here reiterates that memorizing someone else's words does not mean being able to put them to work in a new context.[49] Exhibiting a particular sensitivity to presentation, Galileo suggests that Tasso's clumsy assembly of conceits and phrasing from classical poetry draws the reader out of the verisimilar setting and calls attention to the fabrication of his text in a negative way.

In a philosophical context the concern for patchwork mosaics of earlier texts takes on an imaginative and poetic identity: the chimera. This mythological monster traditionally appears as an assemblage of three different animals, often a lion, snake, and goat. Figuratively, the trope of a chimera was used to identify any difficult or unexplainable idea. In Galileo's iteration of the problems created by Sarsi's text, the innocuous result of crude woodworking becomes an active monster from narrative: the fearful chimera that blocks the reader's attempts to navigate the labyrinth of nature. As part of his literary critique, the Canon of Toledo expresses the apparent incongruities of chivalric fictions and the episodic zigzag narration that plays on digressions in similar terms: "they are made up of so many disparate members that it would seem the author's intention was to create a chimera or a monster rather than a well-proportioned figure."[50] Monsters and chimeras evoke once again the imagery of the Minotaur in the labyrinth, and Galileo makes this explicit when he criticizes Sarsi for essentially false advertising of a mediocre work that draws in a reader with titles and promises, but fails to follow through with their content. As he says in the *Assayer*:

> magnificence of titles and grandeur and number of promises attract the natural curiosity of men and hold them perpetually involved in fallacies and chimeras, without ever offering them one single sample of the sharpness of demonstration, by which the taste might be awakened to the insipidity of its ordinary fare. Hence these will keep an infinite number of men occupied, and that man will be very fortunate who, led by some unusual inner light, shall be able to turn from the dark and confused labyrinths within which he might have gone forever wandering with the crowd and becoming ever more entangled.[51]

The "fallacies" and "chimeras" are dangerous to the presumed audience. Chimeras populate the *Assayer* and *Chief World Systems* as emblems of the dangers of verisimilitude, much like Dante's chimerical Geryon.[52] Galileo predicts (and implies his own candidacy for the role of) a reader who will be able to pull himself out of the confused labyrinths of published philosophy and lead readers away from these monsters.

By emphasizing the poor craftsmanship of Sarsi's text, Galileo can offer instruction on the appropriate form that philosophy should take. In opposition to the dark, enclosed prison of this textual labyrinth would be the potentially well-written document, poetic or philosophical. Recalling Ariosto's own narrative tapestry in the *Orlando furioso*, once again *Don Quixote* provides a literary context for the trope that Galileo uses to express these concerns. According to the Canon a talented author of epic poetry who demonstrates bravura in various fields of knowledge, expresses the pinnacles of morally correct emotion, and shows stylistic acuity in both poetry and prose would create: "a web woven of beautiful and variegated threads, one which when completed would exhibit such a perfected beauty of form as to attain the most worth-while goal of all writing ... to instruct and to entertain."[53] In the *Assayer* Galileo's process of indicating this perfected form is inverted: by pointing out the negative qualities of

Sarsi's writing, he implies its positive counterpart. There is only one place in Galileo's body of writing where he metaphorically uses the idea of a *tela*, or cloth, with its etymology in *textum*, and therefore closely related to writing. In Part XIV of the *Assayer*, while Galileo criticizes the syllogistic rhetorical strategies of Sarsi, he juxtaposes weaving and woodwork to discredit the Jesuit in a way similar to his critiques of the *Gerusalemme liberata*:

> I believe that in the course of weaving of this cloth [*tela*], he is going to get himself so entangled in it (more than he supposes now, when he is laying the warp) that in the end he will voluntarily confess himself vanquished. This will be apparent to anyone who will pay attention to the fact that he will end by saying precisely the same things that Sig. Mario wrote – though covered in gold [*orpellate*] in such a way, and fitted in piecemeal [*intarsiate*] among such a variety of wordy ornaments and arabesques … that perhaps those who consider them less carefully will at first think them somewhat different from what they essentially are.[54]

The passage is as much concerned with the visual arts as it is with the experience of the early modern reader. The gilded, misleading phrases recall Doni's pedant relying on the gold-lettered tome of a presumably learned man instead of using his own intellect. The arabesques and printers' flowers were a device introduced in the mid sixteenth century as part of the architecture of books to indicate textual units. They were widely used to fill white space on pages often intended for a popular audience and were imitated, copied, reused, and rearranged with no indication of authorship or origin.[55] The attention given to the presentation of words on the page anticipates Sagredo's ridicule of the book of disquisitions that Simplicio has had brought to him to assist the discussion in the *Chief World Systems*. When the book arrives, Sagredo asks Simplicio to show them the passage in which the author refutes any terrestrial motion. Simplicio reads the passage aloud followed by another selection, at which point Sagredo takes the book to look at a figure referred to in the text. He expresses his delight at the image: "Oh what beautiful designs, what birds, what balls, and what other pretty things are these?"[56] The comment is a delightful jab at the mode of representation in Jesuit texts, as opposed to those in Galileo's.[57] Rather than hearing amazement from Sagredo about the persuasive force of the content, about which Simplicio was so vociferous, we hear aesthetic remarks about birds and unidentified objects drawn into the figures.[58]

Sarsi's method, according to Galileo, is full of deceit, fabrication, and incongruous ideas. The danger is evident that readers will be confused in this labyrinth of poor publications unless some hero arrives to steer their intellects away from fallacies and chimeras. This comparison of Galileo's quite literary criticism and the Canon's expression of his ideals for a future prose masterpiece highlights the ways in which the literary epistemology is here working to identify and create the new paradigm. Galileo writes against this practice in the very document in which he models it. As Chapter 5 will show, when he crafts the *Chief World Systems* and *Two New Sciences*, Salviati's speech will reflect this open space while Simplicio remains trapped in the labyrinth. Reliance on poetic texts generates a philosophically insecure text, a weakness of which Galileo takes full advantage.

Galileo's characterization of Sarsi and Simplicio highlights the perils of a literal reading of the printed philosophical tradition, as it would seem to be founded on poetic works such as the *Iliad* or *Orlando furioso* that deserve a literary critical reading instead. This tension comes to the fore for all authors in discussions of the senses; language that describes seeing, hearing, or touching is even more difficult to refute than erroneous logic. Cervantes too engages with these questions during the luncheon exchange between Quixote and the Canon near the end of the first part of the book. Quixote counters the Canon's desire to fling the worst of the poems into the fire by saying: "to endeavor to persuade anyone that Amadis never lived, nor any of the other knightly adventurers that fill the history books, is the same as trying to make him believe that the sun does not shine, that ice is not cold, or that the earth does not bear fruit."[59] Quixote appeals to the senses, to what our body tells us about the truth of the world, but he directly equates that truth to the written words in his poetic books. This is the same battle that Galileo fights with his detractors: they can see the Sun move. We have no perception of the Earth being in motion, since we do not go flying off its surface as it spins. Galileo's character Simplicio, who is often the devil's advocate in the *Dialogues* and *Discourses*, will provide a similar reading of Aristotle to suggest that he had completed an experiment: "His language would seem to indicate that he had tried the experiment, because he says: *We see the heavier*; now the word *see* shows that he had made the experiment."[60] Like the authors who do not anticipate figurative statements from the didactic poets, Simplicio does not consider a figurative use of "see."[61] The Canon, in response to the mixture of truth and falsehood in Quixote's reasoning, tries to explain that yes, some of these men did exist, but the truth of their actions as recounted in chivalric romances cannot be verified. The argument is the same that Galileo holds with his Peripatetic opponents, who rely on Aristotle's statements of seeing and doing as proof that he completed experiments described in the *De anima*.

With their similar concerns for interpreting reality both Galileo and Cervantes turn to the same language and imagery to ridicule erroneous logic. The knight errant's point of contention rests on Roland's enormous horn, which Quixote claims is on display at Roncisvalles, the traditional place of Count Roland's defeat and death. The Canon claims to have never seen it, to which Quixote replies that lack of visual confirmation does not negate its existence. The Canon's situation highlights the same paradox that faces Galileo. In this moment of contradictions where seeing is believing, but not seeing does not deny believing, the voice of truth is silenced by the displaced discourse of outdated books. Quixote defends himself by listing the details that the authors include to create a sense of verisimilitude, though he takes them as signs of veracity: "Do they not have every appearance of being true? Do they not tell us who the father, mother, relatives of these knights were, the name of the country from which they came, their age, the feats that they performed, point by point and day by day, and the places where all these events occurred?"[62] This kind of pseudo-logical reasoning based on verisimilitude is the same that will undo Simplicio in the *Dialogues* and *Discourses*. The problem is that these details are distant in time and space, and therefore subject to speculation. Simplicio and Sarsi would then seem to be the Quixotes of philosophy. Aided by the literary concerns of Galileo, their characterization as fools of the old tradition works just as much to discredit them as it does to allow a space for a new dialogue in these debates.

Curiously, both authors will give the final word in their works to the very object of their ridicule. As the last part of his argument, Quixote quickly changes to a discussion of the pleasure that derives from detail and its effect on the reader by giving the example of the story of the Knight of the Lake. Even this anachronistic storytelling can hold an audience rapt; the reader pays attention, demonstrating the power of this manner of thinking. The Canon himself is completely overshadowed by the enchanted, and enchanting, "mad" knight errant. Prior to Simplicio's declaration of Catholic dogma at the end of the fourth day of the *Chief World Systems*, Salviati changes his tone dramatically, excusing himself for many things, including support for a *fantasia* that we would easily admit is a *vanissima chimera*.[63] After 488 pages of discussion in which the opposite associations that have been formed between *fantasia*, *chimere*, and traditional philosophical thought have been maintained, how are readers to respond? While only minimally comprehending the final arguments of the dialogue, Simplicio says that it is the most *ingegnoso* conclusion that he has heard, even as Salviati discounts it. In the same breath that Simplicio invokes the subtitle of *Don Chisciotte*, the *ingegnoso cittadino*, he returns to his mind's eye and evokes the old doctrine to which Salviati and Sagredo immediately acquiesce. Does the literal trump the literary, or have the literary clues been strong enough to show readers the error of these speakers' ways?[64]

Galileo's fictional philosopher errant

In the examples seen thus far, Galileo's criticism of Sarsi and Simplicio has been informed by and presented in terms of literary concerns, but his presentation of his own method also benefits from this same attentiveness to matters of composition and interpretation. The one declaration that we have of Galileo Galilei's scientific method is a picaresque journey in search of the causes of sound that revises Quixote's errors seen thus far.

The so-called Fable of the Sounds is a direct response to the book culture that Galileo feels has provoked the stalemate in intellectual debate of the period. Here we see the most obvious example of the interconnectedness of the epistemologies of the literary and philosophical. As with Galileo, for Cervantes, the old and the new worlds collide.[65] The printed tradition alone pushes readers in one direction, that of anachronistic discourse with the past. For Quixote this disjointedness appears as madness, for Galileo it is outright erroneous.[66] Modern critics of Galileo's prose have commented on the overall structural similarities between his philosophical writing and contemporary forms of fiction. For Battistini the combination of method and prose creates a new genre, a new middle ground: "the scientific account sheet," composed of "the summary of phenomena until then unknown, exposed with that incisive prose, agile for reasoning and economic in argumentation."[67] Many Galilean scholars share the dismay of Stillman Drake when he points out that Galileo, unlike Kepler "did not publish an account of the bypaths and blind alleys into which he wandered before he arrived at his correct results."[68] Yet, at the same time, Galileo does give hints, in more than one text, of what he calls the "thorny trails" (*spinosi sentieri*) that he traversed before arriving at his conclusions.[69] The Greek philosopher Proclus tells the foundational story about this metaphor: "Ptolemy once asked Euclid if there was not a shorter road to geometry than through the *Elements*, and Euclid replied that there was no royal road to geometry."[70] Battistini, in his analysis of the Fable of the Sounds in the *Assayer*, expresses the epistemology of Galilean science: "What else is the description of a scientific experiment if not the story of a trip followed closely upon by curiosity?"[71] The language of the *picaro* and the epic hero, as we shall see, informs much of Galileo's description of his process of reading and self-defense as his champion of truth wanders the paths of knowledge. A close analysis of this fable from a literary perspective shows the interconnectedness of the two epistemologies.

Once again, the identity of the philosopher charged with championing this new paradigm is born from and benefits from a literary treatment of the characteristics that will lead to success. The drama and emotion of the philosopher's quest, as opposed to the result of the quest itself, so important in earlier paradigms of philosophical pursuits, become a new element in the scientific and philosophical environment. The next part of my analysis partially incorporates the work of Maria Luisa Altieri Biagi and Bruno Basile on the positive model of philosophy that Galileo creates. In their introduction to the volume of works by scientists of the seventeenth century they provide a more ample definition of this drama and emotion: "one of the symptoms of the philosophical tension understood in scientific activity was the flowering, in the scientist, of anxieties, agitations, and melancholy that accompany even the most exalted moments of discovery."[72] According to their claim, the identity of the investigator is as important as his findings, which complements Dietz Moss' conclusion that Galileo aims rhetorically to destroy the character of his detractor, and supports my readings of the poetic insults in the *Assayer*. Yet, Altieri Biagi points out just one trait of the new scientist – *umiltà*, humility – or the capacity to admit "I don't know," something that Galileo does not distinguish in his opponents, but himself displays.[73] He begins the *Assayer* with the phrase "Io non ho mai potuto intendere" ("I have never been able to understand").[74] This characteristic goes hand in hand with the recognition that, in spite of the work of humanists and Renaissance scholars to resuscitate the intellectual culture of Antiquity, the number of unknown causes and effects in nature was still infinite compared to the volumes that offered explanations. If anything, our discussion of Galileo's literary personality has shown that the path to an understanding and acceptance of natural philosophy is not a boulevard paved with unquestioned tomes of philosophy.

One of Galileo's most famous characters, aside from the interlocutors in the *Dialogues on the Two Chief World Systems* and the *Discourses on the Two New Sciences*, is emblematic of the above image of the new philosopher and the picaresque figure: the researcher of sounds in the *Assayer*. The researcher of sounds, an epic-picaresque character created between

1618 and 1623) presents several idealized characteristics that we can relate to Galileo as reader, Galileo as author, and eventually to the later Galilean characters of the dialogues. After citing a long passage by his opponent Sarsi on the appearance of rainbows and the substance of vapors, Galileo begins the passage: "Long experience has taught me that with regard to intellectual matters, this is the status of mankind: The less people know and understand about such matters, the more positively they attempt to reason about them, and on the other hand the number of things known and understood renders them more cautious in passing judgment about anything new."[75] Galileo introduces an argument on human nature of seeming universal importance. His introduction recalls the moral of a fable, though he has turned the traditional structure on end by placing the message at the beginning of the text, whereupon he makes sure the reader is well aware of the lesson to be learned from reading, and removes all chances of a misinterpretation.

Galileo then introduces the main character of the fable: a scientific Everyman in search of truth, one who bears a striking resemblance to Galileo himself, Quixote, and even Sarsi. Without using the term *favola*, the first line of the narrative evokes the genre: "There once lived, in a very solitary place, a man endowed by nature with extraordinary curiosity and a very penetrating mind. He raised many birds as a hobby, much enjoying their songs."[76] In a Counter-Reformation context, curiosity was seen as an indicator of either a good or a corrupt soul, and therefore represented a potential threat to established doctrine.[77] The syntax of Galileo's description of the protagonist in the Fable of the Sounds mimics that of the narrator's description of Quixote's voracious appetite for reasoning about the characters he encountered in the poetry of chivalry.[78] In both stories the reader is presented with a catalog of the investigative material the protagonists encounter: lists of the traditional elements of chivalry and a catalog of the known ways of producing sounds. But, of course, the two take different steps as a result. The narrator describes Quixote's moment of inspiration: "At last, when his wits were gone beyond repair, he came to conceive the strangest idea that ever occurred to any madman in this world. It now appeared to him fitting and necessary, in order to win a greater amount of honor for himself and serve his country at the same time, to become a knight-errant and roam the world on horseback, in a suit of armor."[79] Although lacking the armor and the horse, this describes the protagonist from the Fable of the Sounds. Quixote "would go in quest of adventures, by way of putting into practice all that he had read in his books."[80] Our protagonist instead "decided to travel to distant places in the hope of meeting with some new adventure."[81] Books are never mentioned in his journeys, only first-person experience. Not surprisingly, the genre of the fable is associated with an oral tradition, not a written one.

The plot of the *favola* centers on the character's indefatigable search for all methods of producing sounds in the natural world. The first moment of learning actually comes from a misinterpretation: the researcher hears what sounds like a bird call outside his window, and "arriving at the road, he found a shepherd boy who was blowing into a kind of hollow stick and moving his fingers about on the wood, thus drawing from it a variety of notes similar to those of a bird, though by quite a different method."[82] The new philosopher wanders from adventure to adventure observing nature.[83] The first character that this fictitious investigator encounters is a shepherd. The protagonist then wanders into a temple and an *osteria*, a typical setting for many seventeenth-century tales. While the researcher explores these places, Galileo goes so far as to include a nearly encyclopedic list of mechanisms for producing sound that he discovers.

The reader expects to reach a climactic conclusion in which the researcher of sounds reveals a unifying truth that was previously unknown. Instead, to parody philosophical language, Galileo mentions variations of the word *stupore* four times in this journey.[84] The final investigation carried out by the character is more reminiscent of a Marinesque poem than the culmination of hours of investigation. From the birds at the beginning of the tale the researcher eventually arrives at an investigation of a cicada, vividly similar to Marino's nightingale in the *Adone*.[85] The researcher is pushed to drastic measures in his quest:

> ... he found himself more than ever wrapped in ignorance and bafflement upon capturing in his hand a cicada, for neither by closing its mouth nor by stopping its wings could he diminish its strident sound, and yet he could not see it move either its scales or any other parts. At length, lifting up the armor of its chest and seeing beneath this some thin, hard ligaments, he believed that the sound was coming from a shaking of these, and he resolved to break them in order to silence it. But everything failed until, driving the needle too deep, he transfixed the creature and took away its life with its voice, so that even then he could not make sure whether the song had originated in those ligaments.[86]

The vivisection of the cicada is an obvious example of grotesque imagery. Galileo has rendered a tiny insect so significant that the *favola* is nearly two pages long, a tremendous amount of textual importance for an object that is superficially unrelated to astronomy. In the Italian version, the anaphora of *né*, used four times in successive clauses, emphasizes Galileo's apophatic method: that of reaching a justifiable hypothesis by negation of other possible solutions. The conclusion of the *favola* explains the situation of Galileo when faced with questions about the truth: "thereupon his knowledge was reduced to such diffidence that when asked how sounds are generated he used to reply tolerantly that although he knew some of the ways, he was certain that many more existed which were unknown and unimaginable."[87] Knowledge will forever be a work in progress. Galileo's lesson lies in this conclusion to the tale: certainties cannot pass from era to era unchecked.[88]

The conclusion is much like Pliny's observation that the ancient artist Apelles signed his work with a provisional title "as though art was always a thing in process and not completed."[89] The curious irony is that Apelles, according to Pliny, purportedly used this device to skirt criticisms by retreating to the excuse that his work was unfinished. When considered with an eye to the debates on sunspots, Galileo's formulation of method would then also be a correction of Scheiner's misreading of what Apelles represented when Scheiner adopted the name for a pseudonym.

The protagonist holds in his hands a key to understanding sound, another piece in a larger puzzle, but is thwarted in his attempts to look past the shell of the insect to understand what lies beneath it. Importantly he is not trying to make sense of a poetic veil of the type seen in Chapters 1 and 2 to reveal a hidden truth. He investigates common objects, popular places, all of which belong to a certain daily vocabulary that does not require the creation of new terms. Following the argument of Ezio Raimondi, the protagonist of the Fable of the Sounds does not need the *terra incognita* of Ulysses in order to encounter the marvelous, but just to leave his own home.[90] This character represents a slightly transformed Don Quixote. The marvelous of the world needs no poetic covering in order to be marvelous. As Charles Presberg writes, *Don Quixote* "deals with the pursuit of truth beneath appearance. But in doing so, it also portrays, and parodies, the unstable contingency inherent in man, the individual self, society and art – realities fraught with contradiction, subject to temporal processes of change, and continually undergoing construction and reconstruction in human discourse."[91] Galileo's researcher recognizes that the truth exists within the objects around him in spite of the unstable elements of human discourse, of the literary language that carries influences extraneous to the truth. Is the researcher's task equally as epic as Quixote's or that of Ulysses? Yes and no. As Raimondi concludes about the researcher of sounds: "only objects come to life around him, the adventure remains outside the human labyrinth of passions and conflicts."[92] The tale describes objective investigation, without emotion, in which the researcher seeks information he knows already to be present in the object of his inquiry.

To borrow a phrase from the *Assayer*, the *strada al ritrovamento del vero*, the road to the discovery of truth, is guided by various readings, but both the intellect and the senses aid in finding the way, with the former knowing that the philosopher will likely never reach the end of the journey.[93] In spite of his highly literary identity, textual independence separates Galileo's figure of the new philosopher from Cervantes' Quixote. As Andrea Battistini states: "The philosopher and the scientist are like wayfarers because the truth is not a stable and immovable possession inherited from the school of the past, but a conquest that is constructed little by little under the eyes that search for it with felicity, always distrusting their own knowledge."[94] I would only propose a slight modification to Battistini's suggestion that the truth is constructed. Galileo's fable and the ways in which his characters speak of the truth indicate that the truth is discovered; the philosopher reveals what already exists beneath what tradition and passion would have us believe to be true. In this way, the description is consistent with Michelangelo's sonnet that describes removing stone to reveal the statue that already exists within a block of marble, an image that will appear in the *Chief World Systems* and be analyzed in the next chapter. Galileo's story of the researcher of sounds asks readers to keep in mind the often erroneous influence of preconceived ideas based on earlier study. Building the truth on those foundations is inherently unstable. The flute that the researcher of sounds first hears is not a bird as he initially thinks. Furthermore, he dramatizes the act of removing a hard outer shell to expose the vital content, the mechanism, of a sensory experience. Where Quixote misplaces his signifiers, the researcher of sounds searches for the true signified behind them.

It is strangely ironic that the new philosophers come to be associated with a positive and productive wandering since Galileo has been so critical of the restricted, blinded, and sterile errancy of the Peripatetics, the original philosophical wanderers who followed Aristotle's teachings. Quixote is similarly wandering in search of meaning, but still creating it based on a world on paper that perhaps never corresponded with lived reality. Instead, evoking the Platonic cave, Galileo writes of his contemporary group of Aristotelian philosophers: "they are Peripatetics only in name since they do not walk around but are satisfied with worshipping shadows, and they do not philosophize with their own judgment but only with the memory of a few ill-understood principles."[95] Galileo's comment serves to highlight two problems: the discrepancy between a name (a signifier) and what it represents (the signified), as well as the need for the modern philosopher to rely not on the printed word, but on the eyes of the mind and, importantly, the eyes of the senses to maneuver in philosophical debate.

In a way that mirrors the debates surrounding Ariosto and Tasso, Galileo subjects Sarsi and others to an evaluation of their representations of the truth, unity of composition, and engagement with tradition. As a result the vehicle for their philosophical message is destabilized to the point of compromising the message itself. Seeing Galileo's characterization of Sarsi and Simplicio in light of Cervantes' parody of tradition shows the essential value of the literary as a tool for exploring philosophical weaknesses and illustrating the new paradigm. Galileo's next step in this literary epistemology will be to split the protagonist from the Fable of the Sounds into three different characters: the interlocutors of the *Dialogues on the Two Chief World Systems* and the *Discourses on the Two New Sciences*. One will be unmistakably quixotic, clinging to his rhetorical weapons in defense of Aristotle, but lost in the obscure labyrinth of the printed tradition in natural philosophy. One will be a shipwrecked Dantean protagonist of romance who tries to reconcile the disparity between the views of the errant philosopher and those of the third interlocutor. The third, often taken to be a projection of Galileo, is well versed in the language of romance, of parody, and of poetry, and he uses all three to make the next sally of the knights of new philosophy more successful than its predecessors.

CHAPTER FIVE

Shipwrecked, clueless, and quixotic

After approaching the question of the new philosopher via an epistemology of literary criticism in line with the aesthetic and ideological concerns of Cervantes, Galileo's next expression of philosophical doctrines is also his most literary. The *Dialogues on the Two Chief World Systems* (1632) and the later *Discourses on the Two New Sciences* (1638) are the best representation of literary and philosophical epistemologies working in tandem to promote a new vision for natural philosophy. The principal difference between these two final published works is the shift in subject matter, moving from a hypothetical debate about the structure of the universe to what is essentially a manual, in conversation form, for carrying out mathematical demonstrations of kinetics and the evaluation of material strengths. For the first time in scholarship this final chapter analyzes Galileo's three Venetian gentlemen, Simplicio, Sagredo, and Salviati, as literary characters. The fictional interlocutors are loosely based on historical figures and are characterized in a way that reflects different points of view and intellectual preparations in the debate over the structure of the universe. As they read the relevant books on both sides of the controversy, they encounter difficulties, and their responses to those challenges are couched in a figurative language that aligns them with the popular fiction of the period. This literary reading of Simplicio, Sagredo, and Salviati shows that with these characters Galileo creates new fictional figures: the Aristotelian Quixotic Anti-Hero, the Academic Dantean Romance Hero, and the Copernican Knight Errant. Unlike the scattered tropes and figurative language of other natural philosophical dialogues, the poetic formation of these figures makes the case for the legitimacy of the Copernican Theory even without considering the logic of the philosophy they defend. Together, the literary and philosophical epistemologies brought to life by these characters leave readers convinced of what the Inquisition also suspected – that the *Chief World Systems* was never intended to do anything but sustain the validity of heliocentrism.

Understandably the bitter pill of heliocentrism was hard to swallow, and after the *Assayer* Galileo reached for all of the rhetorical sugar coating he had at his disposal to make his argument ultimately more palatable and more convincing. As Marsh and others have argued, the dialogue, beginning in the fifteenth century, was a way to write against authority without threatening it to the point of fearing recrimination.[1] By 1632 for Galileo these authorities were not just the Aristotelians of the universities but also ecclesiastical figures. The Church had ruled in 1616 to ban support of the heliocentric theory of the universe, meaning that Copernican loyalists could not publish material that directly attempted to prove the validity of their interpretation of cosmic data. Although Galileo received papal and Inquisitorial permissions to publish the *Chief World Systems*, they came with certain restrictions, among which was the necessity of presenting the Copernican Theory as a hypothesis. In reference to these tensions, in his presentation of the years surrounding the publication of the *Dialogue on the Two Chief World Systems*, Heilbron divides the chapter of Galileo's biography into the following subheadings: "The Knight," "The Windmill," and "The Tilt."[2] According to Heilbron's anachronistic parallel with a romantic image of Don Quixote, Galileo is the quixotic knight, Pope Urban VIII the windmill, and the publication of the *Chief World Systems* the tilt. Even though I will continue my argument that Simplicio is more accurately the quixotic figure as contemporary readers would have understood him, Heilbron's comparison does bring to light the dangers of publishing the dialogue. The interlocutors accordingly speak in terms of a hypothesis, a convenient fiction, and they are aided by the literary touch of their author.

The dialogue in Galileo's library

In her study of the dialogue tradition, Virginia Cox calls the *Chief World Systems* "a vehicle for one of the first great products of a recognizably modern scientific mentality."[3] As my analysis will show, via a literary and poetic tradition operating in tandem with the philosophical discussion, the *Chief World Systems* is not just a product of that mentality, but both the blueprint and the propaganda to support its creation. Regardless of the field of inquiry, dialogues served as models of conduct, and the most influential dialogues were self-referential when it came to this topic. Works such as Castiglione's *Libro del cortegiano* (*Book of the Courtesan*; 1528), Giovanni Della Casa's *Galateo* (1551-1555), and Stefano Guazzo's *Civil conversazione* (*Civil Conversation*; 1574) depict courtly conversation by acting out dialogue while discussing it, just as Galileo's speakers depict the actions of philosophy while talking about philosophical conclusions. While focusing on the formal rhetorical aspects of the work, Maurice Finocchiaro describes the *Chief World Systems* in similar terms: "It is above all a book of criticism, a work of polemic and struggle; it is at the same time a pedagogical work, and a philosophical work; it is finally a history book, 'The History of Galileo's Mind.'"[4] The dialogue structure provided a format amenable to flexible exploration of intellectual debate, educational workbook, and explanation of method. As Stephen Clucas demonstrates in a brief article that engages both Dietz Moss and Finocchiaro on the literary and rhetorical qualities of Galileo's dialogues, the choice of what is at times a Socratic method is at once both necessary for the argument at hand and a literary choice of model to demonstrate and educate a future generation of natural philosophers. Clucas states: "dialogue enables Galileo to develop the logical arguments in favour of the Copernican hypothesis."[5] As a result the literariness of these philosophical debates cannot be neatly excised from content and argumentation. In addition, these structural advantages allowed for discussion of this controversial (and prohibited) topic.

Moreover, the genre is also indicative of a certain attitude toward dominant cultural trends in a way similar to that of the quixotic undercurrent in the *Assayer*. The dialogue was a flexible outlet for controversial ideas. As Virginia Cox writes: "it seems safe to suggest that the use of the dialogue form may be seen as a symptom of an unease with the conventions which govern the transmission of knowledge within a society, and a desire to reform them by returning to a study of the roots of persuasion."[6] Once again we return to the idea of persuasion, *ethos* and *pathos* in the hands of a skilled rhetorician. This space for multiple voices, according to Cox, "would have particular value, of course, to a reading public with particular reason to be sensitive to the 'tyranny' of monological written discourse."[7] Galileo's own father Vincenzo Galilei chose the dialogue to express his polemical views on dissonance and acoustics.[8] Galileo's dialogues too show the dynamic interaction of what would otherwise have been competing monologues. The genre of dialogue adopts not only authority, but also experience, by allowing the individual to give voice to first-person testimony.[9] Marsh reiterates for the tradition of dialogues what Galileo will attempt to emphasize in his own compositions: "Of paramount importance to the notion, fundamental to Quattrocento dialogue, that knowledge is not fixed eternally; historical context and the fluidity of debate both play a role in the search for truth."[10] Dialogue overall has the ability to provide flexibility to philosophical discussion that Galileo had called for in the Fable of the Sounds. Galileo is neither the first, nor the only, intellectual to use the dialogue format for his text, but since he chose that structure over the treatise and the letter for these major works on astronomy and cosmography, its stylization as a fiction hints at a new moment of complexity in the philosophical tradition.

The arguments in Galileo's dialogues cover a broad expanse of related literature, and the intellectual approach of the three interlocutors to the books they encounter along the way is characterized by affinities with different fictional literary travelers. As Maria Luisa Altieri Biagi has pointed out more generally, "the new science needs to privilege the moment of research over that of discovery, and therefore the moment of discussion over that of acquisition."[11] Even Galileo's philosopher of sounds never arrived at the moment of acquisition he sought. Kepler's mode of writing also prefers the historical presentation of his mistakes and successes over the logical mode of presentation.[12] The journey becomes the focus, not the destination. Epic poetry once again can inform a reading of these works by bringing to light the types of journey that these speakers describe in their investigations. Where Battistini only quickly mentions the military imagery of the *Chief World Systems* without investigating further, my analysis of this language of battle, struggle, and despair is indicative of a fusion between recognizable literary figures and different philosophical methods.[13] What we find is that Sagredo speaks as though he were a shipwrecked hero of a Dantean landscape, Simplicio as a quixotic classical hero who tries to navigate a modern landscape, and Salviati as the philosopher errant who is well versed in the literary travails of his counterparts and the mathematical language that Galileo feels is necessary to succeed in the interpretation of the natural world.

The scholarly conversation figures heavily in various fields of study in Galileo's library and his personal formation, which reflects the mosaic of stylistic elements in his dialogues. There is currently no evidence to show that the likely ancestors of the framed dialogue a Florentine would have known well, such as Boccaccio's *Decameron* (1353) and Baldassare Castiglione's *Book of the Courtier* (1528), were in Galileo's library, but recent scholarship has shown similarities in tone and content between these works and his prose.[14] He would have also likely been familiar with Benedetto Varchi's posthumous *Ercolano* (1570), a dialogue between philologist Vincenzo Borghini and the lawyer Lelio Bonsi on Florentine and Tuscan language. Where Castiglione focused on etiquette, Varchi outlined expression, giving particular privilege to the written language of Dante, Petrarch, and Boccaccio as the most noble (and therefore correct).[15] As written representations of spoken language, dialogues embody the tension between literary tradition and actual use of Italian. The related Florentine political linguistic debates began with Dante, continued with Bembo, and extended for decades through the foundation in 1582 of the Accademia della Crusca, of which Galileo later became a member.[16] As with most of the other literary choices Galileo made, the adoption of the dialogue was also a declaration of certain cultural and courtly values practiced within the genre: a combination of literary tradition and lively spoken language.

Galileo's collection of books shows the range of fields that used the form. This colorful collection of works reflects the variety of styles that authors of dialogues could adopt in attempts to conform to the demands of courtly culture: a spiritual dialogue, an edition of the *Divine Comedy* with a dialogue on the shape and measure of the *Inferno*, several Latin philosophical dialogues by Fortunio Liceti, and one by a Portuguese physician about the rhetorician Eumenius.[17] He also owned Girolamo Borro's (1512-1592) *Del flusso e riflusso del mare,* a dialogue set at the Medicis' Pitti gardens in Florence, to be discussed in more detail. Liceti's *De centro* (1640), discussed in the first chapter for its use of Virgil, Homer, and Lucan, is a dialogue that involves nine different speakers, but it is printed as though it were a treatise, with little indication that the speaker changes between exchanges. On the other hand, his *De terra unico centro motus* (Udine, 1641) is an imagined dialogue between Girolamo Borro and Scipione Chiaramonti, historical figures seen elsewhere for their conflicts with Galileo. The dialogue is notable because it is an explicit confrontation of these two men's books. Liceti's work opens with the two interlocutors discussing Liceti's theories, and in the margins he indicates the places where he cites passages from the authors' works to create the dialogue. These talking books continue to quote from epic poets in the traditional way, to lend authority to their claims about the motion or stability of the Earth in relationship to the Sun. With its emphasis on the literal printed tradition, Liceti's dialogue stands in sharp contrast to the literary Galileo.

Few of the mathematical and philosophical dialogues in Galileo's library make a recognizable effort to characterize their interlocutors, primarily because their texts are not concerned with literary elements but with the validation of their craft and the accessibility of that information. Niccolò Tartaglia's *Quesiti et inventioni diverse* (*Diverse Questions and Inventions*; 1546) provides a strong counterpoint to the stylization of the *Chief World Systems* and *Two New Sciences*. The *Quesiti* is a series of mathematical explanations related to artillery and military strategy presented in the form of discussions, dialogues, and letters with several different interlocutors. Tartaglia's model was the university *quesito*, and the ask–respond structure of these mini-dialogues maintains that institutional stability.[18] Many of the dialogues appear as they would in an early modern schoolbook. Some encounters between Tartaglia and figures as diverse as a duke, artillery specialist, painter, prior, and the Spanish ambassador to Venice are fictionalized; others merely dramatized; others still are transcriptions of actual questions and answers from correspondence. Richard Wentworth, the gentleman from the English court who quoted Ariosto, mentioned in Chapter 2, also appears in this dialogue. The voices of most of these speakers are indistinguishable; without a label to identify them, they could easily be mistaken for one another. The Prior of Barletta is an exception, because he knows Euclid and discusses Euclidian geometry with Nicolo. Among all of these speakers, the Prior has the most defined personality, and takes the most control of the discussions, even pausing to educate Nicolo on the history of the walls of Turin.[19] Interlocutors express confusion but without figurative language. And for as much resistance as they have to an idea, they always agree with Nicolo by the end of the *quesito* with an "havete ragione" ("you're right") or "mi consona molto" ("that agrees with me very much"). At the end of the thirteenth *quesito*, a servant enters to say dinner is ready.[20] Several evenings have passed in the course of this interrogation and no such thing has occurred prior. Yet, overwhelmingly, the literary elements remain ornaments in service to the mathematical or philosophical material being explained.

Girolamo Borro's slightly later *Dialogo del flusso e reflusso del mare* (Lucca, 1561) and its subsequent revised editions (1577, 1583) reflect the next level of literary complexity in mathematical and philosophical dialogues, one that only furthers the philosophical project insofar as it ingratiates the author with his patrons. The dialogue also takes a stand on the nature of language, reacting against the Florentine high culture espoused in Varchi's *Ercolano*. The interlocutors, Nozzolino and Alseforo Talascopio, spend their time discussing the tides as Alseforo tries to recreate conversations that took place over six days at the court of the Marquis and Marchesana of Massa. Borro is clear about the concern for the language in which his theories are expressed. To demonstrate this Alseforo places two limits on Nozzolino's questioning, one relating to the demonstrations, the other making explicit the kind of language to be used in the discussions, asking of his readers:

> excuse me if I, who never read my Tuscan books, mix together in the course of reasoning some of the words that are not weighty enough, and go along amassing them as I find them, without artifice, as my nursemaid taught

them to me when I was a boy speaking commonly, just as whoever is born or raised in my region speaks. [Excuse me if] I offend your learned and well-censored ears, habituated only to hearing this said with the highest of politeness and gracefulness.[21]

Dialogue is innately tied to courtly identity and therefore has the ability to elevate the social status of the art discussed, but runs the risk of either exposing the author's lack of erudition or offending the opposing linguistic camp. As Dietz Moss writes: "The audience for a dialectical disputation, even in its humanistic form, would presumably be an elite audience of knowledgeable people who would be expected to judge the discourse on its specialized content and regard the rhetorical elements as amusing, entertaining or, if not in agreement, as irritating, even insulting. The rhetoric would be recognized and not seen as a meaningful part of the argument."[22] Borro balances ornate linguistic touches he gives to his speakers in order to please the court with a language that allows him to communicate with those who might practice upon the information in the dialogue.

Borro's work on the tides uses familiar tropes for figurative language within the courtly code of dialogue writing. His use of analogy to explain natural laws is restricted to an image of children skipping rocks being similar to light reflecting at an angle from the surface it strikes, and stars in the sky being like knots in wood.[23] The latter image is taken from astronomical debates of the period about whether the celestial spheres were hard orbs (with stars fixed in place like knots in wood) or fluid through which stars moved like fish in water or birds in the air.[24] In Borro's *Trattato dell'inondatione del Nilo* (*Treatise on the Inundation of the Nile*), which accompanies the second and third editions of the *Dialogo del flusso e reflusso*, one interlocutor uses a parable to complain that another is telling them something they already know. When the speaker replies with a curt response, the moderator of the discussion, Giovanna d'Austria, keeps them on track by mentioning a metaphor described in the previous chapter, the tapestry, saying "without breaking the beautiful weave of such a well-ordered tapestry, let us move on …"[25] The speakers model courtly, not philosophical, behavior, and their conversations are not informed by literary tradition.

For the interlocutors of Borro's dialogues on the tides, intellectual obstacles are variously described following banal conventions, but haphazardly, not systematically. One exchange demonstrates the varied nature of these figurative ways for speaking about intellectual obstacles. Nozzolini at one point says to Alseforo: "This (my dear Alseforo) is not a gait for running very quickly, but for going forward slowly," and then raises an objection that the conclusion suggests the corruptibility of the heavenly bodies.[26] Alseforo replies: "speaking with erudition ... you put your hand in a hole where there hides a crab so large that between both you and me we will just barely be able to dig it out."[27] The importance of the question of expressing these kinds of problems was obviously central to Borro's revisions between editions. The crab in a hole is replaced by a more elegant topos for interpretative problems: the knot. In the second edition, using different interlocutors, Borro retains the image of meandering along in investigation at a slow pace, but the response is much different: "You, Mr. Giovanni, speaking with erudition according to your ancient custom, have tied the knot so tight, that between you and me we will just barely be able to loosen it, yet nevertheless I will try to untie it."[28] Scheiner used this popular motif in the sunspot quarrels, and Galileo makes use of the topos in the *Chief World Systems*.[29] These are the only instances where the intellectual process is expressed figuratively in the book, and I would argue that they are neither literary nor indicative of an epistemology.[30]

Galileo's interlocutors

At the most basic level, Galileo's dialogues approach literality via their conformity to conventions of the genre of fictional conversations. As Cox has noted, the dialogue production of sixteenth-century Italy was distinguished by a historical or documentary style in a way that the fictitious dialogues written elsewhere were not.[31] Characters based on historical figures are often well defined to match their counterparts in order to make the dialogue verisimilar, and Galileo follows this rule. Sagredo is named for Galileo's friend and mentor Giovanfrancesco Sagredo (1571-1620), and his character is a layman open to being convinced of the truth in the Copernican system.[32] Sagredo is often too easily combined with Salviati to present polarized dialogues between pro-Copernican philosophers and the lone Aristotelian when he is in fact as independent as the other interlocutors.[33] Sagredo reads, criticizes, doubts, investigates, and questions the nature of philosophy. Accordingly, he provides a point of departure on which we can frame our later discussions of Simplicio and Salviati. Salviati is named for Galileo's Florentine colleague with close ties to Medici court culture, Filippo Salviati (1582-1614): the dedicatee of the *Letters on Sunspots* who hosted Galileo frequently at his villa, including during the dispute on floating bodies that resulted in the publication of the *Discourses on Bodies in Water*.[34] I support Marsh's reading of Salviati as a variation on a stock figure in early dialogues: "those who fully exercise the possibilities of rhetorical freedom often profess to speak more to stimulate others than to express their own opinions."[35] I would add that the patrician roots of the historical figure also weigh on his importance and characterization as a literary figure. Seen in this light, we can appreciate the literary crafting involved in his creation. Salviati, as a character within a character, plays the part of a vivacious courtly Copernican supporter in the dialogue. The elision between the Copernican Salviati and Galileo is aided by Stefano della Bella's engraved title page, which depicts Copernicus with Galileo's features.[36] Although other historical and fictional figures appear in vignettes during the dialogues, Galileo does not appear as a speaking character in these two works, but he plays a large role and is mentioned repeatedly as the "Accademico."

To complete the dialogue is Simplicio, a pseudonym for an unidentified historical person, named both for the sixth-century Aristotelian philosopher Simplicius and, as the Inquisition will assume, for the double entendre of his name.[37] Drake describes Simplicio as the "stubborn Peripatetic patterned on Cesare Cremonini and Ludovico delle Colombe" in the *Chief World Systems*, who becomes "much more reasonable and willing to learn" in the *Two New Sciences*.[38] Salviati explicitly says that because Scipione Chiaramonti cannot answer questions in person, he will ask Simplicio to respond in his place. In the *Chief World Systems*, the character of Simplicio was also made to be the mouthpiece of Catholic dogma, a move of poetic license that was not taken well by the Pope or the Inquisition.[39] In common with Galileo's tone toward Simplicio in the *Dialogues* and *Discourses*, Marsh writes of the earlier Quattrocento dialogues: "within humanist dialogues the group often mocks or isolates dogmatic rigidity, represented in the person of an intractably 'Stoic' interlocutor out of touch with practical realities."[40] Simplicio is a composite of the adherents of dogma who had blocked the acceptance of Galileo's discoveries in various areas, in whom critics have also identified the characteristics of Fortunio Liceti.[41] In his character development, we can also look to the *Assayer* and the quixotic image of Lothario Sarsi.[42] Galileo designs Simplicio's character in a way that shows his incapacity for fully operating in the new world of philosophy. As Paolo Bozzi remarks, although Galileo can still express wonder (*meraviglia*) about the motion of a pendulum thirty years after its discovery, the character of Simplicio never expresses such a sentiment.[43] Given his dynamic, yet stubborn, character, Simplicio has been given a number of interpretations: Calandrino from the Boccaccian tradition; the fool, or *sciocco* more generally; and the emblem of dogma, arrogance, presumptuousness, obstinacy, and superficiality. He has also been seen as an object of

Galileo's tolerance, meant to keep readers from sympathizing with a character that had been too ridiculed or treated too poorly.

Modern commentators have conflicting interpretations of the three speakers, mostly because they attempt to look beyond the characters for a symbolic reading of the two dialogues and for signs of Galileo in their voices.[44] According to one school of thought, they represent different sides of his personality: Salviati is Galileo's mouthpiece and Simplicio is evidence of Galileo's genius as a writer.[45] Dietz Moss calls Salviati "sage and witty" and Sagredo the "affable and sympathetic listener."[46] Maurice Finocchiaro is one of few modern critics to assert that Salviati is not Galileo, Sagredo is not neutral, and Simplicio is far from simple-minded.[47] I have found one twentieth-century critic who has in part proposed a literary aspect of the Galilean interlocutors, but without carrying out the analysis himself. Rauhut, in an essay on Galileo's importance to Italian language and literature, writes:

> One can say: in the *Chief World Systems* in regard to the Copernican doctrine and in regard to the new method, Salviati performs the role of "God's advocate" and Simplicio the "Devil's Advocate." The three characters are not Allegories, nor do they personify any abstract idea, neither had the author simply given them human clothes; they are rather two lively bearers of the philosophy of life and, as such, knowledge-thirsty, educated men. The liveliness of the three characters is from Galileo's own long experience of the dramatic and, for him, dangerous discussion with the lay public and scientific community; from his experiences in his teaching career, correspondence, educated conversation, and mature scientific disputation.[48]

Building on this richer consideration of Simplicio, Salviati, and Sagredo, my analysis will examine the experiences of these characters and their expressions of frustrations and confusion to link them to their literary forbears. Just as we saw with insults coined from Ariosto's verses, these contructs are not mere ornaments, nor are they simply in the service of philosophy. Alongside the geometrical language of the book of nature, their literary language dramatizes the positive and negative models of philosophical behavior.

Galileo's contemporaries immediately recognized in these dialogues the literary work of Galileo as an author who created interlocutors that were more than a one-dimensional voice copied from a pre-existing book. According to Maria Luisa Altieri Biagi, Descartes was the first to notice Galileo's characterizations of the interlocutors in the *Dialoghi*, but his Italian colleagues also quickly wrote about their reactions.[49] Fulgenzio Micanzio wrote to Galileo at the end of July 1632 to praise the decorum with which he brought Sagredo to life.[50] Tommaso Campanella then wrote to Galileo a month later to praise the design of Simplicio as the "laughing stock [*trastullo*] of this philosophical comedy," Salviati as a new Socrates, and Sagredo as the free mind "unadulterated by the schools of thought."[51] This reaction persisted in later decades. In a letter to Marcello Malpighi – his good friend and colleague in the scientific Accademia del Cimento – Giovan Alfonso Borelli recommends the successful model Malpighi should use when composing his new dialogue:

> it would be necessary that you take a look at the first dialogues of Galileo on the world system, where you would see not a few examples of the method that you ought to observe while writing a dialogue to be clear, convincing, and to observe the customs and dignity of the people that play the part of the Master and his adversaries."[52]

Borrelli specifically identifies the manners of Galileo's characters, their literariness, as something to model. With these contemporary reactions in mind, I propose to do something different than what modern criticism has thus far allowed for Galileo's interlocutors: to examine Sagredo, Simplicio, and Salviati as literary characters, not philosophical voices, in order to show the culmination of the literary and philosophical working together to establish a new paradigm.

Working in tandem with this larger project are typical elements of literary ornament to frame the dialogue as a fiction and concerns for elite Florentine tradition, in part to escape immediate censure for writing in support of the Copernican Theory, and in part to satisfy tacit demands of a princely audience. Rhetorical figures in the *Chief World Systems* include ridicule, irony, analogy, metaphor, metonymy, and prosopopoeia (when an absent or imaginary person is represented as speaking). For the *Chief World Systems* the choice of location suited the purpose of the philosophical discussion of tides as much as it reflects a literary tradition of the dialogue. This is even more the case with the *Two New Sciences*, set at the Venetian arsenal. As Marsh's survey indicates, the fifteenth-century dialogues tended to take place in a specific social and historical setting that had implications for the content of the conversations and reflected the intended audience.[53] The location admits for freedom of belief, the company or host for the freedom of organization, and yet the ensemble still reflects society.[54] In this period, the close of the day in a garden at sunset came to indicate a "higher plane of understanding and agreement."[55] Later dialogues built upon these traditions. After explaining his choice of interlocutors, Galileo too provides the frame of the *Chief World Systems*:

These gentlemen had casually engaged in various sporadic discussions, and, as a result, in their minds their thirst for learning had been aroused rather than quenched. Thus they made the wise decision to spend a few days together during which, having put aside every other business, they would attend to reflecting more systematically about God's wonders in heaven and on earth. They met at the palace of the most illustrious Sagredo, and after the proper but short greetings, Salviati began as follows …[56]

The stage is set. The players receive no other introduction from their author. They need none. Occasionally readers are reminded of the frame, particularly at the opening and closing of the days of the dialogues. Just as happens in the Quattrocento dialogue and the Ciceronian models, the *Chief World Systems* also adjourns with proposed future discussions.[57] There are elements of the "plot," such as sending a servant to collect a book for Simplicio and his stranding at low tide, that attempt to root the dialogue in a verisimilar world.[58]

At the same time, the dialogue relies heavily on non-literary elements including geometrical diagrams that complement the discussion. On the use of such diagrams and props in the dialogues of Galileo and others, I agree with Virginia Cox, who writes: "Despite these niceties, however, the effect of the inclusion of such devices in dialogue is to undermine the reader's faith in the fiction of the conversation portrayed and to make him aware of the book before him as a physical object, rather than an utterance."[59] The literary and the mathematical exist in delicate unison to maintain the sense of hypothesis while also demonstrating the certainty of the application of geometry to the questions of astronomy. Even the inclusion of Simplicio being stranded in a gondola at low tide, ostensibly a detail of the literary frame, makes the reader hyper-aware of the focus on the tides, and by extension the questions about the Earth's motion. As far as the literary epistemology is concerned, the equally self-referential comments that the speakers make will also remind the reader of the fictive nature of the work.

Sagredo, Lucretius, and Dante

Sagredo perhaps best represents the study of the innovative application of mathematics to philosophy behind the *Chief World Systems*. He can be seen as the literary representative of many readers of the dialogues. He is characterized as the Venetian consul to Syria, a diplomatic position he held for several years, which portrays him as a representative of culture and politics, as well as an emblem of social credit.[60] In many ways, he is also emblematic of the language of tradition against which Galileo is working, which may in part lead to the neutral evaluation that he has usually been given. My analysis builds on Pierpaolo Antonello's work that connects Sagredo to other Italian literary figures. For example, he ties Sagredo's claim at the end of the *Chief World Systems* about removing excess marble from sculptures to Michelangelo's sonnet "Non ha l'ottimo artista alcun concetto," in which the artist expresses the neo-platonic idea that the finished sculpture exists inside the raw piece of stone.[61] I would add that these frequent allusions to plastic and visual arts could also be connected to the historical Sagredo's fondness for collecting art and his self-styling as a gentleman, as opposed to a man of letters, which he expresses in correspondence.[62] Antonello also sees a possible "vague Petrarchan flavor" in Sagredo's comment on the alphabet at the close of the first day – "Io son molte volte andato meco medesimo considerando" – a self-referential phrase that loses its Petrarchan tone in translation: "I have many times considered within myself."[63] Perhaps not surprisingly, Petrarch and Michelangelo are two Italian poets whose corpus reflects indecisiveness when faced with moral and theological questions. They were also two models for their disciplines, and both subjects of linguistic and cultural debate in Florence in Galileo's lifetime due to Bembo and Vasari. I will argue that in addition to these literary echoes, Sagredo's method itself is tied to the structure and expressions of other poetry. He is concerned with the foundations of communication, the very geometry of language, and the power of the alphabet, linking him to Piccolomini's declarations about Homer and Virgil, the earliest philosophers seen in Chapter 1, as well as many other contemporary authors.[64] It also places him in a position either to follow only models or to study their sources as well, in opposition to the Peripatetics and Aristotle. Like Galileo confronting Tasso's poetic method and Sarsi's philosophy, Sagredo too expresses method by using analogies from the visual arts. As a result of his concern for the building blocks of philosophy, which tie him to Lucretius, he is also sensitive to the possibilities of rearranging those fundamental pieces in order to create something wholly unlike the original structure that still bears the same name as that original.

Sagredo outlines several dangers of this recombinant, atomistic philosophy at the same time that he praises its application – an expressive strategy that places him on the same level as the text-bound Aristotelians but also has the potential to liberate him to join Salviati. Sagredo concludes Day One of the *Chief World Systems* by praising the building blocks of language in a way that will define his approach to philosophy by the end of the dialogues:

> When reading the best poets, what wonder fills those who carefully consider the creation of images and their expression! What shall we say of architecture? What of the art of navigation? But above all stupendous inventions, how sublime was the mind of whoever conceived a means of communicating his most private thoughts to any other person, though very distant in time or place; that is, a means of speaking with those who are in India, or those who have not been born yet or will not be born for another thousand or ten thousand years! And how easy it is, by various arrangements of twenty characters on paper! Let this be the seal for all wonderful human inventions and the end of our reasoning today.[65]

Sagredo concludes: "there is nothing open to investigation that one cannot understand by careful study of its letters."[66] His fascination with the effects of composition in poetry and architecture, along with reading the stars in navigation, can be tied directly to Galileo's library. As if to demonstrate the geometrical nature of language itself, Albrecht Dürer devotes an entire chapter of his *Painter's Manual* to the depiction of the alphabet, starting with the basic unit of the letter "I" from which the majority of other letters are derived.[67] Sagredo's praise is also reminiscent of Boccaccio's story of Carmenta, mother of the Latin alphabet and grammar. In the *Famous Women*, a copy of which Galileo owned in the vernacular, Boccaccio too lists the importance of the alphabet for allowing "a perpetual remembrance of divine and human accomplishments" for future generations, correspondence, friendship, theology, and science.[68] In another volume with which Galileo was familiar, Lucretius says in the didactic poem *On the Nature of Things* that in his verses the words differ even though they are made from like elements:

> it is vital in what order I array
> The different letters that make up my lines, in what position,
> Because the *sky*, the *sea*, the *soil*, the *streams*, the shining *sun*,
> Are drawn from a single pool of letters, and one alphabet,
> Spells *barley*, *bushes*, *beasts*, words not identical, and yet
> With certain letters shared in common, for what really matters,
> What makes a world of difference, is the *arrangement* of the letters.
> The same goes for the physical.[69]

Sagredo's presentation, when viewed from its likely source text, then appears to offer a linguistic atomism that has dangerous implications for the stability of language and its power as a reliable signifier. Rather than turning to Lucretius or Boccaccio in a verbatim quotation as Delle Colombe, Liceti, or Sarsi would have done, Galileo incorporates their themes and images into Sagredo's speech for a spontaneous intertextuality that has none of the rough edges of Tasso's or Capra's clumsy borrowings from other texts.

Beyond the constructive potential for the new, Sagredo here argues for an appreciation of the power of the alphabet, expressed as written communication, to provide a one-way conversation between the past and the future. Manilius too starts with these fundamentals in his didactic poem *Astronomica*. In Book II he outlines his pedagogy, saying that to teach new principles, one must start with the most basic element – in his example, the alphabet. Children should then learn syllables, words, expression, grammatical rules, and finally verse.[70] He goes on to compare the process to building a city.[71] Informed by a literary and philosophical tradition, Sagredo's building-block presentation of the alphabet, when seen in light of Manilius, is also reminiscent of the geometrical figures that form the language of the book of nature.[72]

The difference between Sagredo and these poetic sources that would otherwise tie him to an authoritative tradition, one Galileo has repeatedly discounted, is that he is aware of the inherent potential problem: the letters of any language are interchangeable and alterable until they are fixed to paper. Sagredo focuses on the new, but the existing practice emphasizes this fixed tradition. The "great practice on the texts of Aristotle" that Galileo soundly dismissed in the *Assayer* is a parallel act to recombining the alphabet to create new words according to Sagredo's analogy. The possibilities of dismantling and rebuilding exist with the smallest elements of the linguistic structure, in this case letters, but continue through to entire portions of texts. Early modern readers were avid consumers of piecemeal texts, relying on new and expanding genres of reference works, including the florilegia against which Galileo wrote in the *Assayer*, to excerpt necessary material in order to appear well educated.[73] Both poetry and philosophy would seem to thrive on this process. What Sagredo, Cicero, Boccaccio, and certainly Lucretius have realized is that changing the order of the parts changes the identity of the whole. Several early modern readers had run afoul of the Inquisition for this very practice.[74] Thus, a rearranged Aristotle in the seventeenth century should no longer have the authority of the original Aristotle. Sagredo later creates a demonstrative analogy to show the dangers of such a method of disputing and criticizing, and he ties it once again to the project of epic poetry. What works for one scholar ought to work for another:

> But then, what you and other learned philosophers do with Aristotle's texts, I will do with the verses of Virgil or Ovid, by making patchworks

of passages and explaining with them all the affairs of men and secrets of nature. But why even go to Virgil or the other poets? I have a booklet much shorter than Aristotle or Ovid in which are contained all the sciences, and with very little study one can form a very complete picture of them: this is the alphabet.[75]

This is an obvious allusion to Galileo's advocacy for the geometrical language of nature. Taken to the extreme, Sagredo's example suggests that any text, then, has the possibility to be an authority on the same subjects as Aristotle's. His declaration implies a different approach to verbal expression. Why recompose the sentences or verses of other authors when every intellect has the capacity to start with letters and create an entirely new message? The masters of Latin and Greek epic poetry are compared to Aristotle, and implicitly to the book of nature – the latter immutable and perfect, the former all available piecemeal. He has incorporated Lucretian philosophy to the point of making it an epistemology.

Where Simplicio crafts his arguments from pieces of other texts, Sagredo instead returns to the most fundamental pieces: "There is no doubt that whoever knows how to combine and order this and that vowel with this and that consonant will be able to get from them the truest answers to all questions and the teachings of all sciences and the arts."[76] He goes on to compare the combinatory possibilities of the alphabet with those of the painter's palette, and the means to imitate "all visible objects."[77] He returns to the *poesis* at the core of both epistemologies. Again, the possibilities are endless, with the correct intellect in control of the pen or the brush. The painter's possibilities end, according to Sagredo's analysis, with the visible realm, things of which the painter has had direct sensory experience.

His presentation recalls Galileo's earlier marginal criticism on *De phaenomenis in orbe lunae* (*On the Phenomena of the Lunar Orb*; 1612) by Giulio Cesare Lagalla (1576-1624). Galileo calls attention to the importance of understanding, not just copying, the language of philosophy by suggesting that Lagalla was metaphorically stunted by the study of the masters, rather than growing through the creation of art (or philosophical truth) itself. Since Lagalla's primary dispute with Galileo involved the representations of the Moon that Galileo produced after viewing it with a telescope, the language of visual arts is appropriate. According to Galileo, without moving beyond the model, an author becomes an intellectually blinded copier, seeing and writing only the words of another without ever understanding their meaning. This multipart lesson in the margins of Lagalla's *De phaenominis orbe lunae* includes the following analogy:

> similarly busying oneself always and consuming oneself over the works of others, without ever raising the eyes to the same works of nature, trying to recognize in those the truths already discovered and investigate some of the infinite ones that remain to be found, will never make a philosopher from a man, but only a scholar and expert in the writings of others on philosophy. I do not believe that you would esteem as a talented painter one who had practiced much on the paper and panels of all of the painters so that he could quickly identify this or that manner and habit as coming from Michelangelo, that one from Raphael, that group from Rosso, that other from Salviati, and also knew how to copy them.[78]

Galileo accuses his detractors of privileging precedent to any kind of dynamism observed in the natural world, the subject of artists and philosophers alike. The language of the visual arts and this sense of recycling centuries-old translated documents persists into Sagredo's voice because both the written material and the vision of these readers are limited by choice. Sagredo is not a creator, but a champion of the practice, an imitator who at leasts understands the paradigm. Unlike Salviati, who will be seen later, Sagredo's imagination appears to have no role here in trying to surpass the model. His intellectual curiosity seems blocked at the point where Bembo relied on Petrarch and Boccaccio or Vasari's first edition of the *Lives of the Artists* (1550) that presented Michelangelo as the insurmountable pinnacle of artistic production.

The literariness of Sagredo's philosophical language is further marked by its incorporation of ideas found in Galileo's other works to create a rich intratextuality. Sagredo is intuitive enough to distinguish the quality of sources. When he describes the Aristotelian Scipione Chiaramonti, he uses specific terms taken from the Fable of the Sounds that will be discussed in the conclusion when Chiaramonti responds to the *Chief World Systems* the following year. Sagredo speaks in terms of battle when he describes Chiaramonti as: "A man able to sustain the Peripapetic inalterability of the heavens against a host of astronomers, and one who, to their greater shame, has done battle against them with their own weapons!"[79] Sagredo here supports Salviati's claim that Chiaramonti's work is an embarrassment to all Italian intellectuals that should be passed over in silence because it is not meritorious of reply. He derides his dissimulation and disagreement when faced with principles they do not understand. Salviati then adopts Sagredo's language himself to talk about Chiaramonti's calculations: "The author, I say, in order to attack [*trafiggere*] his adversaries with their own weapons, takes a large number of the observations which they themselves have made as I say, these adversaries with their own weapons, a large number of the observations made by their very selves."[80] Of the few times that variations of *trafiggere* appear in Galileo's work, notably it occurs at the climax of the Fable of the Sounds to describe the researcher's actions that kill the cicada he tries to study. When considered in the context of researcher and object of study, Salviati's comment suggests a self-reflexivity in Peripatetic study that is both sterile and self-destructive.

Even though Sagredo's moments of insight echo Galileo's earlier criticisms, his confusion is indicative of the literary model for his character, one that would push an attentive reader to prefer a different, more successful philosophical model. The final image of Sagredo in the *Chief World Systems* is of a blind man, one who chooses his condition, selecting Salviati as his guide: "I feel myself being gently led by the hand; and although I find no obstacles in the road, yet like the blind I do not see where my guide is leading me, nor have I any means of guessing where such a journey must end."[81] Blindness is not merely an ornamental trope; blindness has serious implications for a philosophy founded on the senses. Salviati responds gently: "There is a vast difference between my slow philosophizing and your rapid insight; yet in this particular with which we are now dealing, I do not wonder that even the perspicacity of your mind is beclouded by the thick dark mists which hide the goal toward which we are traveling."[82] At this point Salviati compares himself to Orlando nearly gone mad in the episode analyzed in Chapter 3. After the explanation of the philosophical problem at hand Sagredo will thank Salviati for leading him out of an infernal landscape:

> You, Salviati, have guided me step by step so gently that I am astonished to find I have arrived with so little effort at a height which I believed impossible to attain. It is certainly true that the staircase was so dark that I was not aware of my approach to or arrival at the summit, until I had come out into the bright open air and discovered a great sea and a broad plain.[83]

In a poetic language evocative of Dante's climb out of the pit of hell, Sagredo has seemingly arrived at the shores of purgatory under the tutelage of his own philosophical Virgil. The implications are at once moral and philosophical – redemption can be had after this unfamiliar philosophical journey made familiar by its literary connotations.

Sagredo continues to dramatize the events of the Dantean journey in the *Two New Sciences*, where he indicates a sense of linear progress through the intellectual problems of the tides, kinetics, and mechanics that, however successful it may be with the aid of Salviati, cannot succeed on its own. In the *Two New Sciences*, during the first discussion of the first day the speakers debate the relative functionality and strength of materials for making machines of different sizes. Similar to the discussion of giants later in the work that turns to Ariosto, Salviati argues that as dimensions of materials grow, proportionality must be sacrificed to maintain strength. Sagredo responds: "My brain already reels. My mind, like a cloud momentarily illuminated by a lightning-flash, is for an instant filled with an unusual light, which now beckons to me and which now suddenly mingles and obscures strange, crude [*indigeste*] ideas."[84] The interpretation of this obscure expression of illumination requires returning to a similar statement in the earlier dialogue and also considering its literary source. In the *Chief World Systems* Sagredo finds himself confused when examining shipbuilding and the relative dimensions of objects larger in size, which he expresses in the following way: "I feel some confusion whirling in my mind; like a dense and dark fog, it prevents me from discerning the clarity and necessity of the conclusion with the lucidity that is usually appropriate in mathematical reasoning."[85] His reaction to this information linguistically resembles Dante's as he approaches the ring of giants that guard the entrance to Cocytus, a focal point in the poem for determining the size of the Inferno, and therefore very familiar to Galileo:

> Just as, whenever mists begin to thin,
> when, gradually, vision finds the form
> that in the vapor-thickened air was hidden,
> so I pierced through the dense and darkened fog;
> as I drew always nearer to the shore,
> my error fled from me, my terror grew.[86]

Even with their guide, both Dante and Sagredo remain distressed. Dante is about to remark that the head of Nimrod was the size of the Pinecone in Rome, using his senses to give a specific numerical indication that would become one of the central measurements for computing the dimensions of hell. Mark Peterson has recently shown that Sagredo's comment cited above is in direct response to Galileo's realization that the model he supported for the Inferno was incorrect, but without examining the literary model for Sagredo's emotional outburst.[87] The similarities between Dante's and Sagredo's language make evident that Galileo borrowed not just number but also imagery from Dante's poem in order to explain this problem of mechanics. Sagredo's later comment in the *Two New Sciences* echoes Dante's own thoughts at the end of *Paradise* when he compares staring into the light of God to the geometer trying to measure the circumference of a circle. Unlike the geometer, Dante receives his illumination from a lightning bolt of divine will.[88] The difference between Dante and Sagredo is that eventually Dante's small boat safely reaches paradise and gains autonomy, while Sagredo sits storm-tossed with an upset stomach waiting for Salviati's assistance.[89] Without a guide, Sagredo cannot complete the tasks at hand. His approach does not fit the successful model of method that Salviati displays, but at least he does represent forward motion.

Simplicio, Quixote, and immobile mobility

Simplicio, on the other hand, moves, but within the confines of his self-imposed intellectual labyrinth.[90] Both the literary and philosophical epistemologies associated with him express immobility, which, of course, is the very point he and his Aristotelian counterparts are trying to make about the Earth. With the help of his guides he navigates that space better at the end of the dialogues than at the beginning, but never leaves its structure. My analysis will show that through the literary touches of Galileo, Simplicio can also be seen as an image of the motion of a relatively stationary object, much like the attributes of the Sun that many Peripatetics denied.[91] In the style of the literary pedant seen in Chapter 3, Simplicio's first statement in the *Two New Sciences* includes a Latin phrase. He exclaims with no introduction that Salviati's first demonstration is: "A very remarkable and thoroughly unexpected [*praeter spem*] accident."[92] In the *Chief World Systems* he cites from the *Aeneid* and *Bucolics* to talk about tides in the style of the authors seen in Chapters 1 and 2.[93] As Armour has recognized, Simplicio is: "both a dummy enemy built for demolition and a precursor of Manzoni's comic pedant, Don Ferrante; by any standards he is a fine product of literary imagination, an entrenched and old-fashioned philosopher such as all ages can recognize."[94] Maria Luisa Altieri Biagi sees more of Manzoni's Don Abbondio in Simplicio, but the overall sense that he is a precursor to characters in Italy's first historical novel seems constant.[95] Yet, Simplicio's literary dynamism is indicative of concerns more essential to the philosophical debate in which Galileo was engaged.

As we have seen, the disputes between the two worlds, the two books, the two schools of thought, and the two systems of the cosmos were epic at all levels of expression in the Galilean project. His characters are tied to the epic project primarily through Simplicio. Simplicio stands on the defensive; as Muscetta has said, Simplicio is "substantially inconvincible and formally undefeated … as befits a hero."[96] His approach to confusing texts and new ideas borrows language from epic poetry, and he is frequently compared by Salviati and Sagredo to a valiant and faithful knight who stands guard at the Aristotelian fortress. His confusion becomes a defense, not an attempt to understand. Simplicio carries the battle meta-phor throughout. He explains that he cannot speak for Aristotle, but he can speak for his followers who write and dispute so that they are not left "without a guide, without protection, and without a head in philoso-phy."[97] Simplicio's confidence is short-lived, though he maintains his ori-ginal linguistic register throughout the dialogue.

As the literary worlds collide with their different methodologies, their philosophical foundations are also tested. The questioning, analyzing, and demonstrations made by Salviati for the benefit of Sagredo and Simplicio do start to take their toll on the security of the Aristotelian dogmatic interpretation of the natural world. Echoing Sagredo's concerns, nearly in despair, at one point Simplicio asks: "But, if one abandons Aristotle, who will be the guide in philosophy? Name some author."[98] Salviati replies in a way that is also an implied critique of Sagredo's willing blindness – what he had described as a Dantean helplessness: "One needs a guide in an unknown and uncivilized country, but in a flat and open region only the blind need a guide; whoever is blind would do well to stay home, whereas anyone who has eyes in his head and in his mind should use them as a guide."[99] For Salviati, if the knowledge cannot be reconstructed following logical reasoning, and a book is required, the validity of the statement is based more on rhetoric than philosophy, more on words than objects.

Salviati continues with a reiteration of the pedant theme from other works: "Is there anything more shameful in a public discussion dealing with demonstrable conclusions than to see someone slyly appear with a textual passage (often written for some different purpose) and use it to shut the mouth of an opponent?"[100] He goes on to combine the language seen previously into a single statement of philosophical best practices:

> If you want to persist in this manner of studying, lay down the name of philosophers and call yourselves either historians or memory experts, for it is not right that those who never philosophize should usurp the honorable title of philosopher. However, we should get back to shore in order not to enter an infinite ocean from which we could not get out all day.[101]

What Salviati outlines for the philosophers is also what Galileo had been advocating and fighting against with philosophy itself: finding a language in which the object and its linguistic term have a direct correspondence. Here, in the literary realm of being adrift in a sea of thought, a topos with significant weight for the Dantean Sagredo, Salviati establishes the dictum for the new philosophical individual. He concludes by directing Simplicio:

"come freely with reasons and demonstrations (yours or Aristotle's) and not with textual passages or mere authorities because our discussions are about the sensible world and not about a world on paper."[102] Salviati has not come to the discussion to debate textual interpretations. Terms have multiple meanings, definitions have various nuances, and even elements of syntax and composition can change the meaning of a text.

Simplicio, and to a certain extent Sagredo, continue to rely on this printed world, similar to Don Quixote's old tradition. Their allegiances are cast in military, political terms that create a discursive space for undermining the old paradigm. Not merely a topos, this labyrinth of philosophy dramatizes both Galileo's literary and his philosophical concerns. Sagredo sympathizes with Simplicio and imagines his internal reflections on the debate at hand, asking: "On whom shall we rely to resolve our controversies if Aristotle is removed from his seat? Which other author shall we follow in the schools, academies, and universities? Which philosopher has written on all parts of natural philosophy, so systematically, and without leaving behind even one particular conclusion?"[103] Sagredo's first concern, as he identifies with Simplicio, is the authority of the written word that sustains various institutions, with keeping the trustworthy guide through the confusion of natural phenomena. Sagredo describes the value of the Aristotelian library to a host of intellectuals calling it the "Prytaneum," or ancient Greek city hall:

> Must we then leave the building in which are sheltered so many travelers? Must we destroy that sanctuary, that Prytaneum, where so many scholars have taken refuge so comfortably, where one can acquire all knowledge of nature by merely turning a few pages, without being exposed to the adversities of the outdoors? Must we tear down that fortress where we can live safe from all enemy assaults?[104]

The Prytaneum fortress calls to mind the earliest monastic libraries, referred to as the *armarium* because the books were locked in cupboards or armoirs. A turn of phrase suggested that a monastery without an *armarium* was like a fort without an armory.[105] Sagredo's stylization of the Prytaneum recalls the monastic structure, isolated stalls and lecterns and a building itself removed from society with chained books and silence, not the technologies of book readers after the advent of the printing press. Sagredo indicates a kind of philosophy that is entirely denied by Galileo's prescriptions for intellectual investigation, and it further advances the war imagery surrounding Simplicio.[106] According to Battistini, the Prytaneum that Simplicio, with the help of Sagredo, hopes to defend is a symbol of *otium* and immobility, which supports my reading of Simplicio as representative of active rest.[107] Sagredo does, however, juxtapose travelers who temporarily shelter at this fortress with the scholars locked, closed, or otherwise operating behind its walls.

For the latter group, the world on paper of this sanctuary or labyrinth is a closed environment, hermetically and also hermeneutically sealed from the "adversities of the outdoors." No new ideas enter and these Arisotelian knights try desperately to preserve the textual walls that protect them. When Salviati responds, he is explicit that the current dispute is a matter of books:

> There is no danger that such a great multitude of clever and shrewd philosophers would allow themselves to be overcome by one or two noise-makers … It is inane to think of introducing a new philosophy by refuting this or that author; one must first learn to remake human brains and render them fit for distinguishing truth from falsehood, something that only God can do.[108]

The "noisemakers" in this criticism echo the metaphoric starlings and Saracens that similarly created such a din over comets in the *Assayer*. Salviati's comment suggests a capacity for change that is impossible in the Aristotelian system. At the end of the *Two New Sciences*, Simplicio still defends the fortress of Aristotelian philosophy, though nearly by presence alone since he is silent for much of that dialogue.

By such devotion to the written word, Sagredo and Simplicio, and more generally the Aristotelian philosophers, close off interpretative possibilities. They are the pedants so ridiculed by Galileo in his marginalia, and by the populace at large in Renaissance and early modern comedies. Salviati cleverly interjects, after Simplicio cites a long passage on luminosity without citing the author: "I am strongly of the opinion that you do not understand it either, but have committed to memory words written by somebody out of a desire to contradict and to show himself more intelligent than his opponent."[109] For Salviati, Simplicio is like Capra, who shows that he has ineptly stolen passages, or Tasso, who has indiscriminately borrowed from other poets. In Tibor Wlassics' study of the literary Galileo, he suggests that M. V. Giovine forces the identification of Tasso's pseudo-Aristotelianism with Galileo's character of Simplicio, but I suggest that they are linguistically and semantically related.[110] Salviati goes on to say that this desire to use someone else's words to show oneself to be more intelligent can only lead to a chain reaction of misinterpretation. Those who argue in such a way are "those who, in order to appear intelligent themselves, would applaud what they did not understand, and form the better opinion of people according to the deficiency of their own understanding; if indeed the author himself is not one of those (and there are many) who write of what they do not understand, and whose writings are therefore not understood."[111] With these key terms, Salviati identifies Simplicio as a companion of Tasso, Capra, and Sarsi. He also echoes Ariosto's warning to the lady readers of the *Furioso* not to read the canto on the unfaithfulness of women:

> Of no importance is the praise or blame
> Of vulgar folk, whose custom is to rail
> Against their betters and to talk the most
> On what they know the least of, like mine host.[112]

The avalanche of misdirection and confusion that results from this closed system of knowledge also resonates with what the physician William Gilbert, an influential author for the *Chief World Systems*, had to say thirty years earlier about the detritus of this battle in the preface to *On the Lodestone* (1600):

> so vast an ocean of books whereby the minds of the studious are bemuddled and vexed; of books of the more stupid sort whereby the common herd and fellows without a spark of talent are made intoxicated, crazy, puffed up; are led to write numerous books and to profess themselves philosophers, physicians, mathematicians, and astrologers, the while ignoring and contemning men of learning.[113]

In the same passage from the preface Gilbert goes on to criticize the "men who have taken oath to follow the opinions of others."[114] As a champion of precise definitions, a practioner of experiential learning, and a skeptic of the common opinions of professors, Gilbert was influential in more than one way for Galileo's philosophical and epistemological development.[115] Salviati will echo this sentiment nearly verbatim on the second day of the *Two New Sciences*, in reference to Gilbert's text.[116] Furthermore, Salviati's criticism suggests that Simplicio is like Don Quixote. At the beginning of Quixote's first sally, the undubbed knight dreams of the future publication of the chronicles of his deeds. The narrator describes the activity: "so he went on, stringing together absurdities, all of a kind that his books had taught him, imitating insofar as he was able the language of their authors."[117] While walking the thin line between logical fiction and absurd fiction, Galileo – via Salviati – and Gilbert before him, were certain to characterize other writing as fables and old wives' tales.[118]

Salviati himself takes part in a literary characterization of Simplicio that allows for criticism of him, his practices, and his philosophy. Unlike many of Galileo's predecessors in writing philosophical dialogues, where the figurative language exists for one exchange, the speakers in the *Chief World Systems* carry their metaphors throughout the dialogue, and the other interlocutors respond to that language, recognizing its implications. Simplicio holds the sword and shield throughout the *Chief World Systems*, and his interlocutors recognize his role as protector of the Prytaneum, the labyrinth in disguise.[119] Salviati explicitly says:

> It is his followers who have given authority to Aristotle, and not he who has usurped or taken it. Since it is easier to hide under someone else's shield than to show oneself openly, they are afraid and do not dare to go away by a single step; rather than putting any changes in the heavens of Aristotle, they insolently deny those which they see in the heavens of nature.[120]

Salviati uses this language of the battle of books throughout the dialogue. On the third day of the *Chief World Systems*, the interlocutors again return to the question of the structure of the universe, and Salviati says: "Against this position I see Simplicio comes well equipped, in particular with the sword and shield of the booklet of mathematical conclusions or disquisitions; it would be good to begin by proposing its attacks."[121] Simplicio's sword is outdated and outmatched. His book of Aristotelian precepts is akin to Don Quixote's copy of *Amadis of Gaul*. Simplicio, ensconced in the labyrinth, like Sagredo wandering the slopes of hell, chooses to be blind, chooses to have Salviati for a guide.

Salviati, literature, and the new philosopher

Salviati, as the interlocutor most commonly associated with Galileo, should then be not only a conglomerate of the characters of Simplicio and Sagredo, but also a product of the wide readings of his creator. Salviati can speak to Sagredo while he is awash in philosophical confusion, and to Simplicio while he meanders through his self-imposed labyrinth of tradition. But in order not to fall into the quagmire of these two images of the library, the philosophical hero must do something new and something salvific to turn the tides and guide his fellow intellectuals to the truth. Salviati is not exempt from the language of epic, but he uses it as a tool rather than as a defensive weapon. He is acutely aware of the path of their discussions and discoveries. If Simplicio is the failing quixotic champion of Aristotelian philosophy, Salviati becomes the knight-errant philosopher of the newly understood cosmos. As we have seen, he already identifies with Orlando at the point where he is about to go mad. His discourse is rife with metaphors, and he easily maneuvers between multiple systems of meanings in the dialogue, particularly in discussions of books. He debates Simplicio on his own territory, the language of epic battles, but with the instruments of the new science. As Salviati speaks he tells two narratives that reflect the epistemologies he embodies. The first describes the possible arrangement of the universe along with possible mechanisms that govern it. The second tells of the misfortunes and successes of Salviati the interlocutor.

Unlike Sagredo waiting for a guide to bring him to port, Salviati describes himself several times as the victim of a shipwreck, a very common element in the popular romance genre of the period.[122] He is not simply nauseous from nautical discussion, but tossed around by the process of investigating the tides. At the opening of the *Chief World Systems* Salviati says: "Quite willingly I will stop because I run the same risk [to be overcome by doubts], and step by step I am about to be lost, while it suits me to sail among rocks and such breaking waves that make me, as they say, lose my bearing."[123] The nautical metaphors return again with his statement: "I see we are once more going to engulf ourselves in a boundless sea … or sail forever lost."[124] After this comment Salviati once again guides the conversation away from general considerations, often ripe with digressions, back to a consideration of necessary demonstrations. His use of the metaphor of shipwreck usually signals the end of a digression, the moment before all is lost and there is little hope of returning to the original conversation topic.

Yet, in terms that recall the moral interpretations of the Pythagorean Y, toward the end of the third day of the *Chief World Systems* Salviati provides a version of the Galilean scientific method for approaching an investigation of the rationale behind previously unknown or unconfirmed conclusions: "One must be lucky enough right from the start to direct one's reasoning along the road of truth. When traveling along that road, it may easily happen that other propositions will be encountered which are recognized as true either through reason or experience."[125] Salviati here reconfigures the classical topos of the Pythagorean Y, the diverging paths of virtue and vice, that had been adopted by early Christian humanists. Salviati's presentation of this choice in discursive roads echoes with many of the early commentators on the Pythagorean Y such as Plato, Cicero, and Saint Jerome, but perhaps most closely with Lactantius, whom Galileo would have known from his library:

> The philosophers at least have been happy for one path to be the path of the virtues and the other the path of the vices, and for the one assigned to the virtues to be initially steep and rough going; if anyone overcomes its

difficulty and emerges on top, for the rest he has a level road, and beautiful open country, and he reaps a fine, rich reward for all his labours; but anyone deterred by the difficulty of the start slides off on to the path of vice, which is a pleasant path to begin with, and much more well trodden, but after a little more progress its pleasant appearance suddenly fades, and it becomes precipitous, rough with rocks at one moment, overgrown with brambles at another, and broken by fast flooding streams at a third, so that strain, stalling, slipping and falling are inevitable.[126]

Early commentators often associated this topos with Aeneas moving to the right in Tartarus, and Dante incorporates this structure into the *Comedy*.[127] Couched as a corrective to the Dantean journey that departs from the *diritta via*, Salviati's paths of intellectual pursuit are thwarted not by monsters, but by problems of logic.

Salviati fully represents the potential for a combined literary-philosophical methodology. The key difference between his language of expression and that of Simplicio or Sagredo is that he explains his descriptions of investigations being sparked by an observed effect, because: "Without this, ours would be a blind journey, or even one more uncertain than that; for we should not know where we wanted to come out, whereas the blind at least know where they wish to arrive."[128] Just like the researcher of sounds, without that contact with the physical world readers are trapped in the Prytaneum's world on paper and need a guide to lead them on the long climb out of the darkness.

Salviati is the Orlando who knows all without going mad, the hapless protagonist of the *romanzo* who is not diverted by the shipwreck, and the knight errant who sees many possible roads but chooses only the most logical among them, even if his journey happens at zigzags à la Ariosto instead of Tasso's straight plot-line. Moreover, Carlos Fuentes' description of Cervantes' literary project rings true with the philosophical challenges I see Salviati facing in literary terms:

> Navigating in a sea where the torments of renovation and the alga fields of immobility alternate, Cervantes must fight against the old and the new with an intensity infinitely superior to that of writers on the other side of the Pyrenees, who, without great dangers, can promote the parallel realms of reason, hedonism, capitalism, unrestricted faith in progress, and the optimism of history entirely oriented toward the future.[129]

One way that Salviati – and thereby Galileo – attempts to maneuver through these torments and dodge the pitfalls that such illicit topics invite is to speak explicitly about the fictional nature of his own statements.

The first example in the *Chief World Systems* occurs after Salviati has previously declared erroneous theories to be poetical, and he suggests that his own reasoning is not based in truth. Salviati breaks character on the second day, just after Sagredo mentions the delicate assayer's crucible, which will determine the refinement of their arguments. He says:

> Before proceeding further, I must tell Sagredo that in these discussions I act as a Copernican and play his part with a mask, as it were. However, in regard to the internal effect on me of the reasons I seem to advance in his favor, I do not want to be judged by what I say while we are involved in the enactment of the play; but what I say after I have put away the costume; for perhaps you will find me different from what you see when I am on stage.[130]

Salviati quickly and graciously bows to the edict as it was understood by Galileo – that the Copernican Theory could only be addressed as a fiction – so he identifies himself as a fictitious narrator. As Marsh points out, even in the Quattrocento, recantation within a dialogue was popular: "in an age in which unpopular or unorthodox opinions were subject to censure, a sort of moral immunity had to be provided for the speaker of an objectionable position."[131] Salviati later speaks of the drama in which he is involved while he also evokes imagery from the Fable of the Sounds. As he tries to reconcile his and Simplicio's author's calculations of the speed of an object falling from the Moon to the center of the Earth he says:

> Who does not know that in the dissection of some organ of an animal, there may be discovered infinite marvels of provident and most wise nature? Yet for every animal that the anatomist cuts up, a thousand are quartered by a butcher. Now in trying to satisfy your request, I do not know in which of the two costumes I shall make my appearance on the stage; yet taking heart from the spectacle put on by this author of Simplicio's, I shall not hold back from telling you – if I can remember it – the method which I used.[132]

Salviati specifically uses the language of theater to describe his approach to the question. His clever comment, like other self-referential statements, pulls the reader out of the fiction of the dialogue and reminds us of its status as a book. This observation is in line with scholarship on Galileo's role in defining the parameters of modern science, insofar as he participates in establishing a space for inventing that is defined by illusions and fictional definitions.[133] These comments ask readers if the fictional packaging truly negates the philosophical claims contained within it.

Salviati goes on further to enforce, and simultaneously dissolve, the literary, fictional nature of their discussion. He embraces his own fictionality and the very human *poesis* involved in generating their discussion. While speaking of digressions, he suddenly calls their conversation on philosophy an epic poem:

> I do not want this epic [*poema*] of ours to adhere so closely to poetic unity as to leave no room for episodes, for the introduction of which the lightest relevance ought to suffice. It should be almost as if we had met to tell stories, so that it is permitted for me to relate anything which hearing yours may call to my mind.[134]

Rather than a simple *poesia*, Galileo chooses to characterize his work as a *poema*, a term reserved for lengthy verse romances or epics. Salviati is well aware of the astructural nature of their discussion, but his admission suggests that the digressions, because they are not entirely separate from the main subject at hand, somehow change the genre of the dialogue to poetry, perhaps similarly to Ariosto's *Orlando furioso*.[135] In this way the dialogue can make obvious its own necessary literariness vis-à-vis conjecture, but also make the reader aware of the growing disjunction between the literary and philosophical. For a point of philosophical comparison, the editor of Christoph Clavius' 1591 edition of Sacrobosco's *Sphere*, discussed in the first chapter, includes marginal labels next to the text that say *Digressio* to help readers who seek linear explanations.[136] For early modern Italian readers, episodes in a *poema* would also recall the Ariosto–Tasso debates of earlier decades, in which one of the most obvious non-Aristotelian aspects of the *Orlando furioso* was its apparent lack of unity due to its episodic and digressive structure. Moreover, as a young man in Naples Tasso had been educated by the Jesuits and embraced Aristotelian poetics to a fault: both biographical details that strengthen the conflation of these philosophical debates of the early seventeenth century with the poetic disputes of the late sixteenth.

Salviati's use of "poem" invites a literary reading of the whole dialogue. In epic poetry, particularly the *Orlando furioso*, the entrelacement of plotlines necessitates and invites authorial interruptions. Giraldi had said that these breaks in narrative were a method of suspense, a way to keep people reading, but as Daniel Javitch says, by the time the reader returns to the interrupted story, "we hardly care" about the outcome.[137] In addition, each break reminds the reader of the fiction of the text. Javitch has shown that this digressive style irritated readers, so much so that later poets such as Bernardo Tasso edited their works to lessen the effect of shifting between narrative lines.[138] By calling attention to the literary sensibilities of readers of this fictional poetry, Galileo, via Salviati, pulls the reader out of the fiction of his philosophical discussion. At the literal level, this claim adheres to the edict of treating the Copernican Theory as a fiction, but because of its impact as a literary device, the statement also shakes the reader from that very sense of reading a fiction.

As master narrator, Salviati claims that the *Chief World Systems* is a comedy, a poem, and a collection of fables. Through Galileo's stylization these fictions are told by representatives of other popular literary genres – epic and romance poetry and their parody. But even these veils were not enough to prevent Galileo's censure, trial, and imprisonment. Between Salviati's comments on the poems and fables that make up the Copernican Theory in the *Chief World Systems* and his next reference to hidden meanings in his language, five years passed. In the interval, Galileo was tried by the Inquisition in 1633, he subsequently abjured any belief in the Copernican Theory of a heliocentric universe, and the Church issued the decree that all of his books supporting this heretical theory, written in the past or to be written in the future, be placed on the Index of Prohibited Books. Hence the reason the *The Two New Sciences* was smuggled out of Italy and published in Leiden in 1638. This final work does not address Copernicanism directly, but is presented as a continuation of the discussion in the *Chief World Systems*. The discussions take place in the Venetian Arsenal, a site that combines the practical matters of shipbuilding with theoretical mathematics and physics.[139] In the *Two New Sciences* Salviati assumes that certain ideas associated with a rotating Earth are true in order to carry out thought experiments related to kinetics. Also noteworthy is the near absence of literary content in the dialogue.

Thus, Salviati's next comment on the poetic fiction of theories of the structure of the universe appeared in a volume smuggled out of Italy to be published in a country where the Church censors did not hold sway. The changes in tone and message are striking. In his first demonstration of the *Two New Sciences* Salviati says: "Please observe, gentlemen, how facts which at first seem improbable will, even on scant explanation, drop the cloak which has hidden them and stand forth in naked and simple beauty."[140] Gone are the pleasant fictions of the *Chief World Systems*. With the correct explanation, that offered by the science of mechanics and kinetics, nature remains transparent. Later Sagredo intervenes with that observation that Antonello connected to Michelangelo's artistic theory: "This way of all knowledge being contained in a book is very similar to that by which a piece of marble contains within itself a very beautiful statue, or a thousand of them for that matter; but the point is to be able to discover them."[141] Sagredo goes on to dismiss astrologers and alchemists for searching for the mysteries of their arts in the fables of the ancient poets.[142] This is no longer delicate linguistic territory. For these Galilean interlocutors, the need for a veiled discussion has been removed.[143] The subtext for the *Two New Sciences* is no longer the poems or novellas of the *Chief World Systems*, but Galileo's treatise on motion. As literary creations of the Galilean author, reading a work by Galileo, they provide our final example of the literary nature of this philosophical project.

Though the figurative language to discuss these intellectual problems is limited, the speakers do occasionally adopt previous metaphors. At the end of the *Two New Sciences*, Simplicio still defends the fortress of Aristotelian philosophy, but without the figurative language of war or poetic language of the epic around him. Salviati continues to make reference to their errancy from the straight path of discussion.[144] Sagredo embraces this approach, moving him ever closer philosophically and poetically to Salviati, saying at one point: "Pray let us enjoy the advantages and privileges which come from conversation between friends, especially upon subjects freely chosen and not forced upon us, a matter vastly different from dealing with dead books which give rise to many doubts but remove none."[145] The Ariostan zigzag style now pairs well with Sagredo's desire for a living philosophy, even though he had sought a linear route in the *Chief World Systems*. Not only is this a philosophically viable method, it is also the method that Galileo suggests to Francesco Rinuccini for comparing the relative merits of Ariosto and Tasso as late as 1640.[146]

Galileo indicates to his readers the deliberate use and valuable foundation of these literary elements. Salviati carries out a geometric proof to resolve an Aristotelian paradox that can be experienced by watching a wheel turn one rotation and travel along the ground a distance equal to the circumference of the wheel. The hub on the axle, a concentric circle fixed in relation to the larger wheel, also moves the same horizontal distance even though its circumference is much smaller and it only completes one rotation. Salviati makes the Lucretian argument that the smaller circle is a polygon with an infinite number of sides that account for the apparent difference in circumferences. Simplicio raises concerns that these discussions of infinites and related indivisibles might lead them into dangerous discursive territory because of the Epicurean connotations of atomism.[147] Salviati concludes the subsequent demonstration by saying:

> In the course of our discussion it may happen that I shall awaken in you, and especially in Simplicio, objections and difficulties which in turn will bring to memory that which, without such stimulus, would have lain dormant in my mind. Allow me therefore the customary liberty of introducing

some of our human fancies [*umani capricci*], for indeed we may so call
them in comparison with supernatural truth which furnishes the one true
and safe recourse for decision in our discussions and which is an infallible
guide in the dark and dubious paths of thought [*scorte inerranti ne i nostri
oscuri e dubbii sentieri o più tosto labirinti*].[148]

Salviati calls out the human fancies that have been a common part of their
discussion. He evokes Simplicio's need for a safe enclosure, Sagredo's need
for a guide, and the still terrifying labyrinth of nature and natural philosophy. While Simplicio is relatively silent in the *Two New Sciences* and
Sagredo seems to display an evolving understanding of Galileo's new philosophy, Salviati maintains an unchanged identity as a figure who can speak
in terms of Simplicio's immobile epic and Sagredo's Dantean journey.

The page that opens the third day of *The Two New Sciences* marks yet
another change in the style of the dialogues. The page itself looks different
than previous days. Instead of announcing the interlocutors present or
identifying the speaker, it presents readers with the title *De motu locali* in
large font, followed by a Latin declaration of the importance of this new
information to human knowledge.[149] This is no longer the Italian first-person voice of the interlocutors, nor is it the Italian voice of Galileo author,
but a Latin plural voice, also written by Galileo and presumably read aloud
by Salviati.[150] Many of the demonstrations taken from this treatise can be
dated to as early as 1589-1592 in the drafts that exist of two unfinished
treatises and the unrealized *De motu antiquiora* dialogue.[151] In the latter,
Alessandro, a teaching figure who represents Galileo's philosophical position, and Domenicus, a general representation of Pisan students, discuss
principles of motion. Galileo started the work when he was still at Pisa,
and he made several changes, most notably the removal of the dialogue
structure, before its publication as a treatise in the *Two New Sciences* in
1638.[152] From these drafts we see that Galileo originally conceived at least
a portion of his treatise on motion as a dialogue itself, not to be the text
under discussion in a dialogue. The presence of the *De motu* as a treatise
only, and one in Latin, within the Italian dialogue combines both ends of
Galileo's intellectual career, making it circular, not linear.

After expending so much effort to establish literary figures who read
philosophical texts as though they were literary documents, Galileo's final
expression of the two epistemologies demonstrates that his new unpoet-
ical paradigm has been able to discover something that all of the literal
study of traditional poetic sources was never able to reveal. On the fourth
day of the *Two New Sciences* Sagredo interrupts to point out a connection between the author (Galileo) and Plato: a connection that Drake

has identified as the *Timaeus*, 38-39 on the composition of the universe.[153] Sagredo says:

> This conception is truly worthy of Plato; and it is to be all the more highly prized since its underlying principles remained hidden until discovered by our Author who removed from them the mask and poetical dress and set forth the idea in correct historical perspective. In view of the fact that astronomical science furnishes us such complete information concerning the size of the planetary orbits, the distances of these bodies from their centers of revolution, and their velocities, I cannot help thinking that our Author (to whom this idea of Plato was not unknown) had some curiosity to discover whether or not a definite "sublimity" might be assigned to each planet.[154]

Not only does the Accademico discover what has not been discussed before, but he finds the hidden meaning in texts that have been known for centuries. Of note here is the explicit mention of the "mask" and the "poetical dress" of Plato's dialogue, the *Timaeus*. Massimo Bucciantini has already pointed out the important distinction to be made here: Galileo reveals the natural law behind this poetic narration, not an allegorical fiction.[155] More than a concern for Platonism per se, I would argue that this is a declaration of method and a final emblem of the two epistemologies working to establish an authoritative new voice in natural philosophy. Simplicio has been played as a fool and is silently locked in place while Salviati is already wandering through the open landscape of the new philosophy, so it must be Sagredo to make this revelation. Sagredo is the voice of the didactic poets Lucretius and Manilius, used as models by Galileo; he is the character who encounters the truths of philosophy as Dante does those of the afterlife, and does so with the insecurities of Petrarch and Michelangelo. As the literary product of so much poetry, it is only fitting that he recognize and discard the poetry of natural philosophy.

After witnessing the conflict of these three literary figures, Galileo's own text – his voice, that is – seems like the logical choice for the new philosopher. The questions of decorum, themes of journeying, and insistence on direct correspondence between signifier and signified that play out in the literary content of the dialogues together champion a figure who is none other than Galileo himself. Battistini's statement seen earlier, "the scientist is like a wanderer," takes on additional implications when considered in the literary context I have provided for the speakers in the two dialogues.[156] To show that these elements of Quixote, Orlando, and Dante were at least in part recognized by contemporary readers, the conclusion will examine one response to Galileo's dialogues and its own attempts to access that literary tradition.

Conclusion

As Jonathan Culler has argued, the form and meaning of a text come from a reader's knowledge of its conventions and procedures.[1] Scipione Chiaramonti's self-defense shows that this literary space, though perhaps not the literary epistemology, in Galileo's prose was in part recognized by his adversaries, and is the strongest literary approach to refuting Galileo's arguments. Chiaramonti clearly understood the game afoot in the *Dialogue on the Two Chief World Systems*. He has been described as the most vicious opponent of Galileo, either for his dogged Aristotelianism or for reasons of professional jealousy. To preserve the Aristotelian tenet that the heavens were unchanging, he rigidly argued against Copernican supporters such as Kepler, and Tychonic supporters such as Orazio Grassi, that the new stars and comets were sublunar phenomena. For his efforts, Chiaramonti earned the derision and passionate criticism of many in Galileo's circle: Mario Guiducci, Cesare Marsili, and Benedetto Castelli, to name a few.[2] Galileo's response had been to treat Chiaramonti's position with sarcasm in the *Chief World Systems* and to have his work supported only by Simplicio. Chiaramonti responded close to one year later with a self-defense of the works that he felt had been attacked by Salviati in Galileo's dialogue: *Difesa di Scipione Chiaramonti da Cesena al suo Antiticone, o libro delle tre nuove stelle* (*Defense of Scipione Chiaramonti of Cesena of his "Antitycho"; or, Book of the Three New Stars* [Florence, 1633]).[3] While the work itself was panned before it even began to circulate, Chiaramonti's rebuttal is more elaborate than the back-and-forth that framed the early disputes between Delle Colombe and Alimberto Mauri. His defense is more stylized than Galileo's line-for-line parsing of Sarsi's *Libra*. Chiaramonti fuses the various structures of the previous debate, the treatise, close-reading, and dialogue, and carves out a space for his own voice within Galileo's text. For this reason it offers a way to examine the success of Galileo's own literary strategies employed in the dialogues.

In the *Difesa*, the author copies passages from the *Chief World Systems* and from his own writings into the body of the text, breaking apart paragraphs and exchanges between Galileo's interlocutors to insert his new defensive material. The French translator of the *Two New Sciences*, Marin Mersenne, had made similar adaptations to the text in *Nouvelles pensées de Galilée* (1639).[4] While Mersenne's approach is collaborative insofar as he adds recent sources and personal experience, Chiaramonti's is combative. Chiaramonti is clear about whose voice is whose: he indicates to readers all quoted passages by placing them in italics. He (or his editor) also includes indications in the margins as to where to find the passages mentioned in the body of the text when he does not cite verbatim. Beyond this revision of the *Chief World Systems* to include his own voice, Chiaramonti also adopts the literary style of Galileo's interlocutors; reinserts the poetry explicitly; and manipulates the voices of Salviati, Sagredo, and Simplicio.

The first book (*Parte prima*) of Chiaramonti's *Difesa* is a direct response to Galileo's criticism of his *Antiticone* (1611). He identifies three places in the *Chief World Systems* where the ideas in the *Antiticone* are called into question. Chiaramonti plays the game that Galileo had started by referring to him throughout the *Difesa* as the "Accademico," just as Simplicio, Sagredo, and Salviati had done. As Chiaramonti examines these three instances and defends himself against Galileo's criticism, the text appears very similar to the *Assayer*, in which passages from the book under scrutiny are copied out and then analyzed in prose. Chiaramonti's text is ripe with seemingly rhetorical questions, but they are not rhetorical at all – they are aimed at Galileo. After a number of spirited accusations, he concludes this first section by comparing the Accademico to a figure best described as a close rhetorical relative to the gambler, nursemaid, traveler to India, and cloth buyer used to describe Sarsi in the *Assayer*. The last line of the concluding chapter of the first book claims: "to me it seems that the Author has done accidently what that good lady did when after having posed her mouth while looking in the mirror spent the day in pain from hunger so that she did not disconfigure her composition until she could look in the mirror again."[5] Chiaramonti goes on to explain that because Galileo had selected sentences in isolation, without considering the prose that followed the phrases he quoted, he would quite literally be bitten as his *motteggi* (jokes or banter) became *punture* (stings) in the second section of the *Difesa*.[6]

The initial chapters of this second book follow the structure of the first, but at one moment in his self-defense, Chiaramonti laments that the point he tried to make was neither represented fairly by Galileo nor defended well by Simplicio. Before dramatically changing the structure and style of his defense, Chiaramonti recognizes the failed epic task of Simplicio, saying: "But neither is it well presented to my simple defender [*semplice mio difenditore*], nor is it answered by him in the words below."[7] What bothers Chiaramonti is a passage from the *Chief World Systems* that he copies into the *Difesa*: a moment from the second day of the dialogue in which Salviati is concerned with how objects in space can be judged to be immobile, and Simplicio quickly and readily agrees that Salviati's summary of Chiaramonti's approach is correct. Aside from slight spelling variations, Chiaramonti copies into his *Difesa* the exchange that prompts Simplicio's docile assent as it is spoken by Salviati, but Chiaramonti lists the speaker as "Accad.," his abbreviation for the Accademico, or Galileo, the unspeaking character so frequently mentioned in the dialogue.[8]

Chiaramonti begins an adaptation of the *Chief World Systems* at a moment in the dialogue when his own work, *De tribus novis stellis* (*On the Three New Stars*; 1628), has been called upon by Simplicio to defend another work, Johann Locher's *Disquisitiones mathematicae de controversiis et novitatibus astronomicis* (*Mathematical Disquisitions on Astronomical Controversies and Novelties* [Ingolstadt, 1614]). The book, referred to as the *Libretto* by the interlocutors, had surfaced during the sunspot debates. Written under the name of Scheiner's student, Locher, it is presumed to have been written by Scheiner himself in order to promote the Tychonic system as a revision of the theories of Martianus Capella.[9] Galileo used the book as an opportunity to attack Tycho. By adaptation, I mean that Chiaramonti starts inserting his own voice into the transcription of the *Chief World Systems* under the heading of "Chiar[amonti]."[10] He admits that Galileo has faithfully translated the passage from *De tribus novis stellis* and placed it in the mouth of Simplicio, but he is not satisfied with how his voice is represented. He takes the matter into his own hands: "The response follows, to which, for reasons of brevity, I will apply hand in hand the replies in the mode of dialogue."[11] Salviati's exchanges are given the heading "Acc.Sal[v].," or "Accad." Chiaramonti edits the passage from the second day of the dialogue, puts Simplicio's words under his own name, and breaks Salviati's single explanation into a series of shorter statements. He rearranges passages and inserts new lines into Galileo's work. In this first example of friendly revisions to a *Chief World Systems* passage, Chiaramonti's approach is a combination of rhetorical strategies. The first exchange from "Chiar." is a direct response to the "Acc.Salv." as though Chiaramonti had participated in the fictionalized discussion, but his second statement is an extratextual criticism of that same discussion. He does the same in the other interjections in this chapter of the *Difesa*. At the start of the next chapter, Chiaramonti recognizes his departure from the structure of the previous section, saying: "But returning from the dramatic to the narrative ..."[12]

This structure begins to shift more toward the dialogue and away from the analytical defensive treatise as Chiaramonti places himself in dialogue with Simplicio too. He addresses the reader about Simplicio's statements: "But permit me to keep for its richness the response that he makes Simplicio say for me; I will place the words and I will return to the dialogue for greater evidence."[13] In this conversation with Simplicio, Chiaramonti recognizes that Simplicio has been inspired by him, saying in response to one of Simplicio's paraphrases of the *De tribus novis stellis*: "This, I, who am the role, do not say."[14] Elsewhere Chiaramonti declares: "This Peripatetic Simplicio is simple, and little accurate with his responses."[15] Simplicio then falls out of the rewritten discussion, and Chiaramonti speaks directly with the Accademico.

At this point, the engagement with Galileo's text becomes even more indicative of the literary and critical elements that readers saw in the *Chief World Systems*. While arguing that Galileo's logic is faulty, Chiaramonti provides a catalog of similarly illogical statements: if something is a man, it is an animal, but if it is not a man, it is also not an animal; if one is Florentine, one is Italian, but if one is not Florentine, one is not Italian; and finally: "Here is another example for you: if someone doesn't have hands, he will not strike like Scanderbergh, this is true. But 'he who has hands will strike like Scanderbergh' is false, because I have hands and I am far from being able to do that."[16] Scanderbergh is none other than the fifteenth-century Albanian hero George Skanderbeg, hero of Margherita Sarrocchi's *Scanderbeide*, mentioned in Chapter 1 for having been sent in draft form to Galileo for commentary. This would seem a peculiar, illogical syllogism to include in the list, were it not for Galileo's reputation regarding Ariosto, and the acknowledged extensive epic theme that underlies the *Chief World Systems* and the earlier *Assayer*.

By the third example from the *Difesa*, Chiaramonti has stopped identifying the individual speakers of the *Chief World Systems* in the passages he rewrites. Not only does he equate Salviati's voice with the Accademico, but here even the statements of Simplicio and Sagredo are placed under the heading "Accad." On the last page of the *Difesa* Chiaramonti will explain that he omitted mention of Salviati or Sagredo by name in order to honor their memories.[17] The argument at hand is about the difference between motion and rest, and Chiaramonti breaks apart a long statement by Sagredo, who interrogates Simplicio about *De tribus novis stellis* at the end of the second day. After he declares that Sagredo's statements misrepresent his text, Chiaramonti says: "Regarding me, he swapped my view, since not only do I say they are not incompatible, but that they are the same principle, and the Peripatetics say this with me, of whom he now dares to make a shield for himself, and from whose arsenal he dares to take arms, but in handling them he has been left wounded."[18] Chiaramonti has pieced together various phrases from the battle imagery of the *Chief World Systems* and recast them here to use as part of his rhetorical weaponry of defense, yet absent the consistency of application or function to produce knowledge or challenge epistemologies.

Chiaramonti begins to match Galileo step for step as the *Difesa* continues, but without the literary complexity or deep philosophical implications for Chiaramonti's project. In a moment of frustration, he includes his first quotation from poets:

> who does not know that the truth consists in adjusting our intellects to things, not the things to our intellects? I say this, that if we do not have a way to understand and penetrate the nature of things and draw true cognition from them, which is necessary for philosophizing, to what end should he line his papers and others theirs? Better would be that saying *Altum nihil agere* of Pliny. And one ought to say with that poet: *I counsel him to work at something else.*[19]

The Pliny referred to here is not the author of the *Natural History* that is so important to many earlier discussions of astronomy, but Pliny the Younger. Chiaramonti paraphrases the sentiment from one of Pliny's letters: "Satius est enim … otiosum esse quam nihil agere," loosely translated as "it is better to have nothing to do than to do nothing." Chiaramonti's poet is Torquato Tasso, and the verse is from the second scene of the second act of the pastoral drama *Aminta*, in which Dafne reproaches Tirsi for suggesting that Aminta be respectful of the lady that he loves: "A lover too respectful is undone. / I counsel him to work at something else / since he is such a one."[20] Following upon the ways in which Galileo used citations from Ariosto as hidden insults to his opponents, we must ask if this use of Tasso can be seen in the same way. Chiaramonti's truncated allusion suggests that Galileo is not suited for his role as his philosopher, just as Aminta is apparently not aggressive enough to be a good lover. The implications of the line cannot be pushed further, since that would imply that Galileo should be even more aggressive in his approach and less respectful, something that Chiaramonti's criticism of the *Chief World Systems* generally recommends against.

Rather than elaborate upon the literary space that is working to undermine his own philosophical epistemology, Chiaramonti instead returns
to the very source of that paradigm, the poetic witnesses, and he uses the
traditional poetic sources as particularly dangerous weapons. In response
to Galileo harshly dismissing one of his passages as "paralogism" and "rhetorical conjecture" Chiaramonti responds that the best way to defend his
work will be again to step foot into written dialogue with Galileo. He
writes: "For this we will do well to see if in exchange for syllogizing I have
paralogized, and for me myself to enter into the rather usurped dialogue
with the Accademico."[21] In so doing, Chiaramonti breaks apart Salviati's
lengthy paragraph on the appopriateness of the Copernican metaphor for
the Sun as God at the center of the universe and defends himself with
quotations from Lucretius. Chiaramonti is well aware of the relationship
between Galileo's thought and Lucretius, grouping the didactic poet among
the "fautori degli atomi, graditi dal Saggiatore" ("champions of atoms,
agreeable to the Assayer"), who nevertheless say that the Earth sits at rest at
the center of the universe as the stars move around her. To prove his point,
he cites two lines from Lucretius and insists: "Wherefore it is not just of
Aristotle and the Peripatetics, such a Universe, but of the ruling assemblies
[*centuriati comiti*] of the men of letters."[22] Like Piccolomini, Chiaramonti
continues with the idea of the marriage of poetry and philosophy. Here
he tries to undo Galileo with what he sees as his own weapons, the verses
of Lucretius. Given the tensions created by the Lucretian undertones of
Sagredo's methodology and Salviati's demonstrations, Chiaramonti's rec-
lamation of this epic didactic poet perhaps is also an attempt to re-establish
the epistemology that Galileo had undermined in the *Chief World Systems*.

Rather than defend or otherwise justify this poetic philosophy,
Chiaramonti continues this section of dialogue for four more pages,
inserting his rebuttals into Salviati's statement, and with false humility admits that he is similar to Ovid himself. After the final objection,
Chiaramonti says:

> Here I will finish the Dialogue, since it adds nothing, if not to talk of the
> site of the great orb between Venus and Mars later, and in the meantime
> saying that they need to leave behind rhetorical flowers and await demon-
> strations. And I will hold onto this praise for being a great rhetor, since even
> though I had every other intent, I was nevertheless rhetorical, in the guise
> of Ovid in poetry: "Anything I set out to say turned into verse." But he
> attempts with these little things [*cosuccie*] to divert the spirit of the reader
> away from the strength of the argument, something that I do not think will
> happen with the learned.[23]

The quotation is from Ovid's *Tristia*, the verse autobiography of the Roman poet, and is Ovid's response to an attempt to stop writing in meter after his father's complaint that a poet earns no money. Returning to the poetic roots of philosophy, Chiaramonti declares that he is akin to the earliest poets. By calling himself Ovid, Chiaramonti immediately inserts himself into the poetic-philosophical paradigm Galileo had tried to discredit when he contrasted the book of nature with the *Aeneid* and the *Odyssey*.

Chiaramonti frequently inserts himself into the dialogue throughout the rest of the *Difesa*, and his use of poets – particularly epic poets – gradually develops into a style closer to that employed by Galileo in the *Chief World Systems*. As Chiaramonti examines the ways in which Galileo slandered him, he yet again includes his own voice in the dialogue:

> My dear Mr. Accademico, let it be permitted me to say again with that poet: "frank sentiments in simple words and few [*Liberi sensi in semplici parole*]." Your grief, which I have written and printed, works against your reputation, not mine, which you secretly know, because the things written by me make all too evident the contrast against your presumptuousness to undo Aristotle. Meanwhile, though, you artfully procure faith in yourself by simulating benevolence.[24]

Here the quotation comes from the *Gerusalemme liberata*: "I shall respond just as I always do – / frank sentiments in simple words and few."[25] Goffredo speaks these lines to the famous flatterer Alete when he arrives in the Christian camp to suggest that they retreat from battle with the Egyptian King. Chiaramonti chooses to identify with Tasso's hero, portrayed as the savior of Jerusalem. By implication, Galileo, or his interlocutors, would be the slippery-tongued Alete, who tries to ruin the Christian forces. The choice of verse emphasizes the strength of Aristotle by Chiaramonti's selection of his retort from the heroic poem that purported to follow Aristotelian precepts for poetic composition.

Chiaramonti does not rely entirely on Tasso for his emotional responses to the attacks that he feels Galileo perpetrates against his work, turning rather to Galileo's favorite poet for stinging insults. When Salviati laments the high praise that Chiaramonti has received for his intelligence and ability to defend the Peripatetics against the *schiera* of astronomers, Chiaramonti's response is literary. To Salviati's bellicose imagery, Chiaramonti responds with two references to Ariosto. The first involves the false humility of the poet: "What great glory is it that the Accademico permits me. Ariosto contented himself that more than four might tip their hats to him, and I have nothing other than 100 Peripatetics, 99 of whom place me above the greatest intellects that exist?"[26] Chiaramonti concludes this passionate chapter on the Accademico's use of *maledicenze* (blasphemies) against him with a passionate self-defense that also includes Ariosto. He provides a history lesson of how the Peripatetics have withstood other attacks and acts incredulous at Galileo's tone: "And you write about the Peripatetics as the most obtuse intellects and inept men under the sun? *Like sheep, futile and unshriven* [*Come di greggi inutili, e mal nati*]."[27] The last line of this passage, and therefore the section, comes from the *Orlando furioso* at the moment in which the poet claims that even in his time there is evidence that God has sent as punishment scourges such as Atila and Ezzelino: "And to us, sheep-like, futile and unshriven, / Ferocious wolves as guardians [He] has given."[28] With the quotation from the *Furioso* he recognizes Galileo's specific use of Ariosto to attack the Aristotelians. Chiaramonti characterizes the Peripatetics as victims of Galileo, here portrayed as a scourge of God, and uses his favorite poet to punctuate the declaration. In this instance he could be said to attempt the "anything you can do, I can do better" approach to poetry that Galileo had adopted with his own poetic citations in the *Assayer*.

Aside from reiterating his philosophical arguments, Chiaramonti also engages with the various literary and philosophical aspects of the characters of the *Chief World Systems* in a way that suggests his comprehension of their larger epistemological significance. When Salviati says that he feels nauseous after reading the book, Chiaramonti replies to Galileo:

> The Accademico must have an upset stomach for some other reason, because neither are my calculations false, nor is the investigation of parallaxes demonstrated by their differences. He only lowers himself to saying that the observations of the astronomers were erroneous. His nausea must therefore be against those astronomers that erred, and not against my book, which until this point contains no errors.[29]

In a work on the tides, where the implications of explaining tidal changes are directly related to establishing the rotation and orbit of the Earth, Chiaramonti's rebuttal also seems to imply a neutralization of the larger, implied threat of this literary moment.

During another small narrative moment in the *Chief World Systems*, Chiaramonti's presumed reaction to the rejection of his measurements that would place the new star below the lunar sphere is compared to an unhappy farmer surveying his ruined crops.[30] Given that comets were popularly considered to be omens of crop blight, extreme weather, and

other disastrous phenomena, Sagredo's vignette could be said to dramatize the Aristotelian comet as a meteorological event, just as Chiaramonti
argues it to be. Chiaramonti's response recasts two of Galileo's favorite
means of attacking an opponent: analogies with the visual arts and support from his favorite epic poem. Chiaramonti replies by citing Boccaccio,
Michelangelo, and Tasso in an elaborate condemnation of Galileo's
practices:

> You would be marvelous at painting the Baronci family, and would take
> the victory from Michelangelo when he won the bet with the other paint-
> ers. But to your point, what you didn't guess is that even if one cannot say
> (about me) what is said about Solimano ... "with dry / Eye you watched
> your realm be destroyed," nonetheless in my day I have withstood several
> encounters with a confident spirit.[31]

The first part of this comment comes from a story told by Boccaccio in
the *Decameron* (VI.6). In order to trick his friends into paying for his
dinner, the quick-tongued storyteller Michele Scalza proves that the
Baronci family are the most noble of Florentine lineages because they
are the oldest. His evidence is the ugly faces of the family, an obvious
sign that they were designed early in creation when God was still learning
how to paint, according to Scalza. When considered through the lens of
Boccaccio's struggle with Dante's rejection of Epicureanism, the Baronci
story anticipates the later problematic embrace of Epicurean materialism
by Cavalcanti in *Decameron*, VI.9.[32] Chiaramonti ironically praises Galileo
as the inept, fallible, and very human artisan that he feels Epicureanism
makes of any deity. The quick reference to this story seems to cut to the
quick of the materialist, atomist, and Epicurean/Lucretian debates surrounding much of the *Chief World Systems*. Rather than equating Galileo's
tale of the farmer dismayed by ruined crops with the very successful realism of Boccaccio's *novella*, Chiaramonti essentially uses Galileo's own
weapons of literary rhetoric against him to imply more than an inferior
skill worthy only of base and ugly subjects.

The second part of the accusation wryly suggests that this style of painting would be superior to Michelangelo pretending to be the worst, mocking among other things Galileo's frequent comparisons of philosophy to
the visual arts. Chiaramonti borrows an anecdote from Vasari's biography
of the artist:

> In his youth, being once with his painter-friends, they played for a sup-
> per for him who should make a figure most completely wanting in design
> and clumsy, after the likeness of the puppet-figures which those make who

know nothing, scrawling upon walls; and in this he availed himself of his memory, for he remembered having seen one of those absurdities on a wall, and drew it exactly as if he had had it before him, and thus surpassed all those painters – a thing difficult for a man so steeped in design, and accustomed to choice works, to come out of with credit."[33]

This competition of feigned incompetence is won not by artistic skill but by recalling an appropriate example from memory. Chiaramonti strips the tale of its courtly implications of *sprezzatura* and virtuosity, focusing only on the ugly and clumsy product that he feels Galileo has created. Where Galileo had argued that practice upon previous works, paintings or texts, does not alone create a skilled artist or author, Chiaramonti uses Vasari's story with its emphasis on memory both to remind readers of the success of that strategy and to imply Galileo's inferiority.

Chiaramonti ends with a quotation from the *Gerusalemme liberata* that completes this threefold attack on the literariness of Galileo's dialogues and makes clear that he feels he has read between the literary lines. He compares himself to a hardened veteran of war who sees his son killed: "You Soliman, weeping ... who stood by / while your realm was destroyed, and your eyes dry."[34] The moment of emotion is short; Soliman's pity for the dead child quickly turns to rage against his murderer. Chiaramonti defiantly presents himself as the opposite of a farmer defeated by a late-season tempest. He declares with this poetic manuever that he has recognized the rhetorical tricks at play and will not lament his losses, only seek revenge for the damage done to him.

Even with the tripartite literary insult to Galileo in the last example, Chiaramonti's attempts to counter Galileo's style are still not as elaborate as the literary-philosophical prose challenge set before him. Chiaramonti's interspersed rebuttals recognize the weapons of this war of words, but are not as consistently steeped in the books or literature that their predecessor had established as the foundations for passionate, emotive, and effective epistemological space. This characteristic is indicative of a general trend in philosophical literature after Galileo, who was well acknowledged as the master in this arena. Literary critics such as Lanfranco Caretti see in Galileo's descendants that even though they share the lucid prose of their master, they are similar to either the dryly technical Buonaventura Cavalieri or the overly elegant Lorenzo Magalotti.[35] Similarly, Peter Armour argues that Galileo found a middle route through the two contradictory trends of Seicento fiction – what he calls "rigid preceptism and extravagant innovation."[36] This middle ground seems to have been difficult to achieve in the philosophical dialogue format. Dialogues inspired by Galileo's work included a projected piece by Cavalieri with Benedetto Castelli as Cavaliere, Cesare Marsili as a Sagredo figure, and Usulpa Ginuldus (anagram of Paulus Guldinus) as the Simplicio character, in *Geometria indivisibilibus continuorum nova quadam ratione promota* (*Geometry, Developed by a New Method through the Indivisibles of the Continua*; 1653). Joining Cavalieri's dialogue is Paolo Casati's *Terra machinis mota* (1658), a conversation among three voices: Galileo, Marin Mersenne, and Paolo Guldino. Future study will reveal the level to which these authors tried to incorporate the elements of style noted by authors as early as Delle Colombe and as late as Chiaramonti.

The ways that epic poetry and the protagonists of popular fiction made their way into Galileo's philosophical project indicates the permeability of these genres at a time when most critics would argue that the two had been separated, and when Galileo himself claimed that they should be so. With one hand Galileo suggests a separation of literal poetry from mathematics; with the other he drafts the literary elements of that same poetry into his attacks on philosophers in order to generate a new idea and model the behavior of the new philosopher. The result makes his final works even more closely assimilated to his favorite poem than just a matter of a few citations. What Peter DeSa Wiggins has said of the *Furioso* could also apply to the *Chief World Systems*: it is an antidote to dogma and, in that regard, a precursor to the novel.[37] This literary analysis supports Antonello, who follows Battistini when they place Galileo in "a system with a novelistic aspect," which Antonello defines as: "the dissolution of a unifying cosmology; a plurilinguism that crosses social levels, genres, and rhetorical conventions; the mask; the parodic-ironic intent; the dialogic structure of the story."[38] Accordingly, Antonello posits Galileo as the Italian representative among the other European masterpieces of the period: *Don Quixote* and *Gargantua*. Such connections are what have allowed critics to place Galileo in a literary genealogy that includes Leopardi, Manzoni, and Calvino.[39] With an understanding of just how Boiardo, Ariosto, Tasso, Cervantes, and other authors of the Italian poetic tradition became part of Galileo's philosophical process, now this affinity can be seen as the true literary genealogy that it is, paving the way for an expanded application of this paradigm for other genres and intellectuals.

Notes

INTRODUCTION

1 For the most recent work on the subject, and related bibliography, see Andrea Battistini, "Galileo tra letteratura e scienza," in *Galileo scienziato, filosofo, scrittore: a quattro secoli dal "Sidereus nuncius,"* ed. Piero Di Pretoro and Rita Lukoshik (Munich: Martin Meidenbauer, 2011), 109–123.

2 Tycho Brahe, *De mundi aetheri recentioribus phaenomenis liber secundus* (Frankfurt: Tampachium, 1610), 286.

3 Eileen Reeves, *Galileo's Glassworks: The Telescope and the Mirror* (Cambridge, MA: Harvard University Press, 2008), 16–21.

4 See also David Quint, *Epic and Empire: Politics and Generic Form from Virgil to Milton* (Princeton University Press, 1993).

5 Patrick Grant, *Literature and the Discovery of Method in the English Renaissance* (Athens: University of Georgia Press, 1985).

6 Isabelle Pantin, *La poésie du ciel en France dans la seconde moitié du seizième siècle* (Geneva: Librairie Droz, 1995).

7 *Ibid.*, 485–491.

8 See Francis Yates, *The Art of Memory* (University of Chicago Press, 2001); and Lina Bolzoni, *Le stanze della memoria* (Turin: Einaudi, 1995).

9 Pierre Gassendi, *Petri Gassendi Diniensis ecclesiae praepositi, et in academia parisiensi Matheseos regii professoris Opera omnia in sex tomos diuisa,* 6 vols., Vol. IV (Lyon: Anisson & Deuenet, 1658), 10.

10 F. Lucius Ferraris, *Prompta bibliotheca,* 8 vols., Vol. V (Paris: J.-P. Migne, 1854), 273–274.

11 Brian Vickers, *Francis Bacon and Renaissance Prose* (Cambridge University Press, 1968), 157.

12 Elizabeth Spiller, *Science, Reading, and Renaissance Literature: The Art of Making Knowledge, 1580–1670* (Cambridge University Press, 2004), 15. On the broader appeal of the genre to Renaissance readers, see Andrew Pettegree, *The Book in the Renaissance* (New Haven: Yale University Press, 2010), 151–171.

13 Spiller, *Science, Reading, and Renaissance Literature*; Juliet Cummins and David Burchell, eds., *Science, Literature and Rhetoric in Early Modern England* (Burlington, VT: Ashgate, 2007); and Howard Marchitello, *The Machine in the Text: Science and Literature in the Age of Shakespeare and Galileo* (Oxford University Press, 2011).

14 See Maria Luisa Altieri Biagi, *Galileo e la terminologia tecnico-scientifica* (Florence: Olschki, 1965).

15 See James J. Murphy, "One Thousand Neglected Authors," in *Renaissance Eloquence: Studies in the Theory and Practice of Renaissance Rhetoric*, ed. James J. Murphy (Berkeley: University of California Press, 1983), 20–36; and Wayne A. Rebhorn, ed. and trans., *Renaissance Debates on Rhetoric* (Ithaca, NY: Cornell University Press, 2000).

16 Jean Dietz Moss, *Novelties in the Heavens: Rhetoric and Science in the Copernican Controversy* (University of Chicago Press, 1993), 1–23.

17 See Aviva Rothman, "Forms of Persuasion: Kepler, Galileo and the Dissemination of Copernicanism," *Journal for the History of Astronomy* 40 (2009): 403–419.

18 See Erwin Panofsky, *Galileo, Critic of the Arts* (The Hague: Martinus Nijhoff, 1954).

19 Fernand Hallyn, *The Poetic Structure of the World: Copernicus and Kepler*, trans. Donald M. Leslie (New York: Zone Books, 1993), 20.

20 Translation found in S. K. Heninger, *Touches of Sweet Harmony: Pythagorean Cosmology and Renaissance Poetics* (San Marino, CA: Huntington Library, 1974), 289. The original is found in Dante Alighieri, *Divina commedia*, with commentary by Cristoforo Landino (Florence, 1481), fo. 8v.

21 See Anthony Grafton's first chapter on the Quattrocento world of books in *Commerce with the Classics: Ancient Books and Renaissance Readers* (Ann Arbor: University of Michigan Press, 1997), 11–52.

22 Rebecca Bushnell, *A Culture of Teaching: Early Modern Humanism in Theory and Practice* (Ithaca, NY: Cornell University Press, 1996), 129.

23 Ann Blair, "Humanist Methods in Natural Philosophy: The Commonplace Book," *Journal of the History of Ideas* 53.4 (1992): 541–555 (543).

24 Grafton, *Commerce with the Classics*, 63.

25 See Dietz Moss, *Novelties*, 34–46.

26 Paul R. Mueller, S.J., "Textual Criticism and Early Modern Natural Philosophy: The Case of Marin Mersenne (1588–1648)," in *The Word and the World: Biblical Exegesis and Early Modern Science*, ed. Kevin Killeen and Peter J. Forshaw (New York: Palgrave Macmillan, 2007), 78–90 (79).

27 Grafton, *Commerce with the Classics*, 224.

28 See Bushnell's chapter, "Harvesting Books," in *A Culture of Teaching*, 117–143.

29 David Quint, *Origin and Originality in Renaissance Literature: Versions of the Source* (New Haven: Yale University Press, 1983), 1–31.

30 *Ibid.*, x.

31 Grafton, *Commerce with the Classics*, 75–76.

32 Paolo Donati, *Theoriche, overo, Speculationi intorno alli moti celesti* (Venice: Osana, 1575), fo. 19r. The original reads: "se Platone fu di questo parere, che le Stelle si movessero per lor medesime è certo, ch'in questo anco egli s'ingannò. Delle bugie di Erodoto chi dubita, essendo ei stimato da tutti un'historico favoloso? Et Pomponio Mella [*sic*] non racconta questo come cosa vera, ma si

come cosa molto maravigliosa, & impossibile da credere." All translations are mine unless otherwise noted.

33 See T. R. Grill, "Galileo and Platonist Methodology," *Journal of the History of Ideas* 31.4 (1970): 501–520.

34 Grafton, *Commerce with the Classics*, 58.

35 All information about Galileo's library, unless otherwise noted, comes from three works by Antonio Favaro: "La libreria di Galileo Galilei, descritta ed illustrata," *Bullettino di bibliografia e storia delle scienze matematiche e fisiche* 19 (1886): 219–293; "Appendice prima alla libreria di Galileo Galilei," *Bullettino di bibliografia e storia delle scienze matematiche e fisiche* 20 (1887): 372–376; and "Appendice seconda alla libreria di Galileo Galilei," in *Scampoli galileiani* Ser. II, Vol. XII (1895–1896): 44–50, repr. in Antonio Favaro, *Scampoli galileiani*, ed. Lucia Rossetti and Maria Luisa Soppelsa (Trieste: LINT, 1992), 368–374.

36 Lisa Jardine, *Francis Bacon: Discovery and the Art of Discourse* (Cambridge University Press, 1974), 4.

37 William Shea, "Looking at the Moon as Another Earth: Terrestrial Analogies and Seventeenth-Century Telescopes," in *Metaphor and Analogy in the Sciences*, ed. Fernand Hallyn (Dordrecht: Kluwer, 2000), 83–104 (83).

38 Gabriel Naudé, *Advice on Establishing a Library*, trans. and ed. Archer Taylor (Berkeley: University of California Press, 1950), 19–20, 35–36. Naudé indicates Copernicus, Kepler, and Galileo specifically among "more than thirty or forty authors of reputation" who have written against Aristotle and should be included (24).

39 See Brendan Dooley, *Morandi's Last Prophecy and the End of Renaissance Politics* (Princeton University Press, 2002), 35–58.

40 See Maria Teresa Biagetti, *La biblioteca di Federico Cesi* (Rome: Bulzoni, 2008).

41 Jardine, *Francis Bacon*, 179.

42 *Ibid.*, 202. See also Vickers, *Francis Bacon and Renaissance Prose*, 174–201.

43 Vickers, *Francis Bacon and Renaissance Prose*, 200.

44 For the case of Bruno, see Janis Vanacker and Sabine Verhulst, "Atteone furioso: La caccia alla divina conoscenza negli *Eroici furori* di Giordano Bruno," *Rivista di storia della filosofia* 65.4 (2010): 695–717.

45 William Eamon, "Science as a Hunt," *Physis* 31 (1994): 393–432 (396, 401).

46 Peter Apian, *Cosmographia, siue, Descriptio vniuersi orbis* (Antwerp: Withagius, 1584), ii (my translation). The original reads: "extant enim passim litterarum clarissimis testata monumentis, summorum Principum ac Heroum res gestae: quibus quam sit Matheseos Cosmographiaeque cognitio utilis ac necessaria."

47 Pierpaolo Antonello, "Galileo scrittore e la critica: Analisi stilistica e interdisciplinarietà," *Quaderni d'italianistica* 23.1–2 (2002): 25–48 (26; my translation). The original reads: "esiti artistico-letterari con gli intenti intellettuali, la formazione storico-sociale con l'impresa scientifica." For a summary of the research completed on Galileo in this area see Giovanni Baffetti, "Scienza e scrittura letteraria: La lezione di Galileo," *Galilaeana* 2 (2005): 301–306.

Portions of the research in this chapter were funded with the support of an Andrew W. Mellon Foundation Fellowship at the Huntington Library, a New Faculty General Research Fund grant from the University of Kansas, and a Salvatori Research Award from the Center for Italian Studies at the University of Pennsylvania.

1 Galileo Galilei, *Le opere di Galileo Galilei: Edizione nazionale sotto gli auspici di Sua Maestà il Re d'Italia*, ed. Antonio Favaro and Isidoro del Lungo, 20 vols. in 21, Vol. X (Florence: G. Barbèra, 1963–1966 [1890–1909]), 423 (my translation). The collection will be referred to as *Opere* throughout, followed by a volume number and page number (e.g., *Opere*, X, 423). The original reads: "Putat enim hoc hominum genus, philosophiam esse librum quendam velut Eneida et Odissea; vera autem non in mundo aut in natura, sed in confrontatione textuum (utor illorum verbis), esse quaerenda. Cur tecum diu ridere non possum?"

2 See Mario Biagioli's excellent discussion of this topos in *Galileo's Instruments of Credit* (University of Chicago Press, 2007), 233–235.

3 Translation in Galileo Galilei, *The Assayer*, trans. Stillman Drake and C. D. O'Malley, in Galileo Galilei, Orazio Grassi, Mario Guiducci, and Johann Kepler, *The Controversy on the Comets of 1618* (Philadelphia: University of Pennsylvania Press, 1960), 183. For analysis of this topos and relevant bibliography, see Eugenio Garin, *La cultura filosofica del rinascimento italiano* (Florence: Sansoni, 1961), 451–465.

4 See Biagioli, *Instruments of Credit*, 242.

5 Galileo, *Assayer*, 183–184.

6 See Albert Van Helden, *The Invention of the Telescope* (Philadelphia: American Philosophical Society, 2008 [1977]); and Carmelo Greco, "Scienza e teatro in G. B. Della Porta," in *Letteratura e scienza nella storia della cultura italiana* (Palermo: Manfredi Editori, 1982), 429–451.

7 See Giambattista Della Porta, *Gli duoi fratelli rivali/The Two Rival Brothers*, ed. and trans. Louise George Clubb (Berkeley: University of California Press, 1980), 3–6. See also William Eamon, *Science and the Secrets of Nature: Books of Secrets in Medieval and Early Modern Culture* (Princeton University Press, 1994); and Louise Clubb, *Giambattista Della Porta, Dramatist* (Princeton University Press, 1965).

8 See Rita Belladonna, introduction to Alessandro Piccolomini, *Alessandro (L'Alessandro)*, trans. and ed. Rita Belladonna (Ottawa: Dovehouse Editions, 1984), 5–17.

9 Tycho Brahe, *Epistolarum astronomicarum libri* (Frankfurt: Tampachium, 1610), 277–281.

10 Anthony Grafton, *Commerce with the Classics: Ancient Books and Renaissance Readers* (Ann Arbor: University of Michigan Press, 1997), 206.

11 *Opere*, IX, 7–57, 196–209, 212–229. See also the recent edition of the Dante lectures: Galileo Galilei, *Due lezioni all'Accademia fiorentina circa la figura,*

sito e grandezza dell'Inferno di Dante, ed. Riccardo Pratesi (Livorno: Sillabe, 2011). For a recent overview of Galileo poems and comedies, see Antonio Daniele, "Galileo letterato," in *Attualità di Galileo Galilei nella vita scientifica di oggi e di domani: Rapporti con la chiesa e con gli scienziati europei* (Padua: Il Poligrafo, 2009), 35–50.

12 These instances can be found throughout Tycho Brahe, *Astronomiae instauratae mechanica: Facsimile Reprint of Wandesburg, 1590* (Brussels: Culture et Civilisation, 1969).

13 See Adam Mosley, *Bearing the Heavens: Tycho Brahe and the Astronomical Community of the Late Sixteenth Century* (Cambridge University Press, 2007), 1–30.

14 Alessandro Piccolomini, *La Sfera del Mondo di M. Alessandro Piccolomini di nuovo da lui ripolita, accresciuta et fino a sei libri di quattro che erano, ampliata et quasi per ogni parte rinovata et riformata* (Venice: Varisco, 1573), 135 (my translation). The original reads: "Stimano li dotti per cosa certissima che antiquissimame[n]te dal principio, che gli huomini, quasi nuovi nel mondo cominciarono à filosofare; fussero tutte le parti della Filosofia, tratte con l'aiuto della facultà poetica: di maniera che li poeti eran quelli, che l'arti, & le scientie insegnavano al mo[n]do."

15 See Luisa Capodieci and Philip Ford, *Homère à la Renaissance: Mythe et transfigurations* (Rome: Académie de France, 2011).

16 See Jean Dietz Moss, *Novelties in the Heavens: Rhetoric and Science in the Copernican Controversy* (University of Chicago Press, 1993), 129–147.

17 Piccolomini, *Sfera*, 135 (my translation). The original reads:

> come quelli, che ben conoscevano, che quei popoli rozi de i primi tempi difficilmente havriano sopportato di odire, ò di apprendere le cose, se fussero state lor poste innanzi, solamente coperte dell'utile, & dell'honesto che portan seco, senza altra coperta di delettatione. La onde perche la Poesia, per il mezo della imitatione, & del verso, che son due cose, per lor natura, delettevoli all'huomo, può ricoprire le cose utili in modo, che con allettamento di dolcezza, le può far bevere à gli animi nostri, nella guisa che li medici sogliano con qualche dolce liquore circondare la medicina amara, che voglian dare à i fanciulli, accioche allettati da quella dolcezza si bevino quella vivanda che ha da giovar loro: di quì nasceva, che li Poeti (come ho detto poco di sopra) eran quelli, che ne i primi tempi trattavano le scientie tutte.

18 Lucretius, *The Nature of Things*, trans. A. E. Stalling (New York: Penguin, 2007), I.932–947.

19 Timothy J. Reiss, *Knowledge, Discovery, and Imagination in Early Modern Europe* (Cambridge University Press, 1997), 84–85.

20 For context, see Michele Camerota, "Galileo e la *accomodatio* copernicana," in *Il caso Galileo: Una rilettura storica, filosofica, teologica. Convegno internazionale di studi, Firenze 26–30 maggio 2009* (Florence: Olschki, 2011), 129–151.

21 Robert Black, *Humanism and Education in Medieval and Renaissance Italy: Tradition and Innovation in Latin Schools from the Twelfth to the Fifteenth Century* (Cambridge University Press, 2001), 9.

22 See Anthony Grafton, "Kepler as a Reader," *Journal of the History of Ideas* 53.4 (1992): 561–572 (561).

23 Fortunio Liceti, *De centro, & circumferentia libri duo* (Udine, 1640), 69.

24 On education in Europe more generally, see Andrew Pettegree, *The Book in the Renaissance* (New Haven: Yale University Press, 2010), 177–199.

25 Paul F. Grendler, *Schooling in Renaissance Italy: Literacy and Learning, 1300–1600* (Baltimore: Johns Hopkins University Press, 1989), 289–299.

26 Marina Beer, *Romanzi di cavalleria: "Il furioso" e il romanzo italiano del primo Cinquecento* (Rome: Bulzoni, 1987), 227.

27 Grendler, *Schooling*, 289–299.

28 *Ibid.*, 299.

29 Teofilo Folengo, *Baldo*, trans. Ann E. Mullaney (Cambridge, MA: Harvard University Press, 2007), III.86–120.

30 Grendler, *Schooling*, 290.

31 *Ibid.*, 298.

32 JoAnn Cavallo, *The Romance Epics of Boiardo, Ariosto, and Tasso* (University of Toronto Press, 2004).

33 Dennis Looney, *Compromising the Classics: Romance Epic Narrative in the Italian Renaissance* (Detroit: Wayne State University Press, 1996), 16.

34 For the other interpretations of Virgil outside the realm of natural philosophy, see Margaret Tudeau-Clayton, *Jonson, Shakespeare and Early Modern Virgil* (Cambridge University Press, 1998).

35 *Opere*, XIX, 627 (my translation). The original reads:

> Fu dotato dalla natura d'esquisita memoria; e gustando in estremo la poesia, aveva a mente, tra gl'autori latini, gran parte di Vergilio, d'Ovidio, Orazio e di Seneca, e tra i toscani quasi tutto 'l Petrarca, tutte le rime del Berni, e poco meno che tutto il poema di Lodovico Ariosto, che fu sempre il suo autor favorito e celebrato sopra gl'altri poeti, avendogli intorno fatte particolari osservazioni e paralleli col Tasso sopra moltissimi luoghi.

36 Peter Armour, "Galileo and the Crisis in Italian Literature of the Early Seicento," in *Collected Essays on Italian Language and Literature Presented to Kathleen Speight*, ed. Giovanni Aquilecchia, Stephen N. Cristea, and Sheila Ralphs (New York: Barnes and Noble, 1971), 144–169 (161).

37 Lanfranco Caretti, "Galileo uomo di lettere," in *Studi di letteratura e di storia di memoria di Antonio Di Pietro* (Milan: Vita e Pensiero, 1977), 107–123 (109; Caretti's emphasis, my translation). The original reads: "scrittori schietti e concreti, cioè … verso gli scrittori di *cose* e non di *parole*."

38 *Opere*, IX, 278.

39 See Tudeau-Clayton, *Jonson, Shakespeare and Early Modern Virgil*, 21.

40 *Opere*, VI, 343.

41 See Nereo Vianello, *Le postille al Petrarca di Galileo Galilei* (Florence: Sansoni, 1956); and Giuseppe Ottone, "*Postille e Considerazioni* galileiane," *Aevum* 46 (1972): 312–324. Eraldo Bellini has identified some specifically Dantean vocabulary in Galileo's prose; see *Stili di pensiero nel Seicento italiano: Galileo, i Lincei, i Barberini* (Pisa: ETS, 2009), 12–24.

42 *Opere*, XVI, 294.

43 For an analysis see Vittore Branca, "Galileo fra Petrarca e l'Umanesimo ven-
    eziano," in *Galileo Galilei e la cultura veneziana: Atti del Convegno di Studio
    promosso nell'ambito delle celebrazioni galileiane indette dall'Università degli
    Studi di Padova (1592–1992), Venezia, 18–20 giugno 1992* (Venice: Istituto
    Veneto di Scienze, Lettere ed Arti, 1992), 340–343.

44 See Leonard Olschki, "Galileo's Literary Formation," trans. Thomas Green
    and Maria Charlesworth, in *Galileo, Man of Science*, ed. Ernan McMullin
    (New York: Basic Books, 1968), 140–159 (146). More recently, see Mark
    Peterson, *Galileo's Muse* (Cambridge, MA: Harvard University Press, 2011),
    214–236.

45 *Opere*, XIX, 645 (my translation). The original reads: "Fu familiarissimo d'un
    libro intitolato 'l *Ruzzante*, scritto in lingua rustica padovana, pigliandosi gran
    piacere di quei rozzi racconti con accidenti ridicoli."

46 *Ibid.*, XIX, 644 (my translation). The original reads: "Ben spesso havea in
    bocca i capitoli di Francesco Berni, del quale i versi e sentenze in molti prop-
    ositi adattava al suo proposito, niente meno che se fossero stati suoi proprii,
    con somma piacevolezza."

47 See *ibid.*, IV, 446; XII, 156; XVIII, 145; VI, 330; IX, 23–24, 65; XIV, 296; XVI,
    75, 351.

48 For information and bibliography related to Vincenzo Galilei, see Claude V.
    Palisca, introduction to Vincenzo Galilei, *Dialogue on Ancient and Modern Music*,
    trans. Claude V. Palisca (New Haven: Yale University Press, 2003), xv–lxix.

49 *Ibid.*, 354.

50 *Ibid.*, 371.

51 *Ibid.*, 372.

52 *Ibid.*, 212–213.

53 Vincenzo Galilei, *Discorso intorno all'opere di Gioseffo Zarlino* (Florence,
    1589), 96 (my translation). The original reads: "rispondo, ch'egli l'ha con quel
    Sintono natural, et con quel Sintono artifiziale; & io torno a dire che Tolomeo
    fece un solo Sintono Diatonico, al quale non dette nome, ne cognome alcuno
    di natural, ne d'artifiziale."

54 *Ibid.*, 96 (my translation). The original reads: "Il dir poi, che cosi piace a lui,
    mi pare la medesima ragione che usava Orlando nel colmo del suo furore."

55 *Ibid.*, 96–97 (my translation). The original reads: "se al suo scampo non ha
    altra difesa che questa; più honore era il suo acconsentire alla verità subbito,
    che conobbe d'essere in errore, che cercar di difendersi con mezzi come questi,
    da fare l'offesa maggiore."

56 J. L. Heilbron, *Galileo* (Oxford University Press, 2010), 11–12. On the *Alterati*
    see Arjan Van Dixhoorn, *The Reach of the Republic of Letters: Literary and
    Learned Societies in Late Medieval and Early Modern Europe* (Leiden: Brill,
    2008), 285–308.

57 Ian F. McNeely, "The Renaissance Academies between Science and the
    Humanities," *Configurations* 17.3 (Fall 2009): 227–258 (239).

58 Heilbron, *Galileo*, 5.

59 See Biagioli, *Instruments of Credit*, particularly 77–134.
60 See Valeria Finucci, *Renaissance Transactions* (Durham, NC: Duke University Press, 1999).
61 These titles come from the ninth volume of the National Edition, though I find no history of them in the manuscript tradition.
62 Tibor Wlassics, *Galilei critico letterario* (Ravenna: Longo, 1974), 16–17. Varanini points out that Galileo was working with a problematic edition of the *Gerusalemme liberata*; Giorgio Varanini, *Galileo critico e prosatore: Note e ricerche* (Verona: Fiorini-Ghidini, 1967), 56. Dante Della Terza was able to demonstrate that the passages criticized by Galileo in the *Gerusalemme liberata* are "all or almost all changed in the *Conquistata*, if they are not suppressed altogether"; Dante Della Terza, "Galileo Man of Letters," in *Galileo Reappraised*, ed. Carlo L. Golino (Berkeley–Los Angeles: University of California Press, 1966), 1–22 (9).
63 *Opere*, XII, 81–82.
64 See Peter DeSa Wiggins, "Galileo on Characterization in the *Orlando furioso*," *Italica* 57.4: Renaissance (Winter 1980): 255–267 (258).
65 Tibor Wlassics, "La genesi della critica letteraria di Galileo," *Aevum* 46 (1972): 215–236 (234).
66 Heilbron, *Galileo*, 19.
67 Armour, "Galileo and the Crisis," 149.
68 Fernand Hallyn, *The Poetic Structure of the World: Copernicus and Kepler*, trans. Donald M. Leslie (New York: Zone Books, 1993), 198; G. Marzot, "Variazioni barocche nella prosa del Galilei," *Convivium* 23 (1955): 43–67; Raffaele Colapietra, "Caratteri del seicentismo galileiano," *Belfagor* 8 (1953): 570–578; Raffaello Spongano, *La prosa di Galileo e altri scritti* (Messina–Florence: Casa Editrice G. D'Anna, 1949).
69 Wlassics, "La genesi della critica letteraria," 218–219; Armour, "Galileo and the Crisis," 152.
70 DeSa Wiggins, "Galileo on Characterization," 260.
71 Jonathan Unglaub, *Poussin and the Poetics of Painting* (Cambridge University Press, 2006), 124.
72 Galileo Galilei, *Scritti letterari*, ed. Alberto Chiari (Florence: Le Monnier, 1970); my translation of the original headings, which read: "sentenze, comparazioni, iperboli, difficoltà e oscurità, richiami generici, correzioni della stampa del 1572, emendamenti di Galileo, confronti e postille, censure, sottolineature, duelli, descrizioni astronomiche, durezze di costrutto, citazioni e segni generici."
73 Ludovico Ariosto, *Orlando furioso*, II.54; IV.10.4–5; IV.50.3–4; and IV.47.1–2.
74 Torquato Tasso, *Gerusalemme liberata*, III.17.
75 Favaro, "Libreria di Galileo," entries 396, 397. Favaro lists Archivio di Stato di Firenze, Fondo Notarile Moderno, Protocolli, 15676–15685 (Silvestro Pantera, 1646–1650), MS 3483.3 (hereafter Arch. MS 3483.3), and Biblioteca Nazionale Centrale di Firenze, Manoscritti Galileiani, MS 308 (hereafter Gal. MS 308) as sources for this title, but those archival materials suggest one of the many

editions of Dolce's combined volume in which the events of the *Aeneid* follow directly after the *Iliad*; Arch. MS 3483.3, fo. 114r, line 27 reads "l'Anchise et Enea del Dolce," and Gal. MS 308, fo. 167v, line 18 says "L'Achille, e l'Enea del Dolce. 4°." Favaro, "Libreria di Galileo," entry 369 indicates only "Virgilius," but Gal. MS 308, fo. 171v, line 25 indicates a small edition, "Virgilius 32," which only appears to have been printed in Italian in 1623.

76 See *Opere*, XX, 76. During his trial by the Inquisition Galileo responds that he does not remember what was discussed at dinner with Della Porta. See particularly item 69 and the response.

77 For Pulci: Favaro, "Libreria di Galileo," entry 424. Arch. MS 3483.3, fo. 114r, line 23: "Criffo Calvani." Biblioteca Nazionale Centrale di Firenze, Manoscritti Palatini, MS 1195 (hereafter Palat. MS 1195), fo. 196. For Dragoncino da Fano: Favaro, "Libreria di Galileo," entry 457; but Antonio Legname also wrote a poem entitled *Guidon Selvaggio* (Vinegia, 1535, in 8vo). Gal. MS 308, fo. 171r, line 26 lists "Guidone selvaggio. 12," and Gal. MS 308, fo. 170r, line 12, "Guidon Selvaggio. 8°." This could also refer to Michiele Pietro's *Del Guidon Selvaggio canti tredici* (Venice, 1649, in 12mo). I have not found other titles in 12mo. For Guazzo: Favaro, "Libreria di Galileo," entry 409. Arch. MS 3483.3, fo. 114r, line 26: "Astolfo." Gal. MS 308, fo. 169r, line 18: "Astolfo furioso. 4°." For Oriolo: Favaro, "Libreria di Galileo," entry 425 gives the following: "Galluzzi, Cesare. *Ruggero. Poema diviso in XI canti*, Ferrara, 1550, per Giovanni de Buglhat e Comp. in 4°." The above title more closely fits the information in the inventory: Gal. MS 308, fo. 171r, line 19: "Canti di ruggiero. 8°." For Lauro: Favaro, "Libreria di Galileo," entry 330. Arch. MS 3483.3, fo. 115r, lines 7–8: "Rethorica di Polando del Lauri."

78 For *Aspramonte*: Favaro, "Libreria di Galileo," entry 454 gives an edition without a date or size: "Fiorenza, Jacopo di Carlo e Piero Bonaccorsi." Gal. MS 308, fo. 169v, line 24: "Aspramonte. 8°." Favaro, "Libreria di Galileo," entry 460. Favaro attributes a 1534 work, *Il gigante*, to Leone Santi (1585–1636). I have chosen the earliest edition in 8vo of the anonymous work with a similar title to the inventory entry instead: Gal. MS 308, fo. 171r, line 11: "Gigante morante 8°." For *Rogello*: Gal. MS 308, fo. 168v, line 26: "Don Rocello di Gregia 8." The adventures of Don Rogello were reprinted in the 1590s with a slightly different title, and as a six-volume set in 1610. For *Antifor*: Favaro, "Libreria di Galileo," entry 453. Gal. MS 308, fo. 170v, line 24: "Antifior di Barosia. 8°."

79 Favaro omitted the title from his original catalog, but the indication appears in Gal. MS 308, fo. 168v, line 20: "Poesie in lingua rustica padovana." This corresponds most closely to Brentelle's *Poesie in lingua rustica padovana: Madrigali, Bradamante irata, Isabella e Zerbino, Orlando addolorato; Lamenti raccolti et imitati da' leggiadri canti dell'Ariosto* (Venetia: Bissuccio, 1612).

80 Favaro, "Libreria di Galileo," entry 458. Arch. MS 3483.3, fo. 115r, lines 15–16: "Il Piccariglio." Gal. MS 308, fo.170v, line 9: "Il picariglio castigliano 8°."

81 Favaro, "Libreria di Galileo," entry 455 suggests the 1622 second edition edited by Peiresc. Arch. MS 3483.3, fo. 115r, line 13: "Argleniede"; Gal. MS 308, fo. 167v, line 4: "Argenide del Barclaio latina 4."

82 Gal. MS 308, fo. 169r, line 14: "Palladio poemetto 4°." Favaro, "Libreria di Galileo," entry 390 also lists Arch. MS 3483.3 as a source, but I cannot find such an indication in the document.

83 Favaro, "Libreria di Galileo," entry 391. Arch. MS 3483.3, fo. 115r, line 7: "Parto della Vergine, del Calamai." Gal. MS 308, fo. 170r, line 24: "Il parto della Vergine poema 8°."

84 Favaro, "Libreria di Galileo," entry 408. Gal. MS 308, fo. 168r, line 14: "Il Polemidoro del Gualterotti 4."

85 See Eileen Reeves, *Painting the Heavens* (Princeton University Press, 1999), 51–54.

86 *Opere*, XVIII, 410.

87 Favaro, "Libreria di Galileo," entry 399. Gal. MS 308, fo. 171v, line 23: "Lamento d'Emereno 24."

88 Favaro, "Libreria di Galileo," entry 456. Arch. MS 3483.3, fo. 115r, lines 4 and 5: "Don Chisciotte" and "Don Chisciotte Parte 2:a."

89 For Chiabrera: Favaro, "Libreria di Galileo," entry 392. Arch. MS 3483.3, fo. 115r, line 25: "Firenze Poema." For Peri: Favaro, "Libreria di Galileo," entry 421 lists this 1621 edition, but the volume also appeared in 1619. Arch. MS 3483.3, fo. 114r, line 27: "Fiesole distrutta." For Strozzi: Favaro, "Libreria di Galileo," entry 426. Arch. MS 3483.3, fo. 115r, line 16: "La Venetia Poema." For Marino: *Opere*, XIII, 145–148.

90 *Opere*, XI, 324. Sarrocchi's poem has recently been translated into English and edited: Margherita Sarrocchi, *Scanderbeide: The Heroic Deeds of George Scanderbeg, King of Epirus*, ed. and trans. Rinaldina Russell (University of Chicago Press, 2006). See also Serena Pezzini, "Ideologia della conquista, ideologia dell'accoglienza: *La Scanderbeide* di Margherita Sarrocchi (1623)," *MLN* 120.1: Supplement (2005): 190–222; and the discussion in Virginia Cox, *The Prodigious Muse* (Baltimore: Johns Hopkins University Press, 2011), 167–212.

91 *Opere*, X, 241 (my translation). The original reads: "La S.ra Sarrocchi ringratia V.S. del favore fattole in mandarle il giuditio dello stile del suo poema, e della diligenza che dice di voler fare sopra ogni parte di esso." Luca Valerio had been asked by Sarrocchi to present the *Scanderbeide* to Galileo for his criticism, which he did in his letter to Galileo from April 4, 1609 (*Opere*, X, 241). The manuscript was sent to Galileo on May 23, 1610 according to Valerio's letter (245–246). Sarrocchi goes into more detail about the nature of Galileo's corrections in her letter to him from January 13, 1612 (*Opere*, XI, 261–262).

92 *Ibid.*, XI, 265.

93 The letters regarding Galileo's commentary on Sarrocchi's manuscript can be found in *Opere*, X, 241, 245–246. Rinaldina Russell touches on this correspondence in the introduction to her prose translation of Sarrocchi's *Scanderbeide*, 9. Sarrocchi was also one of the recipients of Galileo's *Discourses on Bodies in Water* (1612). See Michele Camerota, *Galileo Galilei e la cultura scientifica nell'età della Controriforma* (Rome: Salerno, 2004), 235.

94 Gal. MS 308, fo. 171v, line 10: "Avinoavolittone berlinghieri poema 12." Favaro, "Libreria di Galileo," entry 388. Favaro notes that he found only a 1643 edition and I have found nothing earlier either.

95 See Monica R. Gale, *Lucretius and the Didactic Epic* (London: Bristol Classical Press, 2001).

96 D. Mark Possanza, *Translating the Heavens: Aratus, Germanicus, and the Poetics of Latin Translation* (New York: Peter Lang, 2004).

97 See Aaron Poochigan, "Introduction" to Aratus, *Phaenomena*, trans. Aaron Poochigan (Baltimore: Johns Hopkins University Press, 2010), xxiii–xxvii.

98 Possanza, *Translating the Heavens*, 86.

99 See Alison Brown, *The Return of Lucretius to Renaissance Florence* (Cambridge, MA: Harvard University Press, 2010), vii.

100 See Pietro Redondi, *Galileo Heretic*, trans. Raymond Rosenthal (Princeton University Press, 1987).

101 For a recent account of the rediscovery of Lucretius in the Renaissance and his importance for subsequent fields of study, see Stephen Greenblatt, *Swerve: How the World Became Modern* (New York: Norton, 2011).

102 See Michele Camerota, "Galileo, Lucrezio e l'atomismo," in *Lucrezio: La natura e la scienza*, ed. Marco Beretta and Francesco Citti (Florence: Olschki, 2008) 141–175 (141–142).

103 Favaro, "Libreria di Galileo," entries 353 and 354; Gal. MS 308, fo. 171v, line 6: "Lucretius 12"; Palat. MS 1195, fo. 185. In addition to Palat. MS 1195, Favaro cites Arch. MS 3483.3 as a source, but the archival material does not show any indication that I have seen.

104 See Camerota, "Galileo, Lucrezio e l'atomismo," 160–161.

105 Vladimir Janković, *Reading the Skies: A Cultural History of English Weather, 1650–1820* (University of Chicago Press, 2000), 21. See also L. A. S. Jermyn, "Virgil's Agricultural Lore," *Greece and Rome* 53 (1949): 49–69; David Scott Wilson-Okamura, *Virgil in the Renaissance* (Cambridge University Press, 2010), 82.

106 Giambattista Della Porta, *De distillatione Libri IX* (Rome: Rev. Camerae Apostolicae, 1608), 3; Fabio Colonna, *Fabii Columnae Lyncei Purpura hoc est, De purpura ab animali testaceo fusa de hoc ipso Animali aliusque rarioribus testaceis quibusdam cum iconibus ex aere ad vivum representatis* (Rome: Jacobum Mascardum, 1616), 4; Pierre Gassendi, *Petri Gassendi Diniensis ecclesiae praepositi, et in academia parisiensi Matheseos regii professoris Opera omnia in sex tomos diuisa*, 6 vols. (Lyon: Anisson & Deuenet, 1658), IV, 6.

107 Janković, *Reading the Skies*, 137.

108 Manilius, *Astronomica*, trans. G. P. Goold (Cambridge, MA: Harvard University Press, 1977), III.31–35.

109 *Ibid.*, III.385–442.

110 Grafton, *Commerce with the Classics*, 198.

111 In Galileo's library, this would have been found in Aristotle, *Operum Aristotelis ... omnium longe principis, nova editio ... nunc primum in lucem prodeunt, ex bibliotheca Isaaci Casauboni* (Lyon, 1590), 377.

112 Liceti, *De centro, & circumferentia libri duo*, 81; Fortunio Liceti, *Litheosphorus, sive, De lapide Bononiensi lucem in se conceptam ab ambiente claro mox in tenebris mire conservante* (Udine: Schiratti, 1640), 13.

113 Fortunio Liceti, *De terra unico centro motus singularum caeli particularum disputationes* (Udine, 1641), 49.

114 *Ibid.*, 102–103. Liceti also uses Ovid, *Metamorphoses*, 1.45–51 for this proof.

115 Fortunio Liceti, *De luminis natura & efficientia, libri tres* (Udine, 1641), 123.

116 *Ibid.*, 207 (unpublished translation by Cara Polsley). The original reads:

> ut ob multos errores in victu, & ob alias caussas [*sic*], facile sibi potest huiusmodi temperamentum labefactare, vitaeque spacium sibi diminuere; unde recte, Didonem iuvenem ob Aeneae discessum se gladio transverberantem, poeta dixit nec fato, nec debita morte periisse suavissimis e metris "Tum luno omnipotens longum miserata dolorem, / Difficilesque obitus, Irim demisit Olympo, / Quae luctantem animam, nexosque resolveret artus. / Nam quia nec fato, merita nec morte peribat, / Sed misera ante diem …"

The verses are Virgil, *Aeneid*, IV.693–697.

117 Giambattista Della Porta, *Ioan. Baptistae Portae Neap. de refractione optices parte. Libri Novem* (Naples: Carlino & Pace, 1593), 167. Virgil, *Aeneid*, trans. Sarah Ruden (New Haven: Yale University Press), IV.469–70.

118 See James R. Lattis, *Between Copernicus and Galileo: Christoph Clavius and the Collapse of Ptolemaic Cosmography* (University of Chicago Press, 1994), 1–21.

119 See *ibid.*, 180–216.

120 Christoph Clavius, S.J., *Christophori Clavii Bambergensis ex Societate Iesv In sphaeram Ioannis de Sacro Bosco commentarius* (Venice: Ciotto, 1591), 308–309. Virgil, *Georgics*, trans. Janet Lembke (New Haven: Yale University Press, 2005), I.233, 239; and Ovid, *Metamorphoses*, trans. and ed. Charles Martin (New York: Norton, 2010), i.45, 51.

121 Clavius, *In sphaeram*, 309–310 (my translation of the phrases "in confirmationem"and "testimonium," respectively).

122 *Ibid.*, 310 (translation found in Lucan, *Pharsalia*, trans. Susanna H. Braund [Oxford University Press], III.248).

123 Clavius, *In sphaeram*, 207. The verses are: "Circuitus circi per septem multiplicetur, / Per duo viginti productum deinde secato: / Hinc numerus, Quotiens qui dicitur, est diametrus. / Per duo viginti si multiplices diametrum, / Per se[p]temq[ue] seces numerum, qui prodiit inde: / circuitum circi Quotiens numerus tibi reddet."

124 The titles in question are: Christoph Clavius, S.J., *Christophori Clavii Bambergensis e Societate Iesu Epitome arithmeticae practicae* (Rome: Basa, 1583); its translation, *Aritmetica prattica composta dal molto reuer. padre Christoforo Clauio … Et tradotto da latino in italiano dal Signor Lorenzo Castellano* (Rome: Basa, 1586); and *Christophori Clauii Bambergensis e Societate Iesu, Geometria practica* (Rome: Zanetti, 1604).

125 The full title is Christoph Clavius, S.J., *Gnomonices libri octo in quibus non solum horologiorum solariu[m], sed aliarum quoq[ue] rerum, quae ex gnomonis umbra cognosci possunt, descriptiones geometricè demonstrantur auctore Christophoro Clavio Bambergensi Societatis Iesu* (Rome: Zanetti, 1581).

126 The full title is Christoph Clavius, S.J., *Christophori Clavii Bambergensis Astrolabivm* (Rome: Grassi, 1593).

127 Galileo, *Assayer*, 304; *Opere*, VI, 343.

128 Piccolomini, *Sfera*, 135–136 (my translation). The original reads:

> Per la qual cosa havendo essi tra le molte cose, che son lor proprie per adornare li lor poemati, bisogno di molte, & diverse descrittioni: accio che potendo meglio così variare il lor versi, maggio diletto apportasseno, con descrivere le stesse cose in diversi modi: questo medesimo usarono nell'Astrologia: si come tra l'altre cose lo fecero nel nascere, & nel nascondersi delle Stelle: accioche con assegnar diversi modi di nascimento, & d'ascondimento, si potessero variamente descrivere, & quasi disegnare le varie stagioni dell'anno, & li diversi tempi dell'hore, & de i giorni, & altre cose simili, secondo che da Homero, da Vergilio, da Horatio, da Ovidio, & da altri buoni Poeti esser veggiamo usato.

129 *Ibid.*, 144 (my translation). The original reads:

> "con questa dottrina si possono intendere molti luoghi loro: poscia che per far più bella tessura, & più vario, & ricco il poema, vanno in diversi modi descrivendo le stagioni dell'anno, li giorni, & le hore secondo che leggendo li poeti buoni, come ho gran piacer di far io, potrà ciascheduno per se stesso veder benissimo."

130 *Ibid.*, 245 (my translation of the prose). The verses are from Dante Alighieri, *Paradiso*, trans. Allen Mandelbaum (New York: Bantam, 2004), IV.40–42. The original reads:

> come Aristotile afferma ne i suoi Libri dell'Anima, & altrove ancora. Et Dante parimente lo manifesta, quando dice, Così parlar conviensi à nostro ingegno: / Peroche solo da sensato apprende / Ciò che fa poscia d'intelletto degno. Et quel che segue. Et essendo questo, non sarebbe maraviglia se gli Astrologi in molte cose, & specialmente nel mostrare le quantità, & grandezze de i detti corpi luminosi del Cielo, & le distantie loro dalla terra, no(n) arrivassero così à punto al segno della verità.

131 Gassendi, *Opera omnia*, IV.16 (unpublished translation by Cara Polsley). The original reads:

> Quo loco vides obiter, eundem Autumnum exprimi, a Virgilio quidem per Occasum, ab Ovidio vero per Ortum earundem Pleiadeum. Sed videlicet prout ille Occasum Cosmicum intelligit; Pleiades enim per illud tempus mane occidunt: iste Ortum Acronychum; caedem enim tunc vespere oriuntur. Acronychi Occasus rariora sunt exempla; nam quod volunt quidem Sagittarium intelligi Occasu hoc occidere, cum Lucanus expressurus crepusculum, proxime aestivum Solstitium, ait, Nam Sol Ladea tenebat / Sidera, vicino cum lux altissima Cancro est, / Nox tum Thessalicas urgebat parva Sagittas. [Lucan, *Pharsalia*, IV.527–529] Constat non posse Sagittarium occidere tunce, nisi Cosmice, oriente puta Sole cum Geminis; ac fortiri dumtaxat posse occasum Acronychum, dum Sol est in ipso, ac una cum eo occidit.

132 See Ward W. Briggs, Jr., *Narrative and Simile from the "Georgics" in the "Aeneid"* (Leiden: Brill, 1980); and Emma Gee, *Ovid, Aratus and Augustus* (Cambridge University Press, 2000).

133 For more on Gassendi see Antonia LoLordo, *Pierre Gassendi and the Birth of Early Modern Philosophy* (Cambridge University Press, 2007).

134 For Kepler, see specifically Johannes Kepler, *Mysterium cosmographicum: The Secret of the Universe*, trans. Alistair M. Duncan; ed. Eric J. Aiton (New York: Abaris Books, 1981), 13.

135 Original verses given in Liceti, *Litheosphorus*, 3. The passage in question is: "Verùm id non rudi quadam, cressaq[ue] Minerva, sed suis causis, & rationibus facere condiscat. Mathematicas novisse disciplinas oportet, & praesertim Astrologiam: nam demonstrat *Ardua quo coeli rapiantur sydera motu, / Quid caligantem modo cogat hebescere Lunam, / Quo circa certis dimensis partibus orbem, / Per duodena regat mundi Sol aureus astra.*" The first verses are Agrippa's own; the last two lines are from Virgil, *Georgics*, 1.231–232.

136 For an example as late as an eighteenth-century text, see Pliny, *Histoire naturelle de Pline*, trans. Louis Poinsinet de Sivry, 12 vols. (Paris: Chez la veuve Desaint, 1778), Vol. X, 144.

137 Arielle Saiber, "Flexilinear language: Giambattista Della Porta's *Elementorum curvilineorum libri tres*," *Annali d'Italianistica* 23 (2005): 89–104.

138 Giambattista Della Porta, *De aeris transmutationibvs libri IIII* (Rome: Mascardi, 1614), 71–72.

139 Giovanni Battista Benedetti, *Diversarum speculationum mathematicarum, & physicarum liber quarum seriem sequens pagina indicabit ad serenissimum Carolum Emanuelem Allobrogum, et Subalpinorum ducem invictissimum* (Turin, 1585), 417–418.

140 Galileo Galilei, *On the World Systems*, trans. and ed. Maurice A. Finocchiaro (Berkeley: University of California Press, 1997), 121; *Opere*, VII, 134–135.

141 See Paul Lawrence Rose, *The Italian Renaissance of Mathematics* (Geneva: Librairie Droz, 1976), 26–75.

142 See Alexander Marr, *Between Raphael and Galileo* (University of Chicago Press, 2011).

143 See Mario Biagioli, "The Social Status of Italian Mathematicians, 1450–1600," *History of Science* 27 (1989): 41–95.

144 The full titles are Rafael Bombelli, *L'algebra opera di Rafael Bombelli da Bologna divisa in tre libri con la quale ciascuno da se potrà venire in perfetta cognitione della teorica dell'arimetica* (Bologna, 1579); Girolamo Cardano, *Hieronymi Cardani, praestantissimi mathematici, philosophi, ac medici Artis magnae sive, de regulis algebraicis Lib. unus. Qui & totius de Arithmetica, quod opus perfectum inscripsit, est in ordine Decimus* (Nuremberg, 1545); and Luca Valerio, *Quadratura parabolae per simplex falsum, et altera quàm secunda Archimedis expiditior ad martium columnam Lucae Valerij* (Rome, 1606), and *De centro gravitatis solidorum libri tres* (Rome, 1604).

145 See for example Giovanni Antonio Magini, *Breve instruttione sopra l'apparenze et mirabili effetti dello specchio concavo sferico del... Gio. Antonio Magini* (Bologna, 1611).

146 See Giovanni Antonio Magini, *Ephemerides coelestium motuum Io. Antonii Magini Patavini … ab anno Domini 1611 usque ad annum 1630 quibus additum est eiusdem Supplementum isagogicarum ephemeridum* (Venice, 1616).

147 Giovanni Battista Benedetti, *Resolutio omnium Euclidis problematum aliorumque ad hoc necessario inventorum una tantummodo circini data apertura per Ioannem Baptistam de Benedictis inventa* (Venice, 1553).

148 The full title is Niccolò Aggiunti, *Nicolai Adiunctii Burgensis Oratio de mathematicae laudibus habita in florentissima Pisarum Academia* (Rome, 1627). Mark Peterson's recent suggestion that this oration was actually the work of Galileo because of its Galilean undertones would be strengthened if it contained more of the poetic style elaborated in later chapters. See Peterson, *Galileo's Muse*, 272–291.

149 Samuel Edgerton, *The Heritage of Giotto's Geometry: Art and Science on the Eve of the Scientific Revolution* (Ithaca, NY: Cornell University Press, 1991), 183.

150 Niccolò Tartaglia, *Ragionamenti sopra la sua travagliata inventione* (Venice, 1551), Fiiii verso (my translation). The original reads: "si a loro gli pare che una promessa non sia promessa se quella non è fatta con publico istrumento & per man di notaro."

151 *Ibid.*, Fiiii verso. Ludovico Ariosto, *Orlando furioso*, XXI.2.1–8 (my translation). The original reads:

Con questo vostro dire mi haveti redutto in memoria una sententia del Ariosto sopra à tal mateia, qual dice in questa forma: "La fede unqua non debbe esser corrotta / o data a un solo, o data insieme a mille; / e così in una selva, in una grotta, / lontan da le cittadi e da le ville, / come dinanzi a tribunali, in frotta / di testimon, di scritti e di postille, / senza giurare o segno altro più espresso, / basti una volta che s'abbia promesso."

152 For an example see Johannes Kepler, *Epitome of Copernican Astronomy*, trans. Charles Glenn Wallace (Chicago: Encyclopaedia Britannica, 1952), 860.

153 Grafton, "Kepler as a Reader," 561.

154 Kepler, *Mysterium cosmographicum*, 55. From Ovid, *Fasti*, I.297–298.

155 Kepler, *Mysterium cosmographicum*, 69.

156 *Ibid.* The allusion is to Terence, *The Self-Tormentor*, IV.3.41.

157 Johannes Kepler, *Optics: Paralipomena to Witelo and Optical Part of Astronomy*, trans. William H. Donahue (Santa Fe: Green Lion Press, 2000), 275.

158 Kepler, *Mysterium cosmographicum*, 117.

159 Virgil, *Aeneid*, IV.569.

160 Pietro Pitati, *Almanach novum* (Venice, 1542), 23r.

161 Kepler, *Mysterium cosmographicum*, 179.

162 Translation found in Carola Baumgardt, *Johannes Kepler: Life and Letters* (New York: Philosophical Library, 1951), 49.

163 Kepler, *Mysterium cosmographicum*, 83.

164 Copernicus too is very light with quotations, limiting his verbatim borrowings from other authors to two passages from Plutarch, and one each from Hermes Trismegistus and Sophocles. The latter two are related to Copernicus' view that the Sun is deserving of its position at the center of the known universe. See Copernicus, *On the Revolutions of the Heavenly Spheres*,

trans. Charles Glenn Wallace (Chicago: Encyclopaedia Britannica, 1952), 527. Copernicus made use of Horatian undertones in his preface to the *De revolutionibus*; see Robert S. Westman, "Proof, Poetics, and Patronage: Copernicus's Preface to *De revolutionibus*," in *Reappraisals of the Scientific Revolution*, ed. David C. Lindberg and Robert S. Westman (Cambridge University Press, 1990), 181–184.

2 STARRY KNIGHTS

1 William Eamon, "Court, Academy, and Printing House: Patronage and Scientific Careers in Late Renaissance Italy," in *Patronage and Institutions: Science, Technology, and Medicine at the European Court 1500–1700*, ed. Bruce T. Moran (Rochester, NY: Boydell Press, 1991), 25–50.

2 Mary Baine Campbell, *Wonder & Science: Imagining Worlds in Early Modern Europe* (Ithaca, NY: Cornell University Press, 1999), 129.

3 Steven Shapin, *A Social History of Truth: Civility and Science in Seventeenth-Century England* (University of Chicago Press, 1994), 126.

4 See Robert S. Westman, *The Copernican Question* (Berkeley: University of California Press, 2011), 403.

5 See David Freedberg, *The Eye of the Lynx* (University of Chicago Press, 2003), 84–91.

6 Galileo Galilei, *Galileo against the Philosophers in His "Dialogue of Cecco di Ronchitti" (1605) and "Considerations of Alimberto Mauri" (1606)*, trans. Stillman Drake (Los Angeles: Zeitlin & Ver Brugge, 1976), 23. See for context Marisa Milani, "Il 'Faelamento' di Rovigiò Bon Magon e Tuogno Regonò a Galileo Galilei," *Giornale storico della letteratura italiana* 165 (1988): 545–577. For an overview of the changing view of Galileo's role in Cecco's text, see Lorenzo Tomasin, "Galileo e il pavano: Un consuntivo." *Lingua nostra* 69.1–2 (2008): 23–36.

7 J. L. Heilbron, *Galileo* (Oxford University Press, 2010), 122–125.

8 See also Westman, *The Copernican Question*, 384–390.

9 Heilbron, *Galileo*, 122–123.

10 For a synopsis of Galileo, Kepler, and the *nova*, see Massimo Bucciantini, *Galileo e Keplero* (Turin: Einaudi, 2003), 117–143.

11 For more on Kepler's larger goals in *De stella nova*, see Westman, *The Copernican Question*, 393–401. The Biblioteca Nazionale Centrale di Firenze holds a copy of this work with Galileo's annotations: Gal. MS 47.

12 Johannes Kepler, *De stella nova in pede Serpentarii, et qui sub ejus exortum de novo iniit, trigono igneo* (Prague, 1606), 69–70 (translation by Cara Polsley). The original reads: "quo in coelum recepto, jam coepisse Poetas cogitare de fabulis."

13 *Ibid.*, 69–70 (translation by Cara Polsley). The original reads: "Tanta est Poetarum licentia, ut hoc Idolum quotidie de mare in foeminam transmutent: quid mirum si quibusdam & effoeminatus fingitur?"

14 *Ibid.* (translation by Cara Polsley). The original reads:

> Per Pontanum igitur licet vel Apollinem dicere, Pythonis, vel Cadmum, Draconis Bocotij inter-
> fectores, vel Jasonem, qui Colchidos Draconem sopivit, vel Aesacum, Egeries nymphae necem in
> serpente ulciscentem, vel quam ipse dicit Eurydicen: At quid si Lesbium illum Draconem dixeris,
> a Phoebo in saxum conversum, illum qui caput Orphei rosit? Cernis ut reflexo collo ad coronam,
> & quae hanc non longo intervallo sequitur, Orphei lyram, etiamnum in corona caput Orphei,
> qui lyrae dominus erat, quaerere videatur? Sin hoc minus placet; Aristaeum in Serpentario agno-
> scito, Proteta in Serpente; ut luctae causa pateat.
>
> At nihil accommodatius Laocoonte Virgiliano, quem serpentes ab exitio / filiorum avertentem /
> Corripiunt spirisque, ligant ingentibus: & jam / Bu medium amplexi, bu collo squamea circum /
> Terga dati, superant capite & cervicibus altu / Ille simul manibus tentat divellere nodos. Frustra
> quidem omnia. Nulla fabula quadrat. Refutat Manilius uno versu: Semper erit paribus bellum:
> quia viribus equant. Omnes vero hactenus commemorati aut vicerunt aut victis sunt. Nunc a
> ludicris ad calculos, a Poetis ad Mathematicos veniamus.

15 *Ibid.*, 121 (translation by Cara Polsley). The original reads:

> Spero me aequis auribus exceptum iri, a Brenggero praesertim alijsque, qui censuerunt,
> non posse sidus [*sic*] hoc naturae transcribi, nisi & novam Physicen corporum coeles-
> tium comminiscamur. Primus igitur ego sententiam dicam: ut habeant caeteri materiam
> dicendi tanto copiosorem. Ac nescio quid mihi Virgilianum hie occinat Pythagoreus ali-
> quis. / Principio coelum ac Terrae, camposque liquentes, / Lucentemque globum Lunae,
> Titaniaque astra / Spiritus intus alit; totumque, infusa per artus, / Mens agitat molem, &
> magno se corpere miscet [*Aeneid*, VI.721–727]. quibus verbis Scaliger existimavit duci nos
> in abdita naturae mysteria.

16 See Nuccio D'Anna, *Virgilio e le rivelazioni divine* (Genoa: ECIG, 1989).

17 Heilbron, *Galileo*, 123.

18 Galileo, *Galileo against the Philosophers*, 64. For the current state of the debate, see Westman, *Copernican Question*, 387–388; Heilbron, *Galileo*, 123–124.

19 See Emilio Lovarini, *Studi sul Ruzzante e la letteratura padovana,* ed. Gianfrancesco Folena (Padua: Antenore, 1965).

20 Heilbron, *Galileo*, 125 126.

21 Lodovico Delle Colombe, *Risposte piaceuoli e curiose di Lodouico delle Colombe alle considerazioni di certa Maschera saccente nominata Alimberto Mauri, fatte sopra alcuni luoghi del discorso del medesimo Lodouico dintorno alla stella appa-rita [sic] l'anno 1604* (Florence: Caneo and Grossi, 1607), IV (my translation). The original reads: "Io, che cerco godermi il cielo, filosofando de'suoi bei lumi, e fuggo le gare, se, affrontato, stringo il nimico, perche scusa meritar non debbo? anzo potrò io ben dir col Veniero il medesimo che nella sua Idalba Tragedia egli disse. Mie difese sforzate, han lor colpe punite."

22 See Margaret F. Rosenthal, *The Honest Courtesan: Veronica Franco, Citizen and Writer in Sixteenth-Century Venice* (University of Chicago Press, 1992), 42–56.

23 Delle Colombe, *Risposte piaceuoli*, IV (my translation). The original reads:

> Hora, perche noi, signora Maschera, ò vero Alimberto Mauri, desideriamo, che quegli, a
> cui aggradirà la lettura di queste risposte, e difese … non siano aggravati di doppia fatica
> nel dover prender più libri nelle mani … ma possano in questo solo per facilità, e chiarezza
> maggiore agiatamente vedere ogni cosa a questa materia appartenente, con ischiettezza, e

sincerità di scrittura trasportata; cominceremo dal principio delle considerazioni vostre … e immediatamente à ciascuna seguirà la risposta.

24 Alimberto Mauri, *Considerations on Some Places in the Discourse of Lodovico delle Colombe*, trans. Stillman Drake, in Galileo, *Galileo against the Philosophers*, 77.

25 In the first consideration, Alimberto Mauri declares that he is an experienced Ulysses, and this prompts him to offer generous advice to those who will follow in his intellectual footsteps:

> I think it would be little admirable, and rather ungrateful to and unworthy of the grace of the studious, if in plowing the waves of this sea of the sciences, I should see danger of their ultimate ruin and not point out to them those sirens whose nature and place I have detected (so far as befits the ability of my feeble mind, working for some time under the most competent Pilot), in order that they, safe from fears of rough passage and not detained by vain ideas, may hold continuously swift the course of their desire to true knowledge.

(Mauri, *Considerations*, 77.)

26 Delle Colombe, *Risposte piaceuoli*, 3r (my translation). The original reads:

> Io tengo per certo, che se Torquato Tasso havesse potuto usurpar cosi bella descrizione, egli la cacciava nel suo poema, per dipinger più al vivo quelle vaghe notatrici lusinghevoli, che aspiravano co' loro allettamenti ad arrestare i passi di que due guerrieri, acciò che non richiamassero al campo il valoroso Rinaldo, che nell delizie del giardin d'Armida se ne stava con essa tra le lascivie innolto [*sic*].

27 Richard Wistreich, *Warrior, Courtier, Singer: Giulio Cesare Brancaccio and the Performance of Identity in the Late Renaissance* (Burlington, VT: Ashgate, 2007), 271–272.

28 Delle Colombe, *Risposte piaceuoli*, 3v–4r (my translation). The original reads: "Non vedete, che questa puntura inzuccherata si ritorce contro di voi, posciache non bastandovi far l'arte dell'indovinare, volete / spacciar ancor del filosofo, e del Teologo, sì che di voi si può dir garbatamente quel verso del Tasso. *Confonde le due leggi à se mal note?*"

29 Only once Delle Colombe will choose lines from Tasso's sonnet that served as the preface for the Dominican Sebastiano Castelletti's short heroic poem *La trionfatrice Cecilia vergine e martire romana* (*The Triumphant Cecilia, Roman Virgin and Martyr*; 1594), to show the durability of bronze. See Delle Colombe, *Risposte piaceuoli*, 40r. Also in Torquato Tasso, *Opere*, ed. Bruno Maier, 5 vols., Vol. II (Milan: Biblioteca Universali Rizzoli, 1963), 329.

30 Delle Colombe, *Risposte piaceuoli*, 6r–v (my translation). The original reads:

> Guardate, che l'amor non v'inganni, e faccia parer come disse il Petrarca. *Donne, e donzelle, e sono abeti, e faggi*; Percioche elle appaiano come disse il Tasso, *Figlie delle salvatiche cortecce.* Orsù volete, ch'io ve la dica? A me elle paiono honeste, appunto, qual fu la figliuola del Soldano di Babilonia, che nove fiate fu contaminate, e ad ogni modo si vende per pulzella. Ma voi non havete cosi ben saputo ricoprirle, che donzelle violate non si dimostrino: e come che voi vogliate far testimonio della purità di esse, alle vostre parole non si dee prestar fede, che padre vi appellate di quelle, e ne siate l'adultero.

31 *Ibid.*, 5r, 6r, 14v, 22r–v, 56v.

32 *Ibid.*, 90v–91r; Francesco Petrarca, *Petrarch's Lyric Poems*, trans. and ed. Robert Durling (Cambridge, MA: Harvard University Press, 1976), poem 128, lines 9–10 (my translation of the prose). The original reads:

> Pian un pò Signor Alimberto, che le cose vanno molto bene; poiche, havendomi voi conceduto, per ragion la nuova stella poter esser nel Primo mobile, vi resta solo una difficultà, ed è questa, che, per non esser penetrabile alla veduta nostra il ciel cristallino, vero esser non può, che tale stella sia stata veduta nel Primo mobile. In una difficultà minima, in un capello consiste tutta la vostra forza. Orsù leviamo il capello a questo Niso, che in vero un capello è, che vi tien, che non vi arrendete: e posso ben dir contro di voi le parole del Petrarca. *Vedi Signor cortese, / Da che leve cagion, che crudel guerra.*

33 Delle Colombe, *Risposte piaceuoli*, 18r (my translation). The original reads:

> In questo sentimento fece l'impresa sua Cardinale Don Luigi da Este, la quale era una Sfera, o Orbe celeste, il motto *In motu immotus.* E ben veramente l'impresa, egli s'impresse nell'animo, poiche, come dice Torquato Tasso, nel dialogo dell'Imprese tra i movimenti della fortuna, e delle guerre, stette sempre immobile, e costante appunto come sta la mia dottrina al combatter della vostra.

34 Fortunio Liceti, *Litheosphorus, sive, De lapide Bononiensi lucem in se conceptam ab ambiente claro mox in tenebris mire conservante* (Udine: Schiratti, 1640), 25, 65–66, and 76, respectively.

35 Daniel Javitch, "The Imitation of Imitations in *Orlando furioso*," *Renaissance Quarterly* 38.2 (1985): 215–239.

36 Liceti, *Litheosphorus*, 14–15 (translation by Cara Polsley). Berni's verses from *An Anthology of Italian Poems 13th–19th Century*, ed. and trans. Lorna de' Lucchi (New York: Alfred A. Knopf, 1922), 136–137. The original Latin prose reads:

> Equidem concedo lapillum asperum, nomine scrupum, maiori molestia calcari, quam lapillum leni superficie; sed concedere nequeo, lapillum durissimum, ob solum sui laevorem calcantibus molestum non esse, ac intra calceamentum si forte inciderit, non augere laeder-eque calcantem; nequicquam ad molestiae carentiam conferente illius exiguitate; nam duritie solum impense laedit; unde bellissime festivus Poeta noster inter molestissimas molestias non ultimo loco posuit, cum Bartholino, cognominato dal Canto de' Bischeri, calculum in calceamento gestare, hoc Epigrammate … Ceterum hie homo fortasse Xantippe cuipiam nupserat, aut Megerae. Galenus, agens de Simplicium medicamentorum facultatibus, lapidem facit commune genus ad pumicem, ostracitem, Iaspidem, magnetem, gagatem, Assium, & alias plures species …

37 Liceti, *Litheosphorus*, 19.

38 See Albert Van Helden, introduction to Galileo Galilei, *"Sidereus nuncius"; or, "The Sidereal Messenger" [Starry Messenger] of Galileo Galilei*, trans. and ed. Albert Van Helden (University of Chicago Press, 1989), 1–24.

39 Richard S. Westfall, "Science and Patronage: Galileo and the Telescope," *Isis* 76.1 (March 1985): 11–30.

40 Galileo, *Sidereal Messenger*, 29. Galileo's language is strikingly similar to that of Boccaccio in the preface to his *Trattatello in laude di Dante* – or, in English, *The Life of Dante* (*c.* 1374). Of the Florentine master, Boccaccio writes:

> Although I am not sufficient for so great a task, nevertheless, what the city ought to have done for him in a magnificent fashion, but has not done, I will endeavor to do, according to my own poor ability. This will not be with a statue or noble burial, the custom of which has now perished among us (nor would my power suffice), but by my writing, which is a humble instrument for so great an undertaking.

(Giovanni Boccaccio, *The Life of Dante*, trans. J. G. Nichols [London: Hesperus Press, 2002], 7)

41 Galileo, *Sidereal Messenger*, 30.

42 Eileen Reeves, *Galileo's Glassworks: The Telescope and the Mirror* (Cambridge, MA: Harvard University Press, 2008), 142–143; Ladina Bezzola Lambert, *Imagining the Unimaginable: The Poetics of Early Modern Astronomy* (Amsterdam: Rodopi, 2002), 54.

43 Jean Dietz Moss, *Novelties in the Heavens: Rhetoric and Science in the Copernican Controversy* (University of Chicago Press, 1993), 81.

44 *Opere*, X, 299 (my translation). The original reads: "Resta hora che si procuri che questa azione, la quale per sua natura è la più eroica et sublime maniera di spiegare et propagare all'eternità le glorie de i gran principi, sia con ogni maggiore splendore et grandezza ricevuta dal mondo."

45 See Mario Biagioli, *Galileo's Instruments of Credit* (University of Chicago Press), 77–134.

46 *Opere*, X, 299 (my translation of "belli ingegni").

47 Heilbron, *Galileo*, 165–166.

48 *Opere*, X, 300–301 (my translation). The original reads: "et io son sicurissimo, che conoscendo Iddio benedetto l'ardentissimo affetto et devozion mia verso il mio clementissimo Signore, già che non mi haveva fatto né un Virgilio né un Homero, mi è voluto esser donatore di un altro mezo non meno peregrino et eccellente per decantare il suo nome, registrandolo in quelli eterni annali."

49 For a more detailed overview of these works, see Westman, *Copernican Question*, 468–477.

50 Girolamo Sirtori, *Hieronymi Sirturi mediolanensis Telescopium* (Frankfurt, 1618).

51 Simon Mayr, *Mundus Jovialis* (Nuremberg: Lauri, 1614). See also Heilbron, *Galileo*, 246.

52 Mayr, *Mundus Jovialis*, B2v.

53 Karl S. Guthke, *The Last Frontier: Imagining Other Worlds from the Copernican Revolution to Modern Science Fiction*, trans. Helen Atkins (Ithaca, NY: Cornell University Press, 1990), 88.

54 Westman, *Copernican Question*, 481–484; Heilbron, *Galileo*, 170–177.

55 Heilbron, *Galileo*, 208–212.

56 For an overview of this period in terms of its courtly context see Mario Biagioli, *Galileo, Courtier: The Practice of Science in a Culture of Absolutism* (University of Chicago Press, 1993), 159–209.

57 Andrea Battistini, *Galileo e i Gesuiti: Miti letterari e retorica della scienza* (Milan: Vita e Pensiero, 2000), 88 (my translation). The original reads: "non è altro che una replica più o meno eristica a critiche e opposizioni messegli contro da avversari tanto più combattivi e tenaci quanto meno attrezzati in sede epistemologica."

58 Pliny, *Natural History*, Book XXXV.

59 Dietz Moss, *Novelties*, 103.

60 *Ibid.*, 126.

61 Galileo Galilei and Christoph Scheiner, S.J., *On Sunspots*, trans. and ed. Eileen Reeves and Albert Van Helden (University of Chicago Press, 2010), 230.

62 *Ibid.*, 289. Reeves and Van Helden put the verb "vedere" in the present tense, but Galileo had cited the original text from Ariosto, which reads "si vidde."

63 *Ibid.*, 289 n. 58.

64 Heilbron, *Galileo*, 192.

65 *Ibid.*, 177–183.

66 See Michele Camerota, *Galileo Galilei e la cultura scientifica nell'età della Controriforma* (Rome: Salerno, 2004), 227–238.

67 See Biagioli, *Galileo Courtier*, 173.

68 Galileo, *Galileo against the Philosophers*, xx.

69 *Opere*, IV, 51 (my translation). The original reads: "sostener viva la mia proposizione ed, insieme con lei, molte altre che la conseguono, salvandole dalla voracità della bugia da me atterrata ed uccisa."

70 *Ibid.* (my translation). The original reads: "Non so se gli avversarii mi averanno di buon grado di così fatta opera."

71 *Ibid.* (my translation). The original reads: "o pure se, trovandosi con giuramento severo obbligati a sostener quasi che religiosamente ogni decreto di Aristotile, temendo forse che egli, sdegnato, non eccitassi alla lor destruzione un grosso stuolo di suoi più invitti eroi, si risolveranno a soffogarmi ed esterminarmi, come profanatore delle sue sante leggi."

72 Ariosto, *Orlando furioso*, XI.46–47.

73 *Opere*, IV, 51 (my translation). The original reads: "imitando in ciò gli abitatori dell'Isola del Pianto irati contro di Orlando, al quale, in guiderdone dell'aver egli liberate da l'orribile olocausto e dalla voracità del brutto mostro tante innocenti verginelle, so movevano contro, rimorsi da strana religione e spaventati da vano timore dell'ira di Proteo, per sommergerlo nel vasto oceano."

74 Citations in English from Ludovico Ariosto, *Orlando furioso*, trans. and ed. Barbara Reynolds (New York: Penguin, 1977), XI.46.2, 4; and in the Italian from Ludovico Ariosto, *Orlando furioso*, ed. Lanfranco Caretti (Turin: Einaudi, 1992), XI.46.3.

75 *Opere*, IV, 51 (my translation). The original reads: "se ben l'avriano fatto se egli, impenetrabile, ben che nudo, alle lor saette, non avesse fatto di loro quello che suol fare l'orso de i piccioli cagniuoli, che con vani e strepitosi latrati importunamente l'assordano." All references are to *Orlando furioso*, XI.49–50.

76 *Opere*, IV, 51 (my translation). The original reads: "Ma io, che non sono Orlando, né ho altro d'impenetrabile che lo scudo della verità, disarmato e nudo nel resto, ricorro alla protezione dell'A.V., al cui semplice sguardo cadranno in terra le armi di qualunque, fuori di ragione, contro alla ragione imperiosamente vorrà muovere assalti."

77 *Opere*, IV, 13.

78 *Opere*, IV, 673–674; and Ariosto, *Orlando furioso*, XXVIII.101.7–8 (my translation). The original reads:

A un'altra esperienza di alcuni Peripatetici, che avevano scritto, un uovo galleggiar nell'acqua salsa e descender nella dolce per esser la salsa più crassa e corpulenta, risponde il Sig. Galileo, questa essere una sciochezza grande, perchè con altrettanta ragione e con i medesimi mezzi si proverà, l'acqua dolce esser più grossa della salsa ... A questa ragion il Sig. Colombo risponde così: *Quella sperienza dell'uovo è del medesimo sapor dell'altre*; nè più oltre si distende la sua risposta. Ma che tal sapor non piaccia al Sig. Colombo, potrebbe per avventura non esser la colpa nella sua insipidezza, ma in quel che l'Ariosto scrive di Rodomonte: "Ma il Saracin, che con mal gusto nacque, / Non pur l'assaporò, che gli dispiacque." Però se voi non mostrate con miglior ragione la sciocchezza di quest'esperienza, credo che la risposta del Sig. Galileo resterà, quale ella è, efficacissima.

79 *Opere*, IV, 299 (my translation). The original reads: "come poverissimi anzi ignudi totalmente di niuna difesa, s'inducono, astretti da estrema miseria, a confessare per errori e fallacie le loro medesime proposizioni, non potendo trovarne tra le mie, pur che resti loro un poco di speranza di poterle far credere per cose mie."

80 *Ibid.* (my translation). The original reads: "lo strano partito del rival di Grifone alla cena di Norandino."

81 Ariosto, *Orlando furioso*, trans. Reynolds, XVII.90.3–8.

82 The popular motif has origins in Paracelsus, gains popularity through medieval commentators, and finally appears in common usage by the Renaissance. See Ernst Robert Curtius, *European Literature and the Latin Middle Ages*, trans. Willard R. Trask (Princeton University Press, 1953), 320–326.

83 Ariosto, *Orlando furioso*, trans. Reynolds, XVII.91.1–8.

84 *Ibid.*, XVII.92.1–8.

85 *Opere*, V, 285 (my translation). The original reads:

Ma se loro, contenendosi dentro a' termini naturali né producendo altr'arme che le filosofiche, sanno d'essere tanto superiori all'avversario, perché, nel venir poi al congresso, por subito mano a un'arme inevitabile e tremenda, che con la sola vista atterisce ogni più destro e esperto campione? Ma, s'io devo dir il vero, credo che essi sieno i primi atterriti, e che, sentendosi inabili a potere star forti contro gli assalti dell'avversario, tentino di trovar modo di non se lo lasciar accostare.

86 See Ariosto, *Orlando furioso*, X.48, 110; XV.10, 49; XX.76, 82, 88; XXXIII.125; XXIV.4; XLIV.19.

87 Shapin, *Social History of Truth*, 287 and 410 (original emphasis).

88 Dietz Moss, *Novelties*, 254.

89 Tibor Wlassics, "La genesi della critica letteraria di Galileo," *Aevum* 46 (1972): 215–236 (220; my translation). The original reads: "è in parte, gran parte, iniziativa dello stesso Galilei."

90 Andrea Battistini, "Galileo tra letteratura e scienza," in *Galileo scienziato, filosofo, scrittore: A quattro secoli dal "Sidereus nuncius,"* ed. Piero Di Pretoro and Rita Lukoshik (Munich: Martin Meidenbauer, 2011), 109–123.

3 SARSI AND THE SARACENS

1 Pietro Redondi, *Galileo Heretic*, trans. Raymond Rosenthal (Princeton University Press, 1987), 36–51.

2 J. L. Heilbron, *Galileo* (Oxford University Press, 2010), 22 and 245.

3 Mario Biagioli, *Galileo Courtier: The Practice of Science in a Culture of Absolutism* (University of Chicago Press, 1993), 309; *Opere*, XIII, 448.

4 Heilbron, *Galileo*, 228.

5 *Opere*, XIII, 37–38 (my translation). The original reads: "non vengha fuori a duello direttamente." All translations from Italian are mine unless otherwise indicated.

6 See Jean Dietz Moss, *Novelties in the Heavens: Rhetoric and Science in the Copernican Controversy* (University of Chicago Press, 1993).

7 Jean Dietz Moss and William A. Wallace, *Rhetoric and Dialectic in the Time of Galileo* (Washington, DC: Catholic University of America Press, 2003), 5.

8 William A. Wallace, "Antonio Riccobono: The Teaching of Rhetoric in 16th-Century Padua," in *Rhetoric and Pedagogy: Its History, Philosophy, and Practice. Essays in Honor of James J. Murphy*, ed. Winifred Bryan Horner and Michael Leff (Mahwah, NJ: J. Erlbaum, 1995), 149–170 (158).

9 Redondi, *Heretic*, 29.

10 William J. Kennedy, *Rhetorical Norms in Renaissance Literature* (New Haven: Yale University Press, 1978), 81.

11 Eileen Reeves, "Daniel 5 and the *Assayer*: Galileo Reads the Handwriting on the Wall," *Journal of Medieval and Renaissance Studies* 21 (1991): 1–27 (10).

12 Peter Armour, "Galileo and the Crisis in Italian Literature of the Early Seicento," in *Collected Essays on Italian Language and Literature Presented to Kathleen Speight*, ed. Giovanni Aquilecchia, Stephen N. Cristea, and Sheila Ralphs (New York: Barnes and Noble, 1971), 150.

13 *Ibid.*, 150.

14 *Opere*, VI, 380 n. 6 (my translation). The original reads: "non producete (ed anco troncamente) altro che quei luoghi da i quali vi par di poter rappresentar contradizzioni o altre fallacie, la falsità delle quali troppo chiaramente si conoscerebbe da chi avesse in pronto l'opera mia."

15 See Federico Barbierato, *The Inquisitor in the Hat Shop* (Farnham, VT: Ashgate, 2012), 168–171, 291–294.

16 Stillman Drake, *Galileo at Work: His Scientific Biography* (University of Chicago Press, 1978), 359.

17 See Massimo Bucciantini, *Galileo e Keplero* (Turin: Einaudi, 2003), 129, 132.

18 For a summary of this period in Galileo's life see Heilbron, *Galileo*, 233–251.

19 For a summary, see Camerota, *Galileo Galilei e la cultura scientifica nell'età della Controriforma* (Rome: Salerno, 2004), 363–398.

20 Galileo Galilei, Orazio Grassi, Mario Guiducci, and Johann Kepler, *The Controversy on the Comets of 1618*, trans. Stillman Drake (Philadelphia: University of Pennsylvania Press, 1960), xv–xvii.

21 See Ottavio Besomi and Michele Camerota, *Galileo e Il Parnaso Tychonico: Un capitolo inedito del dibattito sulle comete tra finzione letteraria a trattazione scientifica* (Florence: L. S. Olschki, 2000).

22 For a recent quantitative analysis and close reading in the case of the annotations to the *Libra* see Ottavio Besomi, "Galileo Reader and Annotator," in *The Inspiration of Astronomical Phenomena VI: Proceedings of a Conference Held October 18–23, 2009 in Venice, Italy*, ed. Enrico Maria Corsini (San Francisco: Astronomical Society of the Pacific, 2011), 43–54.

23 Armour, "Galileo and the Crisis," 164.

24 Ian Maclean, "The Interpretation of Natural Signs: Cardano's *De subtilitate* versus Scaliger's *Exercitationes*," in *Occult and Scientific Mentalities in the Renaissance*, ed. Brian Vickers (Cambridge University Press, 1984), 231–252 (233).

25 Galileo Galilei, *Considerazioni al Tasso*, in *Scritti letterari*, ed. Alberto Chiari (Florence: Le Monnier, 1970), I.26.

26 *Ibid.*, II.14.5–8 (my translation). The original reads: "da riempire canton voti, insipida, disgraziata e al solito pedantesca."

27 *Opere*, VI, 121 n. 31 (my translation of "arcipedanterie") and *Opere*, VI, 133 n. 68 (my translation).

28 Galileo, *Considerazioni al Tasso*, I.36 (my translation). The original reads: "impiasterete di molte carte, e farete una paniccia da cani."

29 *Opere*, III, 254 n. 4 (my translation of "palesandosi sopra tutti gl'ignoranti ignorantissimo") and *Opere* VI, 467 n. 122, respectively.

30 *Ibid.*, VII, 714 and 748 (my translations).

31 Galileo, *Considerazioni al Tasso*, II.40.7–8; II.52.8; VI.13.7; respectively (my translations).

32 *Opere*, III, 255.

33 *Ibid.*, II, 289 n. 1 (my translation). The original reads: "solo amator e defensore delle scientie matematiche contro dell'ignoranti calumniatori."

34 *Ibid.*, II, 289 n. 2.

35 Galileo, *Considerazioni al Tasso*, II.49.5; V.37.8; VI.27; XVI.24, 27.

36 *Opere*, II, 292 n. 6; and 456 n. 24.

37 Accademia della Crusca, ed., *Vocabolario degli Accademici della Crusca*, vers. 1.0, CRIBeCu, 2001, http://vocabolario.signum.sns.it/ (my translation). The original reads: "Quegli che guida i fanciulli, ed insegna loro, al qual noi diciam pedante."

38 Francesco Belo, *Il pedante*, in *Commedie del Cinquecento*, ed. Nino Borsellino, 2 vols., Vol. II (Milan: Feltrinelli, 1967), 99–191 (109; my translation). The original reads: "La comedia si chiama *El pedante*, quale è persona che, con le lettere in mano, defenderà le ragioni sue."

39 *Ibid.* (my translation). The original reads: "affumati procuratori [abietti pedanti] che parlano peggio de un todesco quando si Sforza de parlar italiano."

40 See Antonio Stäuble, *Parlar per lettera: Il pedante nella commedia del Cinquecento e altri saggi sul teatro rinascimentale* (Rome: Bulzoni, 1991).

41 For example, Galileo, *Considerazioni al Tasso*, II.5.3–4: "pedantone."

42 *Ibid.*, II.10.3–4; II.17.7–8; and II.40.7–8.

43 *Ibid.* III.41.7–8; and III.45.8. The full relevant comments are, respectively: "Come è possibile che questo autore, che pur dice delle cose buone, non abbia orecchio da conoscere queste putterie?" and "Parmi pur di vedere il pedantino tutto giubilare, intenerirsi d'allegrezza, nel riconoscere i tesori più cari delle sue eleganze, e sentirsi per tutti li membri, e insino alle radici de' capelli, scorrere un certo burlichio, non meno di quello che si faccia la cara madre guardata dal figliuolo, mentre gli pare che esso, o nel ballo o nel canto o in altra onesta operazione, vinca i suoi coetanei fanciulli."

44 *Opere*, VI, 150 n. 120 (my translation). The original reads: "Noi aviamo imparato da Tolomeo, e non da i pedantuzzi; però non vi maravigliate se non aviamo sapute queste cose, e voi sì: e se voi avesse imparato dal medesimo, non direste queste gofferie."

45 Galileo Galilei, *The Assayer*, trans. Stillman Drake and C. D. O'Malley, in *The Controversy on the Comets of 1618* (Philadelphia: University of Pennsylvania Press, 1960), 198.

46 *Opere*, VI, 160, 266, 283, and 356, respectively. For more information on the use of these vignettes, see Crystal Hall, "Galileo's Rhetoric of Fable," *Quaderni d'Italianistica* 31.2 (2010): 91–112.

47 See Henrique Leitão, "Galileo's Telescopic Observations in Portugal," in *Largo campo di filosofare,* ed. José Montesinos and Carlos Solís, Eurosymposium Galileo 2001 (La Orotava: Fundación Canaria Orotava de la Historia de la Ciencia, 2001), 903–913.

48 Giovanni Camillo Glorioso, *Responsio Jo. Camilli Gloriosi ad controversias de Cometis Peripateticas* (Venice, 1626), 15 (translation by Cara Polsley):

> Ac monet me tandem, ut pro certo habeam viros eruditos nunquam opinaturos me talem esse Homerum, a quo suus Virgilius orationis flosculos delibare voluerit; profecto si Homerus ego non sum, nec ipse Virgilius est: tamen pro certo habeo illum a me multo meliora, quam orationis flosculos delibasse; & qui sunt isti viri eruditi, qui hoc nunquam sunt opinaturi? fortassis illi duo, aut ad summum tres Scholares novitij, & imberbes, cum quibus per Gymnasium, & per civitatem pompam facit? alios non credo equidem.

49 Galileo Galilei, *Postille all'Ariosto*, in *Scritti letterari*, x.24.7–8. The original reads: "si chiamano le persone, e non i nomi."

50 *Opere*, VII, 748 (my translation of "distanza da chi, Sig. Rocco?").

51 *Ibid.*, III, 273 n. 30.

52 Galileo, *Considerazioni al Tasso*, XVI.7.

53 *Ibid.*, II.60.8 (my translation). The original reads:

> Credo che senza altre presunzioni ciascheduno potrà da per sé stesso conoscere, quanto questo *In guise pur d'uom grande e non curante* sia pedantesco e ampulloso: solo avvertisco

che si comincia a metter mano alla scatola del *grande*, per condire, come si vedrà nel progresso, molte e molte minestre di *gran* capi, c.3, st.52, *gran* tauri, c.3. st.32, *gran* corpi, c.6, st.23, *gran* cavalli, e di molte altre *gran* cose; il qual condimento al gusto di questo poeta, se io non m'inganno, è molto a proposito per fare lo stil grande.

54 *Ibid.*, III.35.4 (my translation). The original reads: "Tocca pur su, con quel maledetto *grande*! Dovevano esser due gran facchini, chè tanto è in lingua toscana dir *gran figli.*"

55 *Opere*, VII, 719 (my translation). The original reads: "Il nome ... appresso di voi si tira in consequenza l'identità della sostanza? Oh, Signor mio, non chiamate ancora *stella* quella piccola macchietta Bianca per la quale un cavallo si dice stellato in fronte? non si nomina *stella* la girella dello sperone? niuna di queste è che differisca più da una reale stella del cielo."

56 Galileo Galilei, *Galileo against the Philosophers in His "Dialogue of Cecco di Ronchitti" (1605) and "Considerations of Alimberto Mauri" (1606)*, trans. Stillman Drake (Los Angeles: Zeitlin & Ver Brugge, 1976), 39.

57 For an expansive discussion of Galileo's lexicon, see Maria Luisa Altieri Biagi, *Galileo e la terminologia tecnico-scientifica* (Florence: Olschki, 1965).

58 Galileo *et al.*, *Controversy on the Comets*, xx.

59 *Opere*, VI, 380–1 n. 7 (my translation). The original reads: "Io, alla vostra imitazione, potrei dire che il nome *Simbellatore* vien da i zimbelli, che sono alcuni piccoli sacchetti pieni di crusca, legati in capo di una cordicella, con i quali i nostri fattori il carnovale soglion sacchettare e zimbellare le maschere."

60 Galileo, *Assayer*, 218.

61 *Opere*, VI, 128 n. 53 (my translation). The original reads: "Messer Lottario, voi ci vorresti cambiar le carte in mano; e come la balia toglie il gioiello al bambino, e mostrandoli il cielo dice: 'Ve' ve' gli angiolini,' e supone in luogo della gemma una castagna, così vorresti voi con diverticoli gettarci la polvere negli occhi, e trattarci da insensati. Non è già questa dottrina Gesuitica."

62 Galileo, *Assayer*, 279.

63 See Antonio Favaro, "La libreria di Galileo Galilei, descritta ed illustrata," *Bullettino di bibliografia e storia delle scienze matematiche e fisiche* 19 (1886): 219–293.

64 Galileo, *Postille all'Ariosto*, VII.66.2 (my translation). The original reads: "Ragionando così la maga venne: sarà miglior verso, e la parola *venne* sarà posta tre volte, e sempre in diverso significato." The line in question from Ariosto is "così parlando, la maga rivenne."

65 *Opere*, IV, 443 (my translation). The original reads: "Non mette conto il mettersi a confutare uno che è tanto ignorante, che, per confuter tutte le sue ignorantaggini (essendo quelle più che le righe della sua scrittura), bisognerebbe scriver volumi grandissimi, con nissuna utilità degl' intendenti e senza vantaggiarsi niente appresso il vulgo."

66 Galileo Galilei and Christoph Scheiner, S.J., *On Sunpots*, trans. and ed. Eileen Reeves and Albert Van Helden (University of Chicago Press, 2010), 104, 126, 292, and 259–262, respectively.

67 Galileo, *Considerazioni al Tasso*, I.33 7 (my translation). The original reads: "Diremo che chi non sa quel che si dire, e pur vuol empiere il foglio, bisogna che scriva di queste gentilezze." The second citation is translated in Galileo, *Assayer*, 269.

68 Galileo, *Postille all'Ariosto*, VII.42–43 (my translation). The original reads: "Di grazia, Sig. Lodovico, contentatevi che queste due stanze si levino, perché questa esagerazione è un poco lunghetta, e va nel fine languendo e scemando l'agitazione."

69 Galileo, *Considerazioni al Tasso*, III.II (my translation). The original reads: "S'è consumata una intera stanza in raccontare il grido del talacimanno; e ora delle provisioni che deve fare Aladino per la difesa di Ierusalemme, sopragiungendoli il nimico, si disbriga con due parole."

70 Galileo, *Assayer*, 198.

71 *Opere*, II, 499 n. 128 (my translation). The original reads: "Ecco il suo fiero destino, il quale fa constare, dalla falsità di quanto dice qui, che quello che ha detto di sopra non è sua farina."

72 Francesco Petrarca, *Trionfo della Fama*, III.48; and Ludovico Ariosto, *Orlando furioso*, IV.30.5.

73 Galileo Galilei, *Le postille al Petrarca*, ed. Nereo Vianello (Florence: Sansoni, 1956), 356 (III.48).

74 Ariosto, *Orlando furioso*, IV.30; XXX.28; XXXIX.78; XLII.37.

75 Heilbron, *Galileo*, 103.

76 *Opere*, VI, 152 n. 123 (my translation). The original reads: "Se il Sarsi tassa in certo modo il Sig. Mario di copiatore, il quale tutta via scrive moltissime cose non scritte da altri, come non sarà egli il medesimo che il P. Grassi, che non scrive cosa non detta da molti altri? Questo sarebbe un voler perdonare a sè stesso quei difetti che in altri condanna e biasima."

77 Steven Shapin, *A Social History of Truth: Civility and Science in Seventeenth-Century England* (University of Chicago Press, 1994), 268.

78 Favaro, "Libreria di Galileo," entry 83.

79 Anton Francesco Doni, *The Moral Philosophy of Doni Popularly Known as "The Fables of Bidpai" (A Collection of Sanskrit, Persian, and Arabic Fables) 1570*, ed. Donald Beecher, John Butler, and Carmine Di Biase, trans. Sir Thomas North (Ottawa: Dovehouse Editions, 2003), 11–27.

80 Anton Francesco Doni, *Le novelle. Tomo I. La moral filosofia. Trattati*, ed. Patrizia Pellizzari (Rome: Salerno Editrice, 2002), 17–18 (my translation). The original reads:

> Non facciamo adunque come quel poco accorto uomo ignorante, che desiderava d'esser tenuto literato e molto ornato nel favellare, onde pregò un suo grande amico, poeta e buon retorico, che gli volesse dare alcuna cosa scritta dotta ed eloquente, la quale imparata, la potesse recitare in compagnia degli altri sapienti, per non parer da manco di loro. L'amico lo sodisfece, onde sopra un libretto tutto dorato e ben ligato gli scrisse molte sentenze e molti detti sapienti: tal che egli cominciò a imparare a mente questa autorità, e durato un tempo giorno e note fatica a mandarle a memoria, si deliberò di mostrar che anco egli era dotto. Trovatosi adunque a ragionamento (non sapendo le parole imparate

quel che le volessero significare, per essere in altra lingua che nella sua natia) cominciò ad allegare questi suoi detti fuor di proposito; così fu ripreso e fattosi beffe di lui. Egli, quasi adirato, come ostinato ignorante rispose: – Come posso io errar, che tutto questo ho imparato d'un libro fatto da valente uomo? ed è tutto messo d'oro! – Allora ciascun rise della sua ignoranza.

81 *Opere*, VI, 234.

82 Battistini identifies this strategy as "slittaggio" and gives the following example from the discussion of falling objects as evidence for the rotation of the Earth:

> la relatività del moto in una nave è esteso per analogia a *tutti* i casi di moto, sia terrestre sia celeste: in termini di *elocutio*, dopo il "trucco" della metafora che alla torre sostituisce il pennone di una nave di cui si ammette in anticipo il movimento, si assiste ora a una sineddoche del tipo *pars prototo*, con cui il moto ammesso per ipotesi, trasferito alla terra, diventa il risultato finale della dimostrazione.

(Andrea Battistini, *Galileo e i Gesuiti: Miti letterari e retorica della scienza* [Milan: Vita e Pensiero, 2000], 131.)

83 Galileo, *Assayer*, 189. *Opere*, VI, 236. The Italian reads: "volano a stormi dovunque si posano, empiendo il ciel di strida e di rumori."

84 Heilbron, *Galileo*, 248–250.

85 Lanfranco Caretti, "Galileo uomo di lettere," in *Studi di lettere e di storia di memoria di Antonio Di Pietro* (Milan: Vita e Pensiero, 1977), 113.

86 See Daniel Javitch, "The Imitation of Imitations in the *Orlando furioso*," *Renaissance Quarterly* 38.2 (1985): 215–239.

87 Ludovico Ariosto, *Orlando furioso*, trans. and ed. Barbara Reynolds (New York: Penguin, 1977), XIV.110.1–3.

88 *Opere*, VI, 270 (translation given in Galileo, *Assayer*, 225). Drake translates the plural *balene* in the Italian to a singular whale. I have corrected this in the text.

89 Galileo, *Assayer*, 369 n. 17; and Galileo, *Saggiatore*, ed. Ottavio Besomi and Mario Helbing (Rome: Antenore, 2005), 529 nn. 12, 16.

90 Ariosto, *Orlando furioso*, XI.36–39.

91 *Opere*, VI, 310 (my translation). The original reads: "qui poi non ci è altro da fare per l'oppugnatore se non istringersi nelle spalle e tacere. Quando si ha da convincer l'avversario, bisogna affrontarlo colle sue più favorevoli, e non colle più pregiudiciali, asserzioni; altrimenti se gli lascia sempre da ritirarsi in franchigia, lasciando l'inimico come attonito e insensato, e qual restò Ruggiero allo sparir d'Angelica." Drake and O'Malley give a slightly different translation in Galileo, *Assayer*, 268: "Here there is nothing for us to do except shrug our shoulders and remain silent. If Sarsi is to win over his adversaries, he must confront them with their own most favorable assertions, and not with those most prejudicial to them; otherwise he allows them to escape every time, leaving their enemies feeling stunned and foolish – as Ruggiero felt at the disappearance of Angelica."

92 Daniel Javitch, "The Poetics of *Variatio* in *Orlando furioso*," *Modern Language Quarterly* 66.1 (2005): 1–20.

93 Ariosto, *Orlando Furioso*, trans. Reynolds, XI.vi.2–4.

94 *Opere*, VI, 317; Galileo, *Assayer*, 276.

95 *Opere*, VI, 330 (my translation of the prose). The original reads: "E qui mi fa sovvenire del detto di quell'argutissimo Poeta: Per la spada d'Orlando, che non ànno / e forse non son anco per avere / queste mazzate da ciechi si dànno." Drake gives the translation: "Here Sarsi reminds me of the saying of that most witty poet: 'By Orlando's sword, which they have not, / And perhaps which they never shall have, / These blows of the blind have been given.'" (Galileo, *Assayer*, 290.) The translation and original are provided in Matteo Maria Boiardo, *Orlando innamorato*, trans. Charles Stanley Ross, ed. Anne Finnigan (Berkeley: University of California Press, 1989) III.vi.50,3–5.

96 Boiardo, *Orlando innamorato*, trans. Ross III.vi.50: "Dicea Rugiero: Io gli ho pregati in vano, / Ma di partirli ancor non ho potere. / Per la spata de Orlando, che non hano, / E forse non sono anco per avere, / Tal bastonate da ciechi si dano, / Che pietà per me ne vien pur a vedere: / E certo di prodezza e di possanza / Son due lumiere agli atti e alla sembianza."

97 Galileo, *Assayer*, 298. Galileo is not the only author to refer to intellectual obstacles as chimeras. Near the end of the first book of Tartaglia's *Quesiti*, in interrogation 28, the gunner says to Nicolo: "Queste vostre ragioni certamente me ingrassano, & questo procede perche le comenzo à inte[n]dere è per questo mio intendere, qua[n]do che mi credeva di puor fine à miei quesiti, le vostre argumentazioni me inducono nove chimere nella me[n] te mia, over novi dubbi de adimandarvi, ma dubito di non farvi fastidio" (Niccolò Tartaglia, *Quesiti et inventioni diverse de Nicolo Tartalea Brisciano* [Venice: Ruffinelli, 1546], fo. 31r.)

98 Galileo, *Assayer*, 299. *Opere*, VI, 338. Galileo cites Ariosto, *Orlando furioso*, XXX.49.

99 See also Sergio Zatti, *The Quest for Epic: From Ariosto to Tasso*, ed. and trans. Dennis Looney (University of Toronto Press, 2006), 77–78.

100 *Opere*, VI, 375 (my translation of the motto "Discordes animos compone, hasque opprime flammas").

101 Ariosto, *Orlando furioso*, XXXVII.60.1–2 (my translation). The original Italian, as cited in *Opere*, VI, 375 n. 1, reads: "Simula il viso pace, ma vendetta / Chiama il cor dentro, e ad altro non attende."

102 For an analysis, see Eric Nicholson, "Romance as Role Model: Early Performances of *Orlando furioso* and *Gerusalemme liberata*," in *Renaissance Transactions: Ariosto and Tasso*, ed. Valeria Finucci (Durham, NC: Duke University Press, 1999), 259–261.

103 Galileo Galilei, *On the World Systems*, trans. and ed. Maurice A. Finocchiaro (Berkeley: University of California Press, 1997), 90.

104 Ariosto, *Orlando furioso*, XIX.48.6; and Torquato Tasso, *Gerusalemme liberata*, XI.51.5.

105 Ariosto, *Orlando furioso*, XIX.48.5–6 (my translation). The original reads: "Sul mare intanto e spesso al ciel vicino / L'afflitto e conquassato legno toma."

106 Galileo Galilei, *Concerning the Two Chief World Systems*, trans. Stillman Drake (Berkeley: University of California Press, 1967), 446–447; *Opere*, VII, 472.

107 Ariosto, *Orlando furioso*, XXIII.102.

108 *Ibid.*, XXIII.102–120.

109 Maurice Finocchiaro, *Galileo and the Art of Reasoning: Rhetorical Foundations of Logic and Scientific Method* (Dordrecht–Boston: Reidel, 1980), 64.

110 Galileo, *Chief World Systems*, 447; *Opere*, VII, 472.

111 *Opere*, VIII, 169 (my translation).

112 Galileo, *Dialogues Concerning Two New Sciences*, trans. Henry Crew and Alfonso de Salvio, ed. and commentary Stephen Hawking (Philadelphia: Running Press, 2002), 100; *Opere*, VIII, 169; Ariosto, *Orlando furioso*, XVII.30.1–2.

113 Boiardo, *Orlando innamorato*, trans. Ross, III.iii.28.3.

114 Erwin Panofsky, "Galileo as a Critic of the Arts, Aesthetic Attitude and Scientific Thought," *Isis* 47 (1956): 3–15 (6). Panofsky had just expressed his opinion on the interpretation of this passage:

> Galileo here credits his favorite poet with more physical insight than he possessed. What Ariosto means to say is that, if the *width* of the giant [Panofsky's note: "*grosso*, incorrectly translated by 'size' in the *Two New Sciences*, trans. H. Crew and A. de Salvio, 131"], which should be comparatively easy to estimate because he stands on the same level as does the beholder, is "beyond measure," the giant's *height*, extending far beyond eye level, is quite impossible to calculate.

115 Mark Peterson has recently added to the interpretation of this passage that it was originally intended to counter objections made by a challenger of Galileo's lectures on the *Inferno* decades earlier; Mark Peterson, *Galileo's Muse* (Cambridge, MA: Harvard University Press, 2011), 232–233.

116 Galileo, *Chief World Systems*, 437; *Opere*, VII, 463.

117 Galileo, *Chief World Systems*, 437–438; *Opere*, VII, 463.

118 *Opere*, XX, 64.

119 Torquato Tasso, *Jerusalem Delivered*, trans. and ed. Anthony Esolen (Baltimore: Johns Hopkins University Press, 2000), XII.63. The Italian reads: "Qual l'alto Egeo, perché Aquilone o Noto / cessi, che tutto prima il volse e scosse, / non s'accheta ei però, ma 'l suono e 'l moto / ritien de l'onde anco agitate e grosse" (Torquato Tasso, *Gerusalemme liberata,* ed. Lanfranco Caretti [Turin: Einaudi, 1993], XII.63.1–4).

120 Galieo, *Assayer*, 186; *Opere*, VI, 234.

121 Galileo Galilei, *Opere*, ed. Ferdinando Flora (Milan: Riccardo Ricciardi, 1953), 801.

122 Ariosto, *Orlando furioso*, XLVI.59.1 (my translation). Many thanks to Albert R. Ascoli for calling my attention to this line in the *Furioso*.

123 See Ovid, *Metamorphoses*, VII.402.

4 GALILEO'S LESSON ON *DON CHISCIOTTE* (1622–1625)

1 See Thomas R. Hart, *Cervantes and Ariosto: Renewing Fiction* (Princeton University Press, 1989), 16–54.

2 Galileo Galilei, *Concerning the Two Chief World Systems*, trans. Stillman Drake (Berkeley: University of California Press, 1967), 113; *Opere*, VII, 139.

3 See John Jay Allen, *Don Quixote: Hero or Fool? Remixed* (Newark, DE: Juan de la Cuesta, 2008).

4 Juan Maldonado, *Spanish Humanism on the Verge of the Picaresque: Juan Maldonado's "Ludus chartarum," "Pastor bonus," and "Bacchanalia,"* ed. and trans. Warren Smith and Clark Colàhan (Leuven University Press, 2009), 67.

5 I have found only one suggestive remark on the similar challenges of creating a believable text encountered by the authors of fiction and the new authors of science, namely Cervantes and Galileo, in the work of E. C. Riley, *Cervantes' Theory of the Novel* (Newark, NJ: Juan de la Cuesta, 1992), 189.

6 In Biblioteca Nazionale Centrale di Firenze, Manoscritti Galileiani, MS 308, fo. 171v we see "Avinoavolittone berlinghieri poema 12." The editor of the national edition of Galileo's work, Antonio Favaro, points out that no editions of Bardi's work appear before 1643, one year after Galileo's death.

7 Redondi provides a "blow by blow" account of "Operazione Sarseide" that includes dates and events, such as: "1620, 10–18 maggio. Durante un soggiorno nel palazzo ducale di Aquasparta, vicino ad Urbino, nella residenza di campagna del principe Cesi, il nucleo operativo romano dell'Accademia dei Lincei – Cesi, Ciampoli e Cesarini – decide l'operazione «sarseide», nello stile epico-satirico delle infuocate letterarie del momento." Pietro Redondi, *Galileo eretico* (Turin: Einaudi, 1986), 52.

8 Archivio di Stato di Firenze, Fondo Notarile Moderno, Protocolli, 15676–15685 (Silvestro Pantera, 1646–1650), MS 3483.3 (hereafter Arch. MS 3483.3) lists "pensieri del Tassoni, ii." Tassoni's *Pensieri diversi* were themselves subject to revision because of the 1616 edict and Galileo's attempts on a trip to Rome in 1624 to convince Urban VIII to soften his approach to astronomical questions. See Alessandro Tassoni, *Pensieri e scritti preparatori*, ed. Pietro Puliatti (Modena: Edizioni Panini, 1986), 512–518.

9 Alessandro Tassoni, *De' pensieri diversi di Alessandro Tassoni. Dieci Libri* (Venice: Barezzi, 1646), 395. The original reads: "gli Antichi, non havendo per tanti secoli trovati competitori, si sieno andati avanzando ad un eccesso di fama tale, che 'l passare più oltre paia richiedere ingegno sopraumano."

10 Ezio Raimondi highlights the renewed interest during the early modern period in the world of mendicants and thieves, a world not entirely unrelated to that of the knights errant in heroic tales. See Ezio Raimondi, *La dissimulazione romanzesca: Antropologia manzoniana* (Bologna: Il Mulino, 1997).

11 The full Italian title is *Opera nuoua nella quale si scoprono le fraudi, malitie, & inganni di coloro, che vanno girando il mondo alle spese altrui. Et vi si raccontano*

*molti casi in diuersi luoghi, e tempi successi. Data in luce per auuertimento de'
semplici dal sig. Rafaele Frianoro (A New Work in which Are Uncovered the
Frauds, Maliciousness, and Tricks of Those who Traverse the World at the Expense
of Others: Brought to Light to Warn the Simple by Rafaele Frianoro).* See Favaro's
hesitation in his note to entry no. 461 in "La libreria di Galileo Galilei,
descritta ed illustrata," *Bullettino di bibliografia e storia delle scienze matematiche e fisiche* 19 (1886): 219–293.

12 Andrea Battistini, *Galileo e i Gesuiti: Miti letterari e retorica della scienza*
(Milan: Vita e Pensiero, 2000), 2–3.

13 *Ibid.*, 2 (my translation of "maestro del carnevalesco").

14 Arch. MS 3483.3. This is the 1649 inheritance document compiled at the death
of Galileo's son, Vincenzo Galilei, Jr.

15 Emanuele Zinato writes: "Il decreto anticopernicano del 1616 e la condanna
di Galileo del 1633 si tradussero in tutta Europa in un rincaro nelle strat-
egie della dissimulazione e della menzogna nell'orchestrazione retorica del
discorso scientifico" ("The anti-Copernican decree of 1616 and the condemnation of Galileo in 1633 were translated in all of Europe into an increase
in the practices of dissimulation and lying in the rhetorical orchestration of
scientific discourse" [my translation]). Emanuele Zinato, *Il vero in maschera.
Dialoghismi galileiani: Idee e forme nelle prose scientifiche del Seicento* (Naples:
Liguori, 2003) 165.

16 Much work has been done on the similarities between the content of the
Quixote and that of the *Furioso*. As Thomas Hart has said, "Both *Orlando
furioso* and *Don Quixote* examine the disparity between life as we experience
it and life as it is depicted in books"; Hart, *Cervantes and Ariosto*, 39. Hart
continues: "They demand that we read them as new answers to old questions,
ones posed, perhaps centuries before, in other books" (55).

17 See Howard Marchitello, *The Machine in the Text: Science and Literature in the
Age of Shakespeare and Galileo* (Oxford University Press, 2011).

18 I am going to insist on speaking of narratives of order concerning the universe. Precedent has been set by Foucault, who writes in *The Order of Things*:

> Order is, at one and the same time, that which is given in things as their inner law, the
> hidden network that determines the way they confront one another, and also that which
> has no existence except in the grid created by a glance, an examination, a language; and it
> is only in the blank spaces of this grid that order manifests itself in depth as though already
> there, waiting in silence for the moment of its expression.

(Michel Foucault, *The Order of Things: An Archaeology of the Human Sciences*
[London: Tavistock Publications, 1970], xx.)

19 *Opere*, VII, 302.

20 See Victoria Kirkham, *Laura Battifera and Her Literary Circle* (University of
Chicago Press, 2006), 42–43.

21 For a history of the disbelief associated with the telescope, see Mario Biagioli,
Galileo's Instruments of Credit (University of Chicago, 2007), 111–115.

22 The *Letter to the Grand Duchess* circulated in manuscript form until it was
printed in Latin by the Elsevier brothers in Leiden, 1636.

23 Walter L. Reed, *An Exemplary History of the Novel* (University of Chicago Press, 1981), 71.

24 Ronald Paulson argues in a similar vein about Cervantes and Rabelais: that their "intention of questioning outmoded patterns of thought, the technique of confronting romance with realism, and the ambiguous attitude toward the protagonist were the same"; Ronald Paulson, *The Fictions of Satire* (Baltimore: Johns Hopkins University Press, 1967), 100.

25 This is one reason that Foucault does not consider Galileo to be an author: readers do not return to his texts for new information. See Michel Foucault, "What Is an Author?," in *Twentieth-Century Literary Theory*, ed. Vassilis Lambropoulos and David Neal Miller (Albany: State University Press of New York, 1987), 124–142.

26 Battistini, *Galileo e i Gesuiti*, 7 (my translation of "paladini della tradizione").

27 The full quotation was mentioned at the beginning of Chapter 1: "Philosophy is written in this grand book – I mean the universe – which stands continually open to our gaze, but it cannot be understood unless one first learns to comprehend the language and interpret the characters in which it is written. It is written in the language of mathematics …"; Galileo Galilei, *The Assayer*, trans. Stillman Drake and C. D. O'Malley, in *The Controversy on the Comets of 1618* (Philadelphia: University of Pennsylvania Press, 1960), 183–184.

28 Translation in *ibid.*, 184.

29 Andrea Battistini, "Il libro, il labirinto, la fabbrica del mondo: Metafore epistemologiche della nuova scienza di Galileo," in *Quando l'opera interpella il lettore: Poetiche e forme della modernità letteraria*, ed. Piero Pieri and Giuliana Benvenuti (Bologna: Edizioni Pendragon, 2000), 27–43 (35).

30 Galileo, *Assayer*, 183.

31 Miguel de Cervantes Saavedra, *Don Quixote*, trans. Samuel Putnam (New York: Modern Library, 1998), 27.

32 Perhaps in an ironic twist, we find in Aristotle's *Generation of Animals* the following passage: "distant objects would be seen best of all if there were a sort of continuous tube extending straight from the sight to that which is seen, for then the movement which proceeds from the visible objects would not get dissipated." Albert Van Helden cites this passage in *The Invention of the Telescope* (Philadelphia: American Philosophical Society, 2008 [1977]), 9; he uses A. L. Peck's translation. Galileo mocks this supposition in the *Chief World Systems* by having Salviati tell the story of "a professor teaching at a famous university" who attributes the invention of the telescope to Aristotle by connecting the instrument to a passage on the optics of water wells. Galileo Galilei, *On the World Systems*, trans. Maurice A. Finocchiaro (Berkeley: University of California Press, 1997), 121; *Opere*, VII, 135.

33 Galileo Galilei and Christoph Scheiner, S.J., *On Sunspots*, trans. and ed. Eileen Reeves and Albert Van Helden (University of Chicago Press, 2010), 128.

34 Galileo, *Assayer*, 186; *Opere*, VI, 234.

35 Galileo, *On the World Systems*, 203. *Opere* VII, 231.

36 Galileo, *Chief World Systems*, 233; *Opere*, VII, 259.

37 Horace, *On Poetry: The "Ars poetica,"* ed. and commentary Charles Oscar Brink (Cambridge University Press, 1971), verse 359 (my translation of the verse).

38 Cervantes, *Don Quixote*, 498.

39 *Ibid.*, 499.

40 Galileo Galilei, *Considerazioni al Tasso*, in *Scritti letterari*, ed. Alberto Chiari (Florence: Le Monnier, 1970), I.12 (my translation). The original reads: "Non so quanto abbia di decoro quel far parlare Iddio per interrogazione, domandando perché si cessa o perché non si rinnuovi la guerra; e per avventura avrebbe più del divino il comandare assolutamente, senza altre cirimonie."

41 *Ibid.*, III.17 (my translation). The original reads: "anche in mezzo alla polvere della scaramuccia, che sono cose che a' nostri tempi non si potrian fare nè anche nella distanza d'un ottavo di miglio."

42 See Frédérique Aït-Touati, *Fictions of the Cosmos: Science and Literature in the Seventeenth Century*, trans. Susan Emanuel (University of Chicago Press, 2011), 97–110.

43 Galileo, *Assayer*, 252.

44 Galileo, *On the World Systems*, 155. *Opere* VII, 159.

45 *Ibid.*

46 See Nicolaus Copernicus, *On the Revolutions*, ed. Jerzy Dobrzycki, trans. and commentary Edward Rosen (Baltimore: Johns Hopkins University Press, 1978), 4.

47 Galileo, *Considerazioni al Tasso*, I.1 (my translation). The original reads:

> Uno tra gli altri difetti è molto familiare al Tasso, nato da una grande strettezza di vena e povertà di concetti; ed è, che mancandogli ben spesso la materia, è costretto andar rappezzando insieme concetti spezzati e senza dependenza e connessione tra loro, onde la sua narrazione ne riesce più presto una pittura intarsiata, che colorita a olio: perché essendo le tarsie un accozzamento di legnetti di diversi colori, con i quali non possono già mai accoppiarsi e unirsi così dolcemente che non restino i lor confini taglienti e dalla diversità de' colori crudamente distinti, rendono per necessità le lor figure secche, crude, senza tondezza e rilievo.

48 Cicero, *De oratore*, iii.43. Eileen Reeves ties this to Galileo's criticism of unscientific practices in other contexts; see *Painting the Heavens* (Princeton University Press, 1999), 41–46. For the history of this topos see Eric McPhail, "The Mosaic of Speech: A Classical Topos in Renaissance Aesthetics," *Journal of the Warburg and Courtauld Institutes* 66 (2003): 249–264.

49 In the case of the compass, Capra's plagiarized form is so corrupt that Galileo doubts its effectiveness as a signifier entirely, saying in a marginal note: "Non credo che uomo del mondo possa intender niente; nè anco credo che l'autore sappia ciò che abbia voluto dire, nè che intenda, non che altro, come lo strumento va tenuto in mano" (*Opere*, II, 493 n. III).

50 Cervantes, *Don Quixote*, 499.

51 Galileo, *Assayer*, 189.

52 See Dante, *Inferno*, XVI–XVII.

53 Cervantes, *Don Quixote*, 501.

54 Galileo, *Assayer*, 215.
55 See Francis Meynell and Stanley Morison, "Printers' Flowers and Arabesques," The Fleuron 1 (1923): 1–43.
56 *Opere*, VII, 258 (my translation). The original reads: "Oh che belle figure, che uccelli, che palle, e che altre belle cose son queste?"
57 The best, and perhaps most famous, example from Galileo's library is Franz d'Aguilon's *Opticorum libri sex* (Antwerp: Plantin Press, 1613), for which the famous Flemish artist Peter Paul Rubens designed six engravings of various *putti* (cherubs) examining the eye of the cyclops, measuring the dimensions of the Colossus of Rhodes, and using various instruments of optics.
58 For other examples of these diagrams and illustration see the exhibit organized by William B. Ashworth, Jr. and Bruce Bradley, *Jesuit Science in the Age of Galileo: An Exhibition of Rare Books from the History of Science Collection: March 24–July 31, 1986* (Kansas City, MO: Linda Hall Library, 1986).
59 Cervantes, *Don Quixote*, 515.
60 Galileo, *Dialogues Concerning Two New Sciences*, trans. Henry Crew and Alfonso de Salvio (Philadelphia: Running Press, 2002), 48; *Opere*, VIII, 106.
61 The interpretative strategy is similar to that used by Galileo's detractors in the debate over the passage in Joshua that mentions the Sun standing still in the *Letter to the Grand Duchess*. Unfortunately, similar debates exist about the language of Galileo as proof (or not) of which experiments he actually completed and those he imagined.
62 Cervantes, *Don Quixote*, 519.
63 *Opere*, VII, 487–488.
64 Alban Forcione has argued that the Canon of Toledo represents the complete arc of development of literary criticism of epic poems, and argues effectively that his complaints mirror those of Tasso: structural disorder takes away from the pleasure of the work, as does a lack of empirical possibility for the elements of fiction. Forcione presents Quixote's rebuttal as a statement that truth is always a function of belief, and that belief depends on the individual. See Alban K. Forcione, *Cervantes, Aristotle, and the Persiles* (Princeton University Press, 1970).
65 Carlos Fuentes has said of Cervantes: "las palabras, en su mundo, son el único sitio de encuentro de los mundos" ("words, in sum, are the only site of encounter of the worlds" [my translation]). See Carlos Fuentes, *Cervantes o la crítica de la lectura* (Tabasco: Editorial Joaquín Mortiz, 1976), 32. Fuentes even compares Cervantes to Galileo in passing (36).
66 As Thomas Hart has pointed out: "Don Quixote's error is that he follows his models too literally. He fails to realize something every major Renaissance critic accepted without question: a successful imitation must not follow its original slavishly." Hart, *Cervantes and Ariosto*, 128.
67 Battistini, *Galileo e i Gesuiti*, 21–22 (my translation). In the original, Battistini says of the "rendiconto scientifico" that it is: "il riassunto di fenomeni fino allora ignoti, esposti con quella prosa incisiva, agile nel ragionamento ed economica nell'argomentazione." Battistini further elaborates on the generic

force of the telescope itself, which prompts numerous works such as the *Occhiale* (Venice, 1627) by Tommaso Stigliani (the unskilled editor of the *Assayer*), Scipione Errico's *Occhiale appannato* (Messina, 1647), and Agostino Lampugnani's *Antiocchiale*, all of which are involved in the Seicento *marinisti e antimarinisti* debates. Also of note are the series of voyeuristic episodes inspired by the telescope; see Battistini, *Galileo e i Gesuiti*, 37–42.

68 Stillman Drake, "Galileo's New Science of Motion," in *Reason, Experiment and Mysticism*, ed. Maria Luisa Righini Bonelli and William Shea (New York: Science History Publications, 1975), 131–156 (132).

69 Galileo Galilei, *Operazioni del compasso geometrico*, in *Opere*, ed. Franz Brunetti, 2 vols., Vol. 1 (Turin: UTET, 2005), 197–198 (my translation).

70 Proclus, *A Commentary on the First Book of Euclid's "Elements,"* trans. and ed. Glenn R. Morrow (Princeton University Press, 1970), 57.

71 Battistini, *Galileo e i Gesuiti*, 3 (my translation). The original reads: "Che cos'altro è la descrizione di un esperimento scientifico se non il racconto di un viaggio incalzato dalla curiosità?"

72 Maria Luisa Altieri Biagi and Bruno Basile, eds., *Scienziati del Seicento* (Milan–Naples: Ricciardi, 1980), xiii–xiv (my translation). The original reads: "uno dei sintomi della tensione filosofica sottesa all'attività scientifica sia proprio l'affiorare, nello scienziato, di inquietudini, di turbamenti, di malinconia che accompagnano anche i momenti esaltanti della scoperta."

73 *Ibid.*, xvii.

74 *Opere*, vi, 213 (my translation).

75 Galileo, *Assayer*, 234–5.

76 *Ibid.*, 235. According to Ezio Raimondi this characterization is not limited to the Fable of the Sound alone: "Il *Saggiatore* costituisce il nuovo archetipo del curioso che cerca, esplora, immagina, controlla, sperimenta la «moltitudine» dei fenomeni per un bisogno innato di ordine una volta che si sia posto un problema" ("The *Assayer* constitutes the new archetype of the curious man who seeks, explores, imagines, controls, experiments with the 'multiplicity' of phenomena, out of an innate need for order once a problem has been posed" [my translation]). Raimondi, *La dissimulazione romanzesca*, 21.

77 See David R. Castillo, *Baroque Horrors: Roots of the Fantastic in the Age of Curiosities* (Ann Arbor: University of Michigan Press, 2010), 1–17.

78 The narrator presents the environment that eventually leads to Quixote's adventures: "on those occasions when he was at leisure, which was most of the year around, he was in the habit of reading books of chivalry with such pleasure and devotion as to lead him almost wholly to forget the life of a hunter and even the administration of his estate"; Cervantes, *Don Quixote*, 26.

79 *Ibid.*, 26–7.

80 *Ibid.*, 27. Genette writes: "Delusion or, more precisely, derangement is clearly the operating principle of the type of hypertextuality proper to the antiromance: a weak-minded hero who is unable to distinguish between fiction and reality takes the universe of fiction to be real (and present), assumes that he is one of its characters, and 'interprets' the world around him from that

perspective." Gerard Genette, *Palimpsests: Literature in the Second Degree*, trans. Channa Newman and Claude Dombinsky (Lincoln: University of Nebraska Press, 1997), 150.

81 Galileo, *Assayer*, 235.

82 *Ibid.*

83 In the *Assayer*, Battistini sees "la struttura picaresca della scienza galileiana" ("the picaresque structure of Galilean science"), and he in turn sees Galileo as a picaresque character wandering from conflict to conflict in the fields of astronomy and philosophy (Battistini, *Galileo e i gesuiti*, 3). In the "favola dei suoni" Giorgio Varanini points out the use of the *passato remoto* in the story, that it is not a Vichian myth, but that there is still strong emphasis on *meraviglia*: "la successione delle scoperte, qua, però, s'interrompe; protarla avrebbe contribuito a determinare un ritmo narrativo di tipo fiabesco (la serie delle cose straordinarie in progressione crescente) lontanissimo dallo spirito illuministico di questa parabola" ("the succession of discoveries here, though, is interrupted; carrying it forward would have contributed to establishing a narrative rhythm of fables (a series of extraordinary things in growing progression) very far from the Illuministic spirit of this parable" [my translation]). Giorgio Varanini, *Note e ricerche* (Verona: Fiorini-Ghidini, 1967), 85. Raimondi sees in the fable "lo stesso fine di un mito platonico dove immagine e logos si saldano dialetticamente in un unico contenuto di verità" ("the same end as a Platonic myth where the image and the word dovetail dialectically into a single content of truth" [my translation]). Raimondi, *La dissimulazione romanzesca*, 25.

84 Raimondi speaks to the double nature of the fable: "Il fatto è che la curiosità, insieme con lo stupore, educa lo sguardo al naturalismo di una «sensazione esatta,» all'accuratezza istintivamente artiginale del rilevamento morfologico e del suo valore d'uso, mentre la dignità della rappresentazione viene estesa a tutte le classi, a tutti gli organismi del reale" ("The fact is that curiosity, together with stupor, trains the gaze to the naturalism of 'exact sensation,' to the instinctively artisanal acuity of revealing morphology and the value of its use, while the dignity of the representation is extended to all of the classes, to all of the organisms of the real" [my translation]). Raimondi, *La dissimulazione romanzesca*, 27.

85 See Giambattista Marino, *Adone*, ed. Giovanni Pozzi (Milan: Mondadori, 1976), VII.32–37.

86 Galileo, *Assayer*, 236. The passage is also reminiscent of the image of Democritus using a *stilo* to dissect and a *stilo* to write his conclusions. See Christopher Luthy, "The Fourfold Democritus on the Stage of Early Modern Science," *Isis 91* (2000): 443–479.

87 Galileo, *Assayer*, 236.

88 Emanuele Zinato has commented on this very element of Galilean prose: "La vicenda delle implicazioni filosofiche del galileismo è soprattutto archeologia di strutture discursive, storia carica di inediti generi di prosa, che, come un grande archivio critico-ironico, custodiscono modelli del mondo e progetti

del sapere aperti e suscettibili di accrescimenti e di successive approssimazioni" ("The adventure of the philosophical implications of Galileanism is above all the archeology of discursive structures, history rich with unedited genres of prose, that, like a large critical-ironic archive, curate models of the world and projects of knowing that are open and susceptible to accretions and later approximations" [my translation]). Zinato, *Il vero*, 145.

89 Pliny, *Natural History*, trans. H. Rackham (Cambridge, MA: Harvard University Press, 1979), 26.

90 Raimondi, *La dissimulazione romanzesca*, 24–25.

91 Charles D. Presberg, *Adventures in Paradox: Don Quixote and the Western Tradition* (University Park: Penn State University Press, 2001), 25.

92 Raimondi, *La dissimulazione romanzesca*, 30 (my translation). The original reads: "solo gli oggetti prendono vita intorno a lui, l'avventura resta fuori dal labirinto umano delle passioni e dei conflitti."

93 *Opere*, VI, 282.

94 Andrea Battistini, *Il barocco* (Rome: Salerno Editrice, 2000), 91 (my translation). The original reads: "Il filosofo e lo scienziato sono come viandanti, perché la verità non è un possesso stabile e immoto ereditato dalla scuola del passato, ma una conquista che si costruisce a poco a poco sotto gli occhi che la cercano con letizia, diffidando sempre del proprio sapere." Socrates might be the classical image of just such a character. Not surprisingly, he was immortalized by Plato in dialogue, the very genre Galileo favored. In speaking of forms of communication in scientific documents, Maria Luisa Altieri Biagi writes: "Socrate non è solo un modello di comportamento, ma il coagulo in personaggio di un modo di «intendere» che è un continuo *tendere verso* una verità mai globalmente esplorata e posseduta" ("Socrates is not only a model of behavior, but the coagulation in a character of a means of 'understanding' that is a continuous *moving toward* a truth that is never globally explored or possessed" [my translation]). Maria Luisa Altieri Biagi, "Le forme della communicazione scientifica" in *Letteratura italiana*, ed. A. Asor Rosa, 8 vols., Vol. III: *Le forme del testo*, Part III: *La prosa* (Turin: Einaudi, 1984), 892–947 (910–911).

95 Galileo, *On the World Systems*, 78. *Opere* VII, 30.

5 SHIPWRECKED, CLUELESS, AND QUIXOTIC

1 David Marsh, *The Quattrocento Dialogue: Classical Tradition and Humanist Innovation* (Cambridge, MA: Harvard University Press, 1980), 15.

2 J. L. Heilbron, *Galileo* (Oxford University Press, 2011), 257–285, 285–295, and 296–317, respectively.

3 Virginia Cox, *The Renaissance Dialogue: Literary Dialogue in Its Social and Political Contexts, Castiglione to Galileo* (Cambridge University Press, 2008), 113.

4 Maurice Finocchiaro, *Galileo and the Art of Reasoning: Rhetorical Foundations of Logic and Scientific Method* (Dordrecht–Boston: Reidel, 1980), 28. Finocchiaro cites Alexandre Koyré in the *Etudes galiléennes* as an influence on his conclusions.

5 Stephen Clucas, "Galileo, Bruno and the Rhetoric of Dialogue in Seventeenth-Century Natural Philosophy," *History of Science* 46 (2008): 405–429 (411).

6 Cox, *Renaissance Dialogue*, 7.

7 *Ibid.*, 44.

8 See Vincenzo Galilei, *Fronimo. Dialogo di Vincentio Galilei fiorentino, nel quale si contengono le vere e necessarie regole dell'intavolare la musica del liuto* (Venice: Girolamo Scotto, 1568); and his *Dialogo della musica antica, et della moderna* (Florence: Marescotti, 1581).

9 David Marsh gives the example of Poggio Bracciolini's dialogues in *Quattrocento Dialogue*, 50.

10 *Ibid.*, 34.

11 Maria Luisa Altieri Biagi, *Fra lingua scientifica e lingua letteraria* (Pisa: Istituti editoriali poligrafici internazionali, 1998), 44 (my translation). The original reads: "c'è il bisogno della nuova scienza di privilegiate [*sic*] il momento della ricerca su quello della scoperta, e quindi il momento della discussione su quello dell'acquisizione."

12 Anthony Grafton, *Commerce with the Classics: Ancient Books and Renaissance Readers* (Ann Arbor: University of Michigan Press, 1997), 220.

13 Andrea Battistini, "Il libro, il labirinto, la fabbrica del mondo: Metafore epistemologiche della nuova scienza di Galileo," in *Quando l'opera interpella il lettore: Poetiche e forme della modernità letteraria*, ed. Piero Pieri and Giuliana Benvenuti (Bologna: Edizioni Pendragon, 2000), 27–43 (42–43).

14 See Eraldo Bellini, *Stili di pensiero nel Seicento italiano: Galileo, i Lincei, i Barberini* (Pisa: ETS, 2009), 14–18.

15 See Benedetto Varchi, *L'Ercolano* (Milan, 1804), lxxvi.

16 See Marco Ruffini, *Art without an Author: Vasari's "Lives" and Michelangelo's Death* (New York: Fordham University Press, 2011), 139–150.

17 Antonio Favaro, "La libreria di Galileo Galilei, descritta ed illustrata," *Bullettino di bibliografia e storia delle scienze matematiche e fisiche* 19 (1886): 219–293 (entries 65, 66, 79, 370–372, and 420). The full titles are: Giovanni Panetio, *Dialogo tra Christo e l'anima del P. D. Giovanni Panetio Monaco Celestino, Abbate in S. Stefano di Bologna* (Bologna: per gli Heredi del Cochi, 1625); Dante Alighieri, *Commedia di Dante insieme con un dialogo circa al sito, forma et misura dello inferno* (Florence: Giunti, 1506); Fortunio Liceti, *Lilium maius, sive de natura assistente, Dialogus, ecc.* (Udine: Nicolò Schiratti, 1637); Fortunio Liceti, *Lilium minus, sive de Anima ad corpus physice non propensa, Dialogus* (Udine: Nicolò Schiratti, 1637); Esteban Rodrigo de Castro, *Eumenius, sive de vero amico. Dialogus. Authore Stephano Roderigo Castrensi, Lusitano* (Florence: Zanobi Pignoni, 1626).

18 Raffaele Girardi, *La società del dialogo* (Bari: Adriatica, 1989), 291–292.

19 Niccolò Tartaglia, *Quesiti et inventioni diverse de Nicolo Tartalea Brisciano* (Venice: Ruffinelli, 1546), 70r–v.

20 *Ibid.*, 22v.

21 Girolamo Borro, *Dialogo del flusso e reflusso del mare d'Alseforo Talascopio con un ragionamento di Telifilo, Filogenio della perfettione delle donne*, 1st edn. (Lucca: per il Busdragho, 1561), 12–13 (my translation). The original reads:

che voi mi scusiate, se io; il quale non lessi gia mai a miei libri Thoscani, mescolerò ragionando alcune di quelle parole, che non saranno molto al peso; & le andrò ammassando, come io le troverrò, senza nessuno artificio, e come a me le insegnò la mia Balia, mentre che io ero anche fanciullo, e volgarmente favellando come a punto si favella nella mia patria di chiunque quivi nato, vi si alleva, offenderò le vostre Dotte e ben purgate orecchie, usate solo ad udire cose dette con somma politezza e leggiadria.

22 Jean Dietz Moss, *Novelties in the Heavens: Rhetoric and Science in the Copernican Controversy* (University of Chicago Press, 1993), 265.

23 Borro, *Del flusso*, 1st edn., 27–28. In second edition: Girolamo Borro, *Girolamo Borro Aretino Del flusso, & reflusso del mare & dell'inondatione del Nilo*, 2nd edn. (Florence: Giorgio Marescotti, 1577), 71–72.

24 See Edward Grant, "The Partial Transformation of Medieval Cosmology by Jesuits in the Sixteenth and Seventeenth Centuries," in *Jesuit Science and the Republic of Letters*, ed. Mordechai Feingold (Cambridge, MA: MIT Press, 2003), 127–156 (141–146). The image occurs again in the debates on the *nova* of 1604. See Eileen Reeves, *Painting the Heavens* (Princeton University Press, 1999), 83–84.

25 Girolamo Borro, *Del flusso e reflusso del mare, & dell'inondatione del Nilo. Girolamo Borro Arentino. La terza volta ricorretto dal proprio Autore*, 3rd edn. (Florence: Marescotti, 1583), 199; *Del flusso*, 2nd edn., 222 (my translation). The original reads: "senza ro[m]pere la bella tessitura della già bene ordita tela, lascatel [*sic*] seguitare."

26 Borro, *Del flusso*, 1st edn., 29 (my translation). The original reads: "Questo (M. Alseforo mio) non è passo da correrlo molto velocemente; ma da andarsene oltre pian' piano."

27 *Ibid.*; Borro, *Del flusso*, 3rd edn., 75 (my translation). The original reads: "dottamente parlando … mettete la mano in una buca, dove si nasconde un'granchio tanto grande, che à pena infra voi & io nel potremo cavare."

28 Borro, *Del flusso*, 2nd edn., 75 (my translation). The original reads: "Voi Signor Giovanni, secondo il vostro antico costume dottamente parlando, tanto legate stretto il nodo, che à pena in fra voi & io potremo sciorre: pure comunque io mi potrò, farò pruova di sciorlo."

29 Christoph Scheiner, S.J., *Accuratior disquisitio*, in Galileo Galilei and Christoph Scheiner, S.J., *On Sunspots*, trans. and ed. Eileen Reeves and Albert Van Helden (University of Chicago Press, 2010), 193. See Galileo Galilei, *Concerning the Two Chief World Systems*, trans. Stillman Drake (Berkeley: University of California Press, 1967), 378–379. The motif was used in the title of Jacob Christmann's observations on Saturn and the Jovian stars: *Nodus gordius ex doctrina sinuum explicate* (Heidelberg, 1612). The tradition of Alexander the Great and the Gordian Knot is long, with roots in Quintus Curtius and Justin. See Robin Lane Fox, *Alexander the Great* (New York: Penguin, 2005), 149–151.

30 Because there is no evidence that Galileo owned works by Giordano Bruno, I leave an analysis of his literary style in dialogue for another place. Bruno has been recognized as a Mannerist who staged his philosophical works with careful adoption of literary elements. See for example Nuccio Ordine, *La soglia dell'ombra: Letteratura, filosofia e pittura in Giordano Bruno* (Venice: Mansilio,

2003); Hans Blumenberg, *The Genesis of the Copernican World*, trans. Robert M. Wallace (Cambridge, MA: MIT Press, 1987), 359; and Dietz Moss, *Novelties*, 180. For a study that compares the two, see Clucas, "Galileo, Bruno and the Rhetoric of Dialogue," 405–429.

31 Cox, *Renaissance Dialogue*, 9–21.

32 Aside from his role as mentor, Sagredo was also a frequent visitor to Galileo for astrology consultations. See Nick Kollerstrom, "On the Character of Sagredo: Galileo's Judgment upon His Nativity," trans. Julianne Evans, *Culture and Cosmos* 7.1 (2003): 96–100. Sagredo was also involved in the production of Galileo's first lenses for the telescope; see V. Greco and G. Molesini, "Galileo e Sagredo: Primo enunciato della formula dei fabbricanti di lenti," *Quaderno di storia della fisica* 1 (1997): 35–38.

33 Of note is a recent article by Nick Wilding, "Galileo's Idol: Gianfrancesco Sagredo Unveiled," *Galilaeana* 3 (2006): 229–245. Wilding explores Sagredo's self-presentation through written and visual media as an influence on Galileo's fictional representation of him in the dialogues. More recently see Mariapiera Marenzana, *L'omaggio di Galileo: I personaggi dei dialoghi visti attraverso l'epistolario* (Taranto: Chimienti, 2010), 11–78.

34 See Marenzana, *L'omaggio di Galileo*, 79–94; Mario Biagioli, "Filippo Salviati: A Baroque Virtuoso," *Nuncius* 7 (1991): 81–96.

35 Marsh, *Quattrocento Dialogue*, 12.

36 See Volker Remmert, *Picturing the Scientific Revolution* (Philadelphia: Saint Joseph's University Press, 2011), 47–95.

37 In the unpublished fragments that show a continuation of the *Two New Sciences* Simplicio has been removed and a new character named Aproino has been added. The character is named for a former pupil of Galileo, Paolo Aproino, with whom he had collaborated on a failed ear-trumpet project in the second decade of the seventeenth century. Set to take place a fortnight after the fourth and final day of the *Two New Sciences*, the new dialogue was one that Galileo partially dictated in 1638 on the force of percussion. See Matteo Valleriani, "Galileo's Abandoned Project on Acoustics at the Medici Court," *History of Science* 1 (2012): 1–31; Marenzana, *L'omaggio di Galileo*, 153–176.

38 Stillman Drake, *Galileo at Work: His Scientific Biography* (University of Chicago Press, 1978), 355. As Altieri Biagi points out, Simplicio does pick up and learn the vocabulary of the anti-Peripatetics; Maria Luisa Altieri Biagi, *L'avventura della mente* (Naples: Morano, 1990), 121.

39 Historians generally agree that Galileo did not write Simplicio's character intending to insult the Pope. See Maurice A. Finocchiaro, *The Galileo Affair: A Documentary History* (Berkeley: University of California Press, 1989).

40 Marsh, *Quattrocento Dialogue*, 11.

41 See Marenzana, *L'omaggio di Galileo*, 95–152.

42 Altieri Biagi writes: "A mano a mano che la scrittura procede, il Sarsi diventa sempre più Simplicio, cioè assume autonomia di personaggio e recita parti sempre più dialogate; il canovaccio diventa sempre più 'copione'" ("Little by

little as the writing goes on, Sarsi becomes more and more Simplicio – that is, he assumes an autonomy of character and recites lines that are ever more dialogic; the improvisation becomes more of a script" [my translation]). Altieri Biagi, *Fra lingua scientifica*, 43. But even that identity is not fixed. She says later: "Si potrebbe dire che Simplicio comincia come «Sarsi» ma che, alla fine del *Dialogo*, i suoi comportamenti sono meno legnosi" ("One could say that Simplicio begins as 'Sarsi,' but that, at the end of the *Dialogue*, his behavior is less wooden" [my translation]). Altieri Biagi, *L'avventura della mente*, 120).

43 Paolo Bozzi, "Dalla parte di Simplicio," in *Galileo Galilei e la cultura veneziana: Atti del Convegno di Studio promosso nell'ambito delle celebrazioni galileiane indette dall'Università degli Studi di Padova (1592–1992), Venezia, 18–20 giugno 1992* (Venice: Istituto Veneto di Scienze, Lettere ed Arti, 1992), 313–316. *Meraviglia* was not limited to philosophy alone; see James V. Mirollo, *Poet of the Marvelous: Giambattista Marino* (New York: Columbia University Press, 1963).

44 One exception is the work of Maria Luisa Altieri Biagi, who has argued that the linguistic character of the interlocutors is most pronounced at the beginning of the *Dialogue*, in which Sagredo is less informal, but mimics the spoken register more than Salviati. According to Altieri Biagi, Sagredo demonstrates the "libero movimento orale della sintassi" ("free oral movement of syntax"); Altieri Biagi, *L'avventura della mente*, 119. She has examined the linguistic character of Sagredo compared with Salviati and found an inconstant but distinct difference between the two voices: Sagredo is more informal, more imitative of the spoken language – though these differences are noted mostly at the beginning of the *Chief World Systems*. Since Simplicio speaks with a different rhythm than Salviati, the reader's preference will naturally tend toward Salviati.

45 Carlo Muscetta writes of Simplicio: "Senza la creazione di Simplicio, Galileo resterebbe un geniale scienziato, uno scrittore notevolissimo, ma non sarebbe quel particolare tipo di genio che è riuscito ad essere"; Carlo Muscetta, *Realismo neorealismo controrealismo* (Milan: Garzanti, 1976), 212–213. Italo Calvino writes of Galileo's characters:

> La velocità del pensiero nel *Dialogo dei massimi sistemi* è impersonata da Sagredo ... Salviati e Sagredo rappresentano due diverse sfaccetture del temperamento di Galileo: Salviati è il ragionatore metodologicamente rigoroso, che procede lentamente e con prudenza; Sagredo è caratterizzato dal suo «velocissimo discorso,» da uno spirito più portato all'immaginazione, a trarre conseguenze non dimostrate e a spingere ogni idea alle estreme conseguenze.

(Italo Calvino, *Lezioni americane: Sei proposte per il prossimo millennio* [Milan: Garzanti, 1991], 51.)
Calvino ties these characterizations to Galileo's preference for quick discussions and fast, capable reasoning.

46 Dietz Moss, *Novelties*, 267.

47 Finocchiaro, *Galileo and the Art of Reasoning*, 47.

48 F. Rauhut, "Galileis Bedeutung für die italienische Literatur und Sprache," *Volkstum und Kultur der Romanen* 15 (1942): 157–171 (163; my translation). The original reads:

> Man kann sagen: in dem *Dialogo* spielt hinsichtlich der kopernickanischen Lehre und hinsichtlich der neuen Methode Salviati den "advocatus Dei" und Simplicio den "advocatus diaboli." Die drei Personen sind keine Allegorien, keine personifizierten Abstraktionen, nicht etwa bloß Gedanken, denen der Verfasser menschliche Kleider angezogen hätte, sondern zwei lebendige Träger von Weltanschauungen und dazu an wissensdurstiger Gebildeter; die Lebendigkeit der drei Personen ist aus Galileis eigenem langen Erleben der dramatischen und für ihn gefährlichen Diskussion mit Laienpublikum und Fachwissenschaft, aus seinen Erfahrungen in Lehrberuf, Briefwechsel, wissenschlichem Gespräch und wissenschaftlicher Disputation erwachsen.

49 Altieri Biagi, *L'avventura della mente,* 116.
50 *Opere,* XIV, 350.
51 *Ibid.,* 366 (my translation). The full quotation from the original is:

> Simplicio par il trastullo di questa comedia filosofica, ch'insieme mostra la sciocchezza della sua seta, il parlare, e l'instabilità, e l'ostinatione, e quanto ci va. Certo che non havemo a invidiar Platone. Salviati è un gran Socrate, chef a parturire più che non parturisce, et Sagredo un libero ingegno, che senza esser adulterato nelle scole giudica di tutte con molta sagacità.

52 Maria Luisa Altieri Biagi and Bruno Basile, *Scienziati del Seicento* (Milan–Naples: Ricciardi, 1980), xxii (my translation). The original reads: "sarebbe necessario che V. S. desse una scorsa a i primi dialoghi del Galileo del sistema mondano, dove vedrebbe non pochi esempi del methodo, che dovria V. S. osservare nel dialogare per esser chiaro, convincente, et osservare il costume e la dignità delle persone che fanno la parte del Maestro e degl'avversarii."
53 Marsh, *Quattrocento Dialogue,* 4.
54 *Ibid.,* 13 and 23.
55 *Ibid.,* 60.
56 Galileo Galilei, *On the World Systems,* trans. and ed. Maurice A. Finocchiaro (Berkeley: University of California Press, 1997), 82; *Opere,* VII, 31. The modern critic Carlo Muscetta agrees with Campanella's interpretation: "S'è detto che in Salviati c'è il ricordo del Forestiero e del Socrate platonico"; Muscetta, *Realismo neorealismo controrealismo,* 184.
57 Marsh, *Quattrocento Dialogue,* 11.
58 Maria Luisa Altieri Biagi reads Simplicio's stranding as an allegory for the Peripatetic theories about the tides being left high and dry. See her chapter "*Dialogo sopra i due Massimi Sistemi* di Galileo Galilei," in *Letteratura italiana,* ed. A. Asor, 8 vols., Vol. II: *Dal Cinquecento al Settecento* (Turin: Einaudi, 1992), 891–971 (907–908).
59 Cox, *Renaissance Dialogue,* 105.
60 Wilding, "Galileo's Idol," 230.

61 Pierpaolo Antonello, "Galileo scrittore e la critica: Analisi stilistica e interdisciplinarietà," *Quaderni d'italianistica* 23.1–2 (2002): 25–48 (29). For the theory of the work of art existing within the piece of marble from which it must be liberated by the gifted sculptor see the recent edition of Michelangelo Buonarroti, *Rime e lettere*, ed. Paola Mastrocola (Turin: UTET, 2006), 196–198.

62 *Opere*, XII, 45–46.

63 Antonello, "Galileo scrittore," 29. Sagredo's comment is from Galileo, *On the World Systems*, 115. Galileo uses this same phrase to describe his own actions in a letter to Francesco Rinuccini about the comparison of Ariosto to Tasso (*Opere*, XVIII, 192).

64 See Bellini, *Stili di pensiero*, 23–29.

65 Galileo, *On the World Systems*, 116; *Opere*, VII, 130–131. Eraldo Bellini has recently commented:

> I recenti editori del *Dialogo* hanno proposto nel loro commento quali possibili fonti di questa pagina un passo della *Filosofia naturale* di Alessandro Piccolomini e un brano della *Lezione delle parti della poesia* di Benedetto Varchi. I rinvii sono senz'altro pertinenti, ma forse non è utile ricordare che molteplici suggestioni letterarie, alcune delle quali assai prossime agli ambienti culturali frequentati da Galileo, potrebbero aver indotto lo scienziato ad appropriarsi brillantemente di quello che era ormai senza dubbio un *topos*.

> The recent editors of the *Dialogue*, in their commentary, proposed as possible sources for this page a passage from Alessandro Piccolimini's *Natural Philosophy* and an excerpt from the *Lesson on the Parts of Poetry* by Benedetto Varchi. The references are certainly pertinent, but perhaps it is useful to remember that multiple literary suggestions, some of which are rather near to the cultural environments frequented by Galileo, could have induced the scientist to appropriate brilliantly that which was already without doubt a topos.

(Eraldo Bellini, "Galileo e le 'due culture,'" in *La prosa di Galileo: La lingua, la retorica, la storia*, ed. Mauro Di Giandomenico and Pasquale Guaragnella [Lecce: Argo, 2006], 143–78 [158; my translation].)

66 Galileo, *On the World Systems*, 116; *Opere*, VII, 131.

67 Albrecht Dürer, *Painter's Manual: 1525,* trans. and commentary Walter L. Strauss (New York: Abaris Books, 1977), 303.

68 Giovanni Boccaccio, *Famous Women*, trans. and ed. Virginia Brown (Cambridge, MA: Harvard University Press, 2001), 111. Boccaccio was likely borrowing the conceit from Cicero, *The Nature of the Gods,* trans. Horace C. P. McGregor (New York: Penguin, 1978), II.91.

69 Lucretius, *The Nature of Things*, trans. A. E. Stalling, lines 1014–1020. Lucretius appears twice in Galileo's library: once as a general reference by author as given in Biblioteca Nazionale Centrale di Firenze, Manoscritti Galileiani, MS 308 (hereafter Gal. MS 308), and again in Vincenzo Viviani's inventory, *Poetae ac Philosophi vetustissimi, De rerum natura libri sex* (Lyon: Sebastian Gryphius, 1558) in 16mo. As an Epicurean text, the *De rerum* expounds the atomism that many argue led to the charges against Galileo of heresy.

70 Manilius, *Astronomica*, trans. G. P. Goold (Cambridge, MA: Harvard University Press, 1977), II.749–763.

71 *Ibid.*, II.772–783.

72 For a discussion of the alphabet and the printed word, see Marshall McLuhan, *The Gutenberg Galaxy: The Making of Typographic Man* (University of Toronto Press, 1962).

73 See Ann Blair, *Too Much to Know: Managing Scholarly Information before the Modern Age* (New Haven: Yale University Press, 2010).

74 See Francesco Barbierato, *The Inquisitor in the Hat Shop* (Farnham, VT: Ashgate, 2012).

75 Galileo, *On the World Systems*, 121; *Opere*, VII, 135.

76 *Ibid.*

77 Galileo, *On the World Systems*, 121. Calvino writes: "Lorsqu'ils parle d'alphabet, Galilée entend donc un système combinatoire qui peut rendre compte de toute la multiplicité de l'univers" ("When speaking about the alphabet, Galileo means a combinatory system that can provide an account of the entire multiplicity of the universe" [my translation]). Italo Calvino, "Le livre de la Nature chez Galilée," in *Exigences et perspectives de la sémiotique: Recueil d'hommages pour Algirdas Julien Greimas*, ed. Herman Parret and Hans-George Ruprecht, 2 vols., Vol. II (Amsterdam: John Benjamins, 1985), 684. This is a sentiment he repeats in the *Lezioni americane*: "Anche Galileo vedrà nell'alfabeto il modello d'ogni combinatoria d'unità minime"; Calvino, *Lezioni americane*, 32.

78 *Opere*, III, 395–396 (my translation). The original reads:

> così l'occuparsi sempre ed il consumarsi sopra gli scritti d'altri senza mai sollevar gli occhi all'opere stesse della natura, cercando di riconoscere in quelle le verità già ritrovate e d'investigare alcuna de l'infinite che restano a scoprirsi, non farà mai un uomo filosofo, ma solamente uno studioso e pratico ne gli scritti d'altri di filosofia. Io non credo che voi stimassi per buon pittore uno che avesse fatta una gran pratica nelle carte e nelle tavole di tutti i pittori, sì che prontamente riconoscesse le maniere di questo e di quello, e quell'attitudine venir da Michelagnolo [*sic*], quella da Raffaello, quel gruppo dal Rosso, quell'altro da Salviati, e che anco le sapesse copiare.

79 Galileo, *Chief World Systems*, 279; *Opere*, VII, 302.

80 Galileo, *Chief World Systems*, 280; *Opere*, VII, 304.

81 Galileo, *Chief World Systems*, 446; *Opere*, VII, 472.

82 *Ibid.*

83 Galileo, *Chief World Systems*, 454; *Opere*, VII, 479.

84 Galileo Galilei, *Dialogues Concerning Two New Sciences*, trans. Henry Crew and Alfonso de Salvio, ed. and commentary Stephen Hawking (Philadelphia: Running Press, 2002), 3; *Opere*, VIII, 51.

85 Galileo, *On the World Systems*, 185; *Opere*, VII, 224.

86 Dante Alighieri, *Inferno*, trans. Allen Mandelbaum (New York: Bantam, 2004), XXXI.34–39.

87 Mark Peterson, *Galileo's Muse* (Cambridge, MA: Harvard University Press, 2011), 228.

88 Dante, *Paradiso*, XXXIII.133–141.

89 Sagredo has a turbulent relationship to water throughout the dialogues, which could be reflective of his role as a Venetian consul who frequently traveled the Mediterranean. See *Opere*, VII, 275, 466; and Galileo, *On the World Systems*, 303. Sea imagery seems particularly appropriate in Borro's *Dialogo del flusso e reflusso del mare*, where it occurs only a handful of times. For example, see Borro, *Del flusso* (1583), 34. Vincenzo Galilei makes much more frequent use of this figurative language, with at least five instances of speaking about oarsmen, uncharted waters, rocks, the port, and favorable winds. See Vincenzo Galilei, *Dialogo della musica antica*, 4, 22, 25, and 31.

90 For a discussion of the labyrinth topos, see Sophie Chiari, *L'image du labyrinth à la Renaissance* (Paris: Honoré Champion Editeur, 2010).

91 I say relatively because Galileo supported the hypothesis that the Sun rotated on its access in Galileo and Scheiner, *On Sunspots*, 76 and 90.

92 Galileo, *Two New Sciences*, trans. Crew and de Salvio, 4; *Opere*, VIII, 53.

93 See Galileo, *Chief World Systems*, 146 and 328; *Opere*, VII, 172 and 356.

94 Peter Armour, "Galileo and the Crisis in Italian Literature of the Early Seicento," in *Collected Essays on Italian Language and Literature Presented to Kathleen Speight*, ed. Giovanni Aquilecchia, Stephen N. Cristea, and Sheila Ralphs (New York: Barnes and Noble, 1971), 144–169 (166).

95 Altieri Biagi, "*Dialogo*," 933.

96 Muscetta, *Realismo neorealismo controrealismo*, 181 (my translation). The original reads: "sostanzialmente inconvincibile e formalmente invitto ... come si conviene ad un eroe."

97 Galileo, *On the World Systems*, 98; *Opere*, VI, 76.

98 Galileo, *On the World Systems*, 126; *Opere*, VII, 138.

99 *Ibid.*

100 Galileo, *On the World Systems*, 127; *Opere*, VII, 139.

101 *Ibid.*

102 Galileo, *On the World Systems*, 127–128; *Opere*, VII, 139. On the third day Salviati asks Simplicio to create a second type of world on paper:

> take a sheet of paper and a compass, and let this white paper be the immense expanse of the universe where you have to locate and arrange its parts in accordance with the dictates of reason. First, without my teaching it to you, you firmly believe the earth to be located in this universe; so, take a point of your own choosing around which you understand it to be located, and mark it with some symbol.

(Galileo, *On the World Systems*, 227; *Opere*, VII, 350.)

103 Galileo, *On the World Systems*, 105; *Opere*, VII, 80.

104 *Ibid.*

105 See Nikolaus Pevsner, *A History of Building Types* (Princeton University Press, 1976), 92.

106 Even though any relation between Galileo's work and Bruno's is speculative, Sagredo's statement resonates with the Aristotelian Burchio in *On the Infinite Universe and Worlds*: "Would you then render vain all efforts, study and labours on such work as *De physica uditu* and *De coelo et mundo* wherein so many great commentators, paraphrasers, glossers, compilers, epitomizers,

scholiasts, translators, questioners and logicians have puzzled their brains? Whereon profound doctors, subtle, golden, exalted, inexpugnable, irrefragable, angelic, seraphic, cherubic and divine, have established their foundation?" Giordano Bruno, *On the Infinite Universe and Worlds*, trans. Dorothea Waley Singer (New York: Henry Shurman, 1950), 324.

107 Battistini, "Il libro, il labirinto, la fabbrica del mondo," 42.

108 Galileo, *On the World Systems*, 106; *Opere*, VII, 81.

109 Galileo, *Chief World Systems*, 78; *Opere*, VII, 103.

110 Tibor Wlassics, "La genesi della critica letteraria di Galileo," *Aevum* 46 (1972): 215–236 (227).

111 Galileo, *Chief World Systems*, 446; *Opere*, VII, 103.

112 Ludovico Ariosto, *Orlando furioso*, trans and ed. Barbara Reynolds (New York: Penguin, 1977), XXVIII.1.5–8.

113 William Gilbert, "Author's Preface" to *De magnete*, trans. and ed. P. Fleury Mottelay (New York: Dover, 1958), xlviii.

114 *Ibid.*, xlix.

115 For how this relationship appears in Galileo's correspondence, see Mario Loria, "William Gilbert e Galileo Galilei: La terrella e le calamite del granduca," in *Saggi su Galileo Galilei*, ed. Carlo Maccagni, 2 vols., Vol. II (Florence: Sansoni, 1972), 208–247.

116 Salviati echoes these sentiments again in the *Chief World Systems* (*Opere*, VII, 432) and *Two New Sciences* (*Opere*, VIII, 204).

117 Miguel de Cervantes Saavedra, *Don Quixote*, trans. Samuel Putnam (New York: Modern Library, 1998), 33.

118 See Eileen Reeves, "Old Wives' Tales and the New World System: Gilbert, Galileo, Kepler," *Configurations* 7.3 (1999): 301–354.

119 See for example Galileo, *On the World Systems*, 123; *Opere*, VII, 136–137.

120 Galileo, *On the World Systems*, 123; *Opere*, VII, 137.

121 Galileo, *On the World Systems*, 221; *Opere*, VII, 346.

122 See Hans Blumenberg, *Shipwreck with Spectator: Paradigm of a Metaphor for Existence*, trans. Steven Rendell (Cambridge, MA: MIT Press, 1997).

123 *Opere*, VII, 39 (my translation). The original reads: "Io molto volentieri mi fermerò, perché corro ancor io simil fortuna, e sto di punto in punto per perdermi, mentre mi conviene veleggiar tra scogli ed onde così rotte, che mi fanno, come si dice, perder la bussola." Drake gives a slightly different translation that seemingly oversimplifies the imagery: "I shall willingly pause, for I run the same risk too, and am on the verge of getting shipwrecked. At present I sail between rocks and boisterous waves that are making me lose my bearings, as they say." Galileo, *Chief World Systems*, 15.

124 Galileo, *Chief World Systems*, 44; *Opere*, VII, 69.

125 Galileo, *Chief World Systems*, 408; *Opere*, VII, 434–435.

126 Lactantius, *The Divine Institutes*, trans. A. Bowen and P. Garnsey (Liverpool University Press, 2003), VI.3.2–3. For the reference to Galileo's library see Archivio di Stato di Firenze, Fondo Notarile Moderno, Protocolli, 15676–15685 (Silvestro Pantera, 1646–1650), MS 3483.3, fo. 115r, line 12: "Lattantio";

Gal. MS 308, fo. 169r, line 2: "Lactantius Firmianus 8°"; and Favaro, "Libreria di Galileo," entries 350 and 361. Entry 361 gives the title as *Summa*, attributed to a Pacifico Lattantio (of whom no record exists), but I have found a *Summa* written by Pacifico di Novara that better fits the information given by the inventories.

127 See Olivia Holmes, *Dante's Two Beloveds* (New Haven: Yale University Press, 2008), 205–206 nn. 12–13; and Phillip Damon, "Geryon, Cacciaguida, and the Y of Pythagoras," *Dante Studies* 85 (1967): 15–32.

128 Galileo, *Chief World Systems*, 417; *Opere*, VII, 443.

129 Carlos Fuentes, *Cervantes o la critica de la lectura* (Tabasco: Editoral Joaquín, 1976), 83 (my translation). The original reads:

> Navegante en un mar donde se alternan las tormentas de la renovación y los sargazos de la inmovilidad, Cervantes debe luchar entre lo viejo y lo nuevo con una intensidad infinitamente superior a la de los escritores transpirenaicos que, sin mayores peligros, pueden promover los reinos paralelos de la razón, el hedonismo, el capitalismo, la fe ilimitada en el progreso y el optimismo de una historia totalmente orientada hacia el futuro.

130 Galileo, *On the World Systems*, 153; *Opere*, VII, 157–158.

131 Marsh, *Quattrocento Dialogue*, 31.

132 Galileo, *Chief World Systems*, 220; *Opere*, VII, 246–247.

133 See Isabelle Stengers, *The Invention of Modern Science*, trans. Daniel Smith (Minneapolis: University of Minnesota Press, 2000), 75–80.

134 Galileo, *Chief World Systems*, 162; *Opere*, VII, 188. This echoes Galileo's own sentiments in the letter to the discerning reader that prefaces the *Dialogues on the Chief World Systems*, where Galileo explains his choice of format: "I thought it would be very appropriate to explain these ideas in dialogue form; for it is not restricted to the rigorous observation of mathematical laws, and so it also allows digressions which are sometimes no less interesting than the main topic"; Galileo, *On the World Systems*, 81.

135 Maurice Finocchiaro demonstrates the digressive structure of the *Chief World Systems* in *Galileo and the Art of Reasoning*, 145–150.

136 For examples see Christoph Clavius, S.J., *Christophori Clavii Bambergensis ex Societate Iesv In sphaeram Ioannis de Sacro Bosco commentarius, nunc tertio ab ipso auctore recognitus, & plerisque in locis locupletatus* (Venice: Ciotto, 1591), 217–220.

137 Daniel Javitch, "Narrative Discontinuity in the *Orlando furioso* and Its Sixteenth Century Critics," *MLN* 103.1 (January 1988): 50–74 (54).

138 *Ibid.*, 62–63.

139 See Matteo Valleriani, *Galileo Engineer* (Dordrecht: Springer, 2010), 117–153.

140 Galileo, *Two New Sciences*, trans. Crew and de Salvio, 3; *Opere*, VIII, 52.

141 Galileo, *On the World Systems*, 122; *Opere*, VII, 135. Salviati later says:

> I have no hesitation in agreeing with you. But profound considerations of this kind belong to a higher science than ours. We must be satisfied to belong to that class of less worthy

workmen who procure from the quarry the marble out of which, later, the gifted sculptor produces those masterpieces which lay hidden in this rough and shapeless exterior.

(Galileo, *Two New Sciences*, trans. Crew and de Salvio, 149; *Opere*, VIII, 230.) See above, n. 61, for the the connection of this theory to Michelangelo.

142 Galileo, *On the World Systems*, 122–123; *Opere*, VII, 136.

143 Salviati promises that after the discussion of projectiles he will replicate, as well as he is able, the "fantasies" or "vagaries" of the author that were reached after having spent "thousands of hours in speculating and contemplating" (Galileo, *Two New Sciences*, trans. Crew and de Salvio, 210; *Opere*, VIII, 299). The promise is never fulfilled. Galileo had also provided for new sections of what he called the *Discourses and Demonstrations*, a reprint of the *Two New Sciences*.

144 Galileo, *Two New Sciences*, trans. Crew and de Salvio, 20; *Opere*, VIII, 73.

145 Galileo, *Two New Sciences*, trans. Crew and de Salvio, 20; *Opere*, VIII, 73.

146 See *Opere*, XVIII, 193. Galileo advises: "bisognerebbe sentire i contradditori in voce, o se pure in scrittura, proporre a lungo da una parte e leggere le risposte dell'altra, e di nuovo replicare, et andarsene, per modo di dire, in infinito."

147 Galileo, *Two New Sciences*, trans. Crew and de Salvio, 24; *Opere*, VIII, 77. See also Heilbron's description in *Galileo*, 333–334.

148 Galileo, *Two New Sciences*, trans. Crew and de Salvio, 23–24; *Opere*, VIII, 77.

149 Galileo, *Two New Sciences*, trans. Crew and de Salvio, 116; *Opere*, VIII, 190.

150 For the original treatise, *De motu locali*, see *Opere*, I, 249ff.

151 See Michele Camerota, *Galileo Galilei e la cultura scientifica nell'età della Controriforma* (Rome: Salerno, 2004), 46–50, 61–74, 132–149.

152 See Winifred L. Wisan, "The New Science of Motion: A Study of Galileo's *De motu locali*," *Archive for History of Exact Sciences* 13.2–3 (1974): 103–306. See also Heilbron, *Galileo*, 48–55.

153 Galileo Galilei, *The Two New Sciences*, trans. Stillman Drake (Madison: University of Wisconsin Press, 1974), 233 n. 22. See also Corrado Dollo, *Galileo Galilei e la cultura della tradizione*, ed. Giuseppe Bentivegna, Santo Burgio, and Giancarlo Magnano San Lio (Soveria Mannelli: Robbettino, 2003), 23–62.

154 Galileo, *Two New Sciences*, trans. Crew and de Salvio, 202; *Opere*, VIII, 284.

155 Massimo Bucciantini, *Galileo e Keplero* (Turin: Einaudi, 2003), 303–304.

156 Battistini, "Il libro, il labirinto, la fabbrica del mondo," 39.

CONCLUSION

1 Jonathan Culler, "Prolegomena to a Theory of Reading," in *The Reader in the Text*, ed. Susan R. Suleiman and Inge Crosman (Princeton University Press, 1980), 46–66.

2 See for example *Opere*, XIV, 412; XV, 91–92, 144–145.

3 The full title is Scipione Chiaramonti, *Difesa di Scipione Chiaramonti da Cesena al suo Antiticone, o libro delle tre nuove stelle, dall'oppositione dell'autore de' due Massimi Sistemi Tolemaico e Copernicano. Nella quale si sostiene che la nuova*

stella del 72 non fu celeste: si difende Aristotile ne' suoi principali dogmi del Cielo: si rifiutano i principii della nuova filosofia e l'addotto in difesa e prova del Sistema Copernicano, ecc. (Florence: Landini, 1633).

4 See Renée Raphael, "Galileo's *Discorsi* and *Mersenne's Nouvelles* pensées: Mersenne as a Reader of Galilean Experience," *Nuncius* 23.1 (2008): 7–36.

5 Chiaramonti, *Difesa*, 18–19 (my translation). The original reads: "a me pare, che l'Autore habbia fatto per avventura, come quella buona donna, c'havendo la mattina composta la bocca nello specchio, il dì penò di fame per non disconciarsi la compositione sino a nuova specchiata."

6 *Ibid.*, 19.

7 *Ibid.*, 26 (my translation). The original reads: "Però neben vien proposto al semplice mio difenditore, ne ben da lui risposto nelle sottoposte parole."

8 See *Opere*, VII, 274.

9 See William Shea, "Georg [*sic*] Locher's *Disquisitiones mathematicae de controversiis et novitatibus astronomicis* and Galileo Galilei's *Dialogue on the Two World Systems*," in *Proceedings of the 13th International Congress of the History of Science, Moscow, 18–24 August, 1971* (Moscow: Izdatelstvo "Nauka," 1974), 211–219.

10 The instance in question is in Chiaramonte, *Difesa*, 31–34, but occurs repeatedly in the book.

11 *Ibid.*, 31 (my translation). The original reads: "Seguita la risposta, alla quale per brevità applicherò ancor'io per modo di dialogo di mano in mano le repliche."

12 *Ibid.*, 34 (my translation). The original reads: "Ma dal drammatico al narrativo tornando …"

13 *Ibid.*, 45 (my translation). The original reads: "Però mi favorisca ritener a suo censo la risposta che fa per me dire à Simplicio; Io porrò le parole, e ritornerò al dialogo per maggior evidenza."

14 *Ibid.* (my translation). The original reads: "Questo, io, che son la parte, non dico."

15 *Ibid.*, 62 (my translation). The original reads: "È semplice questo Peripatetico Simplicio, e poco accurato nel rispondere."

16 *Ibid.*, 46 (my translation). The original reads: "Eccovi un'altro esempio: Se non ha mani, non farà i colpi di Scanderbergh è vera: ma se ha le mani farà i colpi di Scanderbergh: è questa falsa: perche io ho le mani, e son lontano dal farli."

17 *Ibid.*, 344.

18 *Ibid.*, 64–95 [*sic*] (my translation). The original reads: "Quanto a me, m'ha preso in cambio, che non solo dico, non esser incompatibili, ma che sono il medesimo principio, e meco lo dicono i Peripatetici, de'quali ha presteso hora farsi scudo, e del loro arsenale pigliar l'armi: ma nel maneggiarle è restato ferito."

19 *Ibid.*, 67 (my translation). The original reads:

chi non sa che la verità consiste nell'aggiustar il nostro intelletto alle cose, e non le cose al nostro intelletto? Io questo dico, che se non habbiamo via all'intendere, & al penetrare la natura delle cose, & a ritrarne vera cognitione, che occorre il filosofare, à che fine vergar [*sic*] egli le carte, & altri le loro. Meglio farebbe quello *Altum nihil agere* Pliniano. E si dovrebbe dir con quel Poeta. *Consiglia pur che faccia altro mestiere.*

20 The Pliny reference is *Epistles* 1.9 (my translation). Torquato Tasso, *L'Aminta: A Pastoral Play*, trans. Charles Jernigan and Irene Marchegiani Jones (New York: Italica, 2000), 71.

21 Chiaramonti, *Difesa*, 80 (my translation). The original reads: "Sarà perciò bene pur vedere, se io in cambio di sillogizzare, habbia paralogizato, far con l'Accademico meco medesimo l'usurpato talhora dialogo." He is making reference to the passage in *Opere*, VII, 292–293.

22 *Ibid.*, 81 (my translation). The original reads: "Laonde non è d'Aristotile solo, e de' Peripatetici tal'Universo, ma de i centuriati comitij de' Litterati."

23 *Ibid.*, 85 (my translation of the prose). The original reads:

> Qui finirò il Dialogo, poi che altro non suggiunge, se non che del sito dell'Orbe magno fra Venere, e Marte parlerà poi, & intanto replica che s'hanno da lasciare i fioretti retorici, & attendere dimostrationi; Et io mi riterrò questa lode d'esser retorico grande, poiche dove ogn'altro pensiero hò havuto, son nondimeno retorico stato: à guisa di Ovidio in poesia *Quidquid conabar dicere versus erat*. Ma tenta egli con tali cosuccie divertire dalla forza degl'argomenti l'animo di chi legge: che non li verrà, credo, fatto appresso i dotti.

The translation of the verse is from Ovid, *Tristia/Sorrows of an Exile*, trans. and ed. A. D. Melville (Oxford: Clarendon Press, 1992), IV.10.26.

24 Chiaramonti, *Difesa*, 109 (my translation). The original reads:

> Sign. Accademico mio, siami lecito ancora à me seco[n]do quel Poeta dire *Liberi sensi in semplici parole*. Il cordoglio vostro, ch'io habbia scritto, e stampato, non è per mia, ma per vostra reputatione, conoscendo voi in ristretto, che le cose da me scritte facciano troppo evidente contrasto alla vostra pretensione d'annullare Aristotele; In tanto però vi procurate artificiosamente fede, simulando benevolenza.

25 Torquato Tasso, *Jerusalem Delivered*, trans. and ed. Anthony Esolen (Baltimore: Johns Hopkins University Press, 2000), II.81.7–8.

26 Chiaramonti, *Difesa*, 112 (my translation). The original reads: "Gloria grande è questa, che mi promettete Sig. Accademico. L'Ariosto si contentava, che più di quattro se gli cavassero il cappello, & io non ho da contentarmi che di cento Peripatetici, i novanta nove m'habiano da porre sopra i maggiori intelligenti, che siano?"

27 *Ibid.*, 115 (my translation). The original reads: "E voi de' Peripatetici scrivete come de'più ottusi ingegni, & inetti huomini, che siano sotto il Cielo? Come di greggi inutili, e mal nati."

28 Ludovico Ariosto, *Orlando furioso*, trans. and ed. Barbara Reynolds (New York: Penguin, 1977), XVII.3.7.

29 Chiaramonti, *Difesa*, 137 (my translation). The original reads:

> Deve per altro l'Accademico havere lo stomaco nauseabundo, poiche, nè sono i miei calcoli falsi, e l'indagine delle parallassi dalle differenze loro è dimostrata: solo egli discende à dire che siano errate le osservationi degli Astronomi. La sua nausea dunque dovrebbe essere contra quelli Astronomi, che hanno errato, e non contra il mio libro, il quale sin qui niuno errore contiene.

30 See Galileo Galilei, *Concerning the Two Chief World Systems*, trans. Stillman Drake (Berkeley: University of California Press, 1967), 318.

31 Chiaramonti, *Difesa*, 238 (my translation). The original reads: "Voi sareste mirabile in dipingere i baronzi, e la torreste a Michel'Agnolo quando vinse la scomessa con gl'altri Pittori. Mà per vostra sè, che non l'havete indovinata: che se non si può dire come a Solimano … *con asciutto / Occhio mirasti il Regno tuo distrutto.* hò però con animo assai franco sostenuto qualche incontro a miei giorni."

32 See Albert Ascoli, "Auerbach fra gli epicurei: Dal Canto x dell'*Inferno* alla vi Giornata del *Decameron,*" *Moderna* 1.1–2 (2009): 135–152.

33 Giorgio Vasari, *Lives of the Most Eminent Painters, Sculptors, and Architects,* trans. Gaston C. de Vere, ed. Kenneth Clark, 3 vols., Vol. iii (New York: Harry N. Abrams, 1979), 1928–1929.

34 Tasso, *Jerusalem Delivered,* ix.86.6–8.

35 Lanfranco Caretti, "Galileo uomo di lettere," in *Studi di letteratura e di storia di memoria di Antonio Di Pietro* (Milan: Vita e Pensiero, 1977), 107–123 (121).

36 Peter Armour, "Galileo and the Crisis in Italian Literature of the Early Seicento," in *Collected Essays on Italian Language and Literature Presented to Kathleen Speight,* ed. Giovanni Aquilecchia, Stephen N. Cristea, and Sheila Ralphs (New York: Barnes and Noble, 1971), 144–169 (146).

37 Peter DeSa Wiggins, "Galileo on Characterization in the *Orlando furioso,*" *Italica* 57.4: Renaissance (Winter 1980): 255–267 (261).

38 Pierpaolo Antonello, "Galileo scrittore e la critica: Analisi stilistica e interdisciplinarietà," *Quaderni d'italianistica* 23.1–2 (2002): 25–48 (45; my translation). The original reads: "dispositivo di carattere romanzesco," and "la dissoluzione di una cosmologia unitaria, un plurilinguismo che attraversa strati sociali, generi e convenzioni retoriche, la maschera, l'intento ironico-parodistico, la struttura dialogica del racconto."

39 Caretti, "Galileo uomo di lettere," 115; Luciano Celi, *Gettar luce nell'oscuro labirinto: Arte, letteratura, scienza in Galileo Galilei* (Rome: Aracne, 2010), 77–90; Jonathan White, *Italian Cultural Lineages* (University of Toronto Press, 2007), 59–86.

Bibliography

MANUSCRIPT COLLECTIONS

ARCHIVIO DI STATO DI FIRENZE
Fondo Notarile Moderno. Protocolli, 15676–15685 (Silvestro Pantera, 1646–1650). MS 3483.3.

BIBLIOTECA NAZIONALE CENTRALE DI FIRENZE
Manoscritti Galileiani. MS 308, fos. 167r–174r. 1668.
Manoscritti Palatini. MS 1195 già 21.5–1126.

PRIMARY PUBLISHED PRINTED TEXTS

Accademia della Crusca, ed. *Vocabolario degli Accademici della Crusca*, vers. 1.0, CRIBeCu, 2001, http://vocabolario.signum.sns.it/. Accessed October 1, 2011.

Aggiunti, Niccolò. *Nicolai Adiunctii Burgensis Oratio de mathematicae laudibus habita in florentissima Pisarum Academia*. Rome, 1627.

Agrippa, Cornelius. *De occulta philosophia: Libri tres*, ed. V. Perrone Compagni. Leiden: Brill, 1992.

Occult Philosophy or Magic, ed. Willis F. Whitehead. New York: Ams Press, 1982.

Alighieri, Dante. *Convivio*, trans. Richard Lansing. New York: Garland, 1990.

Divina commedia, commentary Cristoforo Landino. Florence, 1481.

Inferno, trans. Allen Mandelbaum. New York: Bantam, 2004.

Paradiso, trans. Allen Mandelbaum. New York: Bantam, 2004.

Apian, Peter. *Cosmographia, siue, Descriptio vniuersi orbis. Petri Apiani & Gemmæ Frisij, mathematicorum insignium, iam demùm integritati suæ restituta. Adiecti sunt alij, tum Gemmæ Frisij, tum aliorum auctorum eins argumenti tractatus ac libelli varij, quorum seriem versa pagina demonstrat*. Antwerp: Withagius, 1584.

Aratus. *Phaenomena*, trans. Aaron Poochigan. Baltimore: Johns Hopkins University Press, 2010.

Ariosto, Ludovico. *Orlando furioso*, trans. and ed. Barbara Reynolds. New York: Penguin, 1977.

  Orlando furioso, ed. Lanfranco Caretti. Turin: Einaudi, 1992.

Aristotle. *Operum Aristotelis … ominum longe principis, nova editio … nunc primum in lucem prodeunt, ex bibliotheca Isaaci Casauboni.* Lyon, 1590.

Belo, Francesco. *Il pedante*, in *Commedie del Cinquecento*, ed. Nino Borsellino, 2 vols. Vol. II. 99–191. Milan: Feltrinelli, 1967.

Benedetti, Giovanni Battista. *Diversarum speculationum mathematicarum, & physicarum liber quarum seriem sequens pagina indicabit ad serenissimum Carolum Emanuelem Allobrogum, et Subalpinorum ducem invictissimum.* Turin, 1585.

  Resolutio omnium Euclidis problematum aliorumque ad hoc necessario inventorum una tantummodo circini data apertura per Ioannem Baptistam de Benedictis inventa. Venice, 1553.

Boccaccio, Giovanni. *Famous Women*, trans. and ed. Virginia Brown. Cambridge, MA: Harvard University Press, 2001.

  The Life of Dante, trans. J. G. Nichols. London: Hesperus Press, 2002.

Boiardo, Matteo Maria. *Orlando innamorato*, trans. Charles Stanley Ross, ed. Anne Finnigan. Berkeley: University of California Press, 1989.

Bombelli, Rafael. *L'algebra opera di Rafael Bombelli da Bologna divisa in tre libri con la quale ciascuno da se potrà venire in perfetta cognitione della teorica dell'arimetica.* Bologna, 1579.

Borro, Girolamo. *Del flusso e reflusso del mare, & dell'inondatione del Nilo. Girolamo Borro Arentino. La terza volta ricorretto dal proprio Autore.* 3rd edn. Florence: Marescotti, 1583.

  Dialogo del flusso e reflusso del mare d'Alseforo Talascopio con un ragionamento di Telifilo, Filogenio della perfettione delle donne. 1st edn. Lucca: per il Busdragho, 1561.

  Girolamo Borro Aretino Del flusso, & reflusso del mare & dell'inondatione del Nilo. 2nd edn. Florence: Giorgio Marescotti, 1577.

Brahe, Tycho. *Astronomiae instauratae mechanica: Facsimile Reprint of Wandesburg, 1590.* Brussels: Culture et Civilisation, 1969.

  De mundi aetheri recentioribus phaenomenis liber secundus. Frankfurt: Tampachium, 1610.

  Epistolarum astronomicarum libri. Frankfurt: Tampachium, 1610.

Bruno, Giordano. *On the Infinite Universe and Worlds*, trans. Dorothea Waley Singer. New York: Henry Shurman, 1950.

Buonarroti, Michelangelo. *Rime e lettere*, ed. Paola Mastrocola. Turin: UTET, 2006.

Cardano, Girolamo. *Hieronymi Cardani, praestantissimi mathematici, philosophi, ac medici Artis magnae sive, de regulis algebraicis Lib. unus. Qui & totius de Arithmetica, quod opus perfectum inscripsit, est in ordine Decimus.* Nuremberg, 1545.

Cervantes Saavedra, Miguel de. *Don Quixote*, trans. Samuel Putnam. New York: Modern Library, 1998.

Chiaramonti, Scipione. *Difesa di Scipione Chiaramonti da Cesena al suo Antiticone, o libro delle tre nuove stelle, dall'oppositione dell'autore de' due Massimi Sistemi Tolemaico e Copernicano. Nella quale si sostiene che la nuova stella del 72 non fu celeste: si difende Aristotile ne' suoi principali dogmi del Cielo: si rifiutano i principii della nuova filosofia e l'addotto in difesa e prova del Sistema Copernicano, ecc.* Florence: Landini, 1633.

Christmann, Jacob. *Nodus gordius ex doctrina sinuum explicate.* Heidelberg, 1612.

Cicero. *Cicero on the Ideal Orator ("De oratore")*, trans. James. M. May and Jakob Wisse. Oxford University Press, 2001.

The Nature of the Gods, trans. Horace C. P. McGregor. New York: Penguin, 1978.

Clavius, S.J., Christoph. *Aritmetica prattica composta dal molto reuer. padre Christoforo Clauio ... Et tradotto da latino in italiano dal Signor Lorenzo Castellano.* Rome: Basa, 1586.

Christophori Clavii Bambergensis Astrolabivm. Rome: Grassi, 1593.

Christophori Clavii Bambergensis e Societate Iesu Epitome arithmeticae practicae. Rome: Basa, 1583.

Christophori Clauii Bambergensis e Societate Iesu, Geometria practica. Rome: Zanetti, 1604.

Christophori Clavii Bambergensis ex Societate Iesv In sphaeram Ioannis de Sacro Bosco commentarius, nunc tertio ab ipso auctore recognitus, & plerisque in locis locupletatus. Venice: Ciotto, 1591.

Gnomonices libri octo in quibus non solum horologiorum solariu[m], sed aliarum quoq[ue] rerum, quae ex gnomonis umbra cognosci possunt, descriptiones geometricè demonstrantur auctore Christophoro Clavio Bambergensi Societatis Iesu. Rome: Zanetti, 1581.

Colonna, Fabio. *Fabii Columnae Lyncei Purpura hoc est, De purpura ab animali testaceo fusa de hoc ipso Animali aliusque rarioribus testaceis quibusdam cum iconibus ex aere ad vivum representatis.* Rome: Jacobum Mascardum, 1616.

Copernicus, Nicolaus. *On the Revolutions*, ed. Jerzy Dobrzycki; trans. and commentary Edward Rosen. Baltimore: Johns Hopkins University Press, 1978.

On the Revolutions of the Heavenly Spheres, trans. Charles Glenn Wallace. Chicago: Encyclopaedia Britannica, 1952.

d'Aguilon, Franz. *Opticorum libri sex.* Antwerp: Plantin Press, 1613.

de' Lucchi, Lorna, ed. and trans. *An Anthology of Italian Poems 13th–19th Century.* New York: Alfred A. Knopf, 1922.

Della Porta, Giambattista. *De aeris transmutationibvs libri IIII.* Rome: Mascardi, 1614.

De distillatione Libri IX. Rome: Rev. Camerae Apostolicae, 1608.

Gli duoi fratelli rivali/The Two Rival Brothers, ed. and trans. Louise George Clubb. Berkeley: University of California Press, 1980.

Ioan. Baptistae Portae Neap. de refractione optices parte. Libri Novem. Naples: Carlino & Pace, 1593.

Delle Colombe, Lodovico. *Risposte piaceuoli e curiose di Lodouico delle Colombe alle considerazioni di certa Maschera saccente nominata Alimberto Mauri, fatte sopra alcuni luoghi del discorso del medesimo Lodouico dintorno alla stella apparita [sic] l'anno 1604.* Florence: Caneo and Grossi, 1607.

Donati, Paolo. *Theoriche, overo, Speculationi intorno alli moti celesti del r.p.f. Paolo Donati carmelitano nelle quali senza eccentrici, epicicli, spire, circitori, reuoluenti, ò deferrenti, con nouo modo si saluano le celesti apparentie.* Venice: Osana, 1575.

Doni, Anton Francesco. *The Moral Philosophy of Doni Popularly Known as "The Fables of Bidpai" (A Collection of Sanskrit, Persian, and Arabic Fables) 1570,* ed. Donald Beecher, John Butler, and Carmine Di Biase, trans. Sir Thomas North. Ottawa: Dovehouse Editions, 2003.

Le novelle. Tomo i. La moral filosofia. Trattati, ed. Patrizia Pellizzari. Rome: Salerno Editrice, 2002.

Dovizi da Bibbiena, Bernardo. *La calandria,* in *Commedie del Cinquecento,* ed. Nino Borsellino, 2 vols. Vol. II. 7–97. Milan: Feltrinelli, 1967.

Dürer, Albrecht. *Painter's Manual: 1525,* trans. and commentary Walter L. Strauss. New York: Abaris Books, 1977.

Euclid. *Euclidis elementorum libri xv. Unà cum scholijs antiquis à Federico Commandino Urbinate nuper in latinum conversi, commentarijsque quibusdam illustrati.* Pisa, 1572.

Folengo, Teofilo. *Baldo,* trans. Ann E. Mullaney. Cambridge, MA: Harvard University Press, 2007.

Galilei, Galileo. *The Assayer,* trans. Stillman Drake and C. D. O'Malley, in *The Controversy on the Comets of 1618.* Philadelphia: University of Pennsylvania Press, 1960.

Concerning the Two Chief World Systems, trans. Stillman Drake. Berkeley: University of California Press, 1967.

Dialogues Concerning Two New Sciences, trans. Henry Crew and Alfonso de Salvio. Ed. and commentary Stephen Hawking. Philadelphia: Running Press, 2002.

Discoveries and Opinions of Galileo. New York: Anchor Books, 1957.

Due lezioni all'Accademia fiorentina circa la figura, sito e grandezza dell'Inferno di Dante, ed. Riccardo Pratesi. Livorno: Sillabe, 2011.

Galileo against the Philosophers in His "Dialogue of Cecco di Ronchitti" (1605) and "Considerations of Alimberto Mauri" (1606), trans. Stillman Drake. Los Angeles: Zeitlin & Ver Brugge, 1976.

On the World Systems, trans. and ed. Maurice A. Finocchiaro. Berkeley: University of California Press, 1997.

Opere, ed. Ferdinando Flora. Milan: Riccardo Ricciardi, 1953.

Opere, ed. Franz Brunetti, 2 vols. Vol. I. Turin: UTET, 2005.

Le opere di Galileo Galilei: Edizione nazionale sotto gli auspici di Sua Maestà il Re d'Italia, ed. Antonio Favaro and Isidoro del Lungo, 20 vols. in 21. Florence: G. Barbèra, 1963–1966 [1890–1909].

Le postille al Petrarca, ed. Nereo Vianello. Florence: Sansoni, 1956.

Saggiatore, ed. Ottavio Besomi and Mario Helbing. Rome: Antenore, 2005.

Scritti letterari, ed. Alberto Chiari. Florence: Le Monnier, 1970.

"Sidereus nuncius"; or, "The Sidereal Messenger" of Galileo Galilei, trans. and ed. Albert Van Helden. University of Chicago Press, 1989.

The Two New Sciences, trans. Stillman Drake. Madison: University of Wisconsin Press, 1974.

Galilei, Galileo and Christoph Scheiner, S.J. *On Sunspots*, trans. and ed. Eileen Reeves and Albert Van Helden. University of Chicago Press, 2010.

Galilei, Galileo, Orazio Grassi, Mario Guiducci, and Johann Kepler. *The Controversy on the Comets of 1618*, trans. Stillman Drake. Philadelphia: University of Pennsylvania Press, 1960.

Galilei, Vincenzo. *Dialogo della musica antica, et della moderna*. Florence: Marescotti, 1581.

Dialogue on Ancient and Modern Music, trans. Claude V. Palisca. New Haven: Yale University Press, 2003.

Discorso intorno all'opere di Gioseffo Zarlino. Florence, 1589.

Fronimo. Dialogo di Vincentio Galilei fiorentino, nel quale si contengono le vere e necessarie regole dell'intavolare la musica del liuto. Venice: Girolamo Scotto, 1568.

Gassendi, Pierre. *Petri Gassendi Diniensis ecclesiae praepositi, et in academia parisiensi Matheseos regii professoris Opera omnia in sex tomos diuisa: quorum seriem pagina praefationes proximè sequens continet. Hactenus edita auctor ante obitum recensuit, auxit, illustrauit. Posthuma verò totius naturae explicationem complectentia, in lucem nunc primùm prodeunt, ex bibliotheca illustris viri Henrici Ludouici Haberti Mon-Morii libellorum supplicum magistri*, 6 vols. Lyon: Anisson & Deuenet, 1658.

Gilbert, William. *De magnete*, trans. and ed. P. Fleury Mottelay. New York: Dover, 1958.

Glorioso, Giovanni Camillo. *Responsio Jo. Camilli Gloriosi ad controversias de Cometis Peripateticus, seu potius ad calumnias et mendacia cujusdam Peripatetici*. Venice, 1626.

Horace. *On Poetry: The "Ars poetica,"* ed. and commentary Charles Oscar Brink. Cambridge University Press, 1971.

Kepler, Johannes. *De stella nova in pede Serpentarii, et qui sub ejus exortum de novo iniit, trigono igneo*. Prague, 1606.

Epitome of Copernican Astronomy, trans. Charles Glenn Wallace. Chicago: Encyclopaedia Britannica, 1952.

Kepler's Conversation with Galileo's Sidereal Messenger, trans. and ed. Edward Rosen. New York: Johnson Reprint Corp., 1965.

Mysterium cosmographicum: The Secret of the Universe, trans. Alistair M. Duncan; ed. Eric J. Aiton. New York: Abaris Books, 1981.

Optics: Paralipomena to Witelo and Optical Part of Astronomy, trans. William H. Donahue. Santa Fe: Green Lion Press, 2000.

Lactantius. *The Divine Institutes*, trans. A. Bowen and P. Garnsey. Liverpool University Press, 2003.

Liceti, Fortunio. *De centro, & circumferentia libri duo in quibus diligenter physice, mathematiceque tractatur de centri, & circumferentiae nomine, varietate, natura, speciebus, proprietatibus, & utilitatibus ex rei natura, & potissimum ad aures Aristotelis.* Udine, 1640.

    De luminis natura & efficientia, libri tres. Udine, 1641.

    De terra unico centro motus singularum caeli particularum disputationes. Udine, 1641.

    Litheosphorus, sive, De lapide Bononiensi lucem in se conceptam ab ambiente claro mox in tenebris mire conservante. Udine: Schiratti, 1640.

Lucan. *Pharsalia*, trans. Susanna H. Braund. Oxford University Press, 1999.

Lucretius. *The Nature of Things*, trans. A. E. Stalling. New York: Penguin, 2007.

Magini, Giovanni Antonio. *Breve instruttione sopra l'apparenze et mirabili effetti dello specchio concavo sferico del … Gio. Antonio Magini.* Bologna, 1611.

    Ephemerides coelestium motuum Io. Antonii Magini Patavini … ab anno Domini 1611 usque ad annum 1630 quibus additum est eiusdem Supplementum isagogicarum ephemeridum. Venice, 1616.

Maldonado, Juan. *Spanish Humanism on the Verge of the Picaresque: Juan Maldonado's "Ludus chartarum," "Pastor bonus," and "Bacchanalia,"* ed. and trans. Warren Smith and Clark Colàhan. Leuven University Press, 2009.

Manilius. *Astronomica*, trans. G. P. Goold. Cambridge, MA: Harvard University Press, 1977.

Marino, Giambattista. *Adone*, ed. Giovanni Pozzi. Milan: Mondadori, 1976.

Mauri, Alimberto. *Considerations on Some Places in the Discourse of Lodovico delle Colombe*, trans. Stillman Drake, in *Galileo against the Philosophers in His "Dialogue of Cecco di Ronchitti" (1605) and "Considerations of Alimberto Mauri" (1606).* Los Angeles: Zeitlin & Ver Brugge, 1976.

Mayr, Simon. *Mundus Jovialis anno MDCIX detectus ope perspicilli Belgici, hoc est, quatuor Jovialium planetarum, cum theoria, tum tabulæ … jnventore & authore Simone Mario Guntzenhusano.* Nuremberg: Lauri, 1614.

Naudé, Gabriel. *Advice on Establishing a Library*, trans. and ed. Archer Taylor. Berkeley: University of California Press, 1950.

Ovid. *Fasti*, trans. Anne Wiseman and Peter Wiseman. Oxford University Press, 2011.

    Metamorphoses, trans. and ed. Charles Martin. New York: Norton, 2010.

    Tristia/Sorrows of an Exile, trans. and ed. A. D. Melville. Oxford: Clarendon Press, 1992.

Petrarca, Francesco. *Petrarch's Lyric Poems*, trans. and ed. Robert Durling. Cambridge, MA: Harvard University Press, 1976.

    Trionfi. Milan: Biblioteca Universali Rizzoli, 1984.

Piccolomini, Alessandro. *Alessandro (L'Alessandro)*, trans. and ed. Rita Belladonna. Ottawa: Dovehouse Editions, 1984.

    La Sfera del Mondo di M. Alessandro Piccolomini di nuovo da lui ripolita, accresciuta et fino a sei libri di quattro che erano, ampliata et quasi per ogni parte rinovata et riformata. Venice: Varisco, 1573.

Pitati, Pietro. *Almanach novum*. Venice, 1542.

Pliny, the Elder. *Histoire naturelle de Pline*, trans. Louis Poinsinet de Sivry, 12 vols. Vol. x. Paris: Chez la veuve Desaint, 1778.

Natural History, trans. H. Rackham. Cambridge, MA: Harvard University Press, 1979.

Pliny, the Younger. *Letters and Panegyricus*, ed. and trans. Betty Radice, 2 vols. Vol. i. Cambridge, MA: Harvard University Press, 1969.

Proclus. *A Commentary on the First Book of Euclid's "Elements,"* trans. and ed. Glenn R. Morrow. Princeton University Press, 1970.

Ptolemy. *Almagest*, trans. and ed. G. J. Toomer. Princeton University Press, 1998.

Sachetti, Franco. *Trecentonovelle*, ed. Vincenzo Pernicone. Florence: Sansoni, 1946.

Salviati, Lionardo. *Degli Accademici della Crusca Difesa dell'"Orlando furioso" dell'Ariosto*. Florence, 1584.

Sarrocchi, Margherita. *Scanderbeide: The Heroic Deeds of George Scanderbeg, King of Epirus*, ed. and trans. Rinaldina Russell. University of Chicago Press, 2006.

Sarsi, Lothario [Orazio Grassi]. *The Astronomical and Philosophical Balance*, in *Controversy on the Comets of 1618*, trans. Stillman Drake. Philadelphia: University of Pennsylvania Press, 1960.

Sirtori, Girolamo. *Hieronymi Sirturi mediolanensis Telescopium sive, Ars perficiendi nouum illud Galilaei visorium instrumentum ad sydera in tres partes divisa quarum prima exactissimam perspicillorum artem tradit; secunda telescopii Galilaei absolutam constructionem, & artem aperte docet; tertia alterius telescopii faciliorem vsum & admirandi sui adinuenti arcanum patefacit.* Frankfurt, 1618.

Tartaglia, Niccolò. *Quesiti et inventioni diverse de Nicolo Tartalea Brisciano*. Venice: Ruffinelli, 1546.

Ragionamenti sopra la sua travagliata inventione. Venice, 1551.

Tasso, Torquato. *L'Aminta: A Pastoral Play*, trans. Charles Jernigan and Irene Marchegiani Jones. New York: Italica, 2000.

Gerusalemme liberata, ed. Lanfranco Caretti. Turin: Einaudi, 1993.

Jerusalem Delivered, trans. and ed. Anthony Esolen. Baltimore: Johns Hopkins University Press, 2000.

Opere, ed. Bruno Maier, 5 vols. Vol. ii. Milan: Biblioteca Universali Rizzoli, 1963.

Tassoni, Alessandro. *De'pensieri diversi di Alessandro Tassoni. Dieci Libri*. Venice: Barezzi, 1646.

Pensieri e scritti preparatori, ed. Pietro Puliatti. Modena: Edizioni Panini, 1986.

Terence. *The Self-Tormentor*, ed. and trans. A. J. Brothers. Warminster: Aris & Phillips, 1988.

Valerio, Luca. *De centro gravitatis solidorum libri tres*. Rome, 1604.

Quadratura parabolae per simplex falsum, et altera quàm secunda Archimedis expiditior ad martium columnam Lucae Valerij. Rome, 1606.

Varchi, Benedetto. *L'Ercolano*. Milan, 1804.

Vasari, Giorgio. *Lives of the Most Eminent Painters, Sculptors, and Architects*, trans. Gaston C. de Vere; ed. Kenneth Clark, 3 vols. New York: Harry N. Abrams, 1979.

Virgil. *Aeneid*, trans. Sarah Ruden. New Haven: Yale University Press, 2008.

Georgics, trans. Janet Lembke. New Haven: Yale University Press, 2005.

Viviani, Vincenzo, *Poetae ac Philosophi vetustissimi, De rerum natura libri sex*. Lyon: Sebastian Gryphius, 1558.

SECONDARY MATERIALS

Aït-Touati, Frédérique. *Fictions of the Cosmos: Science and Literature in the Seventeenth Century*, trans. Susan Emanuel. University of Chicago Press, 2011.

Allen, John Jay. *Don Quixote: Hero or Fool? Remixed*. Newark, DE: Juan de la Cuesta, 2008.

Altieri Biagi, Maria Luisa. "*Dialogo sopra i due Massimi Sistemi* di Galileo Galilei," in *Letteratura italiana*, ed. A. Asor Rosa, 8 vols. Vol. II: *Dal Cinquecento al Settecento*. 891–971. Turin: Einaudi, 1992.

"Le forme della communicazione scientifica," in *Letteratura italiana*, ed. A. Asor Rosa, 8 vols. Vol. III: *Le forme del testo*, Part III: *La prosa*. 892–947. Turin: Einaudi, 1984.

Fra lingua scientifica e lingua letteraria. Pisa: Istituti editoriali poligrafici internazionali, 1998.

Galileo e la terminologia tecnico-scientifica. Florence: Olschki, 1965. *L'avventura della mente*. Naples: Morano, 1990.

Altieri Biagi, Maria Luisa and Bruno Basile, eds. *Scienziati del Seicento*. Milan–Naples: Ricciardi, 1980.

Antonello, Pierpaolo. "Galileo scrittore e la critica: Analisi stilistica e interdisciplinarietà." *Quaderni d'italianistica* 23.1–2 (2002): 25–48.

Armour, Peter. "Galileo and the Crisis in Italian Literature of the Early Seicento," in *Collected Essays on Italian Language and Literature Presented to Kathleen Speight*, ed. Giovanni Aquilecchia, Stephen N. Cristea, and Sheila Ralphs. 144–169. New York: Barnes and Noble, 1971.

Ascoli, Albert. "Auerbach fra gli epicurei: Dal Canto x dell' *Inferno* alla VI Giornata del *Decameron*." *Moderna* 11.1–2 (2009): 135–152.

Ashworth, Jr., William B. and Bruce Bradley. *Jesuit Science in the Age of Galileo: An Exhibition of Rare Books from the History of Science Collection: March 24–July 31, 1986*. Kansas City, MO: Linda Hall Library, 1986.

Baffetti, Giovanni. "Scienza e scrittura letteraria: La lezione di Galileo." *Galilaeana* 2 (2005): 301–306.

Barbierato, Federico. *The Inquisitor in the Hat Shop*. Farnham, VT: Ashgate, 2012.

Battistini, Andrea. *Il barocco*. Rome: Salerno Editrice, 2000.

Galileo e i Gesuiti: Miti letterari e retorica della scienza. Milan: Vita e Pensiero, 2000.

"Galileo tra letteratura e scienza," in *Galileo scienziato, filosofo, scrittore: A quattro secoli dal "Sidereus nuncius*," ed. Piero Di Pretoro and Rita Lukoshik. 109–123. Munich: Martin Meidenbauer, 2011.

"Il libro, il labirinto, la fabbrica del mondo: Metafore epistemologiche della nuova scienza di Galileo," in *Quando l'opera interpella il lettore: Poetiche e forme della modernità letteraria*, ed. Piero Pieri and Giuliana Benvenuti. 27–43. Bologna: Edizioni Pendragon, 2000.

Baumgardt, Carola. *Johannes Kepler: Life and Letters*. New York: Philosophical Library, 1951.

Beer, Marina. *Romanzi di cavalleria: "Il furioso" e il romanzo italiano del primo Cinquecento*. Rome: Bulzoni, 1987.

Bellini, Eraldo. "Galileo e le 'due culture,'" in *La prosa di Galileo: La lingua, la retorica, la storia*, ed. Mauro Di Giandomenico and Pasquale Guaragnella. 143–78. Lecce: Argo, 2006.

Stili di pensiero nel Seicento italiano: Galileo, i Lincei, i Barberini. Pisa: ETS, 2009.

Ben-Zakin, Avner. *Cross-Cultural Scientific Exchanges in the Eastern Mediterranean, 1560–1660*. Baltimore: Johns Hopkins University Press, 2010.

Besomi, Ottavio. "Galileo Reader and Annotator," in *The Inspiration of Astronomical Phenomena VI: Proceedings of a Conference Held October 18–23, 2009 in Venice, Italy*, ed. Enrico Maria Corsini. 43–54. San Francisco: Astronomical Society of the Pacific, 2011.

Besomi, Ottavio and Michele Camerota. *Galileo e Il Parnaso Tychonico: Un capitolo inedito del dibattito sulle comete tra finzione letteraria a trattazione scientifica*. Florence: L. S. Olschki, 2000.

Bezzola Lambert, Ladina. *Imagining the Unimaginable: The Poetics of Early Modern Astronomy*. Amsterdam: Rodopi, 2002.

Biagetti, Maria Teresa. *La biblioteca di Federico Cesi*. Rome: Bulzoni, 2008.

Biagioli, Mario. "Filippo Salviati: A Baroque Virtuoso." *Nuncius* 7 (1991): 81–96.

Galileo Courtier: The Practice of Science in a Culture of Absolutism. University of Chicago Press, 1993.

Galileo's Instruments of Credit. University of Chicago Press, 2007.

"The Social Status of Italian Mathematicians, 1450–1600." *History of Science* 27 (1989): 41–95.

Black, Robert. *Humanism and Education in Medieval and Renaissance Italy: Tradition and Innovation in Latin Schools from the Twelfth to the Fifteenth Century*. Cambridge University Press, 2001.

Blair, Ann. "Humanist Methods in Natural Philosophy: The Commonplace Book." *Journal of the History of Ideas* 53.4 (1992): 541–555.

Too Much to Know: Managing Scholarly Information before the Modern Age. New Haven: Yale University Press, 2010.

Blumenberg, Hans. *The Genesis of the Copernican World*, trans. Robert M. Wallace. Cambridge, MA: MIT Press, 1987.

Shipwreck with Spectator: Paradigm of a Metaphor for Existence, trans. Steven Rendell. Cambridge, MA: MIT Press, 1997.

Bolzoni, Lina. *Le stanze della memoria*. Turin: Einaudi, 1995.

Bozzi, Paolo. "Dalla parte di Simplicio," in *Galileo Galilei e la cultura veneziana: Atti del Convegno di Studio promosso nell'ambito delle celebrazioni galileiane indette dall'Università degli Studi di Padova (1592–1992), Venezia, 18–20 giugno 1992.* 313–316. Venice: Istituto Veneto di Scienze, Lettere ed Arti, 1992.

Branca, Vittore. "Galileo fra Petrarca e l'Umanesimo veneziano," in *Galileo Galilei e la cultura veneziana: Atti del Convegno di Studio promosso nell'ambito delle celebrazioni galileiane indette dall'Università degli Studi di Padova (1592–1992), Venezia, 18–20 giugno 1992.* 340–343. Venice: Istituto Veneto di Scienze, Lettere ed Arti, 1992.

Briggs, Jr., Ward W. *Narrative and Simile from the "Georgics" in the "Aeneid."* Leiden: Brill, 1980.

Brown, Alison. *The Return of Lucretius to Renaissance Florence.* Cambridge, MA: Harvard University Press, 2010.

Bucciantini, Massimo. *Galileo e Keplero.* Turin: Einaudi, 2003.

Bushnell, Rebecca. *A Culture of Teaching: Early Modern Humanism in Theory and Practice.* Ithaca, NY: Cornell University Press, 1996.

Calvino, Italo. *Lezioni americane: Sei proposte per il prossimo millennio.* Milan: Garzanti, 1991.

  "Le livre de la Nature chez Galilée," in *Exigences et perspectives de la sémiotique: Recueil d'hommages pour Algirdas Julien Greimas*, ed. Herman Parret and Hans-George Ruprecht, 2 vols. Vol. II. 683–688. Amsterdam: John Benjamins, 1985.

Camerota, Michele. "Galileo e la *accomodatio* copernicana," in *Il caso Galileo: Una rilettura storica, filosofica, teologica. Convegno internazionale di studi, Firenze 26–30 maggio 2009.* 129–151. Florence: Olschki, 2011.

  Galileo Galilei e la cultura scientifica nell'età della Controriforma. Rome: Salerno, 2004.

  "Galileo, Lucrezio e l'atomismo," in *Lucrezio: La natura e la scienza*, ed. Marco Beretta and Francesco Citti. 141–175. Florence: Olschki, 2008.

Campbell, Mary Baine. *Wonder & Science: Imagining Worlds in Early Modern Europe.* Ithaca, NY: Cornell University Press, 1999.

Capodieci, Luisa and Philip Ford. *Homère à la Renaissance: Mythe et transfigurations.* Rome: Académie de France, 2011.

Caretti, Lanfranco. "Galileo uomo di lettere," in *Studi di letteratura e di storia di memoria di Antonio Di Pietro.* 107–123. Milan: Vita e Pensiero, 1977.

Castillo, David R. *Baroque Horrors: Roots of the Fantastic in the Age of Curiosities.* Ann Arbor: University of Michigan Press, 2010.

Cavallo, JoAnn. *The Romance Epics of Boiardo, Ariosto, and Tasso.* University of Toronto Press, 2004.

Celi, Luciano. *Gettar luce nell'oscuro labirinto: Arte, letteratura, scienza in Galileo Galilei.* Rome: Aracne, 2010.

Chiari, Sophie. *L'image du labyrinth à la Renaissance.* Paris: Honoré Champion Editeur, 2010.

Clubb, Louise. *Giambattista Della Porta, Dramatist.* Princeton University Press, 1965.

Clucas, Stephen. "Galileo, Bruno and the Rhetoric of Dialogue in Seventeenth-Century Natural Philosophy." *History of Science* 46 (2008): 405–429.

Colapietra, Raffaele. "Caratteri del seicentismo galileiano." *Belfagor* 8 (1953): 570–578.

Cox, Virginia. *The Prodigious Muse*. Baltimore: Johns Hopkins University Press, 2011.

The Renaissance Dialogue: Literary Dialogue in Its Social and Political Contexts, Castiglione to Galileo. Cambridge University Press, 2008.

Culler, Jonathan. "Prolegomena to a Theory of Reading," in *The Reader in the Text*, ed. Susan R. Suleiman and Inge Crosman. 46–66. Princeton University Press, 1980.

Cummins, Juliet and David Burchell, eds. *Science, Literature and Rhetoric in Early Modern England*. Burlington, VT: Ashgate, 2007.

Curtius, Ernst Robert. *European Literature and the Latin Middle Ages*, trans. Willard R. Trask. Princeton University Press, 1953.

Damon, Phillip. "Geryon, Cacciaguida, and the Y of Pythagoras." *Dante Studies* 85 (1967): 15–32.

Daniele, Antonio. "Galileo letterato," in *Attualità di Galileo Galilei nella vita scientifica di oggi e di domani: Rapporti con la chiesa e con gli scienziati europei*. 35–50. Padua: Il Poligrafo, 2009.

D'Anna, Nuccio. *Virgilio e le rivelazioni divine*. Genoa: ECIG, 1989.

DeSa Wiggins, Peter. "Galileo on Characterization in the *Orlando furioso*." *Italica* 57.4: Renaissance (Winter 1980): 255–267.

Della Terza, Dante. "Galileo Man of Letters," in *Galileo Reappraised*, ed. Carlo L. Golino. 1–22. Berkeley–Los Angeles: University of California Press, 1966.

Dietz Moss, Jean. *Novelties in the Heavens: Rhetoric and Science in the Copernican Controversy*. University of Chicago Press, 1993.

Dietz Moss, Jean and William A. Wallace, *Rhetoric and Dialectic in the Time of Galileo*. Washington, DC: Catholic University of America Press, 2003.

Dollo, Corrado. *Galileo Galilei e la cultura della tradizione*, ed. Giuseppe Bentivegna, Santo Burgio, and Giancarlo Magnano San Lio. Soveria Mannelli: Robbettino, 2003.

Dooley, Brendan. *Morandi's Last Prophecy and the End of Renaissance Politics*. Princeton University Press, 2002.

Drake, Stillman. *Galileo at Work: His Scientific Biography*. University of Chicago Press, 1978.

"Galileo's New Science of Motion," in *Reason, Experiment and Mysticism*, ed. Maria Luisa Righini Bonelli and William Shea. 131–156. New York: Science History Publications, 1975.

Eamon, William. "Court, Academy, and Printing House: Patronage and Scientific Careers in Late Renaissance Italy," in *Patronage and Institutions: Science, Technology, and Medicine at the European Court 1500–1700*, ed. Bruce T. Moran. 25–50. Rochester, NY: Boydell Press, 1991.

Science and the Secrets of Nature: Books of Secrets in Medieval and Early Modern Culture. Princeton University Press, 1994.

"Science as a Hunt." *Physis* 31 (1994): 393–432.

Edgerton, Samuel. *The Heritage of Giotto's Geometry: Art and Science on the Eve of the Scientific Revolution*. Ithaca, NY: Cornell University Press, 1991.

Favaro, Antonio. "Appendice prima alla libreria di Galileo Galilei." *Bullettino di bibliografia e storia delle scienze matematiche e fisiche* 20 (1887): 372–376.

"Appendice seconda alla libreria di Galileo Galilei," in *Scampoli galileiani* Ser. II, Vol. XII (1895–1896): 44–50; repr. in Antonio Favaro, *Scampoli galileiani*, ed. Lucia Rossetti and Maria Luisa Soppelsa. 368–374. Trieste: LINT, 1992.

"La libreria di Galileo Galilei, descritta ed illustrata." *Bullettino di bibliografia e storia delle scienze matematiche e fisiche* 19 (1886): 219–293.

Ferraris, F. Lucius. *Prompta bibliotheca*, 8 vols. Vol. V. Paris: J.-P. Migne, 1854.

Finocchiaro, Maurice A. *The Galileo Affair: A Documentary History*. Berkeley: University of California Press, 1989.

Galileo and the Art of Reasoning: Rhetorical Foundations of Logic and Scientific Method. Dordrecht–Boston: Reidel, 1980.

Finucci, Valeria. *Renaissance Transactions*. Durham, NC: Duke University Press, 1999.

Forcione, Alban K. *Cervantes, Aristotle, and the Persiles*. Princeton University Press, 1970.

Foucault, Michel. *The Order of Things: An Archaeology of the Human Sciences*. London: Tavistock Publications, 1970.

"What Is an Author?," in *Twentieth-Century Literary Theory*, ed. Vassilis Lambropoulos and David Neal Miller. 124–142. Albany: State University Press of New York, 1987.

Fox, Robin Lane. *Alexander the Great*. New York: Penguin, 2005.

Freedberg, David. *The Eye of the Lynx*. University of Chicago Press, 2003.

Fuentes, Carlos. *Cervantes o la crítica de la lectura*. Tabasco: Editorial Joaquín Mortiz, 1976.

Gale, Monica R. *Lucretius and the Didactic Epic*. London: Bristol Classical Press, 2001.

Garin, Eugenio. *La cultura filosofica del rinascimento italiano*. Florence: Sansoni, 1961.

Gee, Emma. *Ovid, Aratus and Augustus*. Cambridge University Press, 2000.

Genette, Gerard. *Palimpsests: Literature in the Second Degree*, trans. Channa Newman and Claude Dombinsky. Lincoln: University of Nebraska Press, 1997.

Ginzburg, Carlo. *The Cheese and the Worms: The Cosmos of a Sixteenth-Century Miller*, trans. Anne Tedeschi and John Tedeschi. New York: Penguin, 1987.

Giovine, M. V. *Galileo scrittore*. Genoa: Società Anonima Editrice Dante Alighieri, 1943.

Girardi, Raffaele. *La società del dialogo*. Bari: Adriatica, 1989.

Grafton, Anthony. *Commerce with the Classics: Ancient Books and Renaissance Readers*. Ann Arbor: University of Michigan Press, 1997.

"Kepler as a Reader." *Journal of the History of Ideas* 53.4 (1992): 561–572.

Grant, Edward. "The Partial Transformation of Medieval Cosmology by Jesuits in the Sixteenth and Seventeenth Centuries," in *Jesuit Science and the*

Republic of Letters, ed. Mordechai Feingold. 127–156. Cambridge, MA: MIT Press, 2003.

Grant, Patrick. *Literature and the Discovery of Method in the English Renaissance.* Athens: University of Georgia Press, 1985.

Greco, Carmelo. "Scienza e teatro in G. B. Della Porta," in *Letteratura e scienza nella storia della cultura italiana.* 429–451. Palermo: Manfredi Editori, 1982.

Greco, V. and G. Molesini. "Galileo e Sagredo: Primo enunciato della formula dei fabbricanti di lenti." *Quaderno di storia della fisica* 1 (1997): 35–38.

Greenblatt, Stephen. *Swerve: How the World Became Modern.* New York: Norton, 2011.

Grendler, Paul F. *Schooling in Renaissance Italy: Literacy and Learning, 1300–1600.* Baltimore: Johns Hopkins University Press, 1989.

Grill, T. R. "Galileo and Platonist Methodology." *Journal of the History of Ideas* 31.4 (1970): 501–520.

Guthke, Karl S. *The Last Frontier: Imagining Other Worlds from the Copernican Revolution to Modern Science Fiction*, trans. Helen Atkins. Ithaca, NY: Cornell University Press, 1990.

Hall, Crystal. "Galileo's Rhetoric of Fable." *Quaderni d'Italianistica* 31.2 (2010): 91–112.

Hallyn, Fernand. *The Poetic Structure of the World: Copernicus and Kepler*, trans. Donald M. Leslie. New York: Zone Books, 1993.

Hart, Thomas R. *Cervantes and Ariosto: Renewing Fiction.* Princeton University Press, 1989.

Heilbron, J. L. *Galileo.* Oxford University Press, 2010.

Heninger, S. K. *Touches of Sweet Harmony: Pythagorean Cosmology and Renaissance Poetics.* San Marino, CA: Huntington Library, 1974.

Holmes, Olivia. *Dante's Two Beloveds.* New Haven: Yale University Press, 2008.

Janković, Vladimir. *Reading the Skies: A Cultural History of English Weather, 1650–1820.* University of Chicago Press, 2000.

Jardine, Lisa. *Francis Bacon: Discovery and the Art of Discourse.* Cambridge University Press, 1974.

Javitch, Daniel. "The Imitation of Imitations in *Orlando furioso*." *Renaissance Quarterly* 38.2 (1985): 215–239.

"Narrative Discontinuity in the *Orlando furioso* and Its Sixteenth Century Critics." *MLN* 103.1 (January 1988): 50–74.

"The Poetics of *Variatio* in *Orlando furioso*." *Modern Language Quarterly* 66.1 (2005): 1–20.

Jermyn, L. A. S. "Virgil's Agricultural Lore." *Greece and Rome* 53 (1949): 49–69.

Kennedy, William J. *Rhetorical Norms in Renaissance Literature.* New Haven: Yale University Press, 1978.

Kirkham, Victoria. *Laura Battifera and Her Literary Circle.* University of Chicago Press, 2006.

Kollerstrom, Nick. "On the Character of Sagredo: Galileo's Judgment upon His Nativity," trans. Julianne Evans. *Culture and Cosmos* 7.1 (2003): 96–100.

Lattis, James R. *Between Copernicus and Galileo: Christoph Clavius and the Collapse of Ptolemaic Cosmography*. University of Chicago Press, 1994.

Leitão, Henrique. "Galileo's Telescopic Observations in Portugal," in *Largo campo di filosofare*, ed. José Montesinos and Carlos Solís. 903–913. Eurosymposium Galileo 2001. La Orotava: Fundación Canaria Orotava de la Historia de la Ciencia, 2001.

LoLordo, Antonia. *Pierre Gassendi and the Birth of Early Modern Philosophy*. Cambridge University Press, 2007.

Looney, Dennis. *Compromising the Classics: Romance Epic Narrative in the Italian Renaissance*. Detroit: Wayne State University Press, 1996.

Loria, Mario. "William Gilbert e Galileo Galilei: La terrella e le calamite del granduca," in *Saggi su Galileo Galilei*, ed. Carlo Maccagni, 2 vols. Vol. II. 208–247. Florence: Sansoni, 1972.

Lovarini, Emilio. *Studi sul Ruzzante e la letteratura padovana*, ed. Gianfrancesco Folena. Padua: Antenore, 1965.

Luthy, Christopher. "The Fourfold Democritus on the Stage of Early Modern Science." *Isis* 91 (2000): 443–479.

Maclean, Ian. "The Interpretation of Natural Signs: Cardano's *De subtilitate* versus Scaliger's *Exercitationes*," in *Occult and Scientific Mentalities in the Renaissance*, ed. Brian Vickers. 231–252. Cambridge University Press, 1984.

Marchitello, Howard. *The Machine in the Text: Science and Literature in the Age of Shakespeare and Galileo*. Oxford University Press, 2011.

Marenzana, Mariapiera. *L'omaggio di Galileo: I personaggi dei dialoghi visti attraverso l'epistolario*. Taranto: Chimienti, 2010.

Marr, Alexander. *Between Raphael and Galileo*. University of Chicago Press, 2011.

Marsh, David. *The Quattrocento Dialogue: Classical Tradition and Humanist Innovation*. Cambridge, MA: Harvard University Press, 1980.

Marzot, G. "Variazioni barocche nella prosa del Galilei." *Convivium* 23 (1955): 43–67.

McLuhan, Marshall. *The Gutenberg Galaxy: The Making of Typographic Man*. University of Toronto Press, 1962.

McNeely, Ian F. "The Renaissance Academies between Science and the Humanities." *Configurations* 17.3 (Fall 2009): 227–258.

McPhail, Eric. "The Mosaic of Speech: A Classical Topos in Renaissance Aesthetics." *Journal of the Warburg and Courtauld Institutes* 66 (2003): 249–264.

Meynell, Francis and Stanley Morison. "Printers' Flowers and Arabesques." *The Fleuron* 1 (1923): 1–43.

Milani, Marisa. "Il 'Faelamento' di Rovigiò Bon Magon e Tuogno Regonò a Galileo Galilei." *Giornale storico della letteratura italiana* 165 (1988): 545–577.

Mirollo, James V. *Poet of the Marvelous: Giambattista Marino*. New York: Columbia University Press, 1963.

Mosley, Adam. *Bearing the Heavens: Tycho Brahe and the Astronomical Community of the Late Sixteenth Century*. Cambridge University Press, 2007.

Mueller, S.J., Paul R. "Textual Criticism and Early Modern Natural Philosophy: The Case of Marin Mersenne (1588–1648)," in *The Word and the World: Biblical Exegesis and Early Modern Science*, ed. Kevin Killeen and Peter J. Forshaw. 78–90. New York: Palgrave Macmillan, 2007.

Murphy, James J. "One Thousand Neglected Authors," in *Renaissance Eloquence: Studies in the Theory and Practice of Renaissance Rhetoric*, ed. James J. Murphy. 20–36. Berkeley: University of California Press, 1983.

Muscetta, Carlo. *Realismo neorealismo controrealismo*. Milan: Garzanti, 1976.

Nicholson, Eric. "Romance as Role Model: Early Performances of *Orlando furioso* and *Gerusalemme liberata*," in *Renaissance Transactions: Ariosto and Tasso*, ed. Valeria Finucci. 246–269. Durham, NC: Duke University Press, 1999.

Olschki, Leonard. "Galileo's Literary Formation," trans. Thomas Green and Maria Charlesworth, in *Galileo, Man of Science*, ed. Ernan McMullin. 140–159. New York: Basic Books, 1968.

Ordine, Nuccio. *La soglia dell'ombra: Letteratura, filosofia e pittura in Giordano Bruno*. Venice: Mansilio, 2003.

Ottone, Giuseppe. "Postille e Considerazioni galileiane." *Aevum* 46 (1972): 312–324.

Panofsky, Erwin. "Galileo as a Critic of the Arts, Aesthetic Attitude and Scientific Thought." *Isis* 47 (1956): 3–15.

Galileo, Critic of the Arts. The Hague: Martinus Nijhoff, 1954.

Pantin, Isabelle. *La poésie du ciel en France dans la seconde moitié du seizième siècle*. Geneva: Librairie Droz, 1995.

Paulson, Ronald. *The Fictions of Satire*. Baltimore: Johns Hopkins University Press, 1967.

Peterson, Mark. *Galileo's Muse*. Cambridge, MA: Harvard University Press, 2011.

Pettegree, Andrew. *The Book in the Renaissance*. New Haven: Yale University Press, 2010.

Pevsner, Nikolaus. *A History of Building Types*. Princeton University Press, 1976.

Pezzini, Serena. "Ideologia della conquista, ideologia dell'accoglienza: *La Scanderbeide* di Margherita Sarrocchi (1623)." *MLN* 120.1: Supplement (2005): 190–222.

Possanza, D. Mark. *Translating the Heavens: Aratus, Germanicus, and the Poetics of Latin Translation*. New York: Peter Lang, 2004.

Presberg, Charles D. *Adventures in Paradox: Don Quixote and the Western Tradition*. University Park: Penn State University Press, 2001.

Quint, David. *Epic and Empire: Politics and Generic Form from Virgil to Milton*. Princeton University Press, 1993.

Origin and Originality in Renaissance Literature: Versions of the Source. New Haven: Yale University Press, 1983.

Raimondi, Ezio. *La dissimulazione romanzesca: Antropologia manzoniana*. Bologna: Il Mulino, 1997.

Raphael, Renée. "Galileo's *Discorsi* and Mersenne's *Nouvelles pensées*: Mersenne as a Reader of Galilean Experience." *Nuncius* 23.1 (2008): 7–36.

Rauhut, F. "Galileis Bedeutung für die italienische Literatur und Sprache." *Volkstum und Kultur der Romanen* 15 (1942): 147–171.

Rebhorn, Wayne A., ed. and trans. *Renaissance Debates on Rhetoric*. Ithaca, NY: Cornell University Press, 2000.

Redondi, Pietro. *Galileo eretico*. Turin: Einaudi, 1986.

   Galileo Heretic, trans. Raymond Rosenthal. Princeton University Press, 1987.

Reed, Walter L. *An Exemplary History of the Novel*. University of Chicago Press, 1981.

Reeves, Eileen. "Daniel 5 and the *Assayer*: Galileo Reads the Handwriting on the Wall." *Journal of Medieval and Renaissance Studies* 21 (1991): 1–27.

   Galileo's Glassworks: The Telescope and the Mirror. Cambridge, MA: Harvard University Press, 2008.

   "Old Wives' Tales and the New World System: Gilbert, Galileo, Kepler." *Configurations* 7.3 (1999): 301–354.

   Painting the Heavens. Princeton University Press, 1999.

Reiss, Timothy J. *Knowledge, Discovery, and Imagination in Early Modern Europe*. Cambridge University Press, 1997.

Remmert, Volker. *Picturing the Scientific Revolution*. Philadelphia: Saint Joseph's University Press, 2011.

Riley, E. C. *Cervantes' Theory of the Novel*. Newark, NJ: Juan de la Cuesta, 1992.

Rose, Paul Lawrence. *The Italian Renaissance of Mathematics*. Geneva: Librairie Droz, 1976.

Rosenthal, Margaret F. *The Honest Courtesan: Veronica Franco, Citizen and Writer in Sixteenth-Century Venice*. University of Chicago Press, 1992.

Rothman, Aviva. "Forms of Persuasion: Kepler, Galileo and the Dissemination of Copernicanism." *Journal for the History of Astronomy* 40 (2009): 403–419.

Ruffini, Marco. *Art without an Author: Vasari's "Lives" and Michelangelo's Death*. New York: Fordham University Press, 2011.

Saiber, Arielle "Flexilinear Language: Giambattista Della Porta's *Elementorum curvilineorum libri tres*." *Annali d'Italianistica* 23 (2005): 89–104.

Shapin, Steven. *A Social History of Truth: Civility and Science in Seventeenth-Century England*. University of Chicago Press, 1994.

Shea, William. "Georg [*sic*] Locher's *Disquisitiones mathematicae de controversiis et novitatibus astronomicis* and Galileo Galilei's *Dialogue on the Two World Systems*," in *Proceedings of the 13th International Congress of the History of Science, Moscow, 18–24 August, 1971*. 211–219. Moscow: Izdatelstvo "Nauka," 1974.

   "Looking at the Moon as Another Earth: Terrestrial Analogies and Seventeenth-Century Telescopes," in *Metaphor and Analogy in the Sciences*, ed. Fernand Hallyn. 83–104. Dordrecht: Kluwer, 2000.

Spiller, Elizabeth. *Science, Reading, and Renaissance Literature: The Art of Making Knowledge, 1580–1670*. Cambridge University Press, 2004.

Spongano, Raffaello. *La prosa di Galileo e altri scritti*. Messina–Florence: Casa Editrice G. D'Anna, 1949.

Stäuble, Antonio. *Parlar per lettera: Il pedante nella commedia del Cinquecento e altri saggi sul teatro rinascimentale*. Rome: Bulzoni, 1991.

Stengers, Isabelle. *The Invention of Modern Science*, trans. Daniel Smith. Minneapolis: University of Minnesota Press, 2000.

Tomasin, Lorenzo. "Galileo e il pavano: Un consuntivo." *Lingua nostra* 69.1–2 (2008): 23–36.

Tudeau-Clayton, Margaret. *Jonson, Shakespeare and Early Modern Virgil.* Cambridge University Press, 1998.

Unglaub, Jonathan. *Poussin and the Poetics of Painting.* Cambridge University Press, 2006.

Valleriani, Matteo. *Galileo Engineer.* Dordrecht: Springer, 2010.

"Galileo's Abandoned Project on Acoustics at the Medici Court." *History of Science* 1 (2012): 1–31.

Van Dixhoorn, Arjan. *The Reach of the Republic of Letters: Literary and Learned Societies in Late Medieval and Early Modern Europe.* Leiden: Brill, 2008.

Van Helden, Albert. *The Invention of the Telescope.* Philadelphia: American Philosophical Society, 2008 [1977].

Vanacker, Janis and Sabine Verhulst. "Atteone furioso: La caccia alla divina cono scenza negli *Eroici furori* di Giordano Bruno." *Rivista di storia della filosofia* 65.4 (2010): 695–717.

Varanini, Giorgio. *Galileo critico e prosatore: Note e ricerche.* Verona: Fiorini-Ghidini, 1967.

Vianello, Nereo. *Le postille al Petrarca di Galileo Galilei.* Florence: Sansoni, 1956.

Vickers, Brian. *Francis Bacon and Renaissance Prose.* Cambridge University Press, 1968.

Wallace, William A. "Antonio Riccobono: The Teaching of Rhetoric in 16th-Century Padua," in *Rhetoric and Pedagogy: Its History, Philosophy, and Practice. Essays in Honor of James J. Murphy*, ed. Winifred Bryan Horner and Michael Leff. 149–170. Mahwah, NJ: J. Erlbaum, 1995.

Westfall, Richard S. "Science and Patronage: Galileo and the Telescope." *Isis* 76.1 (March 1985): 11–30.

Westman, Robert S. *The Copernican Question.* Berkeley: University of California Press, 2011.

"Proof, Poetics, and Patronage: Copernicus's Preface to *De revolutionibus*," in *Reappraisals of the Scientific Revolution*, ed. David C. Lindberg and Robert S. Westman. 167–205. Cambridge University Press, 1990.

White, Jonathan. *Italian Cultural Lineages.* University of Toronto Press, 2007.

Wilding, Nick. "Galileo's Idol: Gianfrancesco Sagredo Unveiled." *Galilaeana* 3 (2006): 229–245.

"Manuscripts in Motion: The Diffusion of Galilean Copernicanism." *Italian Studies* 66 (2011): 221–233.

Wilson-Okamura, David Scott. *Virgil in the Renaissance.* Cambridge University Press, 2010.

Wisan, Winifred L. "The New Science of Motion: A Study of Galileo's *De motu locali.*" *Archive for History of Exact Sciences* 13.2–3 (1974): 103–306.

Wistreich, Richard. *Warrior, Courtier, Singer: Giulio Cesare Brancaccio and the Performance of Identity in the Late Renaissance.* Burlington, VT: Ashgate, 2007.

Wlassics, Tibor. *Galilei critico letterario*. Ravenna: Longo, 1974.
  "La genesi della critica letteraria di Galileo." *Aevum* 46 (1972): 215–236.
Yates, Francis. *The Art of Memory*. University of Chicago Press, 2001.
Zatti, Sergio. *The Quest for Epic: From Ariosto to Tasso*, ed. and trans. Dennis
  Looney. University of Toronto Press, 2006.
Zinato, Emanuele. *Il vero in maschera. Dialoghismi galileiani: Idee e forme nelle
  prose scientifiche del Seicento*. Naples: Liguori, 2003.

Index